CREOLES
OF SOUTH LOUISIANA

ISBN 13 (paper): 978-1-946160-19-5

Printed on acid-free paper in the United States.

Library of Congress Cataloging-in-Publication Data

Names: Istre, Elista (Elista Dawn), author.
Title: Creoles of South Louisiana : three centuries strong / Elista Istre.
Description: Lafayette, LA : University of Louisiana at Lafayette Press, [2018] | Includes bibliographical references.
Identifiers: LCCN 2017048394 | ISBN 9781946160195 (alk. paper)
Subjects: LCSH: Creoles--Louisiana--Social life and customs. | Creoles--Louisiana--Songs and music. | Creoles--Louisiana--Folklore. | Cooking, Creole. | Creole dialects--Louisiana. | Fables, Creole--Louisiana. | Proverbs, Creole--Louisiana. | Oral tradition--Louisiana.
Classification: LCC F380.C87 I87 2018 | DDC 976.3--dc23
LC record available at https://lccn.loc.gov/2017048394

CREOLES
OF SOUTH LOUISIANA
Three Centuries Strong

BY

ELISTA ISTRE

2018

UNIVERSITY OF LOUISIANA AT LAFAYETTE PRESS

Dedicated to Creoles of all colors,
both past and present,
who strive to make the world a better place
for the future

"Truly, I have a beautiful heritage." Psalm 16:6 (ISV)

Table of Contents

Acknowledgments ix
Introduction xi

1 *Les Créoles*

Origins and Evolution of a Cultural Identity 1

- *Explication de Créole*: Defining "Creole" 1
- *Les Créoles Blancs*: Affluent White Creoles 7
- *Les Créoles Noirs*: Enslaved Black Creoles 10
- *Les Créoles de Couleur*: Free People of Color and Creoles of Color 16
- *Les Créoles D'Aujourd'hui*: Creoles Today 23
- Creole Families in Black and White 30

2 *Allons Manger!*

Cooking in Creole Country 43

- Savoring Survival: Frontier Cooking 49
- Plantation Cuisine: The Big House and Beyond 58
- Black Pots, White Rice, and Brown Gravy: Creole Cooking Today 70
- Creole Specialties in the Kitchen 90

3 *Allons Parler!*

Creole French and the Oral Tradition 109

- New World French: Origins of a Language 111
- Creole French: A "Curious Dialect" 118
- Folklorists: Documenting Oral Tradition 131
- Creole Stories in the Repertoire 140

4 *Allons Danser!*

From Quadroon Balls to Zydeco Halls 155

- African Chants and French Arias: Early Louisiana 156
- Field Hollers and House Dances: From Juré to La La 170
- Dance Halls and Festivals: From Creole to Zydeco 190
- Creole Influences in Music 194

5 *L'Héritage Créole*

Still Going Strong 207

- Creole People: From Invisible to Vocal 208
- Creole Cuisine: Cookin' Up Something Good 214
- Creole French: Let's Talk About It 224
- Creole Music: Play Me Some Zydeco 234
- Creole Culture: Preserving and Presenting Heritage 250
- Creole Heritage in the Modern World 254

Notes 265
Bibliography 291
Image Credits 305
Index 311

ACKNOWLEDGMENTS

Over the years, I have had opportunities to be both an inside participant and outside observer to the place I call home. Through my experiences growing up in Acadiana, as well as my travels and interactions with countless people across the globe, I have come to understand and value my own culture even more. For this reason, I would like to thank all the individuals and groups who have asked questions, challenged assumptions, and offered insights that have enabled me to become a better cultural ambassador for South Louisiana.

I also would like to thank the many Creoles who opened their homes and hearts to me as I asked them personal questions about growing up Creole in a world that often considered them "too dark to be white and too light to be black." For the older generation, these conversations often unlocked painful memories of speaking French in an English-speaking world. For young people, it frequently meant lamenting their inability to speak their ancestors' language in a globalized society that now values multilingualism. Friends, family members, and sometimes even complete strangers shared their stories with me in dance halls, at family reunions, and around kitchen tables. I am honored to share their stories within the pages of this book.

When this publication was still evolving as a dissertation in the hands of my major professor Dr. Brady Banta at Arkansas State University, his understanding of Louisiana history and fastidious attention to detail strengthened my research and writing skills considerably. Equally significant were the "Cajun Humanitarian Aid" packages of *andouille* sausage and *boudin* links he left on my desk at the most unexpected times—gifts that provided both nourishment and comfort to this Louisiana girl living in exile north of I-10. For all this and more, I thank him.

I envisioned a publication that would not only provide an overview of Creole history and culture, but also offer great visual appeal complete with full-color images and creative layout designs. My dream became a reality when this book was placed into the capable hands of Mary Duhé, production manager at UL Press. I cannot adequately express my gratitude to her for the hours of dedication and creativity she committed to making this book even more beautiful than I imagined.

Last, but certainly not least, I would like to thank my family. For years, they have endured phone calls, dinners, and road trips where discussions of this book dominated the conversation. They have shared my frustrations, celebrated my victories, and helped me keep the faith and maintain balance throughout the process. I am eternally grateful to them for believing in me and for encouraging me to pursue my passions.

Introduction

Hé, Cajun.
Et toi, Créole,
cofaire to pélé to même
blanc où noir? Qui donnein toi noms-yé?
Nous tous descendants des Français, Espagñols,
Africains, Indiens, Acadiens, Haitiens,
et tout z.autres Gombo People qui té vinir à
la Louisiane. Epice-yé té fait le Gombo . . .

C'est nous—les franco-louisianais, fiers de
nous l'heritage Francais et Africain . . .

Mais mon ami, pas garrochez l'épice
Parce que li trop blanc où trop noir.
Si vous fait ça, to sa pas gain Gombo
jamain plus, mais un ragout fondu salé-là
fait avec la chair niée de to l'ancestre-yé . . .

Hey, Cajun,
and you, Creole,
how come you call yourself
white or black? Who gave you these names?
We are descendants of the French, the Spanish,
the Africans, the Indians, the Acadians, the Haitians,
and all the other Gombo People who came to
Louisiana. These spices made the Gombo . . .

We are the Louisiana French, proud of
the French and African heritage . . .

But my friend, do not throw away the spice
because it is too light or too dark.
If you do that you will not have Gombo
ever again, but a foul melted stew made up of
The denied flesh of your ancestors . . . [1]

Mamaw's kitchen. Bits of conversation punctuated by bursts of laughter waft across half-empty cups of black coffee on the table. Children dart in and out, absorbed in their games but drawn to the kitchen by aromas that tempt even the pickiest of appetites to pull up a chair and linger for a bit. The velvety texture of roux folds over itself at the bottom of a well-loved pot as steady hands methodically brown the cream-colored mixture of flour and oil to perfection. A large, red-trimmed, enameled bowl offers a temporary holding place for delicately smothered okra picked from the garden. Nearby, smaller bowls of various sizes and colors containing diced onions, bell peppers, and celery line the worn counter top. Chicken quarters and coin-shaped bites of smoked sausage—the kind of smoked sausage found *only* in South Louisiana—stand ready to impart their own rich flavor to the bubbling cauldron. Deft hands, softened by age and seasoned by experience, add ingredients to the pot, tossing in a good measure of spices to tickle the taste buds. A steaming pot of rice waits patiently, ready to be drowned in the soup-like concoction known as "gumbo." Like green confetti, dashes of *filé*—ground-up leaves plucked and dried from the sassafras tree—top the hearty servings for good measure. For the uninitiated, the first bite offers a tantalizing foray into a world full of promise. For the experienced, each bite serves as a reminder of where they have come from and the long road that has brought them to where they are today.

Perhaps there is no way to describe South Louisiana's melting pot of cultures better than comparing it to a pot of gumbo. Featuring ingredients such as okra from Africa, spices from the Caribbean, *filé* from North America, and a base of roux from Europe, the blending of many cultures over the past three centuries has created a cultural mélange in the Bayou State that truly sets the region apart from the rest of the United States.

Thanks largely to the tourism industry, many outsiders associate South Louisiana with Cajun culture only. Few realize that Creoles inhabited the region long before the Cajuns arrived, and many are unaware that the Creole heritage continues to play an important role in the area's cultural landscape. Several factors contribute to the complexity of Creole identity, both past and present. Even the definition of Creole has changed over time as Louisiana's native-born population either claimed or rejected its European or African ancestry. Although the debate over "true" Creole identity continues, throughout the prairies of South Louisiana, the term typically refers to French-speaking individuals of varying skin tones and diverse ancestral roots who share a similar culture and heritage.

For many Creoles, three important cultural elements distinguish them from other ethnic groups: foodways, oral tradition, and music. Despite outside pressure to fully assimilate into mainstream American culture, Creoles take

Cajuns and Creoles have experienced a resurgence of cultural pride over the last several decades that has encouraged many to claim their diverse heritage publicly.

For three centuries, Creoles have kept their culture alive through the food they cook, stories they share, and music they enjoy.

pride in the fact that they still prepare regional dishes such as chicken fricassée and crawfish étouffée, speak a unique type of French found only in certain parts of South Louisiana, and play a style of accordion and rubboard-driven music commonly known as "Zydeco." Although some cultural elements have been lost or adapted over time, recent years have seen a renewed interest in not only preserving, but also presenting South Louisiana's rich Creole heritage. Through a variety of venues such as museum exhibits and cultural attractions, educational programs and workshops, as well as food and music festivals, Creoles celebrate their culture and seek out ways to share it with others around the world.

Over the past several decades, many Louisiana scholars have published works that illuminate Cajun history. Their cultural counterpart, the Creole community, has not yet enjoyed such attention. Despite the undeniable historical connection between Creoles of all colors, due to the work of early twentieth-century historians, genealogists, and novelists, much of the written literature excludes Creoles of Color and proposes a "whites-only" definition of the term.[2]

Although the academic world neglected the study of black Creole culture for many years, several scholars have recently attempted to balance the scales by providing insight into the experience of Creoles of Color. For example, Carl A. Brasseaux, Keith P. Fontenot, and Claude F. Oubre collaborated on an important work entitled *Creoles of Color in the Bayou Country*; James H. Dormon published a collection of essays entitled *Creoles of Color in the Gulf South*; and Sybil Kein offered an additional collection of essays in her work *Creole: The History and Legacy of Louisiana's Free People of Color*.[3] These works are all significant in that they were among the first scholarly efforts to recognize and legitimize the existence of South Louisiana's black Creole population. These researchers laid the groundwork, yet it is important to continue making inroads in the field of Creole studies.

With so much confusion surrounding usage of the term "Creole," even among scholars, it is not surprising that many people bring their own idea of "*créolité*" or "creolism" to the table. For some, New Orleans's colonial aristocracy represents the "true" Creoles, while others consider francophone[4] blacks in the rural communities of Acadiana[5] to be today's "authentic" Creoles. Still others believe that Creoles of Color are those who descend from Louisiana's free people of color, while some argue that the Creoles were comprised of Louisiana's enslaved population. The reality is that all of these definitions are correct.

Creoles of all colors and walks of life lived side-by-side for centuries, frequently sharing recipes, stories, and musical styles. Sometimes they even shared beds. While some sources have certainly illuminated various aspects of Creole history and culture, most of the scant scholarship that currently exists offers only an examination of either black Creoles or white Creoles. This academic segregation falsifies the realities of their integrated heritage.

Unable to find a source that addresses the various definitions of Creole and discusses how the lives of black and white Creoles were inextricably intertwined through the food they cooked, language they spoke, and music they danced to, I was prompted to attempt the task myself. It is my intent to not

Festivals invite people from all walks of life to dance their cares away.

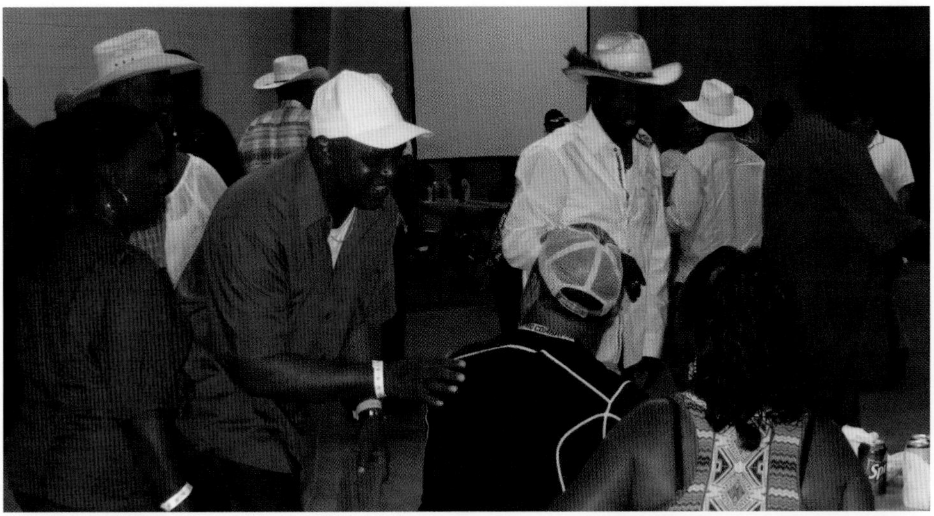

Gatherings like church bazaars, dances, and family get-togethers offer opportunities for Creoles to socialize with each other and welcome others into their world.

only bring clarity to the confusion surrounding South Louisiana's Creole identity, but also to address significant cultural aspects that distinguish them from other people in the Bayou State.

Thriving Creole communities currently exist in places such as Louisiana's Cane River region,[6] east Texas, and California, but I limited my area of focus to South Louisiana. I found it vital to include the history, culinary talents, oral traditions, and musical heritage of both black and white Creoles in New Orleans in this work since they contributed significantly to the development of South Louisiana's Creole culture as a whole. When addressing twentieth- and twenty-first-century Creole culture, however, I shifted my focus to the black Creoles in the prairie regions of Acadiana.[7] I based this decision on the fact that many outsiders are somewhat familiar with New Orleans's famous Creole food and music. Rural francophone Creoles in the prairies of South Louisiana, on the other hand, are less widely known and sometimes mistakenly identified as "black Cajuns."

My purpose in writing this book is to offer both academic and general audiences the first integrated study of South Louisiana's Creoles. My hope is that the historic legacy and enduring spirit of the region's Creole people will be revealed through this examination of their history, foodways, language, musical traditions, and efforts to preserve, celebrate, and share their heritage. Most of all, I desire to inspire all Creoles, regardless of skin color, linguistic preferences, age, occupational experience, or educational background, to become more interested in their shared heritage and appreciate the contributions that we all have made to the Bayou State's cultural gumbo.

1

Les Créoles
Origins and Evolution of a Cultural Identity

Explication de Créole: Defining "Creole"

What does "Creole" mean? Is it an ethnic label? A signifier of socio-economic status? A mark of racial "purity" or evidence of racial "tainting"? Is it a means for becoming assimilated, or a way of resisting assimilation? Is it a culture? A language? A kind of food? Perhaps the reason the word "Creole"[1] has created so much confusion in South Louisiana is simply because the answer is "yes" to all of the above. Over the years, the word's meanings, implications, connotations, and associations have changed, oftentimes crossing ethnic, social, and economic boundaries in the process. To some, the term "Creole" conjures up images of affluent members of the antebellum planter class who descended from French and Spanish aristocracy. To others, "Creole" refers to the descendants of Louisiana-born slaves or free people of color who claim mixed ancestry, including Spanish, French, African, and American Indian. For some, it signifies a regional cuisine or the rhythmic sounds of Zydeco music. To still others, it denotes the unique type of French that originated with African and Caribbean slaves. To most, it encompasses several of these aspects. "Creole" is a way of life, a culture, something to be proud of—a heritage worth preserving.

Anthropologist James Deetz defines creolization as "the interaction between two or more cultures to produce an integrated mix which is different from its antecedents."[2] Although people have been engaged in this type of cross-cultural contact since the beginning of time, scholars initially limited usage of the term "creole" to languages that evolved out of colonial-period contact between Europeans and others, especially African and Indian slaves.[3] For example, some have described Louisiana's French Creole dialect as "an exceedingly interesting example of the influence on a European tongue of negro speech and character."[4] However, as prominent French

Creole scholar Robert Chaudenson points out, many early intellectuals "treated contact between European and non-European languages . . . like a mixture of bodies in a test tube or a retort in a chemistry experiment."[5] Most considered pidgin and creole languages to be nothing more than corrupted versions of standard European languages and sought to discover the "pure" origins of the language.

Over the past several decades, however, scholars have begun to realize that although languages play an integral role in the development of distinct cultural identities, they are not the only significant cultural aspect worthy of academic attention. The relatively young discipline of Creole studies has expanded its traditionally narrow focus on Creole linguistics to include additional fields of study, such as history, anthropology, sociology, literary criticism, and cultural studies.[6] This cross-disciplinary approach lends itself to addressing the complexities of mixed cultures that transcends traditional ethnic, social, and economic norms across the globe.

By examining the concept of *créolité* from a variety of sources, it is clear that "people of all colours can affirm a creole identity through elective processes—speaking a creole language, through friendships and relationships, or simply by identifying with the many expressions of creole popular culture (music, art, dancing, food, syncretic religion, and forms of material culture) that are prevalent in their region."[7]

According to the *Harvard Encyclopedia of American Ethnic Groups*, "Creole [uppercase "C"] refers to people, to culture, to food and music, and to language. Originally from the Portuguese *crioulo* . . . probably derived from the Latin *creare* (create), it became *criollo* in Spanish and *créole* in French."[8] Simply put, the term creole (lowercase "c") originally referred to anything created or developed in the New World, including native varieties of livestock and vegetables such as creole ponies, creole tomatoes, and creole onions.[9]

Although Louisianians are the focus of this book, they are certainly not the first people to be considered Creoles. In the 1460s, Portuguese mariners began settling Cape Verde, an archipelago located some five hundred miles west of Senegal. Within a decade's time, the Cape Verde islands became integrated into the trading system of Africa's Atlantic coastline. A plantation economy consisting of cotton, sugar, and an enslaved black labor force quickly developed.[10] Although other Atlantic islands such as Madeira and the Canaries had previously used North African and Sub-Saharan slaves, Cape Verde was the first "locale in which slavery began to adopt the racial stripe which would henceforth characterize it in the Atlantic."[11] Sociologist Robin Cohen and social anthropologist Paola Toninato add, "as few Portuguese women were landed in Cape Verde, the Portuguese settlers increasingly married or had sexual relations with African women, creating the first population described as Creole."[12]

The French Market Creole Tomato Festival in New Orleans celebrates the many uses of this locally-grown product through cooking demonstrations, food booths, live music, and other family-friendly events.

Beginning with Cape Verde in the fifteenth century, and continuing up through the present, groups of people around the world have been labeled Creole or self-identified as such. For example, in eighteenth-century Mauritius, "Creole" referred to whites, primarily of French descent, who lived in Mauritius or on other islands in the Indian Ocean. By the twentieth century, however, Creole had come to mean "people of mixed origins."[13] In Sierra Leone and other parts of West Africa, blacks who had been awarded their freedom for supporting the British during the American War of Independence comprised the Creole (or "Krio") population. After a brief stint in Nova Scotia, about one thousand of these free blacks established the colony of Sierra Leone. About four thousand blacks from London joined the initial colonists, and later on, "recaptives," or those slaves who had been captured by Portuguese and Spanish slavers first, also became part of Freetown's population. Creole descendants of these early settlers enjoyed an elevated position in Sierra Leone until the native-born Temne majority came into its own in the 1960s. In Trinidad, the fifth largest island in the West Indies, "Creole" typically referred to those of African descent who acquired their freedom and "were early beneficiaries

European influences on this African woman are clearly obvious in *Portrait of an African Slave Woman*, attributed to Annibale Carracci, c. 1580.

of education [who] moved into the ranks of the colonial civil service, professional employment, and political leadership."[14] The Caribbean island country of Haiti is perhaps the most recognized Creole nation in the world, with the majority of its nearly ten million inhabitants speaking *Kreyòl*, one of the country's two official languages.[15]

Historians like Ira Berlin,[16] Linda M. Heywood, and John K. Thornton[17] employ the term "Atlantic Creole" to describe the African-born population of mixed African and European parentage that ended up in North America. Berlin explains that their "combination of swarthy skin, European dress and deportment, knowledge of local customs, and multilingualism gave them inside understanding of both African and European ways" and distinguished them from strictly European, African, or even North American culture.[18] Berlin commented that this prompted many Atlantic Creoles who lived in the early settlements along North America's Atlantic Coast to make a distinction between their national or creolized identities, despite their status as indentured servants or slaves. For instance, names like Paulo d'Angola, Simon Congo, and Jan Guinea indicated African origins, while names such as Carla Criole, Jan Creoli, and Christoffel Crioell exhibited creolized heritage.[19]

Throughout the Americas, people began calling themselves Creoles; but a common denominator was having colonists of Spanish, Portuguese, or French extraction settle in the region. As historian Joyce E. Chaplin points out, English-speaking colonists preferred to maintain their British ties. They consciously rejected the term "creole," and, until they rebelled and called themselves "Americans," these British subjects did not favor a New World identity, despite their obviously creolized culture.[20] It seems ironic, then, that recent scholars have published works with titles such as "Chesapeake Creoles: The Creation of Folk Culture in Colonial Virginia,"[21] *Creole Gentlemen: The Maryland Elite, 1691-1776*,[22] and *Friends and Strangers: The Making of a Creole Culture in Colonial Pennsylvania*.[23]

In Louisiana, Creole populations emerged in three distinct geographical locations—along the Cane River around Natchitoches,[24] throughout the prairies and swamps of Acadiana, and in and around New Orleans. Several histories, including *Africans in Colonial Louisiana: The Development of Afro-Creole Culture in the Eighteenth Century*,[25] *Creoles of Color of the Gulf South*,[26] *Creoles of Color in the Bayou Country*,[27] and *Creole: The History and Legacy of Louisiana's Free People of Color*[28] have made remarkable contributions to our understanding of South Louisiana's black Creole culture. Yet they provide no single, clear definition that accurately reflects the cultural amalgamation found in the area, and the debate over who the "true" Creoles are continues. Currently, some argue that Creoles are of mixed ethnic heritage, while others are convinced the term refers to those of strictly European (French and Spanish especially) ancestry. Since the concept of creole is such a complicated one, even within one region of one state on one continent, it is worthwhile to examine how, when, and why certain people in South Louisiana came to use the term at different times and in specific places.

The earliest known use of the word "Creole" dates back to its Spanish usage in the 1560s and originally applied "exclusively to Negroes." In the early 1600s, Garcilaso de la Vega, nicknamed "The Inca," wrote that "the name was invented by the Negroes . . . to mean a Negro born in the [West] Indies . . . to distinguish those who come from this side and were born in Guinea [West

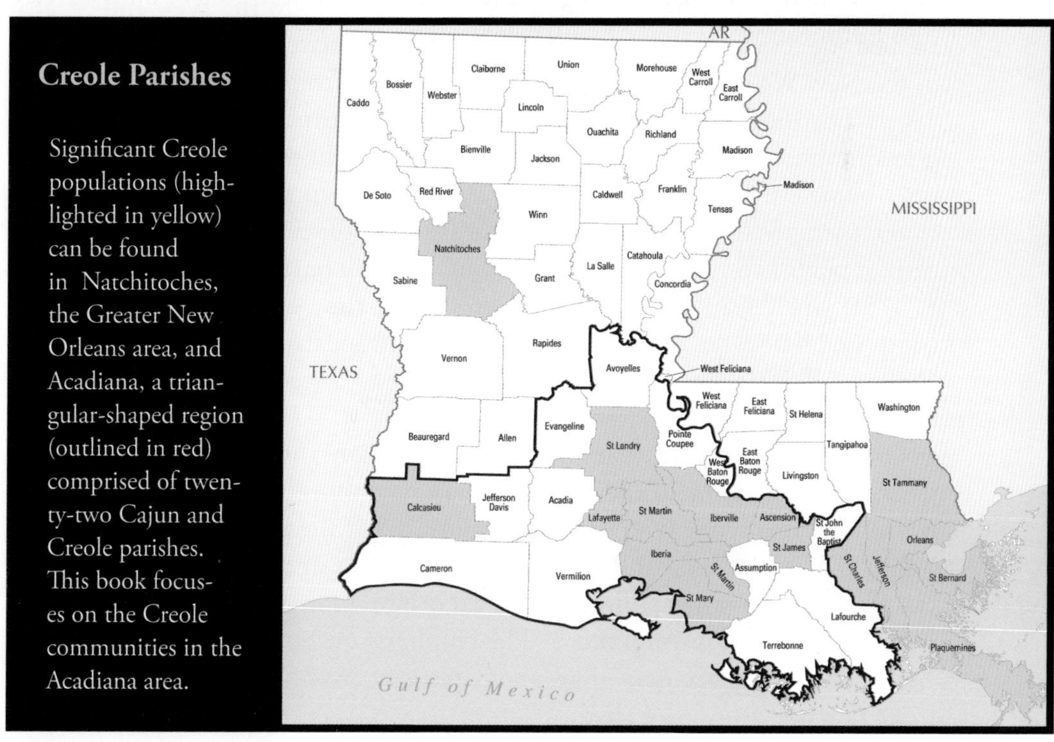

Creole Parishes

Significant Creole populations (highlighted in yellow) can be found in Natchitoches, the Greater New Orleans area, and Acadiana, a triangular-shaped region (outlined in red) comprised of twenty-two Cajun and Creole parishes. This book focuses on the Creole communities in the Acadiana area.

Linen Day, Roseau, Dominica—A Market Scene by Agostino Brunias, c. 1780, captures the ethnic and socio-economic diversity in the West Indies that resembled Colonial Louisiana.

Africa] from those born in the New World."[29] In his four-volume travelogue, published in 1722, Father Labat, a French missionary to the West Indies, also applied the term to blacks, making a distinction between "Creole slaves" born in the New World and "traded slaves" who hailed from Africa.[30]

"The Inca" claimed that the Spanish later usurped the term and applied it to all those born in the New World, regardless of European or African ancestry.[31] Some even began excluding blacks from the equation and used "Creole" to refer strictly to New World inhabitants of European ancestry. In fact, the earliest published reference to Louisiana Creoles in particular occurred on July 1, 1751, when Jean-Bernard Bossu wrote that the New Orleans population comprised four types of inhabitants, namely Europeans, Indians, Africans, and "half bloods." He described Creoles exclusively as "those born of French fathers and French, or European, mothers."[32]

Despite Bossu's explanation, most Louisianians throughout the eighteenth century imitated their West Indian neighbors and used the term Creole to refer to anyone who was native-born, regardless of skin color or ethnic origin.[33] Therefore, during the colonial period, "Creole" distinguished both black and white native children "of local origin" from other African, European, and American immigrants.[34] The emphasis on birthplace made "Creole" "more about displacement than about place; a *creole* is 'from here' but with roots that are 'from over there.'"[35]

Les Créoles Blancs: Affluent White Creoles

From its inception, white Creole society in Louisiana modeled itself after the French feudal system. Although not wealthy, landed, or titled, many white colonists considered themselves to be an emerging colonial aristocracy, complete with converted Indians acting as peasants and the black population serving as convenient serfs. Despite desperate living conditions and the constant threat of starvation, the appearance of status remained essential to their identity. For example, disputes commonly erupted over the location of their family's pew in church or who could stand at the front of religious and military processions. Marrying well became such a preoccupation that one woman sent to Louisiana in 1704 as a prospective bride refused to marry beneath her, and not even entreaties from France's minister of the Navy and Colonies could sway her opinion.[36]

When France turned Louisiana over to Spain and England in 1763, several Louisiana officers in the French garrison retired.[37] Only four of these former officers actually possessed titles. Although their claim to nobility was legitimate, they were merely chevaliers, a position considered to be the "absolute lowest rung of the French nobility." While others proudly claimed to be chevaliers in the Military Order of St. Louis, they received this honorary title for contributing twenty years of meritorious military service, not because of their noble birth or aristocratic lineage. In France, these titles would have been sneered at, but in Louisiana's wilderness environment, they offered prestige and power to their possessors.[38]

Whether they boasted legitimate claims of nobility or not, white Creoles disdained work and viewed farming as a viable means of income only if it were a large-scale international operation, complete with slaves. Managing vast plantations with the support of "armies of field hands and legions of domestic servants" was simply another method of flaunting their wealth and status.[39] White Creoles aspired to embody the epitome of elegance, grace, affluence, and refined tastes, an effort that garnered them respect "as the most cultured people in the world."[40]

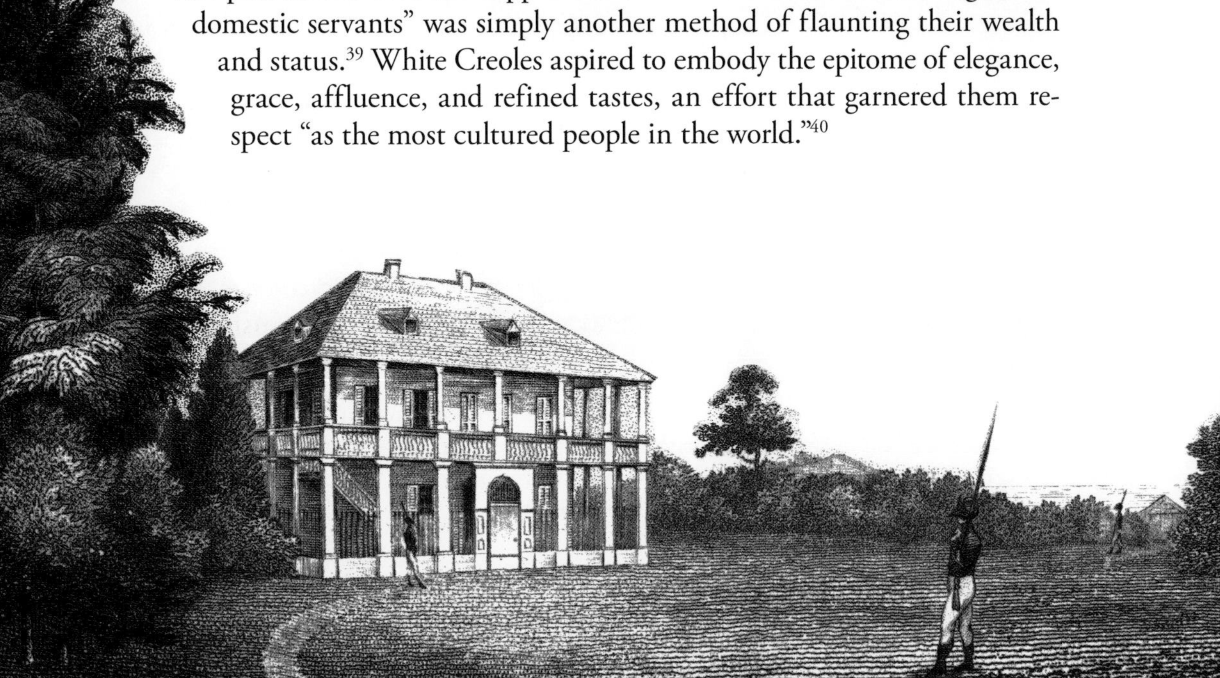

When white Creole refugees fleeing the island of Saint-Domingue[41] during the Haitian slave revolt arrived in New Orleans in the early nineteenth century, they quickly established theaters that featured ballets and operas. Many worked as lawyers, doctors, and government officials. Since these Saint-Domingue Creole refugees[42] shared the same values as their Louisiana counterparts, they too only engaged themselves in "noble" professions. The aristocratic ideals of Louisiana's white Creole population, combined with those of the Saint-Domingue immigrants, contributed to their demise, beginning with the arrival of Anglo-American immigrants after the Louisiana Purchase in 1803. When Louisiana attained statehood in 1812, even more American immigrants began flooding the region, eager to seize economic opportunities. Since Creole society considered work beneath them, during financial crises or crop failures, they often sold prized land along major rivers to Americans in order to acquire the cash necessary for maintaining their opulent way of life. Sacrificing landholdings in order to maintain appearances caused many to lose their estates as well as their elitist positions.[43]

During the Americanization process of Louisiana, white Creoles clung to their glorious past in the midst of economic difficulties and declining social status. They held to their image as long as possible, and as late as the 1930s, journalist Lyle Saxon boasted, "The New Orleans Creole is our finest product. The women are lovely. The men are brave. They have charming manners. They are exclusive. They are clannish. Can anyone blame them? They have their own language, their own society, their own customs . . . They still speak a pure French."[44]

During the Haitian slave revolt, white Creoles fled Saint-Domingue (present-day Haiti). Many survivors reestablished themselves in New Orleans where they socialized during "the season" between January and March. The other nine months, they stayed in the country to oversee their sugarcane plantations.

A Creole Plantation

Cultivation and exportation of sugarcane made Saint-Domingue one of France's most lucrative landholdings in the New World. Louisiana's planter class, including Guillaume Duparc, a French naval veteran of the American Revolution, used the island as a model to develop their own plantation sugar economy. In 1804, Duparc purchased Laura Plantation in Vacherie, Louisiana. Sugarcane cultivation continued there until 1981.

Not all observers bestowed such glowing reports on the Creoles. After fleeing Saint-Domingue during the slave revolts, sugar planter Pierre Louis Berquin-Duvallon noted in 1802 that Louisiana's "first settlers were either needy French or German adventurers, who scarcely improved their fortune to mediocrity." He further expounded that "the Creoles of Louisiana being all of base extraction . . . were naturally illiterate, ignorant, and rude; qualities inherited and preserved by their descendants. In fact, the present race seem[s] to have degenerated from their ancestors." He relayed a conversation in which a Creole told him "with great naiveté" that "a never failing method to make him fall asleep, was to open a book before him." His criticism continued. "They are the greatest egoists in the world; their conversation is eternally about themselves. They are vulgarly familiar with their equals, insolent towards their inferiors, cruel to their slaves, and inhospitable to strangers."[45]

Despite such criticism, those who still claim to be of white Creole extraction often uphold lofty ideas of a planter aristocracy that stood far superior to the region's Anglo-American "invaders." Yet documentation proves that French Creoles and Anglo-Americans were more than eager to form alliances and often intermarried in order to preserve their elitist status. During the antebellum years, maintaining control over the region's growing slave population became a much more serious threat and source of concern than any Anglo-French tensions.[46]

Les Créoles Noirs: Enslaved Black Creoles

Whereas white Creoles boasted racial, social, and economic privilege, enslaved black Creoles formed the lowest ranks of Louisiana's three-tiered population.[47] Yet, without their knowledge, skills, and labor, Louisiana never would have survived as a colony. As early as 1699, Louisiana's governor requested permission to travel to Guinea for the purpose of buying slaves, but his request was initially denied. Within a few years, census records indicate that a handful of blacks inhabited the fledgling colony, most of whom undoubtedly were smuggled in as slaves[48] since the first two sanctioned ships laden with five hundred enslaved Africans did not reach Louisiana's shores until 1719.[49]

Although the French slave trade peaked in the 1730s, none of these slaves reached Louisiana, mostly due to New Orleans's inconvenient distance north of the Caribbean sugar islands and its location some one hundred miles up the Mississippi River. For French slavers, it was more practical to drop off their "highly perishable and rebellious" human cargo at the first available port where they could be sold for a profit. Therefore, islands like Saint-Domingue, Martinique, and Guadeloupe became the primary ports for slave-transporting vessels. Due to the lack of imported slaves, the New Orleans slave force soon became one of the most aged and most creolized slave populations in the New World. By 1741, approximately two-thirds of Louisiana's entire slave population was native-born.[50]

By Dutillet & Peyrellade.

On Wednesday the 7th day of Nov. next, will be sold at the said auction,

A negro creole, a good cook and intelligent servant, 30 years old.

A negro man from Africa, since 5 years in the country, a servant of 20 years old.

A negro woman from Africa, since 7 years in the country, a good washer and servant, 20 years old, with her child, a mulatto girl from 3 to 4 years old.

A negro woman from Africa, since 6 years in the country, a good servant.

Since Creoles typically fetched higher prices, auction ads like this one from the *Orleans Gazette* in 1810 noted which slaves were of Creole origin and which ones came from Africa directly. Women and children were no exception. For instance, the "good washer" was only thirteen when she arrived from Africa. Now twenty, her three to four-year-old mulatto daughter joined her on the auction block. Meanwhile a thirty-year-old "negro creole" is described as a "good cook and intelligent servant."

New Orleans's St. Louis Hotel hosted aristocratic Creoles and visiting Europeans. As depicted in this engraving, its ornate rotunda housed an auction block where the wealthy could buy and sell slaves.

Creole slaves from Louisiana and other French colonies, unlike those hailing directly from Africa, typically sold for higher prices on the auction block because they were "considered to be more docile, seasoned to the climate, trained for field work or domestic tasks, and, most important, French-speaking."[51] From 1766 to 1785, the first two decades of Spanish administration of Louisiana, New Orleans's black population grew from 3,971 to 10,420, with the majority of the population increase attributed to natural reproduction.[52]

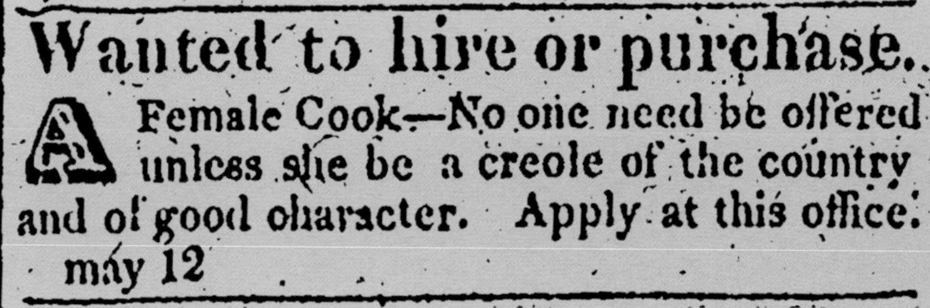

Wanted to hire or purchase.

A Female Cook—No one need be offered unless she be a creole of the country and of good character. Apply at this office.

may 12

This advertisements from the *Orleans Gazette* in 1820 specifically requests a Creole cook.

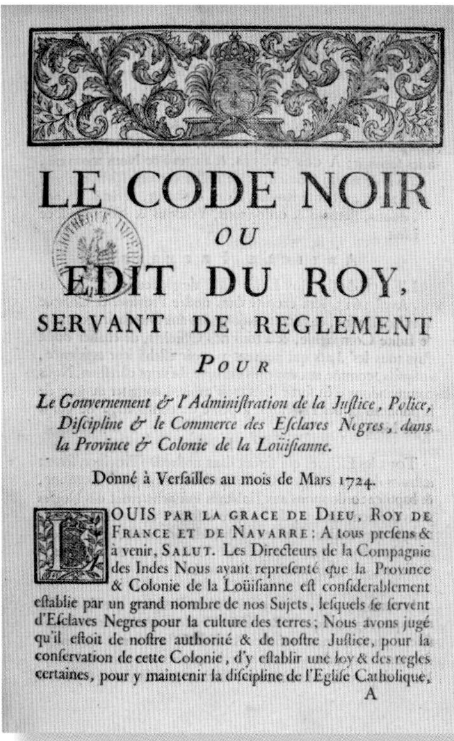

LE CODE NOIR

OU

EDIT DU ROY,

SERVANT DE REGLEMENT

POUR

Le Gouvernement & l'Adminiſtration de la Juſtice, Police, Diſcipline & le Commerce des Eſclaves Negres, dans la Province & Colonie de la Loüiſianne.

Donné à Verſailles au mois de Mars 1724.

LOUIS PAR LA GRACE DE DIEU, ROY DE FRANCE ET DE NAVARRE: A tous preſens & à venir, SALUT. Les Directeurs de la Compagnie des Indes Nous ayant repreſenté que la Province & Colonie de la Loüiſianne eſt conſiderablement eſtablie par un grand nombre de nos Sujets, leſquels ſe ſervent d'Eſclaves Negres pour la culture des terres; Nous avons jugé qu'il eſtoit de noſtre authorité & de noſtre Juſtice, pour la conſervation de cette Colonie, d'y eſtablir une loy & des regles certaines, pour y maintenir la diſcipline de l'Egliſe Catholique,

A

The *Code Noir* granted enslaved people unprecedented rights and privileges in Louisiana.

Louisiana's adoption of the *Code Noir* of 1724[53] set it apart from the rest of North America. Under these "black codes," slaves could report their masters to the authorities if treated inhumanely or if denied proper food and clothing. Owners had to educate and baptize their slaves in the Catholic faith. Slaves did not have to work on Sundays and holidays, and within a short time they were exempt from work on Saturday afternoons, as well. Slaves could sell foodstuffs in the public marketplace, including garden produce they cultivated, nuts and berries they gathered, and fish and game they hunted and trapped. Slaves could also hire themselves out and keep their wages. With the money earned, they were able to purchase not only clothing and personal supplies, but in some cases, their freedom, as well.[54] As one scholar noted, "What made French Louisiana different was that slaves there came early to be recognized as having the right to use their free time virtually as they saw fit, with little or no supervision. Such a conception, much less such a practice, never prevailed anywhere in the rest of the South."[55]

Although no slave cited overwork as a reason for fleeing during the colonial period, some did run away from their masters.[56] Known as "maroons," these runaways—almost all of whom were former Creole slaves—formed self-contained communities in the swamps and bayous of Louisiana. Already familiar with their environment and comfortable with their surroundings, maroons did not retreat from society. Instead they engaged in business with not only other Creole slaves, but also white businessmen in the city of New Orleans. They cut and sold cypress timber, made willow baskets, sifters, and tubs for processing indigo, and grew and sold foodstuffs.[57] Practical economic demands apparently overrode idealized principles regarding the subjugation of the enslaved population.

Unlike their Anglo-American counterparts, Louisiana's maroon population typically included entire families of runaways, but the inclusion

Maroon communities comprised of runaway slaves often included entire families. This 1873 illustration from *Harper's Weekly* depicts how some maroons survived in the swamps and bayous.

of women and children in maroon camps did not impede their successful attempts to escape bondage. In addition to the maroons' ability to live off the land and negotiate business deals, they were capable of fending off those who tried to recapture them since many were armed. It was common for masters to provide their adult male slaves with weapons so they could defend their master's property against raids, as well as hunt and provide food for the master and his family. During French rule, most runaways succeeded in escaping. In fact, it was not until 1764, one year after Spain officially acquired Louisiana, that the first organized slave patrol was even implemented.[58]

Slaveholders in colonial Louisiana usually complied with the relatively lenient elements of the *Code Noir*, but often ignored stricter regulations, such as those regarding interracial relations. Since the provincial government could not possibly enforce rules on a local level, lax control coupled with

Runaway slave illustration recreated in pen and watercolor by Bernarda Bryson, c. 1935.

voluntary compliance contributed to Louisiana's enslaved population enjoying unparalleled privileges. In essence, French Louisiana slaveholders followed rules when they considered them to be "conducive to the efficient management of slaves" although they ignored "articles viewed as unnecessarily restrictive or impractical."[59] For example, the law permitted slaveholders to punish runaways by cropping their ears or branding them with a fleur-de-lis, but most chose not to mark potential problem slaves permanently in order to try to sell them for a good price in the future.[60]

Although French rule introduced slavery to Louisiana, the number of slaves in the colony increased dramatically during the Spanish (1763-1802) and early American periods (1803-1812). Realizing that Creole slaves were accustomed to enjoying certain rights and privileges under the French, and recognizing the fact that many runaways had established successful maroon communities, Spanish and American administrators began enforcing more stringent laws regarding the importation of slaves in order to minimize the threat of insurrection. The remarkably successful slave revolt in Haiti proved what creolized slave populations were capable of, and Spanish and American authorities hoped to thwart any possibility of a similar uprising occurring during their administration. As a result, under Spanish rule, nearly all slaves brought into Louisiana came directly from Africa, and roughly three-fourths of the imported slave population came from Africa during early American rule. Out of the estimated 24,000 to 29,000 slaves arriving between 1763 and 1812, at least 20,000 to 22,000 of these slaves came directly from West African shores.[61]

Administrators hoped these fresh-off-the-boat slaves would be less likely to cause trouble than their Creole counterparts. This influx of African-born slaves undoubtedly contributed to the Creole slaves' ability to maintain their own identity and somewhat higher status as native-born residents of the region. Many became house slaves and overseers, while the newly arrived African slaves took their place working as field hands and common laborers since they "knew nothing of the religion, language, law, and social etiquette that Europeans equated with civilization." In order to maintain their status as Creoles, many tried to separate themselves from the influx of recently imported Africans by forging new biracial and triracial identities and even passing for white.[62]

A FIELD-HAND.

ANGOLA:
From African Shores to Louisiana's State Penitentiary

Angola's National Museum of Slavery

In addition to French Senegambia, the Portuguese colony Angola provided Louisiana with a significant number of enslaved laborers. In 1720, just two years after the founding of New Orleans, *La Néréide* set sail from La Rochelle, France, and picked up its human cargo in Cabinda. Between 1719 and 1731, Cabinda provided 300 of the 5,500 deported Africans in Louisiana. Angola's National Museum of Slavery, located in the capitol city of Luanda, is housed in a building that once served as a center for slave trafficking. The stairs leading from the museum down to the Atlantic Ocean were the last bit of earth the feet of untold thousands of Africans touched before boarding the ships for their trans-Atlantic voyage. As depicted in one of the museum's exhibits, slaves were often chained together and shackled with weights to minimize their ability to flee.[63]

Five years after the Civil War ended and slavery was abolished, Confederate Major Samuel James acquired the lease for Louisiana prisoners. In exchange for housing and feeding the inmates, he turned a profit by subleasing them to build levees and dig ditches. In 1880, he purchased Angola, an 8,000-acre plantation in West Feliciana Parish that had been named for the former slaves' country of origin. He used the plantation's old slave quarters to house some of the inmates. Today Angola State Penitentiary is Louisiana's oldest and only maximum-security prison.

Louisiana's Angola Penitentiary, 1934.

Les Créoles de Couleur: Free People of Color and Creoles of Color

In Louisiana's three-tiered society, whites formed the pinnacle of the socio-economic pyramid, while enslaved blacks formed the lowest rank. What set Louisiana apart, however, was its surprisingly large middle strata of *gens de couleur libre*, or free people of color. Despite their inability to reach the social status of whites, many *gens de couleur libres* acquired their freedom through various means and became extremely successful businessmen, plantation owners, and slaveholders who enjoyed significant wealth and prestige. After the Civil War eliminated their position of distinction as "free people of color," this segment of Louisiana's population began referring to themselves as *Créoles de Couleur*. As Creoles of Color, these individuals were able to continue maintaining a marked distance between themselves and the newly freed former slave population during the difficult years of Reconstruction.

Within a decade of the first slaves' arrival in Louisiana, blacks had begun attaining their freedom. Some of the earliest *gens de couleur libres* earned their freedom by fighting Indians in the Natchez Wars (1729-31).[64] Since the Spanish colonial government prohibited Indian slavery, some were emancipated during the Spanish period if they could prove American Indian ancestry. Still others purchased their own freedom with the proceeds of their hired-out labor and market endeavors.[65] Due to the leniency of the *Code Noir*, some slaves even earned their freedom by tutoring their masters' children.[66] According to Louisiana law, any master older than twenty-five years of age was permitted to manumit his slaves, and many did, typically as a reward for faithful or heroic service.[67]

Marie Philomene Donato Olivier

At the age of four, Marie was emancipated by her father Martin Donato, one of St. Landry Parish's largest slaveholders. Donato had purchased Marie's mother Julie and grandmother Nelly in 1819. When Donato's wife died in 1832, it seems as though Julie became his concubine; she gave him seven children. In his last will, dated September 2, 1847, Donato emancipated thirty-two-year-old Julie and the children born to their union: Eugenie (14), Emile (12), Uranie (11), twin sisters Feliciane and Felicie (8), Marie Philomene (4), and Didier (15 months).[68]

A gold band graces the left hand of a New Orleans woman in this portrait simply entitled *Creole in a Red Turban* by Jacques Aman, c. 1840.

With the passage of time, however, faithful service was rewarded less. The increase in numbers of the free black population more commonly resulted from masters manumitting their slave mistresses and mulatto children.[69] Since marriages between whites and blacks were officially prohibited, *plaçage*, a system of "placing" women of color in extramarital unions, conveniently suited the needs and desires of Louisiana's black and white populations. Due to the lack of white women in colonial Louisiana, many white males fostered relationships with women of color. Much to the chagrin of early Louisiana visitors who documented their travel experiences, Spanish military officers "and a good many of the inhabitants live[d] almost publicly with colored concubines" and did not even "blush" when baptizing the children born out of these unions.[70]

Quadroon balls offered ample opportunities for these biracial liaisons to be formed. One New Orleans visitor described quadroon[71] women as "almost white and all free. They are prohibited from intermarrying with whites & they *will not* marry mulattoes. They prefer being kept mistresses which is assign'd as a reason for there being such a number of Single Women in this Country."[72] *Plaçage* offered these free women of color a lucrative alternative to undesirable or prohibited marriages. At these formal dances, mothers made arrangements for their daughters to be placed with suitable white men who could offer financial stability and protection.

According to one eighteenth-century observer, "the mulatto [or quadroon] women have not all the faults of the mulatto men. But they are full of vanity, and very libertine; money will always buy their caresses. They are not without personal charms; good

Nineteenth-century illustration of a *Colored Lady of New Orleans* strolling through a park in high fashion.

In this detail from *Free Women of Color with their Children and Servants in a Landscape*, Agostino Brunias (c. 1764–96) artistically captured the blending of European, North American, and African cultures in the Caribbean. Louisiana experienced a similar phenomenon.

shapes, polished and elastic skins. They live in open concubinage with the whites; but to this they are incited more by money than by attachment."[73]

Despite outside criticism, these relationships were recognized publicly and often lasted for life. Louisianians did not attach any social stigma to white males who engaged in these interracial relationships, even if they later married white women. In many cases, these men provided for both their black and white children by passing on their family name to them, baptizing them in the Catholic Church, and leaving behind a sizeable inheritance for them to divide equally. By 1850, about 80 percent of Louisiana's free people of color population was comprised of mulattoes and others of mixed blood, irrefutable evidence of the long history of mutually beneficial sexual liaisons between white males and women of color in the colony.[74]

Although many children of color were born into freedom, not all received such privilege at birth. Some slaves, as previously stated, obtained their freedom by purchasing it or being rewarded for faithfulness or exemplary military service. Others, however, gained their freedom through highly unusual means. For instance, the case of the slave Jeannot sheds light on the remarkable power some slaves wielded, especially in colonial Louisiana.

Lacking a public executioner, the Superior Council, Louisiana's judicial and military oligarchy, ordered Jeannot to fill the position and, recognizing how unsavory the job was, promised to reward him with freedom. Jeannot, however, adamantly refused to execute people who had not harmed him personally, even though he could attain his freedom by doing so. His prayers and petitions to the Superior Council went unheeded until he cut off his right arm and sent it to the councilmen. Greatly impressed by his fortitude, the council decided to grant Jeannot his freedom anyway.[75]

The story of François Tiocou and his wife Marie Aram is particularly poignant. A free man born in Senegal but living in New Orleans, Tiocou made an arrangement to work seven years without pay at the Charity Hospital for the Poor in exchange for his wife's freedom. After faithfully keeping his promise, Tiocou's request was granted, and his wife was awarded "the privileges of persons born free" in 1744.[76]

A freed slave had two restrictions placed upon him by the *Code Noir*—he could not house fugitive slaves and he had to show respect to his former master and the master's family. Otherwise, according to the *Code*, all manumitted slaves were granted "the same rights, privileges, and immunities which are enjoyed by free-born persons." As a result of these "rights, privileges, and immunities," free people of color were able to sue whites in court and often won. The case of Raphael Bernard proves this point. In March of 1724, Bernard loaned a white man two hundred francs. When the loan was not paid by the end of the stipulated month, Bernard petitioned the court. The white defendant was ordered to not only repay the loan to the free man of color, but also to pay interest on the loan and reimburse Bernard for all court costs.[77]

Regardless of how they acquired their freedom, Louisiana's free people of color continued to flourish financially and, under Spanish rule, enjoyed the same property rights as whites. Even if they never attained quite the same social status as their white counterparts, upwardly mobile free people of color continued climbing the ladder of economic success, regardless of the color of their skin. Travelers to South Louisiana were often shocked by the large numbers of wealthy people of color they encountered, commenting that "Negroes [were dressed] in purple and fine linen," the young women were "pretty and accomplished," and the men were "opulent, intelligent colored planters."[78]

By 1860, only one-tenth of New Orleans's free people of color worked as common laborers. Most monopolized skilled trades and became mechanics, carpenters, tailors, barbers, and shoemakers, among other things. New Orleans could not survive without "an urban middle class to work at the skilled trades, to run the hundreds of retail shops, and to perform commercial transactions. The free people of color filled this basic need. . . ." The communities of freed people of color ran their own schools, churches, and theaters, and supported their own artists, writers, and educators.[79]

Not all free people of color were tradesman. Many were affluent plantation owners and slaveholders who comprised the nation's wealthiest group of free blacks in the nineteenth century. As the following chart indicates, all but four of the nation's wealthiest "black" entrepreneurs were Louisiana Creoles, and two of them were women.[80]

Most of these wealthholders had inherited property and slaves from their white fathers, and, like their white planter associates, were often too preoccupied with their own prosperity and status to consider the slaves' situation. For example, after the death of her husband in the late 1830s, a free woman of color "sold two children away from their mothers, disposed of an old

Wealth of Leading U.S. Black Entrepreneurs, 1820-1865
(Minimum property values, $100,000)

Surname	Location	Business Activity	Assessed Wealth
Leidesdorff	San Francisco, Ca.	Merchandising, real estate	$1,500,000
Smith	Philadelphia, Pa.	Lumber merchant, real estate	500,000
Soulie	New Orleans	Merchant broker, capitalist	500,000
Lacroix	New Orleans	Tailor, real estate	300,000
Lacroix	New Orleans	Grocer, real estate	250,000
Ricaud*	Iberville Parish	Sugar planter	221,500
DuBuclet	Iberville Parish	Sugar planter	206,400
Pottier	New Orleans	Cotton commission broker	200,000
DuPuy	New Orleans	Capitalist	171,000
Reggio	Plaquemines Parish	Sugar planter, overseer	160,000
McCarty*	New Orleans	Merchandising, money broker	155,000
DeCuir	Point Coupee Parish	Sugar planter	151,000
Logoaster	New Orleans	Landlord	150,000
Colvis	New Orleans	Tailor	150,000
Metoyer	Natchitoches Parish	Cotton planter	140,958
Durnford	Plaquemines Parish	Sugar planter	115,000
Metoyer	Natchitoches Parish	Cotton planter	112,761
Casenave	New Orleans	Commission broker, undertaker	100,000
Donato	St. Landry Parish	Cotton planter	100,000
Forten	Philadelphia, Pa.	Sailmaker	100,000
Sprawlding	Louisville, Ky.	Barber, real estate	100,000

*Indicates female entrepreneurs. Madame McCarty was a plaçée who accumulated her vast fortune over a period of fifty years. The widow Ricaud and her son owned over 150 slaves before 1860.

Built by the Metoyer family in the 1830s, Melrose Plantation in Natchitoches stands as perhaps the most well known Louisiana plantation owned by free people of color.

woman for fifty dollars, and tried in vain to sell several other slaves described as 'sickly' and 'infirmed.'" One anonymous slave explained to a Louisiana traveler in the mid-1850s, "You might think, master, dat dey would be good to dar own nation; but dey is not. They is very bad masters."[81] As late as 1856, Louisiana's Supreme Court upheld the idea that "in the eyes of Louisiana law there is . . . all the difference between a free man of color and a slave that there is between a white man and a slave."[82] But that soon changed.

Throughout the 1850s, Louisiana's state legislature and the city of New Orleans began blurring the legal lines between free blacks and slaves by passing ordinances such as the one that forbade people of color, whether slave or free, to assemble. Conditions became ludicrous when Louisiana passed a state law in 1859 that "allowed" free people of color to choose their masters and become slaves for life.[83] Naturally, this was not considered a desirable offer, and many began fleeing the state. An 1860 article printed in the New Orleans *Daily Delta* reported, "scarcely a week passes but a large number of free persons of color leave this port for Mexico or Hayti [*sic*]."[84] Mexico was a good choice for those interested in business ventures, but Haiti, as the world's first free black nation, was an appealing location for people of color to resettle. Far outnumbered by enslaved and free blacks, many whites strongly encouraged this outward migration. The *Daily Picayune* proclaimed, "As for us in New Orleans, we say let them go and God speed them; we can get along quietly enough with our contented and faithful slaves."[85]

Despite encouraged emigration, not all *gens de couleur libres* left home. Many stayed behind, in fact, and fought for the Confederacy in order to preserve their status as wealthy landowners and slaveholders. Some even helped to build Southern fortifications by donating their slaves' labor. In the aftermath of the Civil War, these affluent free people of color, like their white counterparts, also endured heavy losses financially, socially, and politically.[86]

A darker-skinned servant poses for a portrait with this Creole of Color couple and their nine children, c. 1900.

Free people of color suffered additionally during Reconstruction when they were stripped of their *gens de couleur libres* status. While some were able to pass for white or successfully carved out niches of power for themselves in the new government, for most former free people of color, their carefully constructed three-tiered world crumbled around them, leaving them in a heap of rubble on the bottom half of a structure in which whites were on top. These once-prosperous and powerful families "abandoned by their white 'allies' and 'friends,' forced off the land or dividing it up into small plots . . . were no longer a privileged group in a slave society."[87] With little more than their French ancestry to cling to, and in an effort to distinguish themselves from the newly freed slave population, the former *gens de couleur libres* and their descendants began referring to themselves as *Créoles de Couleur*.

In the post-war frenzy of racial tensions, whites were horrified with the attachment of *couleur* to the term *Créole* and desperately began taking measures to prove their racial purity.[88] In an ironic twist of fate, white Creoles who had given little thought to their interracial relations via systems like *plaçage* were now plagued with the stigma of having associated with "tainted" blood. Immediately, they began making great efforts to cover their tracks and asserted that "Creole" excluded *all* people of color, regardless of skin tone or antebellum status. White Creoles tried to convince themselves and others that they had no connection with their darker neighbors, business associates, and oftentimes, even family members. In claiming that Creole meant "of pure French and/or Spanish ancestry," they excluded the possibility of any blackness being associated with the glorified mythology of their past.[89] At the close of the nineteenth century, the term "Creole" meant white purity for whites and miscegenation for blacks.[90]

Les Créoles D' Aujourd'hui: Creoles Today

The debate over the "correct" definition of Creole continues. Despite the obvious historical connection between Creoles of all colors, due to the work of early twentieth-century historians, genealogists, and novelists, much of the written literature excludes Creoles of Color and proposes a "whites-only" definition of the term. For example, when Charles Gayarré published his four volumes on Louisiana history, he adamantly opposed the idea that "the basest of races" (i.e. blacks) should be "ingrafted on the trunk of a much nobler race" (white Creoles), considering "this process of propagation by incision" to be "fit only for plants and trees, not for human beings."[91] When Grace King, a genealogist and author mentored by Gayarré, compiled and published her findings in 1895 and 1921, she "carefully extract[ed] those of African descent from the leading white Creole families."[92] Novelist Edward Larocque Tinker introduced his major work *Toucoutou* in 1928 with a definition of Creole that asserted it could "mean only one thing and this is a pure white person born of European parents in Spanish or French colonies."[93]

The keeper of the baptismal records at New Orleans's St. Louis Cathedral admitted that it was "quite common to find colored persons registered on the registry of white persons [but that] it is very seldom that white persons are inscribed on the registry of colored persons. . . . When such a case occurs,

Many Creoles still maintain close-knit familial ties, despite the conveniences and distractions of modern lifestyles. For instance, the Fils family of four lives in rural Sunset, sharing the same street with close relatives.

there is a marginal note made correcting the error." Therefore, even official documents can be altered rather easily to correct "mistakes," changing racial identity with the stroke of a pen and creating additional challenges to those trying to understand New Orleans's complex ethnic makeup.[94]

Nowadays, especially in New Orleans and its environs, the families who can trace their ancestry back to Louisiana's first French and/or Spanish settlers still claim their white Creole heritage proudly and deny any association with the black Creole community. New Orleans's darker-skinned Creoles, on the other hand, still argue that Creole signifies someone of mixed racial ancestry. While both black and white Creoles of New Orleans usually exhibit pride in their respective heritage, they oftentimes struggle with acknowledging Creole people whose skin color is different from their own. Some blacks have dealt with this issue by simply "passing" to the other side of that perceived racial barrier.

As evidenced by cases of passing, some limitations imposed by race were superseded by social and economic opportunities. For instance, Creoles of Color who possessed lighter skin, straight hair, and even blue eyes were capable of denying or hiding their African heritage. By passing into the white world they were able to enjoy greater socio-economic status and opportunity.[95] Although racial boundaries based on skin tones clearly exist between white and black Creoles, as one scholar noted, "the act of passing depends on the construction, maintenance, and transgression of [those] boundaries." Some have successfully negotiated these boundaries to their benefit.[96]

A very different perception of Creole exists outside of New Orleans, however. As one scholar observed, "In present-day southwest Louisiana, individuals who call themselves Creoles are descendants of both free people of color and freed slaves. . . . Black identity and French heritage are thought of not only as compatible but as inseparable."[97] Contributing to this "colored-only" definition of Creole is the fact that many less affluent white Creoles who eventually settled in rural areas began assimilating into the white Francophone world of Cajun[98] culture. The integration of these rural white Creoles was so complete and successful that today, many of these "Cajun" families honestly believe they are of Acadian descent and are completely unaware that their

An unidentified girl shows off her doll in Frilot Cove, a small Creole community located in St. Landry Parish.

Creole youngsters sport their Western clothes at a rodeo in Lake Charles.

family surnames are actually Creole.[99] In the world of twentieth-century Jim Crow segregation, the emphasis placed on racial "purity" reinforced many indigent Creoles' claim of Acadian heritage. To be Cajun was to be white, while being Creole implied having a drop of "colored" blood.

In recent years, the phrase "Creole of Color" has dropped out of usage, but the terms "black Creole" or simply "Creole" are still used to describe the darker-skinned people of Southwest Louisiana's prairie regions. In practical usage, "Creole" now refers to people of mixed African and European heritage who speak French (or have grandparents who did), eat gumbo and jambalaya at family gatherings, wear cowboy hats, boots, and pressed Wranglers, participate in trail rides and *boucheries* (communal pig roasts), and dance to Zydeco music. For many black Creoles, a rural upbringing differentiates them from their urbanized and oftentimes darker-skinned African American neighbors with whom they sometimes struggle to identify. One black Creole explained, "Whites think we're black, and blacks think we're stuck up." Another frustrated Creole described his dating dilemma: "We can't go with white girls *or* black girls."[100]

Norbert Auzenne, vice president of a Creole group known as the Inseparable Friends Benevolent Society, recalls his difficult childhood growing up Creole in a segregated world:

> I can remember as a young boy . . . being light-skinned,
> going to school with the darker-skinned Negroes.
> They looked at us sort of as inferior because our skin was lighter than theirs.
> And because of this we got into a lot of fights.
> The whites didn't have much use for us either
> because our skin color was . . . light,
> our hair was straight.
> And they would look down on us.[101]

Couples grace the dance floor and friends strike a pose at the Creole Renaissance Festival in Opelousas.

Even in the popular world of music, some Creoles have struggled with their identity. For example, Alphonse "Bois Sec" Ardoin, a darker-skinned Creole musician who passed away in 2007 at the age of ninety-one, remembered,

> In those days, you stayed in your own neighborhood. People didn't mix very easily. Take, for example, the people from *La Pinière*.[102] You see, those people didn't want to mix with us. They were lighter-skinned. They were mulattoes. And we couldn't go to their dances. I was able to go because I played music for them, but I couldn't bring a friend. They didn't allow that. It was just like trying to go to a white dance in those days. . . . Then, later, when people started behaving like people, we all got to be like brothers and sisters.[103]

Jeffery Broussard, a well-known Creole Zydeco accordionist, recounted his experiences playing music at a local dance hall called the "Triangle Club."

> It was a real nice place, real huge.
> It would stay packed just about every weekend.
> There was only one thing that was different about it,
> and excuse me for saying this,
> but I felt that it was wrong . . .
> it was like all the blacks were on the left-hand side,
> and the lighter people
> —they called themselves mulatto—
> were on the right-hand side.

Eventually, Broussard explained that the "the young generation blew that out of the water" by transcending those barriers.[104]

In addition to the complex internal struggles some Creoles have in finding common ground within their own segregated communities of color is the more difficult challenge of making outsiders understand that they are not Cajuns just because they live in South Louisiana, speak French, and eat spicy food. For example, Creole Zydeco artist Stanley "Buckwheat Zydeco" Dural was adamant about showcasing his Creole heritage, despite marketing ploys that have incorrectly labeled southwest Louisiana "Cajun Country." In 1988, he and his manager put out a press release to clarify common misconceptions regarding his culture and style of music. He began by explaining that "Cajuns are the *white* descendants of the original French settlers of Nova Scotia, which was originally known as Acadia," but that "all the French-speaking black people of southwestern Louisiana refer to themselves as *Creole* . . ." The release went on to say, "Calling Buck[wheat] a Cajun is sort of like calling an Irishman English, and referring to Zydeco as Cajun music is like calling reggae calypso

People around the world still celebrate their Creole heritage like these French-speaking musicians from Reunion Island, a small country in the Indian Ocean where cultures from Africa, India, and Madagascar blend together.

music. . . . The band is not from New Orleans, and Zydeco is not New Orleans music. The band, as well as most Zydeco bands, is based in and around the small city of Lafayette, which is over a hundred miles west of New Orleans—on the other side of the Mississippi River and the great Atchafalaya Swamp. Once again, it is as distinct a difference as Jamaica is from Trinidad, or Ireland is from England."[105]

From the moment the first European colonists and enslaved Africans set foot on Louisiana's soil, the Creoles of South Louisiana have been defining and redefining what it means to be a "Creole." Although popular media and literature have contributed to the romanticized notion that Creoles are Louisiana's unsullied aristocracy prior to the "invasion" of *les Américains*, the term Creole is much more complex and multilayered than what may initially meet the eye. The historical record proves that identifying oneself as a Creole involved racial, social, economic, and political implications. Creole is much more than an ethnic label, an indication of race, or a signifier of ancestry or heritage. The benefits or drawbacks of being labeled "Creole" depend not only on the perceived color of one's skin or the geographical setting in which one is located, but also the historical context in which the term is placed. To be white Creole in antebellum New Orleans was to be a part of the upper echelon of society. To be black Creole in the rural prairies of Southwest Louisiana today is to be more culturally similar to blue-collar Cajuns than affluent *gens de couleur libres* ancestors.

Although the question "what is a Creole?" may not have a rigid answer, the fact that South Louisianians are still grappling with ways to come up with an answer helps to explain why the term has been so confusing throughout the passage of time. In a world that tries to categorize people on the basis of skin color or ethnicity, language or ancestry, the very concept of Creole transcends racial, social, and economic boundaries. Perhaps the struggle to understand, define, and maintain their unique identity as a people will eventually enable Creoles of all colors, ancestries, and socio-economic backgrounds to unite in understanding and appreciating their shared culture and heritage. As one scholar noted, "Ethnic identity is not a thing outside the self-imposed by 'acculturation'; nor is it an automatic consequence of 'descent.' Rather it is a dynamic mode of self-consciousness, a form of selfhood reinterpreted if not reinvented generationally in response to changing historical circumstances."[106] Maybe one day we will begin to realize that as two scholars claim, "Creole is thus not a 'hard' racial category with strongly policed edges defined by 'blood' or colour, but a 'fuzzy' or 'soft' identity with highly permeable frontiers."[107] As one Louisiana woman explained, in one way or another, "Honey, we's all Creoles!"[108]

Members of the Metoyer family enjoy eating boiled crawfish together at home.

Creole Families In Black and White

"Back in the day, they swept it under the rug. Nowadays, it doesn't matter. They're proud of it."

–Theresa Thibodeaux

Creoles of South Louisiana are part of a culture—not a race. Consequently, their skin tones, socio-economic levels, educational backgrounds, and places of origin vary greatly. Understanding this reality helps explain why many families are not "pure Cajun" or "pure Creole." Culturally, they may identify with one group more closely than another, but many factors play significant roles in determining how individuals self-identify.

Throughout the prairies of South Louisiana, people commonly believe Cajuns are white and Creoles are black, or at least partly black. I was born and raised in Lafayette, the "Heart of French Louisiana" and the "Home of the Ragin' Cajuns." I assumed, as many do, that I was Cajun. My maternal grandmother reinforced this concept by telling us we were "100% Cajun." She was not entirely correct. Nor was she entirely incorrect. Culturally, I do consider myself to be primarily Cajun. However, my lineage is much more complex than that. When I started tracing our family roots, I made some rather interesting discoveries.

Domingue family members gather under the shade of oak trees at a reunion.

I was just a child when I met my grandmother's Uncle Stanley at a family reunion in Lake Charles. Like generations before, we gathered under the shade of sprawling moss-draped oak trees on July Fourth to celebrate the extended Domingue family. Surrounded by distant relatives I barely knew, Uncle Stanley stood out in the crowd. His ruddy cheeks and snow-white beard reminded me of Santa Claus, and I immediately felt drawn to him.

As I munched on a slice of cold watermelon, the chatter of adults flew back and forth over my head. I perked up when Uncle Stanley mentioned that he had been working on our family's genealogy. He explained, "I've traced the Domingue family line all the way back to the Canary Islands. I got as far back as about 1740." Then he added with a chuckle, "I found myself getting a little too close to Africa for comfort, so I had to stop the research there." At the time, I wasn't aware that the Canary Islands are a Spanish territory located a mere sixty miles off the Atlantic coast of Morocco. I later realized that Uncle Stanley's concern about possibly discovering a black branch of our family tree was unfounded since Morocco is a French and Arabic-speaking country in North Africa and not a part of Sub-Saharan Africa.

I learned that during the eighteenth century, Louisiana recruited Spaniards from the Canary Islands to populate the colony. My ancestors were among those early settlers who immigrated to Louisiana. Known as *Isleños*, these Spanish Creoles continued marrying other Spaniards even though an interesting twist changed our family name from Spanish to French.

On April 17, 1873, Valerian Dominguez married Onezida Domingue. According to family records, Valerian and Onezida's fathers were brothers which meant the newlyweds were first cousins. I remember Uncle Stanley explaining that the priest would not marry first cousins, so Valerian and Onezida got around that by dropping the "z" in her last name so it became Domingue (pronounced

Valerian and Onezida's son Camille Domingue with his wife Leah Guillot.

Ellis and Edma Meyers Domingue

DOH-mang in French). For some unknown reason, their eldest son Camille adopted the French spelling Domingue instead of the Spanish name Dominguez, married a Cajun woman named Leah Guillot in 1898, and passed the surname of Domingue on to his twelve children. Their son Ellis and his wife Edma had many children, including my grandmother Elista Elizabeth Domingue.

Elista Elizabeth Domingue Price

My father's heritage is just as interesting. For most of my life, I thought the Istre side of my family was "pure Cajun." It turns out the surname Istre is not Cajun at all, but rather French Creole. I was surprised to learn there was such a thing as white Creoles and shocked to recognize my family name among them. Like the Domingues, the descendants of the Istres who left France and eventually settled in Louisiana in the 1700s were considered Creoles because they were natives of the New World with lineage from the Old World. Skin color had nothing to do with this distinction.

So why are white Creoles like my great-great grandfather Fastin Istre and his son Denis considered "Cajun"? The answer is fascinating. When Acadian refugees began making their way to Louisiana after being exiled from Canada in the mid-eighteenth century, the established Creole families of New Orleans did not allow them to settle in the Crescent City. As a result, the Acadians were forced to carve out a life for themselves in what was then considered wilderness—the prairies and swamps of South Louisiana. These Acadian survivors later became known as "Cajuns."

Fastin Istre

Although we aren't sure why, many less affluent white Creole families like the Domingues and Istres also settled in the prairies and swamps of Acadiana. Not surprisingly, they found more in common with their rural Cajun friends and neighbors than French and Spanish Creoles in the city. Many established Creole families looked down upon Cajuns as poor and ignorant, but the Creole settlers who were not members of the social elite or landed aristocracy began assimilating into Cajun communities within a relatively short period of time. Generations of enculturation and intermarrying resulted in many Creole families like mine sincerely believing themselves to be of Cajun stock.

Adding to the intriguing explanation as to why Creoles claimed Cajun ties is the fact that well into the twentieth century, Louisiana adhered to the "one drop" rule. This rule considered anyone with even a drop of black blood to be black. During the Jim Crow era it became critical for many blue collar white Creoles and their Cajun counterparts to cling to their white heritage. Educational, vocational, social, and financial opportunities were often at stake. Since Cajuns are of European descent but the term Creole could possibly denote African ancestry, Cajuns, while not highly regarded, could at least boast they were not black. White Creoles who had either already assimilated or wished to distance themselves from the term Creole began calling themselves Cajun.

Denis Istre

Evelyn Amelia Trahan Istre

I began to wonder, so am I Cajun at all? Actually, yes I am. My father's mother Evelyn Amelia was a Trahan before marrying my grandfather Harry Joseph Istre. The Trahans were French settlers who made Acadie (Nova Scotia) their home in the New World. Similar to many other Acadian families, the British forced the Trahans out of Canada and sent them into exile during the French and Indian War in a genocidal event known as the *Grand Dérangement* or Great Upheaval. Like other refugees, the Trahan family made their way to the Bayou State and have called Louisiana home ever since.

Do I have American Indian or African ancestry? I am not sure. My great uncle Bill told me that his father told him he was Indian. Not much more is known. At the time, being labeled Cajun was considered degrading enough. Acknowledging tribal affiliation was perceived as moving one rung lower on the social ladder, so if native blood coursed through their veins, most did not talk about it. If there is any African in me, no one in our family has ever mentioned it. Judging by my fair skin and blonde hair, I would have to guess not much, if any, exists. But who knows? Maybe one day I'll discover more. Perhaps I will never know.

Many years ago, I grew close to a precious Creole couple from Lawtell who consider me one of their granddaughters. The family history of Mamaw Theresa and Papaw Goldman Thibodeaux provides even more examples of how blended South Louisiana's inhabitants are. Mamaw Theresa's maternal great-grandfather was Telesmar

Telesmar Fontenot

Fontenot, a Cajun from Mamou who had relations with a mixed woman named Lovenia Victoria. He never married Lovenia, but he did give his last name to their children including their daughter Elvira. Elvira became a Derousseau and her daughter Lula married Leroy Leday, the son of John Leday and Alicia Matte. Not surprisingly, Alicia's father was also a Cajun. Leroy and Lula had three children including Theresa, my adopted Mamaw.

Papaw Goldman's family tree is also a blend of Cajuns and Creoles of Color. His paternal grandfather was an Acadian named Théodule Thibodeaux whose ancestors have been traced back to Pierre Thibodeaux of Marans, Poitou, France, in 1631. Like the Trahans, the Thibodeaux family left France, immigrated to Nova Scotia, and ended up in Louisiana after being exiled. They settled first in Pointe Coupee, then in St. Landry Parish.

Alicia Matte Leday

John Leday

Théodule Thibodeaux

Théodule was born on June 22, 1838, in Grand Coteau. He legally married two white women, but did not marry the mixed woman he kept on the side. He had thirteen children with his first wife Philomène Latiolais and three children with his second wife Carmalite Sonnier. He fathered four more children with Marie Ophelia Richard, a mixed woman who was Papaw's grandmother. Just like Telesmar Fontenot, Théodule gave his name to their children—Mary, known as *Tante Blanche* (Aunt White), Eva, John, and Anatole. Anatole's first wife died in childbirth, but he later married a woman named Josephine Carrière who gave birth to ten children, including Papaw Goldman.

Like many black Creoles of his generation, Papaw grew up in the country and stayed on the farm to help his parents. His limited access to any type of formal education prevented him from becoming literate in Creole French, his first language, or in English, the mandatory language of the classroom. Despite his inability to read, his poetic soul shines through the music and songs he composes and performs.

Just a few years ago, Papaw made a remarkable discovery. While attending a tribute to Amédé Ardoin, considered by many to be the "Father of Creole Music," he found out he was related to Dr. Darrell Bourque, a retired professor of English at the University of Louisiana at Lafayette

Anatole Thibodeaux and Josephine Carriere

and the poet laureate for Louisiana. How can this be? Well, Théodule and his first wife Philomene's son Jacques married Elmire David. Jacques and Elmire became Darrell's grandparents, a coincidence that makes Théodule both Papaw's grandfather and Bourque's great-grandfather.[109]

Philomène Latiolaais Thibodeaux

Genealogy is fascinating, and family trees in Louisiana are anything but simple. How else can you explain how a black Creole musician who never learned to read and a white Cajun who became Louisiana's poet laureate[110] are related? Amazingly enough, these stories are not unique. For many of us, our family tree is not a monolithic trunk of homogeneity. Instead, it is comprised of a blending of branches that reach out beyond what most of us can imagine. For some, acknowledging branches in the family tree that are darker or lighter feels uncomfortable. For others, learning about our roots inspires us to develop an appreciation for the diversity of people and places that brought us to where we are today.

Although dropping the "z" in Dominguez transformed our family from "pure Spanish" to "pure French" in an instant, it does not change who we are today. It does illustrate, however, how a mere stroke of a pen can change dramatically the story of where we came from. When I learned my surname Istre is French Creole and not Cajun, I was shocked, then intrigued. A whole new world opened to me with the realization that white Creoles even existed. Discovering that my adopted Papaw is related to one of my former English professors completely took me off guard. Through this entire process of self-discovery, I have come to believe even more firmly that truth really is stranger than fiction and infinitely more interesting. Who knows what surprises may lay in store if I continue the quest to learn more about my heritage?

Louisiana Creole Surnames

A
Abat
Aguilar
Albarado
Alexandre/Alexander
Alfred
Allain/Allen
Allemand/Alleman
Allick
André/Andrews
Andrépont
Angelle
Antoine/Anthony
Archon/Archangel
Ardoin/Hardoin
Armand
Armelin
Arnaud
Artacho
Augé/Oger
Auguillard
Auguste
Augustin/Augustine
Auzenne/Ozenne

B
Bacqué
Balderas
Balquer/Balqué
Balthasar
Baptiste/Batiste
Barbé/Barbin
Barnabé
Barras
Barré
Barrière
Bastien/Sébastien
Baudoin
Beauvais/Beauvaie
Bégnaud
Bélisaire
Bellard
Bello
Benjamin
Benoît de Sainte-Claire
Bérard
Béraud
Bernard
Beslin
Bienvenu de Vince
Bijeau/Bijoux
Billeaud/Billiot
Billeaudeaux
Birette
Blachier
Blanchet
Boisblanc
Boisdoré
Bolívar
Bonhomme
Boniface
Bonin
Bonnet
Bonvillian
Borago
Bordelon
Borel
Bossier/Bosset/Basset
Botquin dit St.-André
Bouchard
Boucher de Grandpré
Bougère
Bouligny/Buliñy
Boulrisse
Bouquet
Bourdat/Bourda
Bourdier/Bordier
Bourgeois
Boutté
Boyancé
Brettmayer
Briant
Brignac
Broutin
Brunet
Burdin

C
Cabrera
Calais/Callais
Canty/Canti
Carline/Carlin
Carmouche
Carrière/Carrier
Carrón
Caselard
Caso y Luengo
Castex
Casteyo/Castille
Castillo/Castilló
Castillón
Castro
Catalon
Célestin/Célestine
Césaire/Caesar
Chacheré
Chaix/Shay
Champagne
Chanfreau
Chargois
Charlitte
Charlot/Sharlow
Charpentier
Charpiot
Chauvet/Chauvette
Chemin
Chénier
Chênevert
Cheramie
Cheval
Chevalier
Chrétien
Christophe
Clément
Clermont
Coco
Coirin/Quoirin
Colas/Colat/Nicolas
Colette/Collette
Colomb
Comageur/Commagère
Condé
Condon
Corbet
Coulan
Courtableu
Courteaux
Cousin
Coussan
Couvelier/Cuvelier
Crochet/Crouchet
Croiset/Croizet
Croizeau
Cyr

D
d'Abbadie/Dabadie
Dalcourt
Damas
d'Arbonne/Darbonne
Darden
Dartès/d'Hartesse
Dartez
Daspit de St.-Amant
Darby/de St.-Marc d'Arby
d'Aunoy
Dauphin
Dauphiné/Dauphiney
Daurian/Dorian
Dauterive/d'Hauterive
Dautreuil
David
de Aponte
de Baillon
de Barton dit Robinet
DeBlanc
de Blanc de Neuveville
Découx/Descoux
de Clouet/DeClouet
de Court
Decuir
Dèculus/Lucullus
de Favrot
de Fontenet/Fontenette
de Grandpré
de Grüy/de Gruïs
de Hart
Déjean/Desgens
de Kerlégand/Kerlégon
de la Barthe de l'isle de la Boutiquère
de la Chaise/DelaChaisse
de la Croix
de la Fosse/Delafosse
de la Houssaye/Delahoussaye
de la Lande Ferrières
de la Loire
de la Mirande
de la Morandière
de Latte/Délatte/Deslattes
Delaune
de la Vigne
de la Villeboeuvre
Delcambre
de l'Homme/Delhommer/Delhomme
Delille
de Lino de Chalmette
de Macarty
de Mahy
de Mézilières
de Montchervaux
de Morand
de Müy
de Penne
de Prados
Dérise
d'Erneville
de Rosier
de Rouen
Deroussel
de St.-Marc d'Arby/Darby
Des Autels/Deshôtels
Desbordes
Descuires/Décuir
Desgens/Déjean
Desmarais/Desmarest
de Soto
Despaigney/Despanney
Dessessarts
Destouet
d'Estréhan de Beaupré
Detiège
de Valcourt
de Vauginé
de Verdun
de Ville/DeVilliers
de Villiers/Petit de Livilliers

d'Hartesse/Dartès
d'Hauterive/Dauterive
Dieudonné
di Gradenigo/Gradny
Doliolle de Chalmette
Domengeaux
Domínguez/Domingue
Dominique
Donato
Doré
d'Orville
Doucet
Dozat
Dozier
Drouet/Drouette
Dublucet
Dubois
Dubreuil
Duchamp de Châtaigné
Duchesne/Duchêne
du Closlange
Ducôté
Ducourt
Ducrest
Duhamel
Dumesnil
Dumoulin
Dupérier
Duplanti/Duplantis
Dupléchain/Dupléchien
Dupré
Dupuis
Duralde/Dural
Durand
Durousseau
Dusouchet
Dusuau de la Chaise
Dusuau de la Croix
Dutil
Duval

E
Edgar/Edguard
Émmanuel/Manuel
Esclavon
Esprit
Étienne
Étier

F
Falgou/Falgoust/Falgoût
Fascende
Faucher/Fauché/Faucheux
Favre
Fernández
Figerant
Fitch/Fitche
Flégeance/Flugence
Fleuriau d'Erneville
Folse
Fondal
Fontenot
Fontenot dit Belair
Forneret/Fornerat
Forstal/Forstall
Fourien
Fournet
Fournier
Franchebois
Francis/Francisque
François/Frank
François-Étienne
Frère
Frêtté/Frettier/Freddy
Frilot
Frozard
Frugé
Fuselier/Fuselier de la Claire

G
Gagné/Le Gagneux
Galentine
Gallot
Garbarini
Gardemal
Garrigon
Garrigues de Flaujac
Gathe/Gott
Gaubert/Gobert
Gauthier
Gentil
Georges/George
Gérard/Girard
Girouard
Glapion
Gobert/Gaubert
Gobleur/Goblère
Goguet
Gondron
Gonsoulin
González
Goudeau
Gradny/di Gradenigo
Grégoire
Gremillion
Grèvenberg/Grèvenberg dit
Flamand
Guaigneau
Guérinière
Guidroz
Guigneaux
Guillaume/Williams
Guillory

H
Hardoin/Ardoin
Hardy
Henri/Henry
Henriot
Hernández
Himel/Hymel/Ymel
Hisnard/Isnard/Ignar
Hitter
Hiver
Hollier
Honoré
Hotard
Hoursole
Hulin
Huval
Hyppolite/Polite

I
Isidore
Isnard/Ignar/Hisnard
Istre

J
Jacques/James
Jacquet
Jacquot/Jaco
Jan
Janis
Jardoin
Javier/Xavier
Jean/John
Jean/Jones
Jean-Baptiste
Jean-Louis
Jean-Marie
Jeanminette
Jeansonne
Joe/Dio
Jolivet/Jolivette
Joseph
Joubert
Journée/Journet
Judice
Julien
Juneau/Juno
Jupiter

K
Karsayo/Quersayo

L
La Bauve
L'abbé
Labrie
La Caze/Lacase/Lacasse
La Chapelle
La Coste
La Cour
La Croix/Cross
La Fargue
La Fleur
La Fontaine
La Forêt/La Forest
Lagos
La Grange
La Haye
Lalonde
Lamotte/Lamathe
Lançon
Lanclos
Landreneau
Landrieu
Langlinais
Langlois
La Pointe
La Porte
Larrieux
Lartiques/Lartigues
La Salle
Lasseigne
Lastrappes/Lastrapes
Latil/Latille
Latiolait/Latiolais
Laurence/Lorins
Laurent/Lawrence
Lavergne
Laviolette
Lazaire/Lazare
Le Bon du Fort de St.-Ésprit
Le Bourgeois
Le Bretton de Charmois
Le Camus
Le Clerc/Leclère
Le Compte
Lédé/Lédet/LeDée
Le Doux
Leduc/Leduf
Lefèvre/Lefebvre
Le Gagneux/Gagné
Legnon/Lognon
Leissard/Leyssard/Layssard
Le Kintérec
Le Maire
Lemesle/Lemelle
Le Moyne/Le Moine
Le Normand
Léonard
Léopold/Leopaul
Le Page du Pratz
Le Porche/Porche
Le Sassier
L'étang
Lewis/Louis
Lindor
Livaudait dit Beaumont
Lognon/Legnon
Loisel
López
Lorins/Laurence
Louis/Lewis
Louvière
Lucullus/Dèculus

M
Mœstrict
Malbrough
Mallery
Mallet
Malveaux
Manneau
Manuel/Émmanuel
Maraist
Marcantel
Marchand
Marin
Marinette
Martin

Martinet
Masse
Mateo/Mathieu
Mathieu/Mathews
Mayeux
Meaux
Mèche
Médiamolle
Ménard
Mercier
Meslin
Meuillon/Meullion
Michel/Mitchell
Michot
Mígues/Miguez
Millet
Miragoine
Molless
Monteau de Monbérault
Mora
Morales/Moral
Moreau
Morin

N
Narbonne
Narcisse
Navarre
Nepveux
Neuville/Nèville
Neveu
Nézat
Nicolas/Nicholas
Nicolas/Colas/Colat
Noël
Nora
Norbert
Normand

O
Oger/Augé
Oliberos
Olivier de Vésin
Olivier du Closel
Onésime
Orphé
Orso
Ortego
Ortíz
Ory
Oubre
Ozenne/Auzenne

P
Page
Paillet dit Lanot
Pain
Papillon/Papillion
Parquin
Patin
Patout
Paul
Pavy
Pécôt
Peigner/Pennier
Pellerin
Pelletier
Pennes
Pérault/Perro
Pérez
Perrin
Perrodin
Perron
Petit de Livilliers/de Villiers
Peytavin duriblond
Philippe/Phillip
Picard
Piernas
Pierre
Pierre-Auguste
Pilette
Pineaud
Pinta
Poché
Pognion
Polite/Hyppolite
Pommier
Poras
Porche/Le Porche
Porkine
Potier
Poydras
Pourciau
Prade/Pratt
Pradier
Primeaux
Préjean
Prévôt/Prevost
Provost dit Blondin
Provost dit Collet
Prud'homme/Prudhomme

Q
Quevedo/Québédeaux
Quersayo/Karsayo
Quoirin/Coirin

R
Rabelais/Rabalais
Raguet/Raguette
Ramar
Ramírez
Ramón
Ramos
Raymond
Reaux
Réaux
Régis
Règnier
Reneaud
Rénaud
René
Ricard
Richard
Riché
Rideau
Rivet/Rivais/Rivette
Robin
Rochon
Rodríguez
Roman
Romero/Romère
Rougeou/Rougeot
Rousillon
Roussier/Rouzier
Roy
Royer
Ruíz

S
Sabatier
Salomon/Solomon
Saint-Amand
Saint-André
Saint-Cyr
Saint-Germain
Saint-Julien
Saintt-Laurent
Saint-Martin
Saint-Pierre dit Éscadron
Sêm/Sam
Sandose
Sarasse
Schexnayder
Scipion
Sébastien/Bastien
Segura
Sénégal
Sénet/Sénette
Sénétière
Sharlow/Charlot
Shay/Chaix
Sigur/Sigue
Silvestre
Simien/Symien
Simon
Soileau
Sonness
Sorrel
Stelly
Sterling
Suffier
Symien/Simien

T
Taillefer/Taillaferro
Taison
Talamon
Tauriac
Ternoy
Tessier
Théodule
Thériot
Thierry
Thomas
Tisoneau/Tizoneau
Toussaint
Trudeau
Tureaud
Turpeau

U
No known names

V
Valère
Valéry
Valien
Vallot
Valsin
van Voorhies
Vavasseur
Veasey
Veillon
Vénus
Verdun/Verdin
Vérot
Verret
Vidal
Vidrine
Villator
Villeré
Viltz
Vincent
Vital de Grandpré

W
Webre/Webb
Wiltz

X
Xavier/Javier
Xérèz

Y
Ymel/Himel/Hymel

Z
Zépheryn/Zéphirin
Zéringue

Creolized Anglo and German Surnames

Abshire
Anderson
Andrus
Ashford

Baker
Bell
Boyd
Brown

Carroll
Caruthers/Crédeur
Chatman/Chapman
Cheavers/Chévis/Chavis
Collins
Condley
Conner
Cook

Davis
Dwyer

Ferdinand
Fenwick

Gardiner/Gardner
Goodbeer/Gutebier
Green/Greene

Haik
Halphen
Hamilton
Henderson
Hill
Hunt

Jackson
Jenneford/Jennifer

Nelson

Patterson

Schustz
Shaw
Simms
Singleton
Stelly
Stevenson

Taylor

Vining

Wagner

Saint-Domingue Refugee Surnames

Armelin

Barthélémy
Baudoin
Bercier
Billeaudeau
Boulet
Briant
Buteau

Canonge
Carrière
Casenave
Castaing
Chaillot
Charbonnet
Chauvinet

Dacquin/D'Aquin
DeGeneres
Dejean
De la Fosse
DeMahy
Desbordes
Desdunes
Deslandes
Domengeaux
Dominique
Druilhet
Dubois
Duchamp
Dumesnil
Duperier

Faustin

Garrigues de Flaujeac

Joubert

LaBiche
Lacombe
LaCoste
Lacour
Lafargue
L'Eveque/Lesveques

Martel
Metayer
Morel
Morin

Pecot
Peychaud

Savary
Seveigne

*Compiled from research conducted by Christophe Landry and Carl Brasseaux

Allons Manger!
Cooking in Creole Country

Creole cooks are born as others, less favored, are born poets.

–Charles Gayerré[1]

There is not a more food-conscious and cuisine-rich jurisdiction in the nation than Louisiana, and no other state has a better documented, more interesting, or more diverse food history. . . . In a gastronomic sense, there is only one Louisiana, and it is filled with Creole and Acadian and Southern delights that have inspired chefs, cookbook writers, and literary artists for generations.

–John Egerton[2]

Perhaps the best-known element of South Louisiana's Creole culture is its exquisite cuisine. In fact, when many people hear the word "Creole," their mind instinctively turns to images of New Orleans chefs serving up generous portions of delicious food with a spicy kick. In many circles, the term "Creole" has become associated with good food and good times in "The Big Easy." Although cuisine serves as only one aspect of the entire Creole experience in South Louisiana, its widespread appeal has thrust the region's culinary repertoire onto a national and international stage. For example, in a recent article entitled "America's Best Cities for Foodies," New Orleans was touted as the country's best place for neighborhood cafés and placed second in the nation for its "zesty ethnic fare."[3]

New Orleans has been described as "the old Franco-Spanish city on the banks of the Mississippi, where, of all the cities in the world, you can eat the most and suffer the least."[4] Yet, despite its long history as a culinary mecca, Creole cooking extends beyond the confines of this historic metropolis. White and black Creoles in the city of New Orleans as well as throughout rural and urban communities in Acadiana prepare, serve, and consume what is considered to be Creole food.

Culture does not evolve in a vacuum and neither do culinary traditions. As James C. McCann explained, "Combinations of ingredients and structures of cooking are not carried in the genes, but come from historical experiences shared among peoples and across generations. . . . Cuisine is a product of history, and a meal is a conjuncture of time, place, particular ingredients."[5]

South Louisiana's Creole cooking is a rich amalgamation of European, African, and American influences; and there would be no such thing as Creole cuisine without the convergence of Old and New World ingredients, recipes, and cooking traditions. Africans introduced southern staples such as rice, okra, black-eyed peas, collard greens, yams, benne (sesame) seeds, watermelons, sugarcane, and coffee. The Americas yielded green beans, butter beans, lima beans, capsicum (peppers), Irish potatoes, sweet potatoes, kidney beans, navy beans, maize (corn), peanuts, and tomatoes.[6] Europeans contributed olives, wheat, barley, citrus fruit, onions, and domesticated meats such as pork, beef, and chickens to the New World.[7]

So, what exactly is "Creole cooking?" Louisiana Chef Paul Prudhomme explained, "Creole food, unlike Cajun, began in New Orleans and is a mixture of the traditions of French, Spanish, Italian, American Indian, African and other ethnic groups. . . . Creole cooking is more sophisticated and complex than Cajun cooking—it's city cooking."[8] According to John Folse, another world-renowned Louisiana chef, "Creole is the cuisine of cooks and chefs and is based on European techniques. . . . Though Creole cuisine has French roots as well, it has been greatly influenced by other cultures including Native America, Spain, Germany, England, Africa, and Italy." When comparing it to Cajun cuisine, he stated, "In general, Creole cooking is more sophisticated fare."[9] Food historian Peter Feibleman, noting the differences between Cajun and Creole cuisine, explained that while Cajuns are "a strong people used to living under strenuous conditions," many Creoles historically were "rich planters who led a life of relative luxury." He explained that in Cajun food "the ingredients are cooked together in one pot, sometimes fiercely spiced but almost always gentled by a bed of taste-calming white rice, and always good." The Creole kitchen, on the other hand, "aspires to *grande cuisine*; it is a kitchen of delicate blends, of subtle combinations and separate sauces."[10]

While these explanations may accurately reflect the differences between rural Cajun cooking and the elite white Creole cuisine of New Orleans, they exclude the culinary tradition of black Creoles living in Acadiana. Historically, South Louisiana has been divided along stereotypical boundaries that divide "Creole" New Orleans from "Cajun" Acadiana. Although the majority of the world's Cajun population does live in Acadiana, this does not mean that all Acadiana residents are Cajun. Many, of course, are black Creoles whom tourists and even scholars oftentimes overlook or lump in with

Paul Prudhomme was the youngest of thirteen children born to sharecroppers in Opelousas. He learned how to cook at his mother's side and went on to become a world-renowned chef before his passing in 2015.

Leah Chase, the "Queen of Creole Cuisine," was one of fourteen children. Although she grew up in Madisonville, she made her fame and fortune in New Orleans. Her successful culinary career served as the inspiration for Disney's Princess Tiana in *The Princess and the Frog.*

John Folse was born in St. James Parish, but has brought Cajun and Creole cuisine to an international stage through his travels, publications, culinary school, and film series.

the larger, dominant white Cajun population. Due to their close proximity to one another, the availability of certain foodstuffs within a common natural environment, and their shared low socio-economic position as French-speaking minorities within the larger national Anglophone identity, similar recipes and cooking techniques developed over time between the white Cajuns and black Creoles living in South Louisiana. As food historian C. Paige Gutierrez explains, "Outsiders are sometimes confused by the coexistence of the terms *Cajun food* and *Creole food.* Tourist-oriented restaurants in both Acadiana and New Orleans increasingly advertise their foods as *Cajun-Creole*—a marketing term that suggests a monolithic south Louisiana cuisine (and culture)." She expounds, "Many Breaux Bridge[11] residents say that Creole food is the food of New Orleans and its environs. Some say that Creole cuisine is also the food of the wealthy, white French Creoles, including those who live in Acadiana. These uses of the term *Creole food* are consistent with those of the media in both New Orleans and Acadiana, and of the authors of nationally distributed books on regional cuisine in the United States."[12]

Just as the label "Cajun" seems to encompass all of South Louisiana's French culture, so it also overshadows the similar culinary tradition of the region's Creole population. No definitive work has yet addressed the diet of black Creoles living in Acadiana, but it is safe to state that relatively little distinguishes prairie Cajun cuisine from its Creole counterpart since lifestyles, available ingredients, and cooking traditions are so similar. As folklorist John Laudun has point-

Many restaurants like Café Pontalba in New Orleans's French Quarter advertise Cajun and Creole cuisine. Although the sandwich board boasts a "Cajun" breakfast, menu items include "Creole benedicts" and "Creole Grillades and Grits." Marketing strategies like these blur the lines of authenticity and often confuse visitors about the differences between Cajun and Creole food.

ed out, "limiting Creole cooking to a style 'practiced in the areas in and around New Orleans' . . . drives the Creoles of the Louisiana Prairies to no end of distraction." He explains, "individuals tend to practice traditions that have more in common with their geographic neighbors than with a larger imagined, and super-local, ethnic community. . . . Creoles living in Lawtell make a gumbo that has more in common with their Cajun neighbors than Creoles living in Lake Charles, let alone the Creoles of New Orleans or the Creoles of Cane River."[13]

Thomas "Big Hat" Fields at home.

Black Creole musician Thomas "Big Hat" Fields was born in the rural community of Rayne in Acadia Parish and explained,

> When you cross west of Baton Rouge—
> from here to Lake Charles,
> That's the *real* Creole cooking!
>
> New Orleans—
> you got a lot of that Italian and Creole *mix.*
>
> But this is the *real* Creole and Cajun cooking in the flatlands right here.
> *I'm telling you!*
>
> . . . And the Creole food in New Orleans
> And the Creole food here [in Acadiana]
> is a completely different line.
> You know, they mix Italian and they put bay leaves.
>
> But you know, we got the regular roux and the old time stuff.
> The sure 'nough gumbo.
> *You understand*?
> The *country* type stuff.
>
> When you go up to New Orleans, they doctor it up
> and they put all kind of stuff in it.
> *We got the real deal here!*[14]

Dishes like smothered pork chops with rice and gravy often grace Creole dinner tables.

Unlike the cosmopolitan cuisine of the Crescent City, prairie Creole cooking is typically hardy, simple fare that bursts with flavor and subtle nuances. Elaborate sauces are replaced by stick-to-your-ribs rice and gravy, and homemade cornbread and milk trump delicate creole cream cheese crêpes. Much like "soul food," a term that became popular among urban blacks in the 1960s to describe the kinds of food that slaves typically ate, Creole food is largely a creative use of available foodstuffs. As Chef John Folse explained, "Soul food exemplified the skill of the African cook who created masterful dishes from pork scraps, weeds, and leftovers considered unfit for consumption. . . . Interestingly, soul food derived not from Africa, but from frontier experiences and English and Native American influences and was eaten by farmers and poor whites as well."[15] Perhaps one black Creole cook stated it best when she said, "Creole cooking as we know it today is simply glorified 'Soul Food' with a French accent."[16]

Sides like corn and apple sauce complete the meal.

Savoring Survival: Frontier Cooking

The ambition of every good cook must be to make something very good with the fewest possible ingredients.

–Urbain Dubois[17]

Archaeological evidence indicates that various American Indian tribes inhabited Louisiana some 3,500 years before Columbus "discovered" the New World. Excavations have not indicated that corn, beans, or squash were cultivated that early, but since wild plants, animals, and fish were abundantly available to them, these people probably had no need for agricultural sustenance. Instead, they frequently hunted wild game such as deer, bear, raccoon, rabbit, squirrel, beaver, otter, and alligator; and they foraged for berries, fruits, vegetables, and other plants.[18]

Early European explorers documented their forays into the region. For example, members of Hernando de Soto's Spanish expedition reported that they saw bison roaming Louisiana in 1542. When René-Robert Cavelier de La Salle claimed the Mississippi River and all that it drained for France in 1682, he and his men observed Louisiana Indians hunting buffalo along a bayou they aptly named *Terre aux Boeufs* ("Land of the Buffalo"). Jean-Bernard Bossu, a Frenchman who published accounts of his sojourn through North America in the mid-eighteenth century, documented that opossum was not typically eaten, although one entry indicates that he ate it multiple times and that its size and taste was comparable to a suckling pig. Bossu described native waterfowl hunting techniques that incorporated the use of tame or stuffed birds as decoys. He also

Indian Deer Hunt

According to eighteenth-century historian Du Pratz, "the deer is very frequent in this province [Louisiana], notwithstanding the great numbers of them that are killed by the natives. . . . The natives hunt the deer sometimes in companies [as illustrated here] and sometimes alone."

French artist Alfred Boisseau spent two years in Louisiana. In his 1847 painting *Louisiana Indians Walking Along a Bayou*, a man shouldering a long rifle leads the way while a young boy carrying a long stick, possibly a bow or a blowgun, follows. Two women, one bent under the weight of a burden basket, the other toting a sleeping baby, trail behind.

wrote about extraordinarily large frogs that "croaked louder than a bellowing bull." Refuse heaps with evidence of oysters, clams, crawfish, crabs, and shrimp indicate that Indians were also eating shellfish before European contact. With the exception of totem animals that were considered taboo, it appears that Louisiana's first people, like their descendants, ate almost anything "that didn't bite back" as the popular local saying goes.[19]

It has been estimated that Louisiana's native people knew how to use approximately 250 different kinds of edible wild root plants, in addition to a plethora of fruits, berries, nuts, seeds, and herbs. Perhaps the most famous ingre-

Living history interpreters cook food over an open fire, demonstrating what life might have been like for tribal members during the eighteenth century.

Houma tribal member Zoeanna Verret demonstrates how to make filé gumbo.

dient they passed on to Louisiana's cooking tradition, however, can be attributed to the Choctaw Indians who collected, dried, and ground the leaves of sassafras trees that grew wild along the Gulf Coast. Better known by the name of *filé*, this powdery substance was used by the Choctaw to thicken their soups and stews. Some have suggested the name *filé* has been derived from the French word *fil,* which means "thread," since the powder will become stringy if allowed to boil. For most prairie Cajuns and Creoles the thyme-like flavoring agent is added to the gumbo at the very end of the cooking process since they typically use other ingredients like roux and okra to thicken their gumbo stock.[20]

Botanical drawing of the sassafrass plant

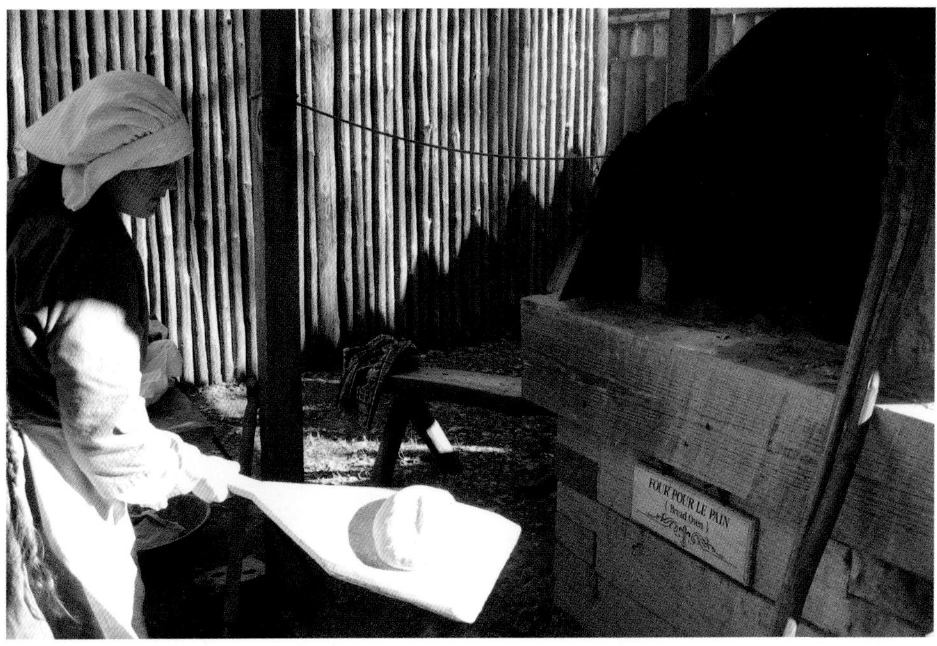

A volunteer bakes French bread in an outdoor oven at
Fort St. Jean Baptiste State Historic Site in Natchitoches.

With European arrival in the Bayou Country came an introduction of new ingredients and culinary traditions. As early as 1706, professional cooks lived in Louisiana, a mere seven years after French-Canadian soldier and adventurer Pierre Le Moyne, Sieur d'Iberville, brought the first permanent French settlers to the Gulf Coast and a dozen years before his brother, Jean-Baptiste Le Moyne, Sieur de Bienville, founded the city of New Orleans. According to census records, artisan bakers were tantalizing taste buds by 1722.[21]

A 1727 bill of fare at a French inn suggests that the French immigrants to colonial America were accustomed to eating "a *soupe* [broth with bread], some boiled meat or a piece of beef, a veal fricassee [*sic*] or some chops, a few vegetables, some roast, and as dessert, some milk, cheese, biscuits, fruit in season. . . ."[22] French cuisine also boasted dishes such as fish-liver turnovers, venison pie with rye flour pastry, eel stew, stewed pigeons, soups thickened with egg yolks, rice, or bread crumbs, pear pies, and sugar tarts.

Naturally, colonial America did not always offer the same types of food, so French immigrants had to substitute ingredients. Life on the frontier demanded a survival existence and food preparation followed suit. Using a single large pot and few utensils, colonists could prepare simple, nourishing soups and stews that could conveniently feed several trappers, soldiers, or hungry families. Food historian Patricia B. Mitchell notes, "As the wilderness was tamed, the more complex food preparation techniques of the French homeland reemerged, and cooks had time, equipment, and ingredients adequate for the creation of food which would be considered 'French-syle'—that is to say, a cuisine characterized by a skillful and artistic use of sauces; the liberal use of wine and herbs; and an expertise in confectionary and pastry making."[23]

Almost immediately after Iberville founded the French colony, enslaved Africans were brought in to provide a labor force. By 1712, there were approximately ten blacks throughout the region.[24] Nearly fifty years earlier, France had claimed her trade monopoly in the Senegambia region of West Africa, located between the Senegal and Gambia rivers, and established trading posts at various locations along Africa's Atlantic coastline. Eighteenth-century French observers praised the Senegal Valley for its vastness, productivity, and fertility. The region's inhabitants were known for their agricultural skills. All of Louisiana's major eighteenth-century crops were grown in the area, including rice, corn, peas, tobacco, indigo, and cotton. Director of the Senegal concession André Brüe described how a supervisory lord, armed with a sword and whip as if going into battle, led a team of *griots*, or overseers, through the fields. The privileged class of *griots* sang and beat drums loudly in order to keep cadence for field gangs who toiled in the nude with long-handled spades that prevented them from having to bend over while cultivating the ground. Alcohol was distributed to *griots* and workers as an incentive to quicken their pace.[25]

African women pounding rice, c. 1797.

Senegalese man in a field, c. 1797.

Louisiana's first slave ships traveled to Africa under strict orders to transport skilled rice cultivators. Within a short time, the grain became indispensable to the colony's survival.

One of the most significant crops in West Africa and later Louisiana was rice. According to some estimates, rice was domesticated as early as 300 A.D. in present-day Mali. Rice cultivation spread along West Africa's coastline from Senegal to Liberia, as well as a thousand miles inland to Lake Chad, and quickly became a dietary staple in Africa. During the first decade of the sixteenth century, Portuguese traveler Valentim Fernandes noted that the people in the old Mali empire were similar to the Wolof in Senegal "except that they eat more rice." Their surplus enabled them to sell it and exchange it for other foodstuffs such as palm wine, oil, and meat.[26]

Although the first handfuls of blacks who arrived in Louisiana were probably smuggled in, sanctioned vessels filled with human cargo quickly followed. The Company of the West (later known as the Company of the Indies)[27] issued strict orders to the captains of the *Aurore* and the *St. Louis*, the first two slave ships, regarding the selection and treatment of their enslaved labor force. Sieur Herpin, captain of the *Aurore*, was instructed to "trade for a few [slaves] who know how to cultivate rice" as well as purchase "three or four hogsheads of rice suitable for planting" when he arrived in the colony. Sieur Du Coulombier, captain of the *St. Louis*, was told to sail directly to Angola to trade for slaves. Like Herpin, he was to trade "only for well-made and healthy negroes" between the ages of eight and thirty who knew how to cultivate rice. In order to maintain their good health, Du Coulombier was responsible for "giv[ing] attention to feeding them well and to preventing their being mistreated by his crew." [28]

One of the characteristics that distinguished the Louisiana slave trade from all others was that "it represents the only clearly recorded, early North American example of the acquisition of African slaves specifically for their agricultural skills—in the cultivation of rice." Within one year of their arrival in Louisiana, enslaved Africans had cultivated rice all along the Mississippi River; within just a few years, Louisiana began exporting surplus grain to the French West Indies. The slaves' familiarity with rice cultivation was indispensable since it was the only reliable food crop that could grow in swampy areas. Even when rain and floods destroyed the corn, when Indian wars forced people to flee the region, when maritime shipping was cut off, and when flour from the Illinois Country did not arrive due to ice blockages or war on the Mississippi River, French Louisiana always had rice. [29] French traveler C.C. Robin wrote at the time of the Louisiana Purchase that rice "is seen on all the tables of the Creoles instead of bread. Boiled rice and cornbread replace wheat completely."[30]

Corn was a staple food item for Louisiana's native population long before French colonization, but normally Europeans fed the grain to cattle and therefore thought it unfit for human consumption. Since French slaveholders viewed their laborers as chattel, they considered corn to be an inexpensive, yet suitable source of nourishment for their workforce. The Company of the Indies gave slaves in their charge one pound of corn per day to subsist on. In 1725, the Superior Council[31] ruled that by increasing the slaves' rations to one and a half pounds of corn, as well as throwing in a half pound of tainted lard, they could simultaneously provide more nourishment to slaves whom they wanted to work harder, avoid wasting lard, and not diminish their own food supply since French settlers and soldiers refused to eat corn or rancid lard.[32] Le Baron de Carondelet, a governor of Louisiana during the Spanish period, decreed in 1795 that "every slave shall punctually receive the barrel of corn allowed" and recommended that masters supplement this ration voluntarily. He stated that work days should com-

Colonists of European descent refused to eat corn since that is what they fed their cattle, but they had no qualms about rationing the New World grain to their enslaved labor force whom they considered chattel.

Cornbread became a staple food item popular among Creoles, as displayed at Longfellow-Evangeline State Historic Site in St. Martinville.

mence at sunrise and cease at sunset, with each slave allotted a break of half an hour for breakfast and two hours for dinner.[33] While sugar planter and Saint-Domingue refugee[34] Berquin Duvallon traveled through Louisiana in 1802, he noted that "The negro, during his hours of respite from labour, is busied in pounding his corn; he has afterwards to bake it with what wood he can procure himself." When an enslaved laborer went to the fields at daybreak, Duvallon commented, he "carries his sorry pittance of a breakfast with him, which he eats on the spot; he is, however, scarce allowed time to digest it. His labour is suspended from noon till two, when he dines, or rather makes a supplement to his former meal. At two his labour re-commences, and he prosecutes it till dark, sometimes visited by the master, but always exposed to the menaces, blows and scourges either of a white overseer, or a black driver."[35]

Initially, poor blacks and whites consumed corn daily. Cooks roasted the ears, parched the kernels, ground the dried kernels into a coarse cornmeal for making hoe cakes or ash cakes, boiled it in water for a corn meal mush, or pounded it into hominy for grits. Eventually Creoles added milk, eggs, and wheat flour to cornmeal to make it better than just unleavened pones cooked over an open fire.[36] By 1803, C.C. Robin observed that in Louisiana,

"The use of corn is universal among the poor and rich. . . . When it is green, Negroes, Creoles, and especially the English, eat the roasted ears, which they call dried corn. It is very tender, and the Creoles prepare it in the same way as garden peas."[37]

The diet of Louisiana's enslaved population consisted primarily of foodstuffs that could provide maximum nourishment at minimal cost, with the latter considered more important than the former in most cases. Berquin Duvallon commented on the regular diet of the enslaved Africans and wrote, "Their ordinary food is indian corn, or rice and beans, boiled in water, without fat or salt. To them nothing comes amiss. They will devour greedily racoon [*sic*], opossum, squirrels, wood-rats, and even the crocodile [*alligator*]; leaving to the white people the roebuck and rabbit, which they sell them when they kill those animals. They raise poultry and hogs, but seldom eat either. They prefer selling them, and purchasing from their profits, cloathing [*sic*] and brandy." He also noted that the free people of color who had obtained their freedom through purchase or through parentage oftentimes resided in the country and cultivated rice and a little cotton to sustain themselves.[38]

Life during the colonial period was challenging at best and food shortages did not affect the slave population only. As historian Carl A. Brasseaux notes, "undernourishment was a fact of life in French Louisiana, and while the slave's diet was similar to his master's in flush times, the bondsmen bore the brunt of the food shortages during the all-too-frequent periods of famine." One official complained to the minister of marine that "every kind of provision is lacking, and we are on the verge of dying of hunger. . . . The colonists are obliged to send their negroes into the woods to gather cane seed to keep them from perishing." [39] Another administrator reported, "The white laborers can barely feed themselves."[40]

South Louisiana's colonial period was marked by the struggle to survive, and frontier realities superseded idealistic notions of the kind of society white Creole settlers hoped to create in the New World. According to census records, 1,721 European settlers and 3,600 enslaved Africans inhabited the Lower Mississippi Delta in 1731.[41] It comes as no surprise, then, that African cooking traditions heavily influenced the diets of Louisiana's colonial inhabitants. As one historian explained, "The cooking of maritime and coastal Africa was as much a sociological phenomenon as a cultural one. If the traders [and slaveholders] were largely male, their cooks, companions, and sexual partners were most often local women, who were usually the domestic managers and cooks who appropriated tastes and ingredients into new mixes that both pleased male bosses or husbands and expanded their palates."[42] Colonial Louisiana followed this precedent well into the plantation culture of the nineteenth century.

Plantation Cuisine: The Big House and Beyond

> *Girls, we will be well fed here; we are fortunate. I have just seen the cook: not a mere black woman that does the cooking, but one bearing a patent stamped by the broad seal of Nature, the type of a class whose skill is not of books or training, but a gift both rich and rare; who flourishes her spit as Amphitrite does her trident (or her husband's, which is all the same); whose ladle is as a royal scepter in her hands; who has grown sleek and fat on the steam of her own genius; whose children have the first dip in all the gravies, the exclusive right to all livers and gizzards, not to mention breasts of fried chicken. . . .*
>
> –David Hunter Strother[43]

During slavery times, little freedoms were afforded those in bondage, but one area in which they were able to express individuality was in the kitchen. Similar to slave artisans like skilled carpenters, ironworkers, and masons, black Creole cooks could be innovative in the preparation of ingredients they received as rations, as well as food they raised in gardens or foraged from the wild. Nineteenth-century writer R.A. Mallard noted, "if there is any one thing for which the African female intellect has natural genius, it is for cooking. . . . French cooks are completely outdistanced in the production of wholesome, dainty, and appetizing food."[44]

Illustration from "Southern Scenes—Cooking Shrimps," *Frank Leslie's Popular Monthly*, 1877.

The interior of a slave cabin at Audubon State Historic Site in St. Francisville illustrates the simplicity of a slave quarter's kitchen.

African women assigned to be cooks often found themselves responsible for providing sustenance for field hands, skilled laborers, and other enslaved workers, as well as for the family and guests of the family to whom they were bound. In Africa, women did almost all of the cooking, so it was only natural for women who worked in New World kitchens to continue cooking as they had been taught. Like their West African ancestors before them, many enslaved women used six basic cooking techniques: boiling in water, steaming in leaves, roasting in the fire, baking in ashes, toasting beside the fire, and frying in deep oil. As one food historian has noted, "The Afro-American cook had certain culinary tendencies: the abundant use of leafy green vegetables; the utilization of okra, or nuts and seeds, as thickeners; the addition of peppery/spicy hot sauces; the use of smoked meat for flavoring; the preparation of various kinds of fritters; and the creation of many one-pot dishes composed primarily of rice with 'enhancements.'"[45] Many women had to make do with substitutions. For example, unable to find banana leaves, they adapted to using cabbage leaves to wrap cornpones, sweet potatoes, and even chickens for roasting.[46]

Like the majority of whites who lived on the frontier during Louisiana's early days of settlement, access to and ownership of more than the most necessary cooking utensils and implements was severely limited. Many slaves had a single cast iron pot to cook in and little else. This required relatively little adjustment for female cooks of African descent who were accustomed to preparing one-pot mixtures of vegetables with a little meat added in as a flavoring agent and nourishing ingredient.[47]

Women who cooked for wealthy masters usually worked in outdoor kitchens that afforded them larger workspaces, more cooking implements, and a greater variety of ingredients. This enabled them to prepare more elaborate dishes than the women who spent their days in the field and were responsible for feeding their immediate family in the slave quarters. Provided with a kitchen separate from the main house, the plantation cook had to ensure that enough wood was chopped to keep the open hearth fire going at all times, tend the garden, prepare the ingredients, and boil, bake, stew, or otherwise prepare enough food to satisfy the needs of the family in the "Big House," as well as any visiting friends, relatives, or business associates who might be staying in the main house. A planter's hospitality was a slave's drudgery. Since most southern travelers stayed with friends, the burden of cooking for guests fell to the cook and her helpers.

White Creole mistresses of plantations were also involved in the culinary activities of the plantation. Although she may not have done the cooking herself, as the woman of the house, she was directly engaged in the meal planning process and had to consult the cook regularly to determine menus, purchase ingredients, and oversee the overall operations of the kitchen staff. Most plantations kept certain specialty items such as rare and expensive spices under lock and key, and it was the mistress's job to dole out the appropriate amount of these items to the enslaved cooks as needed. It was also her responsibility to ensure that the table was set properly and appropriately reflected her household's economic and social status. Having a beautiful and bountiful table was a direct reflection of the household in which she was mistress, and she took pride in her position as hostess.[48]

This elegant dining room in Oakley Plantation dates to 1806.

Women were often burdened with the responsibility of managing vast estates while their husbands were away on business. Auguste Hervieu's 1837 illustration *Clear Starching in Louisiana* depicts a scene in which a mistress scolds an enslaved woman and child.

Mrs. Vincent Perrault, a white woman who was born on a plantation and lived most of her life on one, commented,

> It always amuses me when I hear people say that the mistress of a plantation did nothing in those days before the Civil War. As a matter of fact, the ladies worked from dawn until dark. They supervised everything pertaining to house management. They trained women to sew and cook, they trained women as nurses for the sick. A knowledge of medicine was essential. My mother studied old medical books far into the night sometimes, for there were times when she must know what to do until the doctor could be summoned. There were numerous servants, but they had to be watched, even the best of them, or things went wrong; some of them would shirk and throw the bulk of the work on others. It was very necessary that the plantation mistress keep a firm hand on the household management.[49]

She remembered that there were always ten or twelve people at the table because of the extra guests. Breakfast consisted of hot waffles, buttermilk biscuits, broiled chicken, cane syrup, scrambled eggs, and hominy. Dinner was often a gumbo or soup, baked chicken or turkey, vegetables from the garden, jellies, and fish or shrimp from the river. Supper was essentially the same menu as breakfast with the possible addition of preserved or ripe fruits and sometimes venison or mutton instead of chicken. Every day, the menu was basically

Kitchens that serviced the "Big House," like this one at Destrehan Plantation, often required the talents of several laborers and an arsenal of cooking utensils.

the same, with as much variation as possible, depending on the seasonal availability of certain items. In her household, the cook "did nothing but cook, and she had two assistants, half-grown girls, who helped her."[50]

Most mornings for the antebellum Creole planter class began with a hot toddy or cup of coffee at sunrise and a proper breakfast consisting of things like French bread, salads, strawberries, claret, and more coffee at about nine o'clock. Dinner was served in the early afternoon around two or three o'clock. This main meal typically included seasonal vegetables and whatever else was available for purchase via steamboats that traveled up and down the rivers. Families enjoyed elaborate dinners that might include a variety of dishes such as broth, fowls, beefsteak, peas, asparagus, salad, potatoes, spinach, coffee, and claret. Since steamboats were able to transport ice carefully packed in sawdust, sometimes the mistress was able to serve iced drinks like orange flower water and lemonade, or even ice cream. Supper was served at sunset and consisted mostly of leftovers, although this was sometimes accompanied by custard, milk, coffee, and claret. Apparently, emphasis was placed on the variety of dishes served, not the quantity of food in the dishes.[51]

In 1861, William Howard Russell visited Roman Plantation and described the menu he enjoyed while there. Before taking an early ride to tour the plantation property, a slave served Russell coffee and biscuits. When he returned to the big house at nine o'clock, Russell enjoyed a "proper breakfast" that included "strange dishes of tropical origin." He explained, "There was the old French abundance, the numerous dishes and efflorescence of napkins, and the long-necked bottles of Bordeaux, with a steady current of pleasant small talk." Russell considered mint juleps, the legendary drink of southern aristocracy, to be "a panacea for all the evils of climate" and before breakfast had already enjoyed three glasses of it. A day or two later, Russell started his day at the Burnside Plantation with fish, shrimp, and beef.[52]

Although desserts did not feature prominently on the everyday menus in most households, ice cream was a delightful treat for those who could afford it. Given South Louisiana's long, hot summers, enjoying a cool, refreshing serving of ice cream was a wonderful way to indulge in the finer things of life. Available commercially in New Orleans in the early 1800s, the treat was in such high demand that a year after the Civil War ended, the first mechanical refrigeration plant was built in the city to manufacture ice. Homemade recipes for ice cream are even included in some of the region's earliest recipe books.[53]

While luxury items like ice cream rarely, if ever, graced the tables of Louisiana's enslaved population, plantation slaves probably ate diets similar to their masters. Unless they were hired out or allowed to feed themselves, slaves in town ate almost exactly the same food as masters although the quantity and availability of choice pieces were undoubtedly less.[54] Field hands did not enjoy the same privileges. As one slave recalled, they began working at sunrise and did not eat "mush en things like dat fo breakfast" until eight a.m. when "de folks dat was in de fields would cum home or else de ones at home would tote hit [it] ter 'em." Dinner almost always consisted of a soup or something boiled or fried and was served at half past twelve or one o'clock. Supper was typically cornbread and milk with molasses. "After supper [at six p.m.] us ain't eat no mo 'til de next mornin' at breakfast," he remembered.[55]

Similar to their masters, slaves began their morning with coffee, but instead of claret or mint juleps, they consumed a low-grade rum made of sugarcane syrup known as "tafia." Cornbread might accompany the early morning wake-up call. A more substantial breakfast consisting of soup, dried

ICE CREAM

WILL be prepared every day at the Exchange Coffee-house. Those who wish to procure some, may send from 12 o'clock, a.m. until 10 p. m. may 14

Ice cream has long been a Louisiana favorite as evidenced by this ad from the *Courrier de la Louisiane* dated May 21, 1821.

fish, and molasses might be sent out to the fields around eight o'clock. Since productivity was of primary concern, masters provided their field hands with foods thought to provide "heat and muscle." For example, the midday meal of cornbread, salted or fresh fat meat, peas, a corn pudding, and sometimes milk were sent to the fields. As one cookbook explained, "Corn was for heat, fat meat for muscle power, and peas were considered to contain oil for building muscle." During grinding time, extra rations were often served on sugar plantations to help offset the physically taxing labor and unusually long work days that the sugarcane process required. Before leaving for the fields in the morning, slaves sometimes buried sweet potatoes in the ashes under a cast iron kettle of soup that was set over a fire. Therefore, supper was ready to eat when they came in for the evening. Cornbread and tafia completed the simple meal.[56]

Despite the simplicity of their diet, most slaves were fed an adequate amount of food to sustain their hard labor. As La San Mire, a slave born on Prosper Broussard's plantation in Abbeville, recalled, "We had plenty to eat. Cornbread and grits, beef, 'chahintes' (coons), des rat bois (possum), le couche-couche, and Irish and sweet potatoes."[57] On average, most slaves throughout the South consumed four to five thousand calories daily. Although they ate a lot of pork and fat, surprisingly, they did not suffer from significant amounts of coronary disease. This could be the result of the incredible amount of manual labor they performed, or perhaps due to the fact that other diseases and ailments claimed their lives before heart trouble could become a problem.[58]

La San Mire at the age of 86.

A SLAVE NARRATIVE
La San Mire

La San Mire was born a slave. His father was a Spaniard who spoke Spanish and French, while his mother was French-speaking. Both of his parents were slaves and their master was Prosper Broussard from Abbeville, Louisiana. Mire said they all were considered Creole because they all spoke French, both the slaves and the master. Mire was later freed, and at the age of twenty-one he married a woman from Grand Chenier (Cameron Parish) on the Saturday before Mardi Gras. They had sixteen children together. In 1938 La San Mire was interviewed as part of the Federal Writers' Project slave narratives collections.

Food played a critical role in determining the outcome of the Civil War.
Some blacks, like the one pictured here, became Army cooks.

The Civil War brought hard times for everyone and food shortages became commonplace. Clara Solomon of New Orleans recorded in her journal that in 1861, "We were then summoned to dinner. 'Potato pone' [baked potatoes] and 'molasses candy' the order of the day." In another entry, she wrote, "8 ¼ p.m. . . . We have just repaired from the dining room, where we have been indulging in bread and molasses, and wishing for one of those nice fish suppers, of which nothing but the memory of them, now remains." A month later, she commented, "[W]e proceeded to dinner, the principal items of which were a nice dish of tomatoes Stew, and P.P. [potato pone]."[59] Conditions only worsened as the war dragged on.

Food historian John Egerton explains, "The war years brought physical devastation to the Southern landscape and desperation to the people. Shortages of such staples as salt, sugar, meat, and flour were at first an inconvenience—and then alarming, even terrifying. What little meat there was often spoiled for lack of salt to cure it. Corn, too, was scarce, and that limited the bread, without which there was almost nothing."[60]

For the poor, learning to make do was nothing new. For the planter class, doing without was a novel experience. Those in rural areas typically fared better than their city counterparts simply because they had gardens and easier

The starving people of New Orleans fed by the United States military authorities, seen in *Harper's Weekly*, June 14, 1862.

access to wild game and fish in the nearby woods and water. Regardless of location, however, substitutions became common for everyone. The only cookbook published during the war in the Confederacy was the *Confederate Receipt Book* which offered a variety of recipes and home remedies designed to assist people in coping with shortages. A few of the more interesting suggestions included frying artificial oysters comprised of green corn and eggs, making a pie crust out of potatoes, substituting beaten egg whites for cream when serving tea or coffee, as well as using rice flour instead of wheat flour to bake bread, fry pancakes, or make fritters.[61] Wealthy planters wrote about their frustration with the lack of coffee beans, but for a long time, the poor had been accustomed to creating coffee substitutes out of dried and parched sweet potatoes, parched rye, corn, peanuts, persimmon seeds, and watermelon seeds. Some even experimented with okra and claimed that carefully ground matured okra seeds gave the closest taste to real coffee.[62] Regardless of their antebellum status, most Southerners, whether white or black, rich or poor, were reduced to eating whatever they could find during wartime.

In the post-war years, members of the planter society struggled to regain their former status as society's upper echelon. Egerton explained the situation when he wrote:

> Prosperous or poor, the advantaged white minority sought to recapture its lost glory—and once again, black cooks, maids, and servants did most of the work. . . . There was much irony in these postwar relationships between white and black women in Southern kitchens. They had been there together for a long time, mistress and slave, rich and poor, combining their talents to produce an impressive array of culinary masterpieces. Now, their relative status was altered. The white woman lived with the burden of a reality called defeat, the black woman with the disillusionment of an abstraction called freedom. Everything was changed—and yet, nothing was changed. The black woman was still poor; the white woman, more often than not, still had property and status but not much money, and so was poor too.[63]

Although the South as a whole struggled to reestablish itself after the Civil War ended, New Orleans was especially affected by the additional internal struggle between white Creole society and the ever-increasing American population. One of the arenas in which Creoles continued to dominate, however, was in the area of its superb cuisine. In the fall of 1873, a *Scribner's Monthly* article described New Orleans as a city that boasted "aristocratic restaurants where the immaculate floors are only surpassed in cleanliness by the immaculate linen of the tables, where a solemn dignity . . . prevails, and where the waiter gives you the names of the dishes in both languages, and bestows on you a napkin large enough to serve you as a shroud, if the strange mélange of

CREOLE FINE DINING

Antoine's Restaurant

In 1840, native Frenchman Antoine Alciatore opened Antoine's Restaurant in New Orleans's French Quarter. The restaurant quickly became popular for its French Creole cuisine and expanded to its current location at 713 St. Louis Street. Antoine's continues to serve its Creole fare and signature Oysters Rockefeller to patrons in a number of New Orleans-themed dining rooms. Today, it is both the oldest restaurant in the city and the oldest continually family-run restaurant in the United States.

Well into the twentieth century, black cooks provided nourishment to white employers. The Lepine family from the Laurel Valley Sugar Plantation in Thibodeaux are pictured here with their cooks, c. 1922.

French and Southern cooking gives you fatal indigestion." Prior to 1885, no surviving recipe books documented the Creole culinary repertoire. However, when New Orleans hosted the World's Industrial and Cotton Exposition in 1885, many visitors to the area became enamored with Creole cuisine and in the same year, the first recipe books highlighting the city's exceptional cuisine were published.[64]

The Creole Cookery Book was a collection of recipes edited by the Christian Woman's Exchange. The cover page notes that their contributors consisted of "housekeepers experienced in the science of cookery as practiced throughout the South, and more particularly as it is understood and applied by the Creoles of Louisiana." In their preface, they clearly state, "it is befitting that the occult science of the gumbo should cease to be the hereditary lore of our negro mammies, and should be allowed its proper place in the gastronomical world." Efforts were clearly being made to expose and publicize the expertise of black female cooks for the benefit of primarily white housewives.[65]

That same year, *La Cuisine Creole* was published anonymously by New Orleans author and journalist Lafcadio Hearn who wrote in the introduction that "it behooves the young housekeeper to learn the art of cooking" since

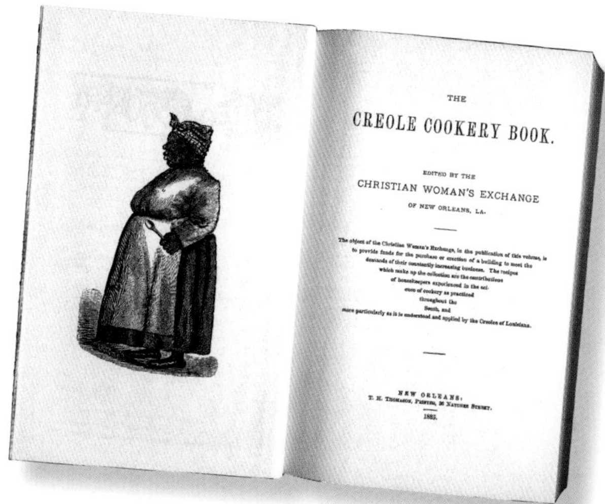

THE

CREOLE COOKERY BOOK.

EDITED BY THE

CHRISTIAN WOMAN'S EXCHANGE

OF NEW ORLEANS, LA.

The object of the Christian Woman's Exchange, in the publication of this volume, is to provide funds for the purchase or erection of a building to meet the demands of their constantly increasing business. The recipes which make up the collection are the contributions of housekeepers experienced in the science of cookery as practiced throughout the South, and more particularly as it is understood and applied by the Creoles of Louisiana.

NEW ORLEANS:
T. H. THOMASON, PRINTER, 36 NATCHEZ STREET.
1885.

The Creole Cookery Book

"food rendered indigestible through ignorance in cooking often creates discord and unhappiness." He went on to explain that "economy and simplicity govern 'La Cuisine Creole'; and its many savory dishes are rendered palatable more as the result of care in their preparation than any great skill or expensive outlay in the selection of materials." He added, "The Creole housewife often makes delicious *morceaux* [morsels] from the things usually thrown away by the extravagant servant. She is proud of her art, and deservedly receives the compliments of her friends."[66]

Some fifteen years later, New Orleans's newspaper *The Picayune* published the *Picayune Creole Cook Book* in order to preserve the "kitchen artistry of 'the Creole negro cooks of nearly two hundred years ago, [as] carefully instructed and directed by their white Creole mistresses.'" Although the paper's publisher feared that "vast upheavels [*sic*] of social conditions" (i.e. emancipation and Reconstruction) would destroy Creole cuisine, his fears proved to be unfounded since Creole cooking only flourished with the passage of time and the additional influences of other immigrant communities. Yet, as Egerton explained, "Creole cooking remained essentially a creation of skilled black cooks and chefs employed by whites."[67]

La Cuisine Creole

Black Pots, White Rice, and Brown Gravy: Creole Cooking Today

> *This was the* brown *area. Everything was pretty much smothered. You took the white flour and cooked it 'til it was brown. And if you wanted to make a fricassée, which is a brown chicken gravy, you cooked it in a black pot and smothered everything down until it was brown. Tomatoes and stuff in the gumbo—that comes from New Orleans. Everything here was* brown.
>
> –Thomas Fields[68]

Much of what the rest of the world has come to associate with South Louisiana cooking is not necessarily what black Creoles ate (or eat) on a daily basis. Despite the popular stereotype that Acadiana residents enjoy gumbo, boiled crawfish, and jambalaya every day, the reality is that many of these dishes are reserved for times when families and friends come together to celebrate special occasions.

According to folklorist John Laudun, "In some ways, the *ur*-dish of the region is not gumbo but rice and gravy. Pork steak. Brisket. Meatballs. Even cowboy stew with potatoes: All are served over rice with gravy. What distinguishes one region from another are the stages of browning." He goes on to explain, "This preference for browning may, in part, come from the roasting practices of 17th-century French cookery. . . . With the addition of West African foodways to the mix, the browning triumvirate—Native American parching, European roasting, and West African frying—was complete."[69]

Naturally, food preferences are directly linked to the availability of certain foodstuffs. With the end of the Civil War and Reconstruction and the dawning of a new century, many former slaves became sharecroppers, but sharecropping did not drastically improve the lifestyle of most freedmen. In fact, many ate more cornbread and pork and fewer fruits and vegetables than ever before. As sharecroppers, generations of poor blacks worked the land and bought most of the flour, cornmeal, lard, and molasses they needed on credit under the crop lien system. Similar to slavery days when blacks received the cheaper cuts of meat from their master's table, the commissary also offered lower grades of pork to those working the land. Blacks continued to eat unusually large quantities of pork—so much so, in fact, the terms "meat" and "pork" became synonymous.[70]

Most Creoles in South Louisiana still consume rice daily. This detail of black workers pitching bundles of rice into a wagon in Crowley is dated 1938.

Laborers employed by Joseph La Blanc [*sic*], a wealthy Cajun farmer, with possum and birds they shot, in Crowley, 1938.

As a result of poor eating habits, many indigent blacks suffered from pellagra, a disease caused by a shortage of niacin attributed to a steady diet of salt pork, cornmeal, and grease. Although the disease probably existed before the Civil War, it was first noted in the early 1900s. New Deal efforts to improve nutrition, as well as the introduction of commercial flour and cornmeal that was fortified with vitamins, undoubtedly helped to decrease the number of pellagra cases from 1933 to World War II. Intestinal worms also plagued the lives of many poor blacks and absorbed much of the nutrition their unvaried diet offered. Some viewed blacks as being lazy, but the reality is that they were probably dealing with a lack of energy due to malnourishment. In 1909, the Rockefeller Sanitary Commission for the Eradication of Hookworm Disease launched an anti-hookworm crusade that Louisiana partnered with the following year. Many hoped the effort would be "a near miracle that would make poor lazy Southerners, black and white, over into energetic Yankees." Although hookworms were not eradicated, the sanitary commission's efforts did help.[71]

Before the Great Depression, some sharecroppers were already hungry because landowners retired marginal land from cultivation, ousting them and their families in the process. The New Deal displaced more sharecroppers as the government instituted crop reduction programs. In the years following World War II, mechanization continued displacing sharecroppers. Employment opportunities in the North and West lured many blacks into cities away from the South's rural areas.[72] Although urbanization brought about change, the fact that cities were still populated by many people who had grown up on farms, or at least had parents who had, caused the shift from rural to urban life to be a slow process. Generations of rural habits could not be changed overnight, and diets did not change instantaneously either.[73] In fact, from the Civil War to World War II, the food consumed in the South remained essentially the same, with corn continuing to be a major source of food for South Louisiana residents.[74]

Those who grew up sharecropping remember how hard they worked. Joann Delafose, a black Creole woman from the Eunice area,[75] explained, "We were farmers, so I had to pick cotton, break corn, dig potatoes, and all that." Describing her sharecropping routine, she recalled,

Joann Delafose with her son Geno

So when you'd get through with the cotton,
then it was corn or the potatoes.
No, the potatoes, and *then* the corn.
The corn was coming in the fall.
And, *girl*, it was so dusty when you'd break that corn and throw it in the wagon!
The two horses would pull the wagon
and you'd walk behind the wagon.
Break the corn
and throw it in the wagon.

And then when you'd get home,
we'd have to *unload* the corn
and put it up
and clean it.

Okay, then when you got through with that, then they had planted some peanuts.
And you'd have to pull all the peanuts up.
And *don't break 'em*
and don't leave none in the holes!
And *then*, when you'd get home,
we'd have to pick 'em
and throw 'em on the old house or barn that wasn't too high
'cause they had to dry.
You had to wait for them to dry.

And once they was dry,
then you had to take 'em off the limbs,
one by one,
and put 'em in something.
We'd pull 'em off the barn and put 'em in a pile.
Then we'd pick 'em up,
break one peanut at a time,
then put 'em in the bucket.[76]

Thomas "Big Hat" Fields was raised by his grandparents on a sharecropper's farm in Rayne.[77] Completely illiterate and unable to speak more than a few words of English, Fields's grandfather "Old Man Frank Sinegal" farmed and raised horses in order to provide for his family of ten children, as well as his grandson. Having grown up on the farm, Big Hat remembered that "everybody worked or done something. Everybody." By thirteen years of age, he was already laboring outside the home for hire. Although raised poor in a large household, Big Hat recalled, "I *never, never* sit to that table one night and cried 'cause we didn't have nothin' to eat. We *always* had plenty to eat."[78]

Even those who did not grow up on a farm usually had close ties to family members who did. For example, Brenda Placide was born in Parks[79] in 1947 but moved to New Iberia[80] as a young girl and has remained there ever since. She recalled,

> My grandfather was a farmer.
> You see, and he was raising cows; he was raising hog.
> They had cotton in the field they picked.
> They had okra to pick, watermelon to pick.
> My grandfather was a farmer.
> And what my mother used to do,
> my mother's mother used to live in Breaux Bridge,
> so for—for the summer, my mother would send us out there
> and they would make us work. [*Laughs*][81]

Unidentified young men work their farm in Frilot Cove.

Sugarcane worker drinking water in the field near New Iberia, 1938.

Living on a farm enabled most black Creoles to be almost entirely self-sufficient. Even with a third of their livelihood going to "the man," with the exception of staple items like rice and flour, most of the meat and vegetables that ended up on the table came from their own gardens or livestock pens. Even relatively small plots of land successfully fed large families and what was not consumed immediately was canned and put up for later.[82]

To start off the work day, most Creoles in the prairie area remember eating *couche-couche* and milk every morning.[83] Lesley "Les" Comeaux was one of sixteen children born to the same parents. A native of Opelousas,[84] he explained, "If we had sugar, that was alright. But fresh milk and *couche*—it would taste so good. You didn't need no sugar."[85] Thomas "Big Hat" Fields recalled that his family always ate early before the sun came up because they

Sharecropper tenant preparing a meal in the kitchen.

had to start working in the fields as soon as it was daylight. He remembers eating cornbread and milk for breakfast, as well as grits, eggs from the chickens in the yard, and a little bacon from the hogs they raised.[86]

Lesley "Les" Comeaux.

Dinner was always the heartiest meal on the farm. When Joann Delafose left school early and married at a young age, she became very close to her mother-in-law. Joann recalled that Mrs. Delafose would begin working in the fields at seven o'clock in the morning. At 10:30, however, she headed back to the house in order to start cooking dinner. When the meal was ready at noon, she waved a white rag for everyone to come in and eat. Much of what she served came from the garden she tended herself. Although it was not a large garden, she had a row for everything—tomatoes, bell peppers, cucumbers, and other vegetables. She often served butterbeans, snapbeans, mustard greens, corn, and biscuits with brown gravy alongside portions of chicken or meat they had raised and slaughtered on the farm.[87]

Thomas "Big Hat" Fields remembered that at 11:30 when they came in from the fields for dinner, his grandmother's table was always "dressed with plenty of food, enough to feed their family and whoever else came." He explained, "And that was a way of life for us. We didn't have new clothes or fancy things, but we always had plenty to eat." Everything they ate was homegrown, whether it was tomatoes or corn, hogs or beef. Breakfast may have been a simple affair, he remembered, "But at noon, you had a *solid* meal."[88]

Les Comeaux's grandmother was also the primary cook in his family. While the older children and adults worked in the fields, his grandmother stayed home with the little ones and cooked. "Everything my grandmother cooked would make you lick your fingers," he recalled with a smile. Sometimes she would walk out to the fields carrying a pan on her head filled with sweet breads or water for the ones who were picking cotton in the heat.[89]

Born in 1941, Merline Herbert grew up in Lafayette, the daughter of a furniture mover father and a stay-at-home mother. When asked what her family usually ate for dinner, she explained, "Oh we cooked rice and smothered meat—cooked meat in a pot with onions and bell pepper and some beans. You always had meat, rice, and a vegetable, yeah—be it beans or greens or whatever, but you always had meat, rice, and vegetables. And we always had that for lunch."[90]

Merline went on to say, "Now at night we ate sandwiches or we had cornbread with milk or maybe biscuits or cous-cous [*couche-couche*] and milk. We never ate meat and rice at night when I was coming up. My daddy did not like eating heavy at night, yeah. And then, you know, when I got married that was the most interesting thing, and my—my sister and my brothers they would sometimes come over and eat at my house because when I got married my husband and I, we worked during the day so in the evening when we got home I'd sometimes fix a hot meal for us. And they thought that was—ah, that was fantastic, some meat and rice at night, wow. So they would come over and eat with us sometimes. Yeah; that was special."[91]

Others recalled eating *couche-couche*, cornbread, or biscuits for dinner as well. Les Comeaux's family rarely ate meat during the week, but relied primarily on *couche-couche* and milk or biscuits and syrup for sustenance.[92] Joann Delafose said, "I went to bed hungry many times 'cause I didn't want to eat cornbread and biscuits." Laughing, she added, "But look how big I am. I did *not* starve!" She shook her head. "Mm. Hm. Hm."[93]

Merline Herbert opened the Creole Lunch House after retiring from teaching.

Children heading off to school carrying their lunches as they leave Lejeune's store in Mix, a community in Point Coupee Parish. Notice the advertisement for Creole Belle Coffee and the African style chair (called *banza mambu* in Angola) to the left of the porch.

Although many children growing up in rural areas were often needed at home, some were afforded the opportunity to gain at least a little bit of formal education. Thomas Fields, for instance, attended the Acadia Parish Training Center on and off for six or seven grades. Yet, he missed so much school, he says that to this day, "I can't read a letter, can't write a letter. *I'm telling you!* I can count. I can add and subtract and that's it. What's wrong with that? Went all over the world [playing music] like that, baby. That's right."[94]

Joann Delafose was able to complete the eighth grade before getting married and working full-time on the farm. She remembers carrying her lunch in a little black pail when she went to school. Although many of her classmates also brought biscuits and syrup to eat, she was ashamed of her meager lunch, especially when she got older and boys were around. "I'd stay all day without eating them. I did, girl, I *did*," she recalled years later. The biscuits got hard when they were cold, but some of the other children had "the good bread." She was jealous of those classmates.[95]

Les Comeaux remembered his mother filling his lunch bucket with an egg or an egg sandwich that he could carry to school. Other times she would make a sandwich out of leftover meat or a fig sandwich using preserves she had made and put up earlier in the year. Since all of the children at his

Children fishing in the ditch in Thomastown, 1940.

school ate lunch at the same time, it was not uncommon for them to swap lunches with each other to get something more desirable.[96]

For the most part, everyday menus during the week changed only with the seasons. Fridays and Sundays were notable exceptions, however. As was Catholic custom, most Creole families did not eat meat on Fridays. While today's modern convenience of refrigeration and transportation makes seafood more available, most prairie Creoles did not have access to seafood products during Lent or on meatless Fridays. Most substituted eggs for meat in their stews or simply ate fish they caught in nearby waterways. For example, Les Comeaux's father usually went fishing on Fridays. Smothered in gravy, the fish was typically served over rice and accompanied by a potato salad.[97]

By far, the highlight of everyone's weekly routine was Sunday dinner. It was not only a day of rest from the physically demanding farm labor, but also a time for the community to worship together and for families and neighbors to enjoy the best meal of the week. Josephine Phillips Cormier of St. Martinville[98] explained that "every Sunday when I was growing up families would get together. We'd go to church in the morning. The adults would go out and—and start cooking. The kids would go out and play . . . [and] each person would cook, or they would cook together you know. One would do the gumbo and one would do the rice and one would do the meats; the other ones would do . . . the melons and one would do the cakes, the desserts—and maybe it was [a tradition] from the family before my dad. I . . . really don't know. All I can remember is every Sunday you had a family day. So obviously they got that from their family because on Sundays no matter what—it was winter, summer, it was always family dinner." She added, "Sunday dinner was always given [at] the family's house, the main house . . . whether it was grandfather's house or grandma's house, and all the siblings and all their children and all the cousins would get together and have a family dinner—family gathering with food and songs and games."[99]

Les Comeaux remembered walking to church on Sunday mornings because they did not own a vehicle. He explained that in those days, the landowner did not want his laborers to have a car because that would give them mobility and they may be enticed to leave the property in order to find work elsewhere. Therefore, the Comeaux family lined up and walked along the railroad track. When the highway was built, they walked along the highway in a row—grandmother, parents, ten boys, and six girls. Les remembered that his grandmother would give them each a nickel for church and a nickel to spend. After leaving church, they would stop at a corner store to buy a pocketful of penny candies and would eat it all as they walked back home. When they got to the house, his grandmother usually cooked a couple of older hens or surplus roosters from the back yard to feed everyone. She normally served the chicken with gravy over rice.[100]

Brenda Placide recalled that she learned how to prepare okra from her grandmother's mother who used to smother the vegetable down "mostly on Sunday for a Sunday meal." She added, "The favorite thing my mother would make that I loved so much back in the days was smothered chicken. Okra and potato salad [and smothered chicken]. That was a Sunday dinner."[101]

Although their family was considerably smaller, Madonna Broussard remembered always going to Sunday dinners at her grandmother's house where "every Sunday was like a big mama style dinner." She added that her grandmother cooked "a Christmas style dinner every Sunday" with yams and other things that she would make after attending church. When asked who normally went to these dinners, Broussard explained that sometimes it was just her parents, her brother, and the two cousins her grandmother was raising. "We were probably maybe six but she had food for 30," Broussard recalled with a laugh.[102]

Merline Herbert remembered that her mother also put out a big spread for the family on Sundays. She explained, "We all sat down at the table and had dinner together. I mean she'd do stuff like a roast or fried chicken, make potato salad, rice, you know, vegetables—all that, sweet peas or yams and all of that. She cooked big dinners every Sunday; that was—yeah that was special, yeah."[103]

Family going to town in a wagon near Opelousas, 1938.

New Year's Day meal consisting of deep-fried turkey, rice dressing, smothered green beans with sausage and potatoes, sweet potato casserole, black-eyed peas, smothered cabbage, and cornbread.

Besides the weekly Sunday dinner, holidays like Thanksgiving and Christmas provided more opportunities for families to gather and enjoy plenty of food. Brenda Placide explained, "My father used to raise hogs and every holiday they would kill a hog. And they would make the red boudin and the white boudin[104] and make hog crackling and smother the backbone, which they call a neck bone now. . . . Christmas, Easter, they would always butcher a hog. That's way back in the days."[105] Joann Delafose remembered that her family typically enjoyed turkey for Thanksgiving with trimmings like cornbread dressing, rice dressing, cole slaw, greens, salad, homemade boudin, cracklins, fresh sausage, sweet potatoes, sweet potato pie, pecan pie, and pumpkin pie. There was also a pot of gumbo on the side for those who wanted gumbo. Since several family members came in from out-of-town and were unable to get some of the locally made items on a regular basis, her family made sure to prepare the special dishes and sent the out-of-towners home with any leftovers.[106]

Desserts were rare treats in Creole households. Les Comeaux remembered that when he was growing up, desserts in his family usually consisted only of things that had been canned and put up—such as a jar of figs that had been mixed with some type of vanilla and put on sweet breads. In the winter when work slowed down on the farm, his family sometimes made popcorn balls. Otherwise, mealtime consisted of simple hearty fare.[107]

Several Creole restaurants in Acadiana such as Brenda's Dine-In and Take-Out in New Iberia, Laura's II in Lafayette, the Creole Lunch House in Lafayette, and Josephine's Creole Restaurant in St. Martinville are keeping the Creole cooking tradition alive through their plate lunches. Menus typically include local favorites such as red beans and rice, smothered chicken, smothered pork chops, meatball stew, rice and gravy, and sides of vegetables like black-eyed peas, smothered okra, and smothered cabbage.

In keeping with Catholic tradition, Fridays are usually seafood days when crawfish étouffée, fried catfish, and other meatless dishes are served. Louisiana specialties like jambalaya, shrimp Creole, and gumbo are rarely served year-round. As Josephine Cormier, owner of Josephine's Creole Restaurant, explained, "Very seldom will I do a gumbo when it's warm unless it's requested, you know." She usually makes her gumbo "when the fall comes in or the first cold weather."[108]

Smothered sausage and rice with corn, greens, and cornbread.

Brenda Placide and her grandson Typann continue a family tradition.

Brenda Placide, owner of Brenda's Dine-In and Take-Out, was born in 1947 and continues the cooking tradition of her mother and grandmother before her. She started her little restaurant around 1990 when her brother asked her if she would cook up some plate lunches for him and about a dozen of his co-workers at the nearby Morton Salt mine. Her business has since grown to serve between seventy and one hundred lunches per day. Although Placide's mother Gustavia David worked in a lot of people's kitchens as a cook, her grandmother cooked at home in order to provide for her ten children. Placide refers to her own cooking as "mama's cooking" and said, "This little place here [Brenda's Dine-In and Take-Out], this type of food, people from all over the world come here to eat because this food is like straight from Mama's and your grandmother, your auntie, like back in the olden days. You could go to different restaurants but you can't find this particular type of food. So that's why the food is so special." When asked if she considered her food to be Cajun, Placide answered, "It's a little Creole, little Cajun—mix all that together and it comes out just right."[109]

Owner and cook at Laura's II, Madonna Broussard was born in 1969 and grew up in Lafayette. Madonna's grandmother Laura Williams Broussard was born in 1920 and first began cooking when she was about ten years old. Standing on a box to reach the top of the stove, she stayed home and cooked for her

Madonna Broussard proudly offers "a Creole experience" to her customers.

siblings while her mother "went out to do some form of laboring" as was common at the time. In the early 1960s Laura started cooking plate lunches out of her home; she opened the first "Laura's" around 1968. As Madonna explained, Laura's "was probably the first soul food plate lunch spot here in Acadiana." She added, "My grandmother back in the day was the Queen of Soul Food." When Madonna took over the family business and opened Laura's II in 2000, she said, "I didn't come in as a more millennium-type young black woman. You know I came in as just—a lot of old school flavor as my grandmother, where we *cher-chered* [short for *chérie* and pronounced 'sha,' meaning dear or darling] everybody, you know, and if you came in and if you spoke French, we can speak French with you."[110]

Pork continues to be a predominant meat although former staples like pork shanks, pig's feet, and roux-based cowboy stew[111] may not be as popular with today's clientele. Still, Madonna says that from time-to-time people still ask her, "Why don't you serve those pork shanks your grandmother had thirty years ago on Tuesday—?" Madonna claims that their gravy is one of the staples "that has made us known." She explains that a lot of men who come through taste her gravy and exclaim, "Wow, my wife does not know how to make gravy." She suggests that using a brown roux gravy is what makes all the difference. "If you put our gravy on a [plate of] rice, it won't just kind of run down. It'll actually stick to the rice. It's brown in color which is also a good thing . . . I've had people to come through that were out-of-towners and say well we don't really know what gravy is. You know, we usually eat rice with a butter or just dried rice, or white sauce. But we actually have a brown roux gravy." She goes on to explain, "We are a Creole experience, so we need to stick to who we are and what we are and what we represent." She expounds that while her grandmother "went as Laura's Soul Food . . . I in turn want . . . to be . . . Laura's II: A Creole Experience."[112]

Josephine Phillips Cormier was born in 1953 and owns Josephine's Creole Restaurant in St. Martinville. She said, "My heritage is Creole, but in this area there's a combination between Cajun-Creole and it's very hard to differentiate it." As she explained, "The cooking is basically the same in this area" due to the combined heritages. Speaking of her family history she offered, "I'm just assuming that they [her father's family] were brought here as slaves and just worked as—as sharecroppers and in the fields, 'cause I do remember when I was little that he [her father] did work on a plantation and we lived on a plantation until further years. I think it was first grade before we moved and they bought a home and we lived there." Her mother's family name, on the other hand, is "Ebow" [113] and she knows that her mother descends from an African tribe.[114]

Josephine Phillips Cormier considers okra to be one of her specialties.

Cormier's shrimp and okra gumbo.

Although her plate lunch menu varies from day-to-day, one of Cormier's specialties is okra. Taking the fresh okra from the fields, she smothers it down with seasoning like onions, bell pepper, and garlic, then adds tasso, smoked sausage, and shrimp. She said, "Anything that you can grow from the fields we grew up with it, especially okra—okra. That's why I put up so many . . . bundles and so many sacks of okra because that's a product of this area that—you know, it's your big market. . . . That's your heritage whether it's Cajun or whether it's Creole in this area. Okra is our heritage." Like most Creole cooks, Cormier never measures anything. She said, "You know, I need X-amount to come up with X-amount of plates for today," so they simply put things in the pot, "give a prayer to God and say, *Please let it come out right* [laughs]."[115]

Merline Herbert, owner of the Creole Lunch House in Lafayette, was born in 1941."Well, I always did enjoy cooking and feeding," she said. "I always did do a lot of cooking with my mom, and I'd help her. And then being the oldest girl [of five children] in the family, very often I would fix dinner for the whole family to come over. And, you know, they would always tell me, 'Oh girl; you cook real good. This was good.' And I said, 'You know, maybe I could make some money doing that since everybody thinks I'm so good. Maybe I need to try that.'"

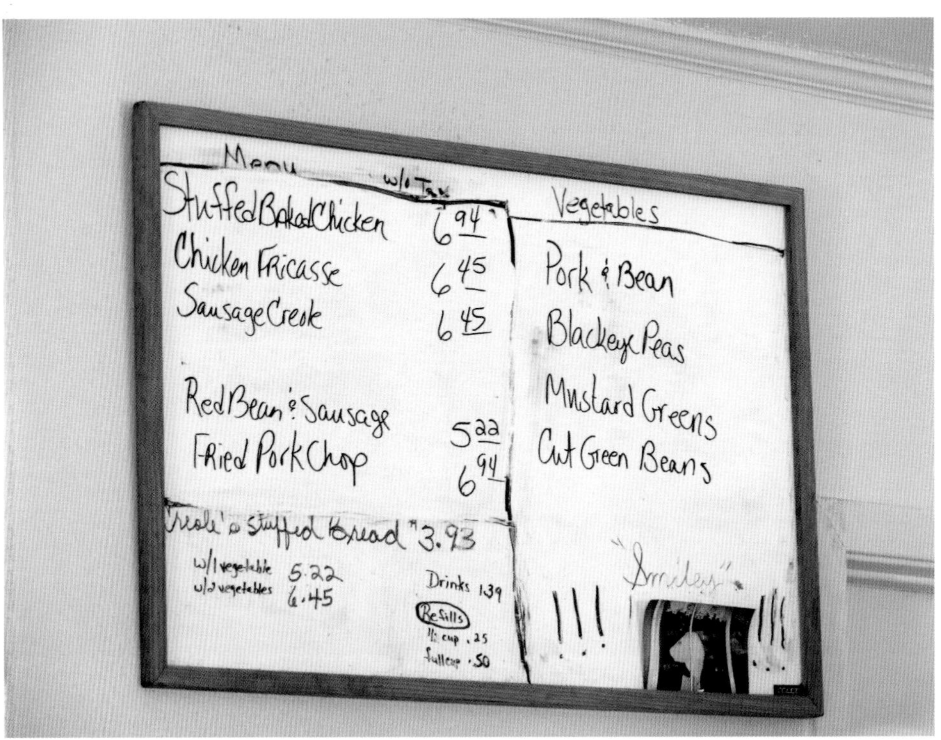

Plate lunch menu board at the Creole Lunch House in Lafayette advertises items like chicken fricassée, sausage Creole, and fried pork chops.

After twenty-two years in the school system, Herbert retired and decided to open her own restaurant. She explained, "Well people like eating meat and rice and gravy 'cause a lot of times this is what you come up with. But then, you know, nowadays parents are so busy, you know, they don't have as much time for cooking. So when you can get some this is great. You know, and too with the restaurant, we're only open five days a week and we only do lunch. We're closed for holidays. I tell my customers, I was a teacher. I don't work on holidays and I don't work on weekends either. And I told them, I said I thought about trying [to close in] the summer, but I said I think that's too long. You're going to starve and I don't want you to starve, so I open during the summer [laughs]."

Acknowledging the importance of rice and gravy in the region, Herbert commented, "It ain't lunch until you have some rice. You know, when we were coming up, like I said, my mama always did cook rice. And we had rice for lunch every day. I mean my dad, I'll never forget; we went to Tennessee to see my brother who was in medical school and they don't do rice. They did green salads; they did potatoes. We stayed there three days. My daddy said, 'Mama next time we come here we going to bring the rice pot.' Yeah. [laughs]." Every now and then someone comes through who does not want rice on their plate.

She said she tells them, "Where you from? What's the matter with you? Oh no; child, you can't eat without no rice. It's not going to work. My meat is not going to stay on that plate [laughs]." She explained that although it is easy to find jambalaya, "there aren't too many places [anymore] where you can really go and get rice and old-fashioned . . . meat cooked in gravy."

Although Creole cooking is considered to be spicy, Herbert said seasoning should not be excessive, and it should be cooked into the meal, not poured on top afterwards. She said with her cooking, "you take a bite and it really tickles the tongue and it excites the mouth" but "it's not abusive." With a laugh she explained that some customers seasoned their food before even tasting it, so she had to stop them and let them know, "We just put that [salt and pepper shakers] on the table so it can look like a restaurant." Eventually, she had to "stop making it look like a restaurant because . . . they were messing up their lunch."

Explaining how she decided upon the name for her restaurant, Herbert said, "Well how we got the name Creole Lunch House, you know, it's—somewhat back in history they talked about how the—in New Orleans the—the ships would come in and dock and they unloaded and they had the Creole ladies would do the cooking for the people coming in. And the Creole ladies did all the cooking. So they—and—and they were like brown-skinned women. And I said well I'm brown skinned and I'm going to cook so I guess we'll call this Creole Lunch House. And that's how we got the name; we were Creole

Locals bring a French guest to the Creole Lunch House for a taste of down-home Creole cooking.

One of the Creole Lunch House's specialties is stuffed bread filled with a spicy mixture of ground meat and sausage.

belles like they call them out in New Orleans and so hey, this is Creole Lunch House. And that's—that's how Creole Lunch House came to be, I mean no really—we cook; we just cook. We cook to make money [laughs]."

When Herbert opened the Creole Lunch House in 1983, she "wanted it to be a place where people could come and relax and feel like they were at grandma's for lunch." When her regular clients, "oldie-goldies" as she calls them, bring in new guests, she serves them the "Rookie Plate" so they can try a little bit of everything. With a laugh, she says, "And sometimes I tell them, 'Now you come back and see us now ya hear. And you can tell your friends and your enemies about me; I'll take care of them.'" [116]

Although New Orleans's traditional cooking has been considered to be "perhaps the closest to that of the West African coast that you can find in the United States,"[117] Creole cooking throughout South Louisiana has been deeply influenced by its African, European, and North American roots. Despite its establishment as a frontier outpost, Louisiana's Gulf Coast did survive to become, as one historian has suggested, "Arguably the most cosmopolitan culture in the North American quarter of the Atlantic world. . . . At the mouth of the Mississippi was the last point of entry of captive Africans in North America. . . . With a cultural mix that also included Spanish, French-Canadian, Native America, and Caribbean cultural infusions, the port city of New Orleans resembled cosmopolitan spots like Luanda (Angola), . . . [and] Dakar (Senegal), . . . where subtropical ecologies and the creolization of cooking and tastes ran parallel to fascinating transformations of language, music, and popular culture."[118]

While Creoles in New Orleans and Acadiana may share the same ethnic label as a result of their mutual heritage, black Creoles in the prairie regions of South Louisiana are quick to point out that the ingredients they use and the cooking traditions they employ are more similar to Cajun foodways than New Orleans cuisine. When asked what a true Creole gumbo was, Thomas Fields responded, "It's like a true Creole [person], you understand? You got everything in it. We are plain. We got the roux . . . a little bit of sausage . . . a little bit of Andouille . . . a little bit of chicken . . . . New Orleans—they got gumbo with—shrimp and everything else. But it's not the same gumbo that we have in the flat land, in the prairies of southwest Louisiana."[119] Whether referring to roux-based gumbo, cowboy stew, chicken fricassée, or smothered pork chops, most prairie Creoles would agree that their cuisine, just like their skin, is more brown than anything else.

Creole Specialties in the Kitchen

Most black Creoles of the prairie regions eat the same foods their Cajun neighbors consume, such as *boudin*, cracklins, rice and gravy, crawfish étouffée, rice dressing, grits, and a host of other regional specialties.[120] It would be impossible to provide a comprehensive collection of Louisiana Creole recipes or significant ingredients since there are as many dishes and variations to these dishes as there are cooks. However, some of the most popular items served up in the Creole kitchens throughout South Louisiana deserve a mention here.

Beans and rice

Although beans and rice was considered to be a lower class meal by upper class white planters, aristocratic households quickly adopted black-eyed peas and rice as a dish worthy of a place on their sophisticated tables.[121] The first cookbook published in America was Mary Randolph's *The Virginia House-wife* cookbook, printed in the 1820s, and this early collection documented the first recipe for black-eyed peas.[122] Elsewhere in the South, "hoppin' john" got its name supposedly as a result of the hopping sound the hard dried peas made when soldiers during the Civil

War put them into boiling pots of water. In French, the term for black-eyed peas is *pois pigon*, or "pigeon peas." It is traditional for Creoles to serve black-eyed peas on New Year's Day in order to ensure good health for the upcoming year.[123]

Red beans and rice is another signature Creole dish. Before the modern conveniences of washing machines and clothes dryers, cleaning clothes was a laborious, time-consuming chore that many women tackled on Mondays. Since red beans and rice is both economical and requires little supervision while cooking, it became popular as a "Monday Wash Day" meal. Cost-effective and simple as it may be, Leon E. Soniat Jr. praised its virtues when he assured his readers that the meal "is not inferior, in any way, to even the finest of the Creole haute cuisine." He explained the dish "also demonstrates the Creole cook's ability to serve an elegant meal at a very small expense."[124]

Boudin

A snack food that can now be found in many local convenience stores, boudin is considered by many to be the region's "fast food." Ground pork muscle meat and organ meat are combined with cooked rice and seasoning vegetables and then stuffed into a sausage casing. Traditionally, cleaned hog's intestines were used for the casing, but today's boudin is usually stuffed into rubbery casing that merely resembles intestines. *Boudin blanc* or white boudin is the most common type found locally and is comprised of a rice dressing stuffed into a sausage casing. *Boudin rouge* or red boudin, on the other hand, contains pork blood usually taken from the hog's neck immediately after being stabbed with a butcher knife. Although health laws prohibit the sale of red boudin, it can still be made for personal consumption.[125] Boudin balls are made by rolling the rice stuffing into a ball, sometimes adding pepper jack cheese, then deep-frying it.

Couche-couche

A popular breakfast dish, *couche-couche* (pronounced coosh-coosh) "pays homage to the cornmeal mush offered at the tables of many different cultures."[126] Folklorist John Laudun explains that the corn mush eaten by the colonial French was derived from an American Indian dish called *sagamite*, a term that spans several native language families. He suggests that the name "couche-couche" probably came as a result of comparisons to the West African dish known as "couscous." Although couscous in Mali was made from rice, not corn, and early gumbos were served over corn mush, not rice, today's Creoles use corn exclusively in the preparation of couche-couche and serve gumbo only over rice.[127] C. Paige Gutierrez explains that the simple dish is nothing more than cornmeal batter fried in a small amount of fat. "As a brown crust forms on the bottom of the batter, the cook stirs the mixture, thus allowing other parts of the batter to brown. This process is continued until the batter has been transformed into a pan of dry, crisp bits, described as being like sand."[128] Most of the time, the fried cornmeal grains were served in a bowl of milk and topped with sugar cane syrup or some other available sweetener. If not served at breakfast, couche-couche made for a quick, inexpensive, yet filling supper meal.

Cracklins

Called *gratons* in French, cracklins are simply pieces of pork fat, sometimes with meat attached, that are deep fried to a crisp and seasoned well for flavor. At *boucheries*, or communal hog butcherings, a common saying is "every part of the pig is used except the squeal." Cracklins are simply a way of making even the pig's tough skin edible. The Port Barre Cracklin Festival in St. Landry Parish has been celebrating the popular snack food since 1985.[129]

Étouffée

The French term *étouffée* simply means "smothered." Although it is not unusual to smother steak, chickens, or potatoes in onions until tender and serve it over rice, probably the most culturally distinct dish is crawfish étouffée.[130] Until the latter half of the twentieth century, crawfish was not widely eaten because the harvesting process was so time-consuming and because crawfish were looked down upon as poor man's fare. Crawfish is now a major Louisiana product and processing plants have made it readily available in all local grocery stores. However, it is still not eaten every day in some households as it is a relatively expensive item and the non-frozen tails are available only seasonally. As Eric Cormier recalled, his mother would cook a gumbo any time but reserved crawfish étouffée for special occasions or when people came over. "For sure we had it in April during Easter season [when the Catholic Lent season prohibited meat and when crawfish were at the peak of their season]. For sure we were going to have it at least once during the [year] . . . between Thanksgiving and Christmas season. She would cook it and have a big group of people over. . . . To this day she probably makes étouffée twice a year."[131]

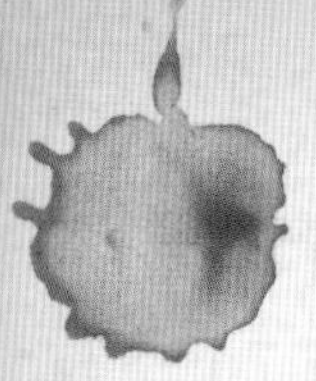

Fricassée

Although a *fricassée* (stew) typically consists of meat or seafood cooked in a dark roux-based sauce and served over rice much like gumbo, according to Gutierrez, "a stew differs from gumbo in that it never contains okra or filé powder" and the sauce of a stew is often thicker than gumbo juice. In the prairie regions, chicken fricassée or smothered chicken is still a very common dish. "Cowboy stew," on the other hand, is not eaten as frequently as before. Comprised of the "small, perishable parts of a freshly butchered cow (the heart, spleen, kidneys, and perhaps part of the liver)," cowboy stew made good use of fresh meat during a traditional *boucherie* (butchering).[132]

Green beans

Perhaps the vegetable most closely associated with Creole culture is the green bean. Touted as the origin for the term "Zydeco," green beans or *les haricots* (pronounced layz-ah-de-koh) are a garden staple. Creoles often answered "*Comment ça va*?" [how are you?] during lean times by saying "*les haricots sont pas salés*," or "the snap beans aren't salty." This literally meant that times were so tough, they could not afford the salt meat to give the beans flavor. Eventually the popular phrase became a song lyric and people at dances would tell the musicians, "Play *les haricots*," meaning "play that song about the snap beans." The spelling evolved into Zydeco, a style of music created and popularized by Creoles.

Gumbo

As a twentieth-century bard once stated, "Sooner or later, Southerners all come home, not to die, but to eat gumbo."[133] Perhaps no other dish characterizes South Louisiana's cultural amalgamation better than the proverbial pot of gumbo. In 2004, Louisiana designated gumbo to be its official cuisine.[134] As folklorist Nicholas Spitzer explains, a gumbo is comprised of "Pots of foreign ingredients—okra from Africa, sassafras from Native America, peppers from the Spanish circum-Caribbean, now all homegrown and stirred with a French sensibility—combined in a new domestic, or even virtual, common space, contributing to the creation of a sauce or roux while retaining essential aspects of their own group primordial."[135]

Described as "perhaps the greatest achievement of all South Louisiana kitchens," there is no one way to make a gumbo. As Chef John Folse explains, "A gumbo is a gumbo in much the way that a snowflake is a snowflake or a fingerprint a fingerprint. All gumbos look alike until you get close to them; then you find that no two are the same."[136]

Gumbo is much more than a soup-like dish. It is symbolic in many ways and represents not only a specific cultural identity, but also a strong sense of community. As the owner of Brigtsen's Restaurant in New Orleans explained, "You don't make gumbo; you make *a* [emphasis added] gumbo. *I'm making a gumbo—y'all come over.* So it's always been to me, again, about people. It's about sharing and getting together over a pot of gumbo."[137] Armand Olivier III of

Olivier's Creole Restaurant in New Orleans was asked what gumbo meant to him personally and culturally. He responded, "Sunday dinner and holidays, that's what it means to me . . . that's what I associate the word with. Holidays, birthdays, guests over, family gatherings—gumbo had to be present for a family gathering."[138]

Gumbo has played a major role in South Louisiana's culinary landscape since its inception. The first reference to the gumbo ingredient known as *filé* that historian Gwendolyn Midlo Hall found was in 1764 by the testimony of runaway slaves living in New Orleans or somewhere nearby. Slaves were sent to the market for shopping and explained they bought *filé* as well as seafood there.[139] Around 1800, Pierre Clément de Laussat recalled a large dinner party thrown in honor of Louisiana's last Spanish governor. Sixty places were set at the main table, twenty-four at the small table, and nearly one hundred fifty guests occupied thirty-two smaller tables. Hundreds more ate standing up. He commented, "As a local touch, twenty-four gumbos were served, six or eight of which were sea turtle."[140]

While traveling through North America at roughly the same time, Fortescue Coming boarded at Madame Legendre's Lafayette Hotel in Baton Rouge and documented his experience:

> The table was covered with different dishes, and a variety of vegetables among which the most conspicuous was a large dish of Gumbo, served

> by the hostess at the head, which seemed to be a standing dish and much in repute. It is made by boiling ocroc [*okra*] until it is tender and seasoning it with a little bit of fat bacon. It then becomes so ropy and slimy as to make it difficult with either knife, spoon, or fork to carry it to the mouth, without the plate being connected by a long string, so that it is a most awkward dish to a stranger, who besides, seldom relishes it, but it is a standing dish among the French Creoles."[141]

Since President Thomas Jefferson was widely known for his love of French cuisine, it comes as no surprise that his cookbook contains several recipes for gumbo and okra soup. One recipe suggests that "gumbo may be made with sassafras leaves dried and powdered, instead of okra, but the sassafras leaves must not be put in until the soup is done. Then add 2 tablespoonfuls of sassafras."[142] Another recipe explains how to first make a roux, then "add 1 fowl which has been disjointed. . . ." After adding water, salt, red pepper and black pepper and cooking for an hour and a half, "just before serving stir in, while stirring constantly, 2 or 3 tablespoonfuls of gumbo (sassafras leaves, dried and pounded) according to the amount of liquid in the pot." They warn against letting the dish boil after the "gumbo" [i.e. sassafras] has been added. The recipe then instructs, "Turn into a soup tureen and serve."[143]

According to Belinda Hulin, author of *Roux Memories: A Cajun-Creole Love Story with Recipes*, "Creole gumbo combines roux and okra, and sometimes tomatoes, to create a dark, rich, thick broth. Once that base has been established, virtually any type of shellfish, sausage, or fowl from the refrigerator can be thrown into the pot."[144] While the New Orleans and Gulf Coast regions had easier access to seafood and people there enjoyed putting tomatoes in many of their dishes, most gumbos prepared in southwest Louisiana's farming and

ranching prairie communities do not include tomatoes. Rather, they utilize fowl and smoked meat or a combination of both since poultry and sausages or other types of smoked meats were readily available to them.

Current Creole cooks in Acadiana still tend to follow these historic trends although modern refrigeration and transportation enable them to add virtually any ingredient they wish to include. For example, Zydeco musician Donna Angelle of St. Martin Parish prepares her gumbo with hen or turkey necks and sausage.[145] Joann Delafose, mother of the well-known Creole artist Geno Delafose and wife of the late John Delafose, puts a combination of hen, smoked turkey necks, smoked sausage, gizzards and hearts into her gumbo.[146] Guinea gumbos are also popular in the prairie regions. Considered to be one of the few food animals indigenous to West Africa,[147] guineas were brought to Louisiana from Africa during the plantation days and were used in soups and stews.[148]

Although not as popular, *gumbo z'herbes* or "green gumbo" is another variety of gumbo comprised of leafy vegetables such as collard greens, kale, mustard greens, beet tops, spinach, cabbage, carrot tops, and peppergrass usually flavored with salt pork. Leah Chase, known widely as the "Queen of Creole Cooking," explained that eating gumbo z'herbes on Holy Thursday before Easter Sunday at the culmination of the Lenten period of fasting is an old Creole tradition. Custom says you cannot use an even number of greens, Chase explained, "But we're not [superstitious]. We just don't take any chances. So don't go into this pot with even numbers. You have to have uneven numbers of greens—5, 7, 9, 11, that kind of thing. Uneven numbers."[149]

JAMBALAYA

Just as each gumbo varies according to the cook, so does the rice-based dish known as jambalaya. Some have suggested that the word *jambalaya* comes from a combination of the French terms *jambon* (ham) à la (with) and the African word for rice *ya-ya.* Others say the dish is a descendent of Spanish *paella*, which bears a close resemblance to Louisiana's saffron-free mixture of rice and meat.[150]

Creole Cookery offered an early recipe for "Jumballaya, A Spanish Creole Dish" in which cooks were instructed to "wash 1 lb. of rice, and soak it an hour; cut up a cold roast chicken or the remnants of a turkey and a slice of ham, which fry in a tablespoonful of lard; stir in the rice, and add slowly, while stirring in a pint of hot water; cover your pot, and set where it can cook slowly. Jumballaya is very nice made with oysters or shrimp."[151]

Although some jambalayas, especially those in the New Orleans area, are known for including canned tomatoes or tomato paste to the base in order to extend and flavor the sauce, most prairie Creoles simply brown the selected meats, seafood items, and vegetables in a large pot to form a gravy. They then add the raw rice and cook the starch in the sauce so that it turns a rich brown color. Unlike rice and gravy or étouffée, jambalayas are not runny; and "the finished product varies in consistency from moist and mushy to dry."[152]

Okra

Okra is a popular vegetable in Creole kitchens. Originating with African cooks who used it as a thickening agent, the slender green pods are oftentimes smothered with tomatoes, fried in batter, or more commonly added to thicken gumbo stocks. In fact, the French word "gumbo" comes from the Angolan word *ki-ngombo* which simply means "okra." The English word "okra" actually comes from *nkruma*, the name for the vegetable in Ghana's Twi language.[153]

Mary Randolph's *The Virginia House-wife* (1824) included the first printed recipe for cooking ocra [okra] and tomatas [tomatoes] in which the cook was to "take an equal quantity of each, let the ocra be young, slice it, and skin the tomatas, put them into a pan without water, add a lump of butter, an onion chopped fine, some pepper and salt, and stew them one hour."[154] An 1876 compilation entitled *Housekeeping in Old Virginia* included a recipe for okra gumbo. Cooks were instructed to "Cut up two chickens, fry slightly with a little onion, and a few slices of pickled pork. Put in three or four quarts boiling water, together with pepper and salt, eighteen okras, one-half peck cut up tomatoes. Stew one hour and a half. It must be dished like soup and eaten with rice; the rice to be boiled dry and served in a vegetable dish; put one or two spoonfuls in a plate and pour the gumbo over it."[155]

Of course, Louisiana's earliest Creole recipe books also recommended a variety of ways for preparing the vegetable. *Creole Cookery* included three recipes entitled "Okra Soup" and other suggestions for drying or boiling the pods.[156] *La Cuisine Creole* included a section entitled "Remarks on Gombo of Okra or Filee [*sic*]" which claimed the dish was "a most excellent form of soup." They provided a recipe for "Simple Okra Gumbo," as well as "Okra and Corn Fricassee [*sic*]." Their suggestion for "A Nice Way to Cook Okra or Gumbo" is "to take a pint of young tender okra, chop it up fine, add to it half as much skinned, ripe tomatoes, an onion cut up in slices, a tablespoonful of butter, a little salt and pepper, and a spoonful of water; stew all together till tender, and serve with meat or poultry."[157]

Pain Perdu

Since white flour was such a luxury item in Louisiana outside of the New Orleans area for so long, white bread was considered to be a treat and none of it was wasted. When no longer fresh, leftover pieces could be coated in beaten eggs, fried in butter and browned on both sides, then sprinkled with confectioner's sugar and drizzled with cane syrup. Known as *pain perdu* or "lost bread" in Louisiana, many other Americans are familiar with the concept via the term "French Toast."[158] Ancient Romans in the first century B.C. had a recipe for *pain perdu* they called *Aliter dulcia*, or "another sweet dish." Their recipe instructed cooks to "Break [or] slice fine white bread, crust removed, into rather large pieces which soak in milk and beaten eggs. Fry in oil, cover with honey and serve."[159]

Roux

Many South Louisiana recipes begin with the phrase, "first you make a roux" since this pasty blend of browned flour and oil forms the basis for many popular regional dishes such as stews, rice and gravy, and of course, gumbo. The seventeenth-century cookbook *Cusinier français* includes the earliest written recipe for roux. French rouxs are typically not cooked as long and as a result are lighter than Louisiana's brown rouxs, which are rich and dark.[160]

Although the French and Africans arriving in the New World knew how to brown meats, it may have been the American Indians who first introduced them to the idea of browning cereals. During his travels in Louisiana in the eighteenth century, French Captain of the Marines Jean-Bernard Bossu described how the Indians took corn flour or maize and roasted it "in just about the way we roast our coffee." When hungry, he explained that "they mix some of the flour with a spoonful of water. . . ." Folklorist John Laudun has suggested that it is possible that this description provides an account of the origins of Louisiana's roux, since the flour and not the butter changes colors, as in a classical French roux.[161]

Leon E. Soniat Jr., author of *La Bouche Creole*, a collection of Louisiana recipes first published in 1981, explained that his *mémère* (grandmother) and *mamete* (mother) "took just about equal amounts of fat (or oil) and flour. They put the oil in a heavy pot and then sprinkled a like amount of flour into the oil. They

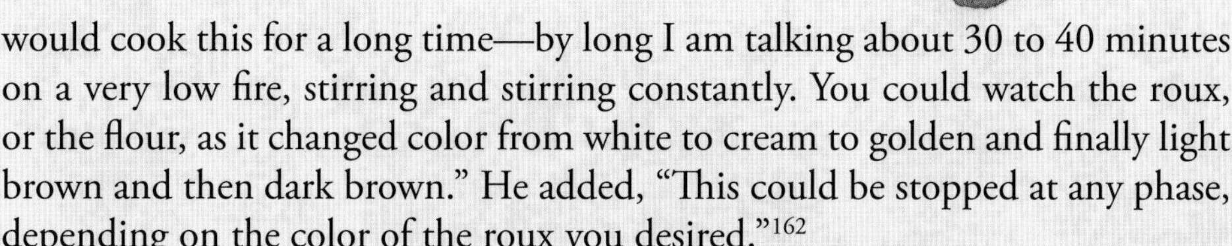

would cook this for a long time—by long I am talking about 30 to 40 minutes on a very low fire, stirring and stirring constantly. You could watch the roux, or the flour, as it changed color from white to cream to golden and finally light brown and then dark brown." He added, "This could be stopped at any phase, depending on the color of the roux you desired."[162]

Tomatoes

In 2003, Louisiana designated the Creole tomato as the official vegetable plant of the state. Creole tomatoes are only grown in certain parts of South Louisiana where the soil is conducive to their cultivation. Sometimes smothered down with okra, tomatoes are also added to some jambalayas to make what is known as a "red jambalaya," a typical New Orleans Creole dish not commonly found in the prairie regions of Acadiana.[163]

Yams

Yams are believed to be indigenous to West Africa, although Fran Osseo-Asara, author of *Food Culture in Sub-Sahara Africa*, explains, "a common misunderstanding outside of Africa is to confuse the yams or sweet potatoes in the United States with African yams, a tropical plant from the morning glory family." The Wolof word for yam is *nyami*, which also means "to eat." In Mende, *yambi* refers to a wild yam. The Portuguese *inhame*, the Spanish *ñame*, and the English word *yam* are thus derived from various West African words for the tuber.[164] In Ibinda, a language spoken in Cabinda, the northern province of Angola, a certain kind of potato is also called *nyami*.[165] During the Middle Passage voyages across the Atlantic Ocean, slaves were often fed yams and descendants of these survivors continue to include yams in their diets.[166]

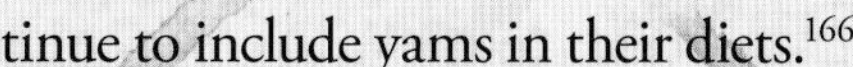

While visiting Louisiana in the early 1800s D.B. Warden observed that three kinds of sweet potato—red, white, and yellow—were "much cultivated" in the area.[167] Throughout the antebellum period, families raised sweet potatoes for home consumption, but after World War I, the need for crop diversification brought about a commercial effort to cultivate the potato. In the early twentieth century, local growers began trying to export their yams to Northern markets at about the same time that Southern blacks began migrating in droves to Northern cities for industrial jobs. Historian Carl A. Brasseaux pointed out that most Southern blacks were used to eating sweet potatoes and their "nostalgic longing for foods left behind undoubtedly helped this emerging Louisiana industry to establish a foothold in the North." He went on to explain, "once 'yams' became part of the national culinary canon for the holidays, the success of the Louisiana sweet potato industry was assured." By the middle of the century, the town of Sunset in St. Landry parish had declared itself the "Sweet Potato Capital of the World"[168] and Opelousas, also in St. Landry Parish, hosted the first annual Yambilee Festival.[169] The sweet potato became Louisiana's state vegetable in 2003.[170]

Desserts

Although desserts have not played a significant role in the culinary tradition of rural Creoles, bread pudding was one significant exception to this general rule. On the farm, milk and eggs were usually readily available. Combined with stale French bread, these ingredients provided a delicious yet inexpensive treat for special occasions. On the frontier and in areas with limited access to pre-packaged goods, sugar was a prized commodity; therefore, sweet candies and desserts were relatively uncommon. In town, however, and especially in the city of New Orleans, many black Creole women made a living by selling homemade treats in the market place. Sybil Kein points out that this was by no means uncommon in other areas. She states, "It is interesting to note that with the making of cakes and candies, the African, West Indian, and Louisiana Creole cooks all hawked their wares with chants about the foods."[171] Even during the slavery period, women made a little extra money by selling pralines and calas on the steps of churches, including New Orleans's St. Louis Cathedral, to hungry parishioners as they left mass on Sundays.[172] As with other dishes, Creole desserts often reflected the cook's ability to transform leftovers into delectable delights. For example, stale bread could be made into bread pudding, cooked rice could be made into calas or rice fritters, sweet potatoes could be baked into pies, and cane syrup could be added to make *gateau de sirop* or syrup cake.

Beignets

Similar to American-style fried doughnuts, "beignets are deep-fried African style, sprinkled with powdered sugar, and served hot with café au lait." Probably the most famous place to order beignets is Café du Monde in New Orleans, a popular tourist spot located in the French Quarter.[173] In 1986, beignets were declared Louisiana's official state doughnut.[174]

Calas

According to some sources, the word "cala" comes from an African word for "rice." Not wanting to waste anything, Creole women could combine leftover rice with flour, sugar, nutmeg, and a few other ingredients and deep-fry the balls. Sprinkled with powdered sugar or drizzled with cane syrup, these fried rice cakes were once as popular as beignets.[175] In fact, the term *calas chaud* (hot rice cakes) first showed up in the nineteenth century when black female merchants known as "cala women" called out chants to hawk their goods.[176]

Pralines

As early as fifteenth-century France, forerunners of the famous praline were being enjoyed. The Creole candy made from sugar, cream, and pecans was supposedly invented by Marshall Dupleses-Preslin's cook (1598-1675).[177] In the 1600s, Field Marshal César de Choiseul, Count Plessis-Plaslin, gave King Louis XIII some of his sugar-glazed almonds, known as his "digestive-aid." The king was so thrilled with the concoction that he named it after his diplomat. When the French arrived in the New World, they substituted pecans for almonds. Black ladies who peddled a modified version of this sweet treat were known as *pralinières*. Using brown sugar and pecans, they created "the smooth and sugary pecan-studded version" most commonly known throughout South Louisiana.[178]

A variation of traditional pecan pralines are the benne pralines that take their name from the Bantu word *benne*, which means "sesame seeds."[179] In 1808, Thomas Jefferson sent Anne Cary Randolph "some seed of the Beny," explaining that it had been brought "from Africa by the negroes" to the Americas where "they bake it in their bread, boil it with greens, enrich their broth & c."[180]

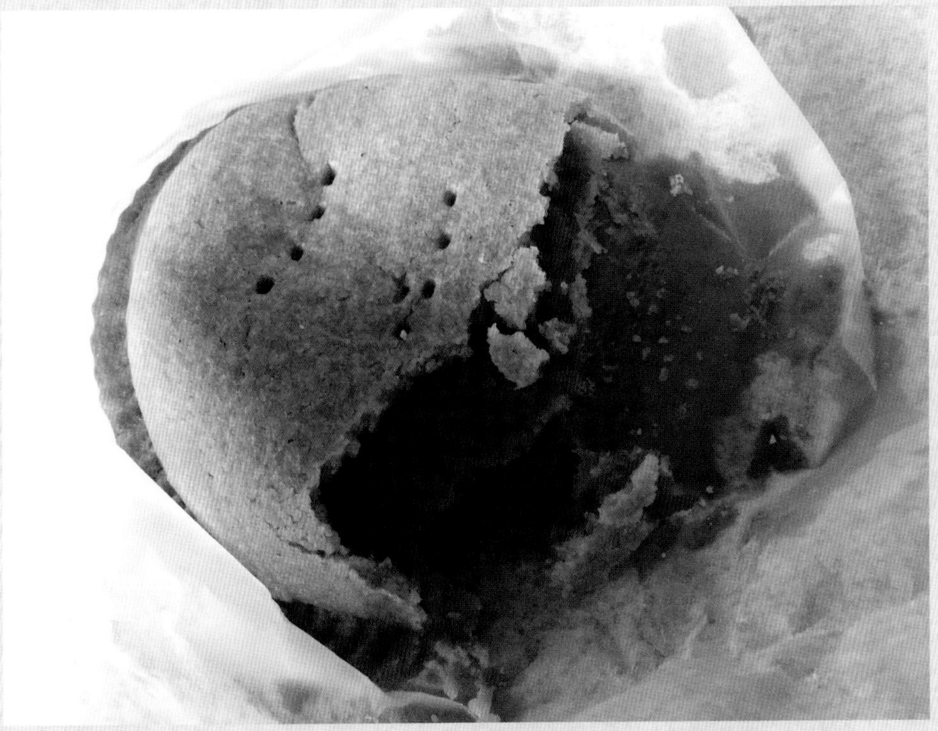

Sweet Dough Pies

Food historians confirm that ancient Romans enclosed meat in a type of pastry made from flour and oil, but according to the *Oxford English Dictionary*, the word "pie" was first used in conjunction with food in 1303. When Europeans emigrated to the New World, they brought this pie-making tradition with them to the frontier for practical reasons. Unlike bread, piecrusts used less flour and did not require brick ovens for baking.[181] In areas where flour was hard to come by, pies provided a convenient alternative.

Creoles traditionally filled their sweet dough pies with seasonal fruits and berries such as peaches and blackberries, or either fig preserves and sweet potatoes they canned themselves. Today, in addition to traditional fillings, some sweet dough pies are stuffed with pineapple pie filling, coconut, or even custard.

In 2011, Grand Coteau, a small community in St. Landry Parish, began an annual Sweet Dough Pie Festival on the the grounds of St. Charles Catholic Church in order to bring more attention to this popular treat often found at festivals and family reunions.[182]

Allons Parler!

CREOLE FRENCH AND THE ORAL TRADITION

One language, one way of thinking. Two languages, two ways of thinking.
–Issiaka Diakité[1]

There was a hobo who had to ask for something to eat somewhere and they didn't want to give him anything because he wasn't Catholic.
So he met another hobo.
He told him, "If you're going to ask for something to eat there, say that you're Catholic, because they won't give you anything if you're not Catholic."
He arrived and he asked for something to eat. They asked him if he was Catholic.
"Oh, yes!" he said. "My father was a priest and my mother was a nun!"
–Lazard Daigle[2]

Virtually anywhere folks gather in South Louisiana, stories and jokes are shared. The setting could be a family barbeque, the deer stand, or around the coffee maker in the office. The region's oral tradition is not only an important cultural element; it is also a way of life. Stories and jokes are used to teach lessons, provide humor, and pass along cultural mores to the next generation. As in the example given, the outsider, or traveling hobo, does not understand the significance of religion within the South Louisiana community he has entered; therefore, his attempt to blend in fails miserably.

Perhaps better known for their Creole cuisine and Zydeco music, one of the most interesting and lesser-known aspects of Creole culture is, in fact, a rich oral tradition that utilizes a distinct type of French found only in South Louisiana. Many black Creoles had limited access to formal education and as a result, relied heavily upon oral, rather than written methods of transmitting information. Despite the fact that most of Louisiana's residents used to speak French, even the type of French the black Creoles developed over time sets them apart from other French speakers. With its European, African, and

Southern porches, like the one attached to this small store near Jeanerette, have always provided a place for friends and family to swap stories, especially during long, hot summers before air conditioning made staying indoors more bearable.

North American influences, the Creole French language is a striking reflection of South Louisiana's cultural mélange. As linguist Michael D. Picone explained, "It would be difficult to find any other region of America having a richer legacy of linguistic diversity—or one facing a bigger threat of dialectal decline at the present time. As a consequence of competition among the French, Spanish, and English for domination of the region and as an outgrowth of the slave trade, European and African languages entered the region and came into contact with each other and with a variety of Native American languages. . . ."[3]

While the language itself may exhibit the results of multicultural contact spanning several centuries, an examination of the region's proverbs, jokes, and stories also reveals links between South Louisiana's Creole repertoire and its African and European roots, as well as its New World influences. Although some argue that the Creole French language and its related oral tradition are in grave danger of disappearing, the work of several folklorists has helped to preserve many elements of this vital cultural component. Despite legislation that once discouraged speaking French in public schools, in recent years, a renewed interest in maintaining and sharing Louisiana's linguistic heritage provides a ray of hope that the Creole oral tradition has a fighting chance for survival.

New World French: Origins of a Language

> *In order to understand a cultural feature, one must understand the context in which it exists. . . . It is trite to say that Louisiana is culturally diverse. The truth is that few people realize the degree of complexity and variation in the cultures of the state.*
>
> –Maida Owens[4]

> *The principal question is not which tales migrated, but which storytellers migrated.*
>
> –Richard Bauman[5]

To many, South Louisiana is like a foreign country. It is a place where locals speak an older dialect of French, eat exotic, spicy food, and dance to the rhythms of Cajun and Zydeco music. Although safely located within the borders of the United States, South Louisiana's distinctive culture invites visitors from all over to have an experience that is "Genuine Cajun, Uniquely Creole," as the Lafayette Convention and Visitors Commission advertises. While the majority of outsiders can successfully identify obvious differences between South Louisiana and mainstream America, most fail to recognize or understand the remarkable ethnic and linguistic diversity found within the region itself.

In seeking to simplify the region's complexity, even self-proclaimed experts like journalists, travel writers, and others passing through the area have contributed greatly to what historian Carl Brasseaux describes as the ongoing perception of South Louisiana's French-speaking community "as a social and cultural, sometimes even a racial, monolith." Unfortunately, many do not realize, Brasseaux continues, that "recent historical, geographical, and ethnograph-

Where Did Cajun French Originate?

In the early 1600s, French peasants immigrated to Nova Scotia. In 1755, the British forced them into exile. Many of these refugees settled in Louisiana and became known as Cajuns. Like Creoles, they passed down their language orally for generations. Many Cajuns still use older French words, although newer words reflect Amerindian, African, Spanish, Caribbean, and even English influences.

French traders purchased Africans at various trading posts, including Gorée Island.

ic studies . . . characterize southern Louisiana's cultural landscape as one of the most complex, if not *the* most complex, in rural North America" [emphasis added].[6] Louisiana's colonial past contributes greatly to the region's incredible diversity. Alternately ruled by the French and Spanish, then acquired by the United States, the area plays host to numerous population groups, including those whose ancestry features roots in Africa, Europe, and the New World. As Picone explains, "Consequently, from its earliest period until today, French in Louisiana has been dialectically diverse and the population of its speakers has always been multiethnic and polychromatic."[7] Yet, before the first European settlers and colonists set foot in the New World, they were quite familiar with the concept of cultural and linguistic diversity in the Old World.

In 1482, a decade before Columbus landed in the Americas, Portuguese entrepreneurs established a trading post in Elmina along Africa's Atlantic coastline.[8] Other European powers quickly followed suit, and by 1664 France had established trading posts at Gorée, St. Louis, and Galam, thereby claim-

Between 1719 and 1808, an estimated 12,000 enslaved Africans were forcibly boarded onto ships bound for Louisiana. Roughly 10,000 survived the grueling sixty-day journey. As illustrated, vessels like the British ship *Brookes* maximized its capacity for transporting human cargo by utilizing every nook and cranny.

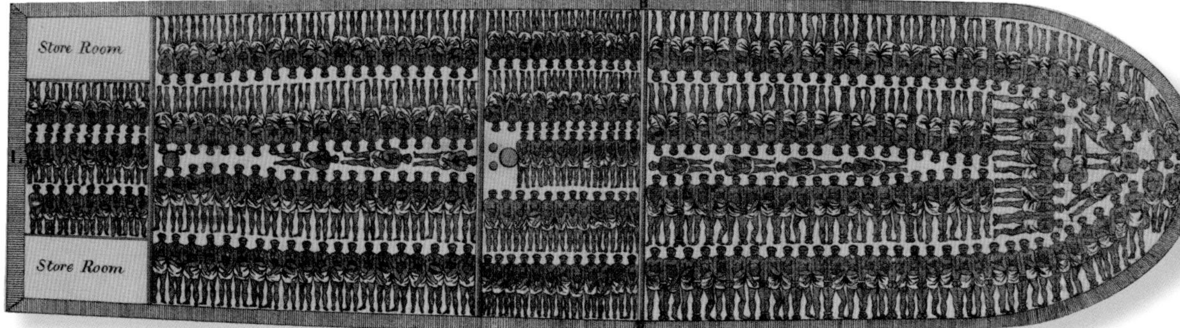

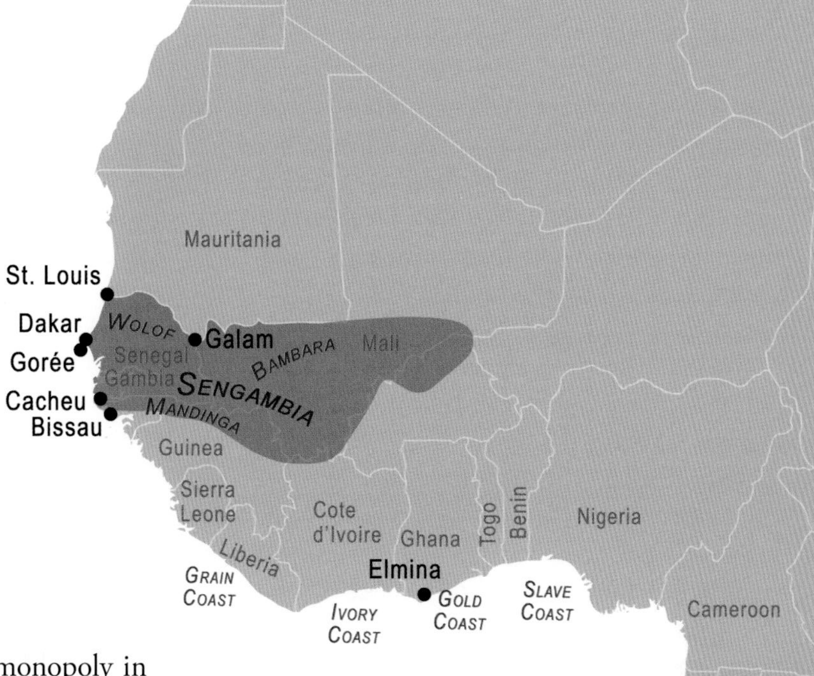

ing a trade monopoly in West Africa's Senegambian region.[9] As trade relations developed and cultures crossed border zones, language, dress, foodways, and other cultural elements were freely borrowed, shared, and adapted as best suited the needs and desires of those involved. European men often found African women to be suitable wives or mistresses, and these liaisons resulted in the development of highly creolized population segments that thrived in and around these trading posts along the West African coastline.[10]

Within a few decades of laying claim to Senegambia, France crossed the Atlantic Ocean and established herself along the Gulf Coast in the New World. Most of the region's earliest soldiers and settlers were, in historian Gwendolyn Midlo Hall's characterization, "the rejects of French society," a motley bunch whose number included deserters, prostitutes, beggars, murderers, and drunkards.[11]

Although many of these emigrants successfully deserted and returned to France, or died during the trans-Atlantic crossing due to mistreatment from ship captains, those who did arrive in the New World suffered extremely high mortality rates that nearly decimated their population.[12] Not surprisingly, the survivors who staggered onto Louisiana's shores and lived long enough to help establish French outposts comprised a remarkably inefficient workforce.[13] Realizing that their imported labor force failed to perform as anticipated, colonial administrators then tried to enslave the local Indians. This plan also proved to be a disaster, and letters sent back to France complained that the Indians were "not appropriate for hard labor."[14] As a result, colonial authorities turned to French outposts on West Africa's coastline for suitable workers.[15]

Since African slavery was a well-established commercial endeavor by the time the earliest French colonists began arriving in Louisiana, it is no surprise that in 1699, colonial administrators petitioned the king for permission to travel to Africa in the king's vessel to purchase slaves. When this request was denied, Louisiana's governor suggested that three Indian captives could be exchanged for every African slave brought in from the West Indies; this request was also denied.[16] Although Louisiana's 1708 census mentions no blacks in the colony (slave or free), by 1712 approximately ten blacks lived in the region, undoubtedly having been smuggled into the colony.[17] The first two slave ships arrived along the Gulf Coast in 1718,[18] and by 1731, census records indicate that 1,721 European settlers and 3,600 African slaves inhabited the Lower Mississippi valley.[19]

Since the French monarch maintained exclusive trade rights in both Louisiana and Senegal, most of the earliest slave ships arrived in the new colony from the Senegambia region. Gorée Island became, as Hall explained, the "main 'warehouse' of the slave 'merchandise.'"[20] Still, some ships such as the *St. Louis* and *la Nériède* picked up their human cargo in Angola,[21] while others hailed from

A SLAVE-PEN AT NEW ORLEANS—BEFORE THE AUCTION. A SKETCH OF THE PAST.

A Slave-Pen at New Orleans—Before the Auction, from *Harper's Weekly*, January 24, 1863.

Louisiana Purchase

Louisiana was alternately under French and Spanish rule throughout the colonial period. French control lasted until 1763 when Louisiana was transferred to Spain. In 1800, Louisiana returned to French rule for a brief period until President Thomas Jefferson incorporated the territory into the United States of America via the Louisiana Purchase in 1803. Louisiana attained statehood in 1812.

Lowering the French flag and raising the American one in New Orleans's Jackson Square signaled the dawn of a new era for Louisiana.

the Congo.[22] Later on, more cultural influences were added to the region when enslaved Africans arrived in Louisiana after stopping over in the French-held sugar islands of the Caribbean. Those slaves born in the New World, whether in Louisiana or in the West Indies, became known as Creoles. These Creole slaves were more highly valued than their African counterparts because they already spoke French, were more resistant to New World diseases, and, having been born into slavery, were deemed less likely to rebel against their masters.

With the passage of time, Louisiana's government was alternately French, Spanish, and finally American; but throughout these periods of change, New Orleans remained the Gulf Coast region's main slave market. According to historian Thomas Ingersoll, "Partly because of its geographical position and partly because of its political history, New Orleans developed a slave population marked by great ethnic variety."[23] Although the influx of enslaved Africans began as a mere trickle, due to increased importation as well as natural increase, by 1850 approximately 245,000 slaves called Louisiana "home."[24]

Regardless of their regions of origin, one thing these enslaved people had in common was their inability to transport to the New World material possessions that could remind them of home. As a result, they preserved their memories and stories from far-off homelands with remarkable tenacity. Long after white immigrants had assimilated and perhaps written down their most popular stories, black communities throughout the South continued to preserve their stories by oral transmission. According to folklorist John A. Burrison, "Nowhere in the United States is storytelling more vital than in the South, where skill with the spoken word has always been emphasized. Strong traditions of storytelling from such Old World source areas of the southern population as Ulster, West Africa, and southern England, reinforced by the physical isolation of dispersed settlements and a conservative mindset that valued the old ways, certainly contributed to this tendency."[25]

Despite its being a part of the American South, however, the social structure found in the French colony of Louisiana produced a slave experience that oftentimes differed from that of other parts of the South. What made Louisiana distinct was not its plantation system that depended upon slave labor, but rather the *Code Noir* or Black Code, issued in 1724, which allowed slaves to earn their freedom. The Black Code also stated that freed slaves could enjoy citizenship privileges "as though they had been born free."[26] According to Article X of the *Code Noir*, a child's status was based on whether or not the mother was free, regardless of the father's condition. Therefore, if the father was enslaved but the mother was free, the children were born into freedom. Although Article VI forbade marriage between whites and blacks, miscegenation[27] was a common occurrence in Louisiana just as it had been in trading posts scattered along Africa's Atlantic coast. Having no legal means of legitimizing the children born to these unions, many white males did in fact emancipate their enslaved mistresses, thereby guaranteeing freedom to their offspring. These children eventually comprised a remarkably large segment of the population known as *gens de colour libre* or "free people of color."[28]

Many free people of color, or "Creoles of Color" as they later came to be known, became slaveholders themselves and blended slave stories from Africa with European stories they heard from their white relatives, neighbors, and

Slave quarters at Evergreen Plantation in Edgard, Louisiana.

New Orleans Slaves

The complexity of Louisiana's racial makeup is evident in this portrait of emancipated slaves. Some of the children are so light-skinned they could pass for white, while others are more clearly of African descent. These emanicapted slaves from New Orleans were brought to New York and photographed in 1863 as part of a campaign to bolster Northern war efforts and raise financial support from Northern sympathizers for newly established schools for blacks in the South. The campaign hoped that dressing the children in fine clothes and including some who looked more white than black would help draw empathy from potential donors when they realized how closely these children resembled their own offspring.

business associates. As a result of tolerant views towards miscegenation and widespread cultural integration, Louisianians, whether of African or European descent, whether slave or free, often crossed racial and cultural boundaries and frequently shared and borrowed traditions from each other.[29] Due to this remarkable mélange of cultures, many traditional African stories brought by slaves to the New World survived, albeit in somewhat modified forms, and have since found their way into Cajun, American Indian,[30] and Creole stories throughout South Louisiana.

Creole French: A "Curious Dialect"

> *The dialect spoken by the negroes in Lower Louisiana and known by philologists as the Creole dialect is an interesting subject for study. . . . It is curious to see how the ignorant African slave transformed his master's language into a speech concise and simple, and at the same time soft and musical.*
>
> –Alcée Fortier[31]

Despite the ethnic diversity of Louisiana's enslaved population, as well as the various native groups and odd assortment of French settlers, soldiers, and administrators who called Louisiana home, within a relatively short period, French became the *lingua franca* of the region. Before even being transported to Louisiana, many slaves in and around the French trading posts in West Africa were familiar with the language, while some learned it upon arrival in the French sugar islands of the West Indies. Similar to the blending of native and European languages in many African regions such as Senegal, Gambia, Angola, and the Congo, Louisiana's American Indian populations also infused their native languages into the various languages European and African immigrants brought with them to the New World. Despite the plethora of languages spoken in colonial Louisiana, with the passage of time, most of South Louisiana's inhabitants, including Native Americans, Creoles, Cajuns, and other immigrant groups, turned to French as their primary means of linguistic communication. Naturally, the language that emerged from this cultural *mélange* was not limited to one kind of French. In fact, Colonial French, Cajun French, Creole French, and International French are among the types of French that are still heard in South Louisiana today.

Although the state's Francophone heritage may be varied and many linguists can trace specific dialects to their historic roots, the origins of Louisiana Creole French continue to be the subject of scholarly debate. As linguist Fehintola Mosadomi explained, French author Jean Raspail considered Creole as spoken by Louisiana's black population to be "inferior because of its simplification, its indicative grammar, its lack of gender and number, its shortened form, and its suppression of prepositions and conjunctions." Viewed in this light, Creole "is thus believed to be a language that will never get beyond its childlike stage." William Read, who published *Louisiana French* in 1931, considered Louisiana Creole to be a substandard dialect of French in which a corruption of French vocabulary was blended with some African words, and then put into an African syntax. Mosadami argued that Margaret Marshall's explanation that "Creole is a variety of French that the slaves were exposed to, a vernacular French characterized by regionalisms and reduced forms" is the most accurate definition of all.[32]

Many Native, European, and African languages influenced or directly contributed to the development of Louisiana Creole French, including the ones listed here.

Rather than debate the validity or illegitimacy of Louisiana Creole, however, perhaps it is more useful to examine the influences that various people had on the language that South Louisiana's black Francophone population speaks today. The base, of course, is French as spoken by the colonists who left various regions of France to settle the New World. Although there are undoubtedly some dialectical variations in the French these immigrants spoke, the current scholarship concurs with Mosadomi that "we can still talk of their base language as a homogeneous French." Thus, despite their geographical or class differences, the majority of French settlers, slave traders, and slaveholders spoke virtually the same kind of French.[33]

Enslaved Africans who found themselves in Louisiana, on the other hand, hailed from many different regions along West Africa's coastline, including present-day Senegal, Gambia, Sierra Leone, Liberia, Ghana, Togo, Dahomey (Republic of Benin), Nigeria, Angola, and the Congo. Naturally, they spoke many different languages before and even after their arrival in Louisiana, such as Wolof, Malinke, Mandingo, Bambara, Foule, Mende, Vai, Twi, Fante, Gâ, Ewe, Fon, Yoruba, Bini, Hausa, Igbo, Ibibio, Efik, Congo, Umbundo, Kimbundu, Serrer, and Pulaar. Yet, upon their arrival in Louisiana, not all slaves were limited to an understanding of certain African languages. With French trading posts having been established along West Africa's Atlantic coastline well before Louisiana was colonized, many Africans, especially in Senegambia, were already conversant in French.[34] Those who were not familiar with the European language had to learn French quickly in order to communicate with their masters. Based on written documentation gleaned from census data, judicial docu-

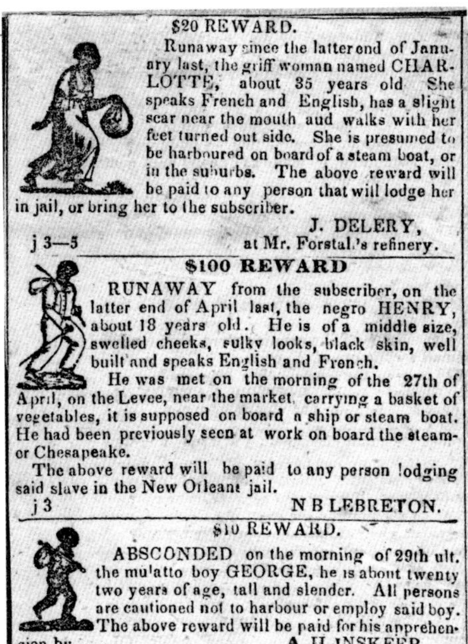

$20 REWARD.

Runaway since the latter end of January last, the griff woman named CHARLOTTE, about 35 years old. She speaks French and English, has a slight scar near the mouth and walks with her feet turned out side. She is presumed to be harboured on board of a steam boat, or in the suburbs. The above reward will be paid to any person that will lodge her in jail, or bring her to the subscriber.

J. DELERY,
j 3—5 at Mr. Forstal.'s refinery.

$100 REWARD

RUNAWAY from the subscriber, on the latter end of April last, the negro HENRY, about 18 years old. He is of a middle size, swelled cheeks, sulky looks, black skin, well built and speaks English and French.

He was met on the morning of the 27th of April, on the Levee, near the market, carrying a basket of vegetables, it is supposed on board a ship or steam boat. He had been previously seen at work on board the steamer Chesapeake.

The above reward will be paid to any person lodging said slave in the New Orleans jail.

j 3 N B LEBRETON.

$10 REWARD.

ABSCONDED on the morning of 29th ult. the mulatto boy GEORGE, he is about twenty two years of age, tall and slender. All persons are cautioned not to harbour or employ said boy. The above reward will be paid for his apprehension by

A H INSKEEP,
june 2—3 58, Canal street.

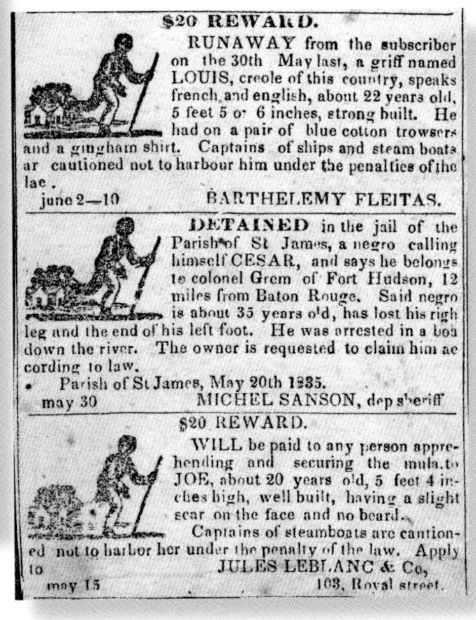

$20 REWARD.

RUNAWAY from the subscriber on the 30th May last, a griff named LOUIS, creole of this country, speaks french and english, about 22 years old, 5 feet 5 or 6 inches, strong built. He had on a pair of blue cotton trowsers and a gingham shirt. Captains of ships and steam boats ar cautioned not to harbour him under the penalties of the lae.

june 2—10 BARTHELEMY FLEITAS.

DETAINED in the jail of the Parish of St James, a negro calling himself CESAR, and says he belongs to colonel Grem of Fort Hudson, 12 miles from Baton Rouge. Said negro is about 35 years old, has lost his righ leg and the end of his left foot. He was arrested in a boa down the river. The owner is requested to claim him according to law.

Parish of St James, May 20th 1835.
may 30 MICHEL SANSON, dep sheriff

$20 REWARD.

WILL be paid to any person apprehending and securing the mulatto JOE, about 20 years old, 5 feet 4 inches high, well built, having a slight scar on the face and no beard.

Captains of steamboats are cautioned not to harbor her under the penalty of the law. Apply to

JULES LEBLANC & Co,
may 15 103, Royal street.

As these notices from the New Orleans *Daily Picayune* indicate, many slaves were bilingual and some were described as "Creoles of this country."

Bambara man and woman

ments, and diaries, Marshall estimates that blacks in Louisiana were already speaking Louisiana Creole by the middle of the eighteenth century.[35]

While slave traders interacted with many different kinds of people in their line of work, many preferred dealing with certain tribes more than others. For instance, French traders like André Brüe wrote in 1722 that Bambara slaves were considered to be "the best in all Africa for work, being strong, gentle, tractable, and faithful; not subject to sullenness, or to run away as the Guinea Negroes frequently are."[36] Considering their position as highly prized slaves, it is not surprising that at one point there were so many Bambara-speaking slaves in Louisiana that the courts had to employ an interpreter named Samba Bambara to assist in the proceedings. Samba had worked for the French in Senegal as an interpreter during the 1720s, but after allegedly joining a slave revolt, he ended up exiled to Louisiana. However, his knowledge of French, Creole, and several African languages landed him a position as an interpreter for Louisiana's Superior Council, and he later became an overseer for the Company of the Indies' largest "concession" or plantation, located across the Mississippi River from New Orleans.[37]

Le Page du Pratz, Louisiana's first historian, recognized the region's linguistic differences and published the earliest known Louisiana Creole phrases. One of the quotes that he documented prior to 1734 was a statement made by Samba Bambara in which Samba reportedly complained, "*M. le Page li diable li sabai tout*" ("Mr. le Page is a devil who knows everything"). If written in International French, the phrase would have read "Mr. le Page est un diable qui sait tout."[38]

French men may have preferred Bambara males as laborers, but they preferred Wolof women to serve as concubines because they considered their *beau noir lustré* (lustrous black skin) to be evidence of pure African blood, unlike the Fulbe women whose association with the Islamic Moors had "imbued them with the reveries of the Koran and, at the same time, ruined their beautiful black color by passing on to them their brown color."[39] Since these Wolof women served as household mistresses and almost always became mothers, they had a profound impact on the creolized culture that liaisons between African women and French men created. Recognizing the fact that these Wolof women often became the primary tradition bearers by passing along linguistic and cultural mores to their children, historian Gwendolyn Midlo Hall argued that "in no other colonial culture of the United States did African women play such a central role."[40]

Due to the significant numbers of Africans living in Louisiana, as well as the close contact they had with French-speaking slaveholders, African influences on Louisiana's French Creole language are undeniable. For example, vocabulary words such as *gris-gris* (a protective place) and *zinzin* (an amulet of support or power) come from Bambara. *Congo* (meaning a snake, a dance, or a region in Central Africa), *gumbo* (okra), *zombie*, and *voodoo* also share African origins.[41] Mosadomi, in paraphrasing Haitian linguist Jules Faine's opinion, explained that "despite the fact that the slaves were forced to learn the language imposed on them by their masters, they nevertheless brought in aspects of their own languages—the harmonious rhythm, the musicality, the tone, the softness, the onomatopoeia, and the system of reduplication such as those found in the Mandingo language, all of which have been observed in Louisiana Creole."[42]

Wolof woman carrying her baby

In some African languages, such as Yoruba, there are no definite articles, a trait commonly found in Louisiana Creole. The following example illustrates the difference between International French and Creole with the symbol Ø indicating the lack of a definite article:

Creole French:	*Ø maringuin perd so temps piquer Ø caiman.*
International French:	*LE moustique perd son temps à piquer LE crocodile.*
English translation:	The mosquito loses his opportunity to bite the alligator.[43]

George Washington Cable explained some additional variations in the French that black Creoles in Louisiana developed as a result of their African origins.

> Certain tribes of Africa had no knowledge of the *v* and *z* sounds. The sprightly Franc-Congoes, for all their chatter, could hardly master even this African-Creole dialect so as to make their wants intelligible. The Louisiana Negro's *r*'s were ever being lost or mislaid. He changed *dormer* ["to sleep"] to *dromi'*. His master's children called the little fiddler crab *Tourlourou*; he simplified the articulations to *Troolooloo*. . . . It was the same thing with many other sounds. For example, final *le*; a thing so needless—he couldn't be burdened with it; *li pas capab'* [instead of *lui est pas capable* or "he is not capable"]! . . . The French *u* was vinegar in his teeth. He substituted *i* or *ei* before a consonant and *oo* before a vowel, or dropped it altogether; for *une* [indefinite article "a" or "one"], he said *eine*; for *puis* ["then"], *p'is*; *absolument* ["absolutely"] he made *assoliment; tu* ["you"] was nearly always *to;* a *mulâtresse* ["mulatto woman"] was a *milatraisse*. . . .
>
> He misconstrued the liaisons of correct French, and omitted limiting adjectives where he conveniently could, or retained only their final sound carried over and prefixed to the noun: *nhomme* [instead of *un homme* "a man"]—*zanimaux* [instead of *les animaux* "the animals"]—*zherbes* [*les herbes* "the herbs"]—*zaffaires* [*les affaires* "the affairs"]. He made odd substitutions of one word for another. For the verb to go [*aller*] he oftener than otherwise used a word that better signified his slavish pretense of alacrity, the verb to run: *mo courri—mo* ["I run—me"] always . . . [44]

In 1895 early Louisiana folklorist Alcée Fortier also noted that Creole stories were told in "a curious dialect." As he explained, "In mouths used to African speech, French has been singularly modified." He follows this statement with "an example [that] will show the character of the dialect."[45]

Edward King's illustration of cabins on a rice plantation, c. 1874.

Creole French:	*In fois yavait in madame qui té si joli, si joli, qué li té jamin oulé marié.*
International French:	*Une fois, il y avait une madame qui c'était aussie jolie, aussie jolie que lui c'était jamais approuver marié.*
English translation:	Once upon a time, there was a young woman that was so beautiful, so beautiful that she would never consent to marry.[46]

For generations, Creole French was spoken throughout Louisiana in addition to Cajun French and Colonial French. Even when Louisiana became a United States territory in 1803 and then a state in 1812, the predominant language of the region was French. For example, during the Battle of New Orleans in 1815, the Creoles of Color had their own war song entitled *"En Avan' Grenadie"* that they sang alongside *Le Marseillaise*:

The English muskets went bim! bim!
Fizi z'Anglé yé fé bim! bim!

Kentucky rifles went zim! zim!
Carabin Kaintock yé fé zim! zim!

I said to myself, save your skin!
Mo di' moin, sauvé to la peau!

I scampered along the water's edge;
Mo zété corps au bord do l'eau;

When I got back it was daybreak.
Quand mo rivé li té fé clair.

Mistress flew into a passion;
Madam' li prend' ein coup d'colère;

She had me whipped at the "four stakes,"
Li fé donn' moin ein quat' piquié

Because I didn't stay with master;
Passequé mo pas sivi mouchié;

But the "four stakes" for me is better than
Mais moin, mo vo mié quat' piquié

A musket shot from an Englishman.
Passé ein coup d'fizi z'Anglé![47]

Free Men of Color sang their own fight song as they took up arms against the British at the Battle of New Orleans.

In 1820, Louisiana boasted thirty-three French-language newspapers and periodicals.[48] Of course, the majority of enslaved Creoles were illiterate, but the *gens de couleur libre* or free people of color were often affluent business owners and tradesmen who had been well educated. Some had even studied overseas in France.[49]

Even after English-speaking Americans began flooding the region in the early nineteenth century, free people of color published their works almost exclusively in French. For example, in 1843, the *L'Album Littéraire, Journal des Jeunes Gens, Amateurs de la Littérature* became the first documented literary

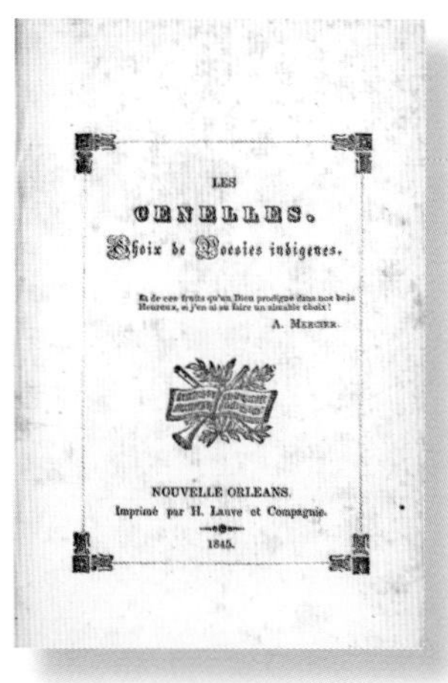

LES

CENELLES.

Choix de Poesies indigenes.

A. MERCIER.

NOUVELLE ORLEANS.

Imprimé par H. Lauve et Compagnie.

1845.

Title page of *Les Cenelles*

publication by Louisiana's free black population. In 1845, Armand Lanusse published *Les Cenelles*, the first collection of poetry to feature black American poets. Seventeen Creole poets contributed to this volume of poems written in French. These authors published their works in International French instead of Louisiana Creole, undoubtedly as a result of their formal educational experience, as well as a reflection of their upper-class social status as free men who wanted to be compared to other French authors both at home and abroad.[50] *Le Meschacébé,* on the other hand, was a French-language publication that recorded several Afro-French fables, songs, and verses in Louisiana Creole from 1858-1877.[51]

It was not until the United States government took an unprecedented interest in homogenizing languages and cultures following the Civil War that the first anti-French legislation was passed. In the Reconstruction Constitution of 1864, the Louisiana Legislature required that "general exercises in the public schools were to be henceforth conducted in the English language."[52] While this may have enacted change legally, it only impacted those parishes occupied by the Union army and affected relatively few Louisiana school children in rural areas because most had limited access to any type of formal education.[53] As linguist Picone explains, "Thus, the first anti-French initiative in Louisiana was as much or more an importation as an expression of local sentiment. As urban centers, New Orleans and Baton Rouge were more vulnerable to the onslaught of the English speaking populations that they naturally attracted. A new Anglocentric infrastructure ensued, partly imposed, partly as a natural outgrowth of the changing demographics."[54]

A photograph taken in 1910 shows three generations of Louisiana Creoles. The grandmother could only speak Creole French, the mother spoke French and English, and the boy only spoke English.

Demographics were not the only thing that changed in the post-war years. Attitudes towards race began shifting, as well. For example, in 1867, several letters written in Creole French were sent to the editor of *Le Meschacébé* as an obvious attempt to make fun of the newly freed black population and their relationship with the people of color who had been free before the war. An excerpt from one of these "letters" demonstrates this phenomenon.

> Creole French: *Li pélé moun tou sort non,* Stinkin, Stilin, Lezi *Niga: cé ça ki soké mouen pli. Vou koné dan tan Rebel yé té di kom ça nég cé nég, grifé cé grief, milat cé milat; a s'tere nou zot cé tou zens koulair, mem ça ki noua kom soudière, yé gainen pou pélé li ein zens koulair. Mo pa tandé Merikien boucou mé mo koné Niga cé pa ein parol pou di ein* Gemman *koulair.*
>
> English translation: He called me all kinds of names, Stinking, Stealing, Lazy Nigger: It is that which provoked me more. You know in Rebel times they said that nigger is a nigger, griffe is a griffe, mulatto is a mulatto; now all of us are people of color, even one who is black as soot, they have to call him a person of color. I don't hear American much but I know Nigger is not a word to say to a *gentleman* of color.[55]

Despite the influence that the printed word may have had in some circles, with the exception of certain urban areas, survival, not literacy, was a priority

Some black children could attend schools like this one in Destrehan, 1938.

Those unable to acquire formal education did the best they could like this mother and children in their Transylvania sharecropper cabin, c. 1939.

for the vast majority of Louisiana's inhabitants even into the twentieth century. Most black Creoles learned French via strictly oral methods just like their indigent Cajun counterparts. While some affluent white Creole planters were financially able to send their mixed-race children to France for higher education, the majority of black Creoles remained in Louisiana where opportunities to acquire formal schooling were rare. For many families to survive, they needed their children's help at home, around the farm, or in the fields. Later on, when school attendance became compulsory, state legislation required twentieth-century Creoles to learn how to read and write in English, not French.

A 1910 photograph of a Louisiana French-speaking grandfather with his grandchild.

CODOFIL

The Louisiana State legislature created the Council for Development of French in Louisiana (CODOFIL) in 1968 as an attempt to reverse the loss of French language usage throughout the state due to previous legislation. Legislative Act 409 authorized the organization to "do any and all things necessary to accomplish the development, utilization, and preservation of the French language as found in Louisiana for the cultural, economic and touristic benefit of the state."

As David Cheramie, former executive director of the Council for the Development of French in Louisiana (CODOFIL),[56] explains, "The Mandatory Attendance Act of 1916 is generally considered to be the first attempt to banish French from schools by forcing Cajun and Creole parents to send their children to English language schools. Until that time, the children remained at home to work the fields and around the house with their parents. [If they did not comply], the parents either had to pay a fine, go to jail, or both, something they could not afford to do."[57] Despite the negative impact this ruling had on French-speaking schoolchildren throughout South Louisiana, the primary purpose of the Mandatory Attendance Act was to afford children the opportunity to attend school, not necessarily prevent them from speaking their mother tongue.

A French-speaking seamstress in Louisiana, 1910.

Although earlier constitutions had recognized French as one of the state's official languages, the Louisiana Constitution of 1921 followed national trends and prohibited the use of any other language except English within the public school system.[58] Teachers strictly enforced the English-only policy and required youngsters to abandon their mother tongue and speak English exclusively in the classroom and other public places. Oftentimes, students were punished or ridiculed for failing to understand their teachers or for speaking French amongst themselves on the playground. As Michael Picone explained, "Virtually every elder French speaker in rural and semirural Louisiana can recite the cruel and humiliating details of the continued implementation of this policy."[59] For example, one man recalled, "I was put

The chalkboard in historic Vermilionville's schoolhouse reminds visitors that French-speaking children were often punished for failing to speak English on school grounds throughout Louisiana.

on my knees in the hallway at school on grains of corn because I spoke French in the playground and got caught." He added, "French was viewed as a language spoken by ignorant people."[60]

Alfred Caesar related his experiences growing up as a French-speaking child who was forced to learn English in school:

> When we started school, we didn't talk American [i.e. speak English]. We learned how to talk American at school—we all spoke Creole. There was a little school here. You went up to the seventh grade in the same schoolroom, all the grades together. But when I got to the third grade, they closed the school. They started bussing us to Oberlin [the parish seat of Allen Parish]. At the Oberlin school, the schoolteacher would stay right beside us to be sure we weren't talking Creole. If they caught us talking Creole, we got a beating. Oh, yes, they didn't want us talking Creole. They knew when the kids from the country got together, we were gonna talk Creole. They would spread us out so we couldn't talk Creole.[61]

As a result of these kinds of experiences, many children grew up believing that speaking French was a shameful part of their heritage and tried to distance themselves from the language either by forgetting or disregarding the

French they had spoken at home. For instance, Earl Barthé, a master plasterer whose family has been in New Orleans since the 1830s, said his relatives spoke Creole; but when his parents called him in, saying "Vien ici, Earl" ("come here, Earl"), the other children would laugh at him. To avoid embarrassment, he asked his parents to speak to him in English. Now that he is an adult who cannot speak French, Barthé regrets his childhood request and admits, "That's the biggest mistake I made in my life."[62]

The vast majority of children who were ridiculed for speaking French grew up and decided to speak English exclusively to their own children in order to help them escape the humiliation and embarrassment they had endured. As Alfred Caesar related, "When we started having children ourselves, we'd had the experience [of being punished for speaking French]. We didn't want our children to go through that. So that is why the language is being lost. Young people don't speak it."[63] Many Francophone parents simply told their children, "You are an American. You need to speak English."[64]

One Avoyelles Parish native wrote, "My grandmother spoke Creole but did not/would not teach it to us because teachers gave Creole speakers a hard time, made fun of them, and thought them less intelligent—so she wanted us to have it 'easier' and to finish school."[65] Another woman explained,

> My father was born in Leonville, outside Opelousas [in St. Landry Parish]. Even though my grandparents moved to a town near Houston where most adults spoke 'French,' the adults did not teach their children the language. The mothers and fathers from Louisiana wanted their children to be 'educated.' Educated meant speaking English . . . only. Unfortunately, the assimilation that was necessary, even required, for approval from teachers, hastened the decline of my grandparents' secret language. MawMaw and PawPaw, along with so many mothers and fathers in this community, only spoke Creole when they didn't want the children to know what they were talking about.
>
> To their credit, these parents did ensure a bright future for their kids. Many of the children my dad grew up with completed undergraduate and graduate programs, becoming a part of the 1960s "first Black to . . ." crowd that enjoyed the professional success their parents only dreamed of. However, our language was nearly lost. Only greeting card phrases remained, and my generation never knew more than, "Yeah, sha. Ca c'est bon!"[66]

Throughout the region, communication barriers that developed within one generation's time caused French-language storytelling traditions to grind to an abrupt halt. Children simply could not communicate with their elders.[67]

Folklorists: Documenting Oral Tradition

> *Preoccupation with European and African antecedents blurred the image of Louisiana French oral tradition unnecessarily. Basically, scholars found only what they were looking for.*
>
> –Barry Jean Ancelet[68]

Due in large part to prohibitions against speaking French, as well as the social stigma attached to being bilingual, numerous traditional stories told throughout Louisiana's Francophone communities were lost over time. However, through the efforts of several dedicated folklorists, many of these stories have been documented via published folktale anthologies. Although folklorists oftentimes infused their own biases and personal interests in the stories they collected, the people they interviewed, and their method of presenting these stories to wider audiences, by preserving elements of Louisiana's French oral repertoire these folklorists have provided an invaluable means for storytellers from previous generations to share their tales with future generations.

In 1892, Alcée Fortier, a Tulane University scholar of Romance languages, founded the Louisiana Association of the American Folk-lore[69] Society in New Orleans. Like Fortier, most of the members in this all-white folklore society were educators. Some were linguists primarily concerned with the preservation of the French Creole language, but others included prominent local color writers from New Orleans who specialized in dialect stories. Since nearly every member of this early folklore society came from a privileged background, Louisiana State University English professors Rosan Augusta Jordan and Frank de Caro reason that by "emphasizing and perhaps creating fictive 'shared understandings' of a plantation culture of the past in which both Blacks and whites played mutually satisfactory roles, the folklorists could make a statement about their 'aristocratic' position, their identities as persons of upper-class status."[70]

Alcée Fortier

Initially, most of the stories collected by the members of Fortier's group were "Negro stories" and Louisiana stories "of African origin." Minutes from their early

Alcée Fortier teaching French at Tulane University, c. 1905.

meetings reveal white perceptions of African and Creole superstitions, dances, and stories. Racist undertones are evident in stories that explained, for instance, "How the negro became black, Flat-nosed and Thick-lipped." The use of phrases such as "old negro nurse," "quaint negro folklore," and "peculiar faculties of an old negro slave" reduced these Afro-Creole storytellers to mere relics of the past and not contributors or participants in their contemporary environment. Whether consciously or not, many of these early folklorists used black Creole stories to solidify their elite white intellectual status within the racially segregated world of post-Civil War Louisiana.[71]

The first scholars who examined French Louisiana's oral tradition followed contemporary trends by focusing on French and African connections to Louisiana. According to Barry Jean Ancelet, "Undoubtedly this approach was due in part to the linguistic and cultural particularities of the region, but it also conformed to the prevailing folklore methodology of the times which placed a premium on European folktales, like those collected by the Grimms in Germany, or on animal tales, like those that inspired Joel Chandler Harris to write his Uncle Remus stories."[72] Indeed, the "Louisiana Folk-Tales" section of the *Journal of American Folklore*'s fall 1894 edition explained that the collected stories "fall into two classes—Animal Tales and Märchen (Fairy-tales)." The African-inspired animal tales featured *Compare Lapin*, the French counterpart to Brer Rabbit, while the fairy tales "appear[ed] to have entered Louisiana through French influence."[73]

Fortier's particular interests led him to focus almost exclusively on animal tales that indicated direct connections between Louisiana and Africa.

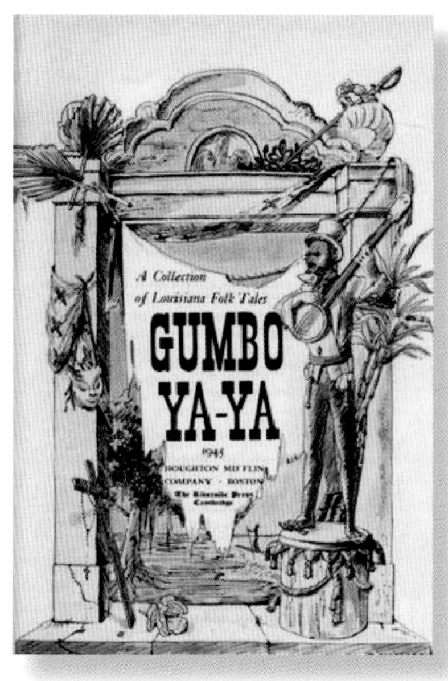

He published his first volume of Louisiana folktales in 1888; seven years later, he published a second volume entitled *Louisiana Folk-Tales, in French Dialect and English Translation*. Indicative of his research within the French-speaking black Creole community, his works are primarily collections of African and Caribbean-style animal fables.[74]

Unlike Fortier, a notable scholar who grew up on a plantation and heard firsthand many of the stories he documented, Lyle Saxon, a native of Washington state, served as director of the Louisiana Writers' Project and its folklore collecting initiative in the Depression era. The work Saxon and his collaborators produced became a compilation of Louisiana stories entitled *Gumbo Ya-Ya: Folktales of Louisiana*. Since Saxon did not grow up on a plantation like many of his predecessors in the Louisiana chapter of the American Folklore Society, as Jordan and de Caro observe, he "reinvented his own past and invented a personal identity as a scion of plantation society. . . ."[75] While his interest in collecting folklore may have been the result of multiple motives, Jordan and de Caro explain that "in his books he took folklore and established it as the area of culture where two racial groups clearly interacted while remaining distinctly apart."[76] *Gumbo Ya-Ya*, published in 1945, is not without its faults. In the words of folklorist Carl Lindahl, its principle weakness lies in the fact that "these tales were not rendered in the actual words of the storytellers, nor were they free of the biases of the collectors. . . . Instead of listening for the values and artistry of the African-American storytellers, the authors of *Gumbo Ya-Ya* simply heard and repeated the tales that reinforced their own prejudices."[77]

In the 1920s and 1930s, even before Saxon and his team began work, Calvin Claudel and Corinne Saucier searched for fairy tales and numbskull stories that shed light on the common

Lyle Saxon

threads that connected Louisiana with its French European heritage. In 1955, Claudel published *The Folktales of Louisiana and their Background*, and in 1962, Saucier published *Folk Tales from French Louisiana*. In the 1940s, Elizabeth Brandon broadened the field's limited perspective when she included more popular genres such as jokes and tall tales in her collection. However, like those who had gone before her, Brandon focused more on the vestiges of the French oral tradition instead of recognizing and acknowledging the evolution and permanence of the genre within its contemporary context.[78]

As pioneers in the developing field of folklore, these early folklorists had an understandably limited view of oral tradition. Lacking the proper training to appreciate a story's context and function, as folklorist Barry Ancelet noted, they found, "little more than the animal tales and fairy tales they asked of their informants." Ancelet went on to explain that due to their limited scope and rudimentary skill in interpreting these oral resources, they unwittingly "created a false impression which led to glum predictions for the future of the tradition."[79]

Within the last few decades, however, folktale anthologies have adopted a more comprehensive and optimistic approach regarding Louisiana's French oral tradition. Ancelet, one of the folklorists who has helped to reshape perceptions of Cajun and Creole storytellers and their repertoires, points out

Stories can be shared anywhere.
The post office in Lafayette provides a backdrop for this conversation in 1938.

Wilson "Ben Guiné" Mitchell relates a tale to folklorist Barry Ancelet as Mitchell's wife looks on.

that "Louisiana is not simply a French or African cultural outpost." Unlike his predecessors who focused almost exclusively on Creole connections to Europe and Africa, he argues, "The fact is that the Cajuns and black Creoles have less connection to France and Africa and more connection to North America (where they have spent the last three centuries) than 'purists' like to admit. While it is true that interesting parallels can be drawn between the Old World and Louisiana, it would be a mistake to neglect the other quite active aspects of the Cajun and Creole cultural blend."[80] His book *Cajun and Creole Folktales: The French Oral Tradition of South Louisiana* serves to illustrate his philosophy. In addition to African animal tales and French magic tales, Ancelet's collection includes jokes, "lies," tall tales, legendary tales, and historical tales that exemplify American South and American frontier influences.

Ancelet's work reflects the opinions of scholars like Richard Bauman who assert that history has proven "the diffusion of folktales frequently involved the telling of stories across group boundaries" and explains that "records and accounts of Frenchmen telling stories to Indians, or African slaves to Englishmen, or Indians to other Indians" certainly exist.[81] Anthropologist Philip M. Peek echoes this line of thinking by asking, "Could not American Indians have been bearers of French tales later passed to British settlers or even to other Frenchmen? What of the various contacts of Africans who came to the United States from Caribbean plantations?"[82] Folklorist Alan Dundes agrees. He suggests that "just as Africanists have wrongly assumed that every tale they collect from an African informant must be an African Tale Type, so European folklorists have wrongly assumed that every tale collected from a European informant must be a European Tale Type." He goes on to say that "what this means to students of the folktale is that each individual tale must be evaluated separately and carefully with respect to origins."[83]

Folklorist Carl Lindahl, Louisiana Folklife Program director Maida Owens, and Louisiana Department of Culture, Recreation, and Tourism field researcher C. Renée Harvison embarked upon an ambitious journey when they decided to canvas the state in an attempt to gather stories that reflect the diversity found within Louisiana's many ethnic groups. Their work *Swapping Stories: Folktales from Louisiana*, published in 1997, provides an impressive sampling of different story types and styles throughout the state. For example, this collection includes Cajun, Creole, African American, and American Indian tales, alongside the stories contributed by more recent immigrants to the state—those Louisianians of Hungarian, Vietnamese, and Italian descent. Similar to Ancelet's work, but broader in scope, *Swapping Stories* provides readers with excellent background information that explains contexts, interprets linguistical nuances, and defines universal elements found within the various oral repertoires.[84]

Although many of the early collectors of Louisiana folklore were concerned with the disappearance of traditional stories and the demise of the Creole French language used to transmit these stories, more recent folklorists have been able to contribute to the preservation of Louisiana's oral tradition by including popular genres that more accurately reflect current trends in Louisiana's storytelling practices. No longer limited by the idea that "traditional"

Even if young Creoles did not grow up speaking French, they consider it an essential element of their cultural identity. For instance, when greeting fans backstage, Rusty Metoyer's tattoo *Famille Créole* (Creole Family) is visible on his right arm.

Older Creoles like Goldman Thibodeaux speak French as their first language and enjoy opportunities to share their stories with young people who have made the effort to learn the language.

elements of a culture should be preserved before its inevitable disappearance in the face of modernization, many present-day folklorists are eager to embrace a broader view of what "traditional" is. Although some folklorists are, and will continue to remain, strict purists at heart, those who fail to recognize the role that cross-cultural exchanges, modernization, and fluid definitions of "tradition" play miss out on the opportunity to document the current state of the world in which they live.

Just like narrowing South Louisiana's diverse cultural landscape into a single French-speaking community creates false impressions and stereotypes, failing to recognize and appreciate the various culture groups whose influences helped create and continue to shape Louisiana's black Creole oral tradition generates a one-dimensional approach that belies the multifaceted nature of their rich storytelling repertoire. In fact, the oral traditions in Francophone communities throughout South Louisiana are not as easily distinguishable from each other as the differences between Creole cooking in Acadiana and New Orleans.

Some estimate that in the early 1990s there were about sixty to eighty thousand Creole speakers throughout Louisiana, with no discernible way of separating them into black and white subgroups.[85] While it may be challeng-

Stories and jokes are often shared between family members like this young man and his grandmother.

ing to draw hard lines of demarcation around certain French-speaking communities based on peculiar vocabulary usage or linguistic syntax, even more daunting a task is attempting to recognize the origins or differences between the stories themselves based on the storytellers' current location. The very nature of oral tradition typically transcends racial, ethnic, and linguistic barriers, as evidenced by centuries of intermingled repertoires. In fact, most folklorists group Creole jokes and tales according to the storyteller's self-identified ethnic background or choice of language.[86]

South Louisiana is far from the ethnically or linguistically homogenous region some outsiders perceive it to be. While French may have been the *lingua franca* throughout the colonial era, American Indians, Spaniards, Africans, and a variety of French-speaking immigrants all contributed to the unique sounds of Creole French. Despite legislative attempts to discourage French from being spoken in schools throughout the Bayou State, the Creole repertoire managed to survive. Over the years, several folklorists have contributed to the preservation of certain Creole folktales via publications, with many of the earliest scholars limiting their research to demonstrating links between Louisiana stories and their African and French origins. In witnessing the declining usage of the French language, as well as the influence of the Americanization process, they predicted that storytelling traditions would fade away. However, as more recent folklorists have argued, Louisiana's French oral tradition is not only alive, but still thrives, albeit via modified means.

Perhaps Barry Ancelet stated it best when he explained:

> Some researchers who claim that oral tradition is dying make this claim because they would like to have the last word on the subject they are studying. Others think of tradition only as a fixed stock of material that is preserved more or less well by an ethnic or regional group under constant threat of modernization. But if tradition is thought of as an ongo-

> ing process, it becomes obvious that, as a culture changes, its traditions are adapted to reflect its new needs and interests. Stories survive, outliving those who predict their demise. We still tell tales that are thousands of years old. Though oral tradition is often described as a fragile thread, it also has the characteristics of a resilient fabric.[87]

The Creole repertoire that once seemed limited to African animal tales and French magic tales has been expanded to include New World genres such as tall tales, jokes, and historical tales. Ancelet points out that although some researchers may have viewed their studies of the Creole oral tradition as "would-be autopsies," it is apparent that "its vital signs seem to be quite healthy."[88] Lengthy magic tales may be replaced with short jokes, and animal tales discussing the escapades of Bouki and Lapin may have moved out of the way to make room for hunting and fishing tall tales, but regardless of the type of story being told, the crucial factor to recognize is that stories are still being told. Traditional cultural elements do not survive when solely preserved in the proverbial Petri dishes of folklore laboratories. However, they can thrive when permitted to develop in a cultural environment that allows room for adaptation and modification.

Theresa Singleton reads her storybook to children during Vermilionville's Creole Culture Day.

Creole Stories in the Repertoire

Si c'est beau, ça a pas besoin d'être vrai; et si c'est vrai, ça a pas besoin d'être beau.

[If it's beautiful, then it doesn't have to be true; and if it's true, it doesn't have to be beautiful.]

–Jean Arceneaux[89]

In 1877, folktale scholar William Owens suggested "the Negroes' fables were most influenced by the Dark Continent and were 'as purely African as are their faces or their own plaintive melodies.'"[90] Although recognizing African elements within the black Creole oral tradition may be a relatively easy task, limiting a study to these links alone would provide an oversimplification of the genre. Rather than trying to prove the exact origins of certain folktales, what is perhaps more interesting and useful is to provide a sampling of stories and jokes from South Louisiana's Creole population that illustrates connections between not only Louisiana and Africa, but also between Louisiana and Africa, Europe, and the New World.

Having discussed the historical context that provides the backdrop for these Creole anecdotes, the origins of the language in which many of these tales were originally told, as well as the work of several dedicated folklorists who collected a variety of these orally transmitted stories, let us now turn our attention to the stories themselves. By comparing several stories, one can begin to recognize the cultural diversity that influenced or contributed to South Louisiana's Creole storytelling heritage.

Animal Trickster Tales

Some of the best-loved and most widely known of all the Creole stories center on two animal characters known as *Bouki*, a strong but foolish hyena, and *Lapin*, a mischievous but clever rabbit.[91] Equivalent to Uncle Remus's Brer Rabbit tales found within African American folktale collections, Bouki and Lapin trickster stories remain popular throughout South Louisiana. Alcée Fortier, who grew up hearing these stories from West African descendants who worked on the plantations surrounding his home in Vacherie, Louisiana, was among the first to collect and write down these tales.[92]

Fortier's collection revealed several significant connections between Africa and Louisiana. For example, the name "Bouki" comes from the Senegalese Wolof word meaning "hyena." It is intriguing to note that although hyenas do not exist in Louisiana, the name "Bouki" has survived in Creole tales, regardless of whether the stories are related in French or English.[93] Another obvious correlation is references to West African locations. In one story Lapin sings,

> Come to the grand ball
> Those that lost their wives
> Beautiful negresses from Senegal.[94]

In other stories, African animals such as lions, elephants, and monkeys play central roles. In "Compair Bouki and the Monkeys," for instance, the monkeys outsmart slow-witted Bouki. The story goes as follows:

> Compair Bouki put fire under his kettle, and when the water was very hot, he began to beat his drum and to cry out:
>
> Sam-bombel! Sam-bombel tam!
> Sam-bombel! Sam-bombel dam!
>
> The monkeys heard and said: "What? Bouki has something good to eat, let us go," and they ran up to Bouki and sang: "Molési cherguinet, chourvan! Chéguillé, chourvan!" Compair Bouki then said to the monkeys: "I shall enter into the kettle, and when I say 'I am cooked,' you must take me out." He jumped into the kettle, and the monkeys pulled him out as soon as he said, "I am cooked."
>
> The monkeys, in their turn, jumped into the kettle, and cried out, immediately on touching the water, "We are cooked." Bouki, however, took his big blanket, and covering the kettle, said: "If you were cooked you could not say so." One little monkey alone escaped, and Bouki ate all the others. Some time after this Compair Bouki was hungry again, and he called the monkeys:
>
> Sam-bombel! Sam-bombel tam!
> Sam-bombel! Sam-bombel dam!
>
> When the monkeys came, he jumped into the kettle again and said: "I am cooked, I am cooked." The monkeys, however, which had been warned by the little monkey which had escaped the first time, did not pull Bouki out, but said: "If you were cooked you could not say so."[95]

Although Compair Bouki ("Brother Bouki") tries to imitate the antics of Compair Lapin ("Brother Rabbit") in many of the stories, he usually ends up getting caught and suffering ill effects for following trickster Lapin's advice. The following story illustrates this concept:

> One day the children of Compair Bouki met those of Compair Lapin, who had on fine Sunday dresses and new shoes. When the little Boukis returned home, they asked their father why he did not give them fine clothes like those of Compair Lapin's children. Compair Bouki went to see Compair Lapin, and asked him where he took the fine things he had given to his children. Compair Lapin did not want to reply, but Compair Bouki annoyed him so much that he said to him: "Go and cut wood in the forest; and when you will be tired, look in the centre of the forest, and you will see a big tree. Go to sleep under it, and when you will awake, say: 'If I were to open, what would you say?' You will reply: 'If you open, I shall be very glad.' When the tree will open, enter into it; it will close up, and you will see many pretty things. Take what you want, and tell the tree: 'Open!' when you wish to depart." Compair Bouki did what Compair Lapin had said, but when he saw all there was in the tree, he wanted to take so many things that he forgot to say: "Tree, open!"
>
> The tree belonged to some thieves, who hid their booty in it. They came back in the woods, and they found Compair Bouki, who was stealing their goods. I need not tell you that they gave Compair Bouki such a beating that he could not move."[96]

Folklorist John Roberts explains the significance of these trickster tales. "In essence, animal trickster tales served to remind enslaved Africans not only of the value of behaviors that they associated with the trickster but also of the consequences of acting like the dupe."[97]

Fairy Tales or Magic Tales

Another popular genre within the older Creole folktale tradition is the fairy tales or magic tales that are said to have originated in France. Having had close contact with the French in both West Africa and Louisiana, it comes as little surprise that black Creoles adopted French stories and included them in their own repertoire. Many of these magic tales show clear European connections through references to such features as kings and castles, but have been, as Ancelet notes, "invariably adapted to the Louisiana experience."[98] Since fairy tales are usually lengthy accounts, storytellers have more difficulty passing on these stories to modern audiences who have become accustomed to fast-paced lifestyles; therefore, retelling these fanciful stories are not as popular as they once were. However, the following serve as excellent examples of magic stories that have been adapted for Louisiana audiences.

The first, collected in 1906 from a Creole woman named Edmée Dorsin, contains an interesting combination of African animals infused into her regional tale. Her story begins,

> Long ago when the lions, the elephants, the tigers, and all this kind of *vermin*, lived on the banks of the Grand Lac, there was a woman who lived with her daughter on the banks of the Bayou Teche.
>
> This woman had a daughter whose lover came to visit daily. The mother, fearing that her daughter would marry the young man and leave her alone, disapproved of the relationship.
>
> Neighbors began asking the mother how it was possible for her daughter to walk in the woods with lions, tigers, and other wild animals without them doing harm to her. The mother was surprised to hear this news and thought her daughter must be unusually kind for the animals not to harm her. One day, the mother decided to feed the animals herself.
>
> To her surprise, the lion chased her and would have devoured her had she not closed her gate. After that the old woman could not put her foot out of her house without a beast coming to run after her. After a while, a little bird told the half-crazy mother that unless she allowed her daughter to marry the young man, the wild beasts would continue to threaten her and be kind to her daughter. The old woman agreed to the marriage to get rid of the wild animals that frightened her.
>
> And there was a grand wedding. In the end, the mother discovered that the young suitor had changed himself into the wild animals in order to frighten the mother into allowing him to marry her daughter.

> The mother was very angry but she was so afraid of him that she did not dare say anything. Fortunately that man is now dead, and he was the last *zombi* (wizard) around here.[99]

A former Creole plantation laborer told a similar story entitled "The Golden Fish." In this fairy tale, the father did not want his daughter marrying, although the young man was a fine prince. The father asked a wizard for help in making the young man leave her alone.

> One day, as the couple sat on a riverbank together, the wizard came along and transformed the suitor into a fish. The father felt confident his wish had come true, so he did not worry when his daughter went to the riverbank day after day.
>
> While sitting there, she sang,
>
> Caliwa wa, caliwa co
> waco, maman dit oui [mama says yes]
> waco, papa dit non [papa says no]
> caliwa wa, caliwa co
>
> Every time she sang her song, a beautiful red fish wearing a golden crown would come out of the water and give her beautiful things to eat.
>
> One day, the girl's father followed her to the riverbank. Realizing what was going on, he brought his gun the next day and killed the fish. He brought the fish home and told his daughter to prepare it for eating. When she got ready to cut the fish, it began singing,
>
> Cut me then, wa, wa
> scrape me then, wa wa
> mix me then, wa, wa
> put some salt, wa wa
>
> The girl cried for the fish, but after it was cooked, her greedy father ate so much that his belly burst, and a quantity of little fish came out and escaped to the water.

The tale ends with the young girl going down to the riverbank where the fish's scales had been tossed out. She cried so much that the earth opened, enabling her to disappear into a hole where she could meet her fish. When her mother came to look for her, she saw only one lock of her daughter's hair, sticking out of the ground.[100]

Jokes and Proverbs

Since fast-paced lifestyles and technological inventions such as televisions and computers claim much leisure time in today's world, short jokes oftentimes replace the magic tales of days gone by. As Ancelet notes, behind every joke, though, is a serious thought that "may conceal deeper psychological or cultural currents."[101] As the following joke reveals, when children educated in English-only public schools were all too eager to distance themselves from their native French tongue, sometimes "lost" linguistic skills came back in a hurry.

> Jean Sot had gone to school to learn English. So he came back to visit his father and mother, and he was acting as though he no longer understood French.
>
> So he went to the garden (his father and mother were working in the garden) to visit. And [he] saw the rakes and the hoe. So he wanted to ask his mother what this garden tool was called. And at the same time, he stepped on the rake. The rake handle came back and hit him on the mouth. "Ah!" he said, *"Mon fils-de-putain de rateau!"* [You s.o.b. of a rake!]
>
> "Ah!" she said, "my son, I see your French is coming back to you!"

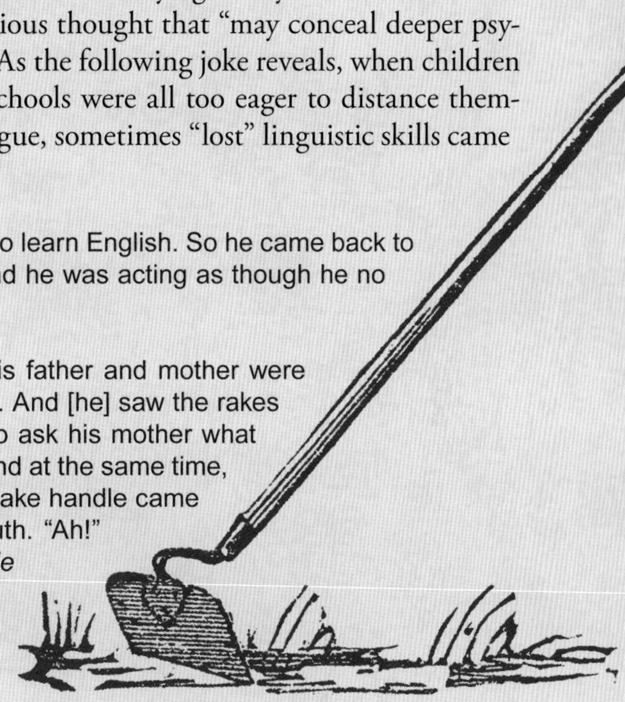

In a slightly different version of the same story, a young man in a market who has "forgotten" his French points at something to ask "what's that?" When a crab pinches his finger, he suddenly remembers how to curse the crustacean in Creole French.[102]

Like jokes, proverbs can also serve as a pithy means for getting a message across; they often incorporate wit or humor for more effect. Some proverbs feature the antics of Bouki and Lapin, the most popular characters in the Creole repertoire. For example, Lafcadio Hearn included one such anecdote in a collection entitled *Gombo Zhèbes: A Little Dictionary of Creole Proverbs* that he published in 1885. As the saying goes, "*Bouki fait gombo, lapin mangé li,*" or "Bouki makes the gumbo and rabbit [Lapin] eats it."[103] Lyle Saxon also recorded what he referred to as "Negro proverbs" in 1929. One states, "White hen mighty pretty, but de black chicken is de luckiest when de hawk come sailin' ovah de chicken yard." This proverb is similar to another that boasts the benefits of being dark-skinned: "De nigger is luckier dan de white man at night," presumably because it is more difficult to see and figure out what a black man is doing when it is dark.[104]

George Washington Cable documented a Louisiana Creole saying that was put to music. This quote recognized the fact that all men, regardless of their skin tone, were interested in trying to get ahead.

> *Neg' pas ca-pa' marché sans mais dans poche,*
> *C'est pou vo-lé poule,*
> *Milâtre pas ca-pa' marché sans la corded dans poche,*
> *C'est pou volé choual,*
> *Blanc pas ca-pa' marché sans la'-zen dans poche,*
> *C'est pou volé filles.*
>
> The black man cannot walk without corn in his pocket,
> To steal chickens,
> The mulatto cannot walk without rope in his pocket,
> To steal horses,
> The white cannot walk without money in his pocket,
> To steal girls.[105]

Cable documented other proverbs as well, including one that warns, "*Pas marré so chien avé saucisse*," or "Don't chain your dog with links of sausage." Another asks, "*Qui zamein 'tendé souris fé so nid dan zoré ç'at?*" or "Who ever heard of mouse making nest in cat's ear?"[106]

Tall Tales and Legends

As inhabitants of the New World for roughly three hundred years, Louisiana's Creole people boast a storytelling repertoire that also reflects the various cultures that surround them. For example, in some tales, American Indians are main characters, while Vieux Nèg ("Old Black") and Vieux Boss ("Old Boss") stories echo the slave experience common throughout the American South. The American frontier's love for tall tales and legends also figure prominently in the current Creole repertoire, while historical tales provide insight into some of the harsh realities of life in South Louisiana during periods of heightened racism. In some instances, cultural crossovers have been so successful that the only way to distinguish between Cajun and Creole stories or jokes is to either recognize the storyteller's use of a particular type of French or to know how that individual self-identifies his or her ethnic heritage.

A prime example of the latter phenomenon is the following story, which resembles the John and Old Master cycles common to the African American oral tradition. In this case, however, a Cajun relates a tale that features an American Indian:

> There were Indians right here at one time. This was their land. And they were eventually run off, but at one time, there were people who had civilized them around here. They spoke well. They were smart people, but they were hunters. There were a few kind and gentle ones who remained.
>
> Whatever they dreamed had to come true. If they dreamed that you gave them something, you had to give it to them. You couldn't fool around with that!
>
> So there was a man who had a fine rifle, a military rifle, a big rifle. And an Indian wanted it. And the Indian had a beautiful saddle horse. The next morning, the Indian arrived. He said, "I dreamed that you gave me your rifle." He went and got his rifle. He gave it to him.
>
> Several weeks later, the white man went to the Indian. He said, "I dreamed that you gave me your horse." And he [the Indian] had the horse on a lead rope. He [the white man] said, "I dreamed last night that you gave me your horse."
>
> He [the Indian] said, "Here, take it, but," he said, "let's not dream anymore!"[107]

"Vieux Nèg" and "Vieux Boss" stories also closely resemble John and Old Master tales popular within the African American slave culture throughout the Deep South. For example, at the beginning of a story entitled "Oh, Fiva!" Creole storyteller Wilson "Ben Guiné" Mitchell from Parks, Louisiana, explains, "There was a boss, a big boss on a big farm, big farm. And they worked all the mules. There were about . . . fifty or so teams. There were a lot of old guys, old black men, who worked all week long. This was like slavery time, you understand?" He then proceeds to describe what happened one day on the farm when one of the mules decided that he would not work on his day off.[108]

In "An Old Black Man and an Old White Man Had a Race," Ben Guiné explains why black Creoles worked the fields and whites did not.

Well, there was a black man—an old black man—and an old white man. They had a race. They announced it in the papers. They advertised it to everyone. There was the old black man and the old white man. They had a race.

Then, well, the old black man and the old white man took off. They took off out of the chute. You could hear the blacks and the whites, "Hey, Mister Tom Jones! Hey, Mister Foff!"

The old black man took off running. He said, "Lord! Lord!" The old black man turned around. The old black man was just in front of the old white man. The old white man had fallen down. The old black man had passed over him.

When the old black man had covered seven arpents, the white man passed him. The old black man got back up in front. He tripped the old white man, and he fell down.

When the old black man arrived, there was one of those big sacks. There was a big sack. Then there was a little old thing like this. He called his friends. He said, "Come and help me." The other old fools were all around. They came. The old black man had won. They yelled, "Heee! He won! He won!"

What do you think was in there [in that big sack]? Some old plows, some old hoes . . . There weren't just any old tools that weren't in there!

The white man came. He picked up the little old sack. There was a book and a pencil—to read and write. Then, the old white man, he was there, but the old black man had to go into the fields. He was miserable all his life.

Eh? Is this not true?[109]

In South Louisiana, hunting and fishing play important roles in daily life. Naturally, many tall tales grow out of these experiences just as they did on the American frontier. While not "lies," they are considered to be acceptable "whoppers." There are stories about the one that got away, as well as the one that did not get away, among others. Sometimes hunters and fishermen are forced to take extreme measures in order to bring in their prize. As one tall tale explains, a man once caught a spotted catfish that was so large that a span of twelve ax handles measured the space between its eyes. To cook the giant fish, they built a pot that was so big that the two men hammering the handles in place, one on each side, could not hear each other's blows because they were so far apart.[110]

Another tall tale, "The Liar and his Black Man," describes the frustration that ensues when a hunter is forced to tell the truth, despite the chiding of his black hunting partner. Unable to embellish his tale, the hunter questions the point of being able to tell the story at all.

> There was a fellow who used to go hunting. And he always had a black man with him to confirm what he had killed. When he lied, the black man had to pull on his coattail. So he shot a raccoon. And it had a tail ten feet long. The black man pulled on his coattail. He said, "Not that long, boss."
>
> So he turned around. "Well," he said, "maybe not ten feet, but," he said, "surely seven feet."
>
> The black man pulled on his coattail again. He said, "Maybe not seven feet, but," he said, "surely five feet."
>
> He pulled again. "Well," he said, "what? Do you expect me to leave it with no tail at all?"[111]

Tall tales are not the only form of legendary stories found within the Creole repertoire. For example, explanations of *feux follets* (mysterious lights seen over marshy places) are popular throughout South Louisiana. Inez Catalon, a Creole woman from Kaplan who was born in 1918, gave her own account:

> You know, the only way I'll believe in these things is if the old folks (I'm talking about nearly a hundred years ago), maybe people were good enough, maybe they saw things like that. But now, people are hypocrites, now, everybody, you know? They're no good because, you see, in the old days, I'm talking about the time of my grandmother. Have you ever heard of a *feu follet*? You never heard of a *feu follet*? Well, I asked Mom what a *feu follet* was. And she told me that it was a child that had died before being baptized. That was a *feu follet*. And they say that at night when you walked and it was really dark, when people walked at night, they would see something like a little light, not much bigger than a candle. The light of a candle.
>
> And if you watched that light, the light would cause you to lose your way. Even though you were on the road, going home. Ah well, you would follow that little light with your eyes, you know. That little light would follow you and would get you lost. And sometimes, you wouldn't find your way until the next morning.
>
> But they say that if ever you saw a *feu follet* and had a pocketknife, you had to open your knife, and stick it on a fence post, if you saw a *feu follet*, that little light. If you stick it on a fence post, you stick it there. And then, that little light will stay. It plays with the knife. Then it leaves you alone.[112]

Historical Tales

Although tall tales and legends may be popular forms of entertainment, perhaps one of the most important genres within the Creole oral tradition is the historical tale. Since many older Creoles had little or no opportunity to acquire a formal education, they placed a special emphasis on maintaining their history through oral and not written methods. In the following historical tale, Westley "Kit" Dennis, a Creole from Scott, poignantly describes the confrontation he witnessed as a mere child when vigilantes came into his own neighborhood.

> I was about nine years old. That's as old as I could have been. And my old father used to go to town every Saturday afternoon in a wagon. We had a pair of mules. One was named March, he was born in March; and the other was called April, he was born in April. And we left to go to town that Saturday afternoon. And there were lots of young fellows who lived on Montgomery's farm. They went to town every Saturday afternoon.
>
> They were going down the road when we arrived. My old father stopped the wagon and then they all climbed into the wagon. There must have been five or six, at least. They climbed into the wagon and we took off for town.
>
> When we arrived in town, they all got out on their respective sides. Then we went into the store, the late Mr. Leon Couvillon's store. The streets were narrow. In those days, they were all dirt streets. They were quite narrow. The store was on this side, the late Leon Couvillon on this side, and on the other side was a Breaux. He stopped the wagon, but we had two young mules. So my father said (they all called me by a nickname, Jack), he said, "Stay in the wagon, Jack, and hold the mules."
>
> So I said, "Okay, Daddy."
>
> So I was holding the mules. They were a little frisky. They were two young mules. So he got down. He went into the store to buy his things. Then a buggy arrived a little later. It came. It pulled up there. But it was too narrow for them to pass. He said I had to move the mules forward.
>
> So my father came to the door, "No, no," he said, "stay right where you are. We were here first."
>
> They were Bergerons, two white men. He had one of those rawhide whips. He got down from his buggy with the whip as though he wanted to whip my father.

So my father said, "If you feel that way, go ahead. I think I'm big enough for your whip to hit."

But it must be that he thought it might have turned for the worse, or something. That's when he went, he climbed up onto his buggy. Then the other Bergeron went into the store. I don't know what he bought, but they came back out right away. They left.

And they went ahead of us about as far as the corner and there was a clump of sage orange trees. One of them went in there to cut some sticks, and the other pretended to be fixing something on his buggy, so that we wouldn't notice anything. And we kept coming. And it was a clump that had briars in it. It was growing along the road, and every Saturday afternoon, people in buggies and on horseback came by and went to town. They were all white. They left Scott, and they went to town. And they went ahead and each rider who went by or each person in a buggy who was on his way to town, among the young people, they stopped them. And then, when we arrived, it was just beginning to get dark. They got in the road with their sticks raised to stop the mules.

So my father told me, "Get down on the floor of the wagon." They started throwing sticks. My father was parrying them off. Then he pushed me down with his elbow like this. And I fell down into the wagon. And while falling down into the wagon—that afternoon we had found one of those cat's heads to use on those big gang plows—and falling down there, I fell on it. I grabbed it and gave it to him. And when I gave it to him, he grabbed it and he hit one of them with it. They kept throwing and throwing, but they couldn't stop the mules. When he called out to the mules, they rushed forward into the gang, like that, and then they took off.

When we had passed the gang, we kept going fast, the mules were galloping. They mounted up and then came and started throwing at the wagon again, but they weren't very lucky. Their horses were going fast and the wagon was going quite fast.

We stopped at the home of an old black man whom we called Jean à Madame Jacques. His woods were about an arpent from his house. And that was before we got to his house. His house was about as far as that old truck there. Well, my father made me get down and I went. I went into the house. And the fellow who was there and my father took sticks and things and when they passed by there to go home, that's when the man who lived there hit one of them in the neck with a stick. He fell down, but got up again just as fast and left with the gang.

> You know, about two weeks after that—it was a house made like this one, but it was along the road and the bed was there and the armoire was there—they passed by, and they shot at the house. If the people had been there, they would have killed the ones in the bed. The bullets passed right over the bed. They shot so much that they caused the armoire door to fall back. They made the armoire door fall in from the shots! And the height of the bullets that struck the door was such that anyone who would have been sleeping in the bed would have been killed.
>
> I was about nine years old in those days. And before that, it was twice as bad.[113]

Historical tales like these transmit to future generations the unwritten past that many Creoles experienced. Whether these stories document accounts of unjust treatment as in the previous selection, or whether they are favorite memories shared at family gatherings, historical tales will probably survive longer than any other genre simply because they are passed down so frequently and often become such a significant part of an individual family's lore. Some may also attribute additional value to these stories because, unlike jokes, proverbs, or magic tales, they are considered to be "true" narratives, not ones merely made up for the sake of entertainment.

Allons Danser!

From Quadroon Balls to Zydeco Halls

If music be the food of love, play on.

–William Shakespeare[1]

If you know how to dance, then you can dance behind someone beating on an old gallon bucket. But if you can't dance to Zydeco, you can't dance, period.

–Clifton Chenier[2]

When people think of South Louisiana, food, fun, and festivals typically come to mind. In an area renowned for its *joie de vivre*, or "joy of living," music plays an integral role in the region's identity and cultural expression. While Cajun music may garner more recognition from the outside world, black Creole music, now known as "Zydeco," has always been an essential part of *le monde Créole*, or the Creole world. Since the eighteenth century when African slaves and French-Acadian refugees began arriving on Louisiana's shores, both Cajun and Creole musicians have maintained traditional elements of their music while integrating contemporary instruments and musical styles. Despite various innovations, the label "Cajun music" has continually applied to music performed by Cajuns who typically sing in French. Creole music, on the other hand, has alternately been referred to as Juré, French La La, Creole music, or simply French music. Although the current term "Zydeco" is now popularly associated with black Creole music, its roots reach deep into Southwest Louisiana's rich prairie soil. Clifton Chenier, the "King of Zydeco," may be credited with giving birth to Zydeco music, but no music is "born." It evolves. Understanding and appreciating this musical progression is of paramount importance to those interested in developing an ability to recognize various forms of Creole music that existed long before the term "Zydeco" was coined.

African Chants and French Arias: Early Louisiana

> *There is the pathos of slavery, the poetry of the weak oppressed by the strong, and of limbs that danced after toil, and of barbaric love-making.*[3]
>
> –George Washington Cable

Perhaps the earliest strains of French music heard in Louisiana were sea chanteys sung by the sailors who first reached the shores of the Gulf Coast in the seventeenth century; or perhaps these initial songs were hymns of thanksgiving offered up by the ship's passengers after surviving a grueling Atlantic crossing. Although it may never be known which French songs were first sung, it is clear from the historical record that missionaries to the colony, interested in converting the Indians to Roman Catholicism, introduced European sacred music to Louisiana's native population. As music historian John Koegel observes, "Despite the many negative aspects of European colonization endured by indigenous peoples throughout North America—disease, warfare, decimation, and cultural and economic subjugation—music usually served as a powerful and positive force, one that was often willingly embraced by local peoples."[4] Mission and parish churches throughout Louisiana, and especially in New Orleans's St. Louis Cathedral,[5] featured sacred music such as psalms, Christmas noëls, hymns, the Magnificat, and the Mass.[6]

In 1725, a mere seven years after the founding of New Orleans, Raphael de Luxembourg, superior of the Capuchin missions in Louisiana, established a school that offered formal music education. Two years later, the Ursuline nuns began a school for girls that offered, among other things, musical instruction. Due to lack of support from the local population, Luxembourg's school lasted for only six years; but the Ursulines enjoyed continued success. In fact, a collection of sacred French music dated 1736 was given to the Ursuline nuns in New Orleans in 1754 and is the earliest music known to have survived from the area.[7]

St. Louis Church (prior to becoming a cathedral), New Orleans, 1794. Although various buildings have been constructed on St. Louis Cathedral's original location, New Orleans residents have been worshiping on that site since the first church opened its doors in 1727.

Despite the importance of sacred music among Louisiana's earliest Catholic settlers and converts, secular music also played a major role in the everyday lives of the region's people. For example, military music regulated the rhythms of daily life in French forts and surrounding communities. Private and public gatherings often featured dance music, instrumental music, and popular songs as forms of entertainment. With an influx of settlers and more leisure time came the increasing importance of more formalized musical expressions through balls and theatrical performances. These events featured professional musicians who, in order to provide a living for themselves and to accommodate their audiences' needs, oftentimes played both sacred and secular music.[8]

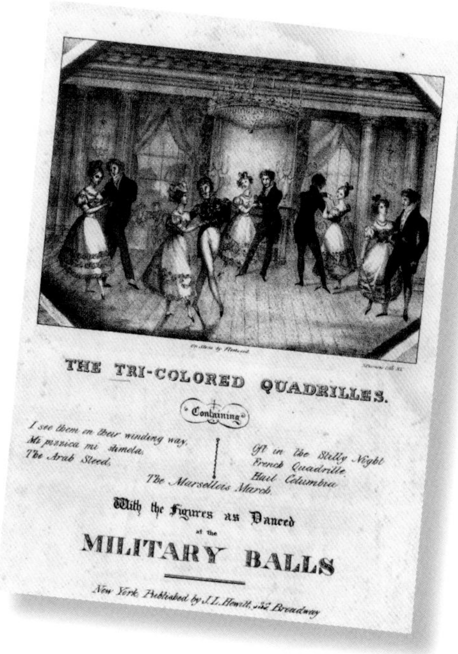

Sheet music cover from "The Tri-Colored Quadrilles," c. 1830.

Concert & Ball.

THE public are informed that on the 2d of next month, Mr. LABADIE, professor of Music, will give a CONCERT *of Vocal and Instrumental Music*, to be followed by a GRAND BALL. He presumes to hope that the public will be satisfied with the pains and care he has taken to unite the talents of the professors and amateurs who have obligingly offered to assist him on this occasion. The particulars of the concert will be announced in the papers of the day. *Nov. 17.*

Ad from the *Orleans Gazette*, November 23, 1807.

During the 1720s, dancing the *calinda* or *kalenda* became a popular pastime in the Caribbean. Slaves later introduced it to New Orleans. François Aimé Louis Dumoulin captured the exuberance of the dance in his 1783 watercolor *Calinda, dance of the Negroes in America.* The popular Cajun song "Allons Danser, Colinda" undoubtedly emerged from this Creole expression.

Regardless of the significance and popularity of music during the colonial period, however, survival remained the primary concern for the region's inhabitants. Within mere decades of France's claim to the entire Mississippi River Valley in 1681, French settlers realized that they needed a substantial labor force to secure the colony's future. Although missionaries had experienced some success in converting the local native people to Catholicism, French colonial administrators had far less success in convincing them to become enslaved laborers. Nicolas de la Salle, Louisiana's first commissary, was responsible for overseeing the royal warehouse and maintaining the financial accounts of official salaries and expenses. Although his request was denied, when la Salle petitioned the king for two hundred African slaves, he complained that the Indian slaves were "not appropriate for hard labor like the blacks."[9] Also appreciating the value of African laborers, French governor of Louisiana Jean-Baptiste le Moyne, Sieur de Bienville, offered to trade three Indian captives for every African slave brought in from the West Indies. In denying his request, the Company of the Indies demonstrated their desire to protect their own trade interests and ruled that the "Colonists of Louisiana will be able to get negroes only when French Vessels bring them [directly from Africa]."[10] Within a short time, Louisiana's colonial administrators, desperate for a labor force, began importing people from various African kingdoms into the fledgling French colony.[11]

Regardless of whether they were enslaved or free, imported forcibly or emigrated voluntarily, the inhabitants of French Louisiana faced a life full of threatening challenges. Starvation was a constant hazard to the French colonists who struggled to carve out a permanent settlement in the midst of a swampy wilderness. Recognizing this harsh reality, colonial administrators encouraged slaveholders to allow their slaves "free days," which absolved slaveowners from the responsibility of feeding those in their charge. On these "free days," which initially were observed on Sundays and holidays and later included Saturday afternoons, slaves were urged to hire themselves out for wages and sell foodstuffs at the local market. By the 1730s, it had become common practice for Louisiana's enslaved African population to gather in Congo Square, an area located on the northern perimeter of New Orleans's French Quarter, to sell their gardens' fresh produce, the fish and meat they caught and hunted, and the nuts and berries they gathered from the land.[12]

Originally a Native trading post along the Mississippi River, the New Orleans French Market has existed in the same location for over two hundred years. Vendors and shoppers representing all corners of the globe still conduct business daily in America's oldest public market, as they have since before Alfred R. Waud illustated a *Sunday in New Orleans—The French Market*, 1866.

Like the *calinda*, the *bamboula* originated in Africa, gained popularity in the Caribbean and was brought to New Orleans by slaves who gathered in Congo Square as depicted in E.W. Kemble's *Bamboula*.

During lulls between haggling with customers, slaves often passed the time dancing and playing music. Just as the French missionaries and settlers had done before them, these Africans from various regions brought with them their styles of music and instrumentation, introducing their own musical heritage to the New World. Using readily available materials, the musicians kept rhythm for dancers by playing drums and scraping bones, sticks, or pieces of metal along the jawbones of large draft animals such as horses and mules.[13] Sometimes they shook gourd rattles filled with pebbles or dried seeds.[14] While most black slaves throughout the South were prohibited from drumming for fear that they were secretly sending messages or planning rebellions, Louisiana's enslaved population suffered no such restrictions under French rule; percussive elements in their music were retained and passed down.[15] Unlike slaves in the English colonies who are primarily known for singing spirituals, the Afro-French slave repertoire included ballads, dance songs, voodoo chants, lullabies, and satires.[16]

Mule jawbones became instruments.

Dancers and musicians of African descent gathered with such frequency that in 1786, when New Orleans boasted a population of only three thousand, the Spanish army[17] outlawed the "nightly congregation" and "dances of colored people" throughout the city. In 1799, a visitor reported seeing "vast numbers" of black men, women, and children drumming, fifing, and dancing on the levee in large rings. Another observer noted that these rings were comprised of various African tribes and nationalities who clustered together in order to sing, dance, and play instruments from their different homelands.[18]

Although blacks congregated in different public areas, eventually Congo Square gained a reputation for being the most important gathering place for the city's enslaved people to conduct business and socialize. According to historian Gary A. Donaldson, "Although subcultures of slaves certainly existed throughout the South (even among the smallest groups on plantations), only at Congo Square did slaves gather for social, cultural, economic, and religious interaction in such large numbers and with such great intensity."[19] Often drawing sizable crowds of mesmerized white observers, hundreds and even thousands of slaves expressed their African heritage through song and dance for generations. This tradition persisted with few interruptions until Federal troops occupied the area during the Civil War and ended the Sunday dances.[20]

Prior to its demise, the weekly gathering garnered significant attention not only from locals who participated in the event, but also from visitors passing through the area. One such observer was Benjamin Latrobe, an American architect and engineer who traveled to New Orleans in the early 1800s in order to build the city's first waterworks system. Latrobe happened

Dancers and musicians still gather in Congo Square as visitors look on.

upon Congo Square one Sunday afternoon after church. Hearing "a most extraordinary noise," he discovered that some five or six hundred people had assembled in several clusters, with some of these groups forming rings approximately ten feet in diameter. He commented that in one of these rings, two women danced, each holding "a coarse handkerchief, extended by the corners, in their hands." He observed various instruments of African origin, including a large drum being played by an old man who "beat it with incredible quickness with the edge of his hand and fingers," and a smaller drum that, when combined with the large drum, "made an incredible noise." He noticed a stringed instrument that he stated was "no doubt imported from Africa." A "very little old man, apparently eighty or ninety years old" played the instrument whose body consisted of a calabash or gourd. A "rude figure of a man in a sitting posture" was carved on the top of the finger board of this stringed instrument. Latrobe also described a woman who used two short sticks to beat another instrument made out of "a calabash with a round hole in it, the hole studded with brass nails." He remarked that a man sung "an uncouth song to the dancing that I suppose was in some African language, for it was not French."[21]

In 1879, nearly two decades after Congo Square's dances were shut down, a New Orleans newspaper reporter recorded his personal recollection of the dances he had observed in earlier years. Much like Latrobe, he recalled that on Sunday afternoons, crowds of at least two to three thousand people gathered "to see the dusky dancers." He wrote, "about three o'clock the negroes began to gather, each nation taking their places in different parts of the square. The Minahs would not dance near the Congos, nor the Mandringos near the Gangas." Filed teeth and tattooed cheeks marked ethnic distinctions between the various tribes. Despite the variety of national identities present, George Washington Cable described the passionate energy all these dancers exuded when he wrote, "Sweat streams from the black brows, down the shining black necks and throats, upon the men's bared chests, and into the dark, unstayed bosoms."[22]

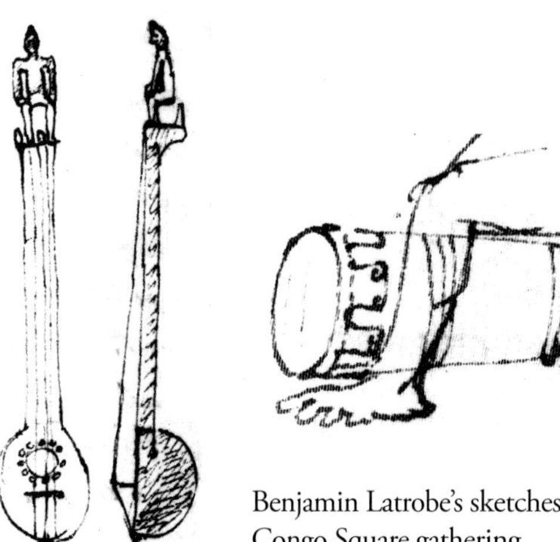

Benjamin Latrobe's sketches from a Congo Square gathering.

Congo Square was much more than just a venue for musical expression. As one reporter noted, it was "a place to renew

A couple dancing in E.W. Kemble's sketch *The Love Song.*

old loves, and to gather new friendships; to talk over affairs of the past week, and lay new plans for enjoyment in the coming ones." Participants turned out in their best finery for the occasion. Women usually wore "stylish bandanas snugly tied about the back part of the head" while "the more independent men . . . made the best show they could in what they inherited of their masters' toilette. . . ."[23] Even the best of finery, however, was scarcely extravagant. Cable explained that "Often the slave's attire was only a cotton shirt, or a pair of pantaloons hanging in indecent tatters to his naked waist. The bondwoman was well clad who had on as much as a coarse chemise and petticoat. To add a *tignon*—a Madras handkerchief twisted into a turban—was high gentility, and the number of kerchiefs beyond that one was the measure of absolute wealth."[24]

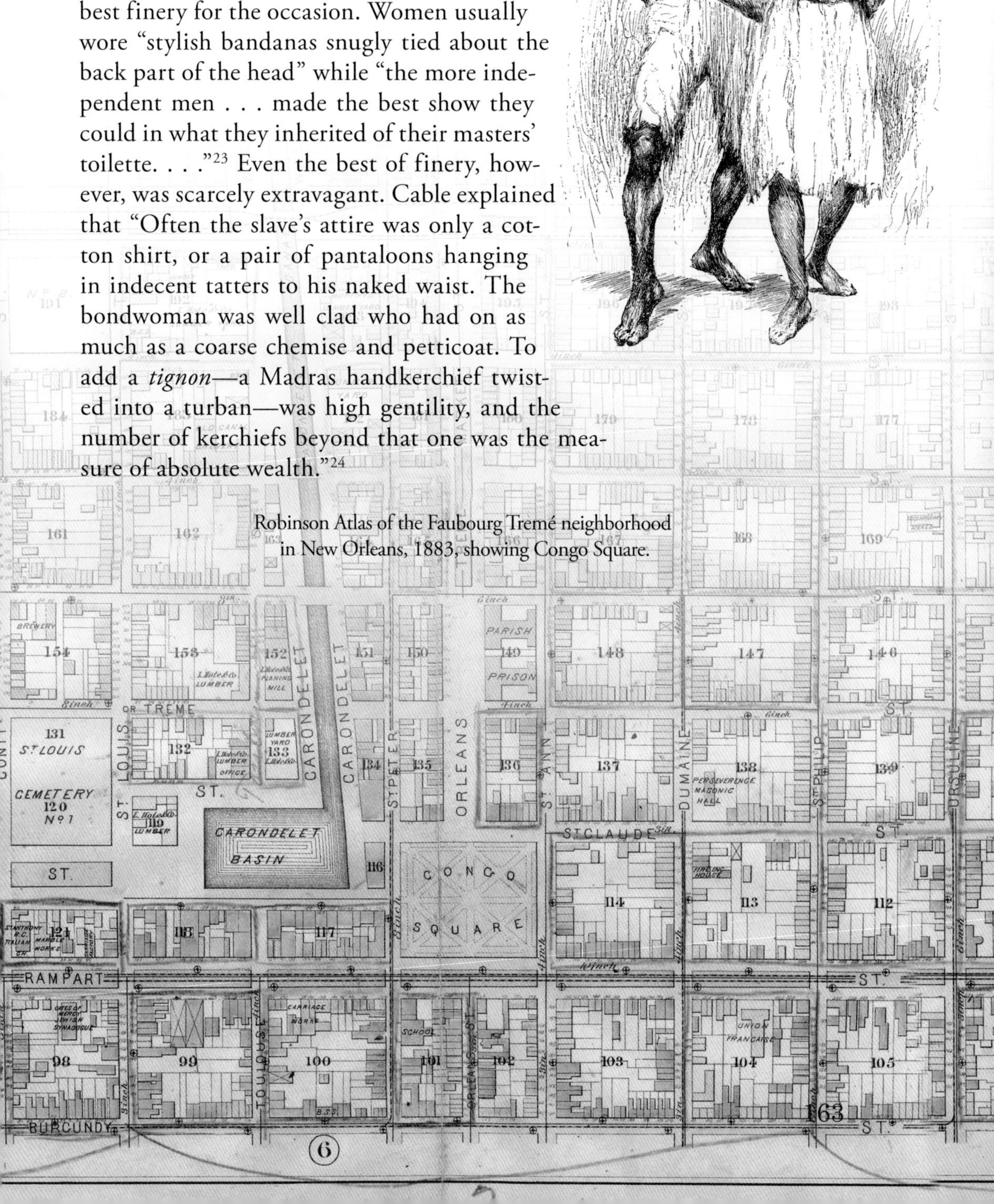

Robinson Atlas of the Faubourg Tremé neighborhood in New Orleans, 1883, showing Congo Square.

While slaves of African descent congregated in places like Congo Square to celebrate their Old World roots, many *gens de couleur libre* or "free people of color" found another venue for socializing. When Louisiana was under French rule, a few blacks arrived in Louisiana as free men, but most acquired their freedom through a variety of means over time. As archivist and author Florence E. Borders explains, "It was, however, during the Spanish period . . . that the free black population experienced its most notable increase during colonial times. This resulted from the more liberal manumission policies of the Spanish and influx of refugees from various Caribbean countries during periods of upheaval and revolution."[25]

It was also during the Spanish period that dance halls catering to blacks opened in Louisiana. The colony's first public dance hall for whites dated from 1792. Shortly thereafter, Governor Francisco Luis Héctor, barón de Carondelet, granted permission for blacks to also hold weekly public dances.[26] By 1805, white men and free women of color were intentionally meeting at dances that eventually became known as "quadroon balls."[27] It was at these dances that women of color discovered a remarkable opportunity to better their economic and social status, as well as secure brighter futures for their children. White women were denied entrance to the dances, and although free men of color often played music at these events, they were not allowed to participate in the dancing.[28] The primary purpose for these quadroon balls was to provide a social setting in which white males and free women of color could meet and form liaisons through a system known as *plaçage.*

Commonly practiced throughout the French and Spanish slaveholding territories, *plaçage* enabled women of color to secure places or become *placée* with free white males as concubines or mistresses. Although laws tried to ban

Washington and American Ball Room.

St. Philip street, between Royal and Bourbon streets.

The Manager respectfully informs his friends and the public generally, that this room having been thoroughly repaired, will be opened for GRAND DRESS and MASQUERADE BALLS every *Tuesday, Thursday, Saturday* and *Sunday* Evening during the season. ☞ *Every Sunday Evening for* QUADROON BALLS.

Admittance—Gentlemen..........................$1 00
Ladies..........................Gratis.

Doors open at half past 7 o'clock.

GEO. STEPHENS, Manager.

No weapons allowed in the Ball Room. o15

Advertisement for a "Quadroon Ball" in the New Orleans *Times Picayune*, December 18, 1884

Plaçage System

Non-whites were racially classified into various groups. An octoroon (*octorón*) was seven-eighths white and one-eighth black. A quadroon (*cuarterón*) was one-fourth black, or the offspring of a white person and a mulatto. Mulattoes (*mulatres*) had one white and one black parent. Full-blooded blacks were considered to be the lowest rung on the social ladder. Women of color of various skin tones, many of whom were the daughters of white fathers and free mothers of mixed parentage, attended quadroon balls in hopes of being suitably placed (*placée*) with a white man who could provide for her and their children under the plaçage system.

Free woman of color and her octoroon daughter in late eighteenth-century New Orleans.

these relationships, the popularity and practicality of the system caused the majority of the population to ignore these prohibitions.

The majority of these women did more than merely survive under the *plaçage* system; in fact, many flourished and became wealthy landowners, slaveholders, and merchants who benefited from the educational refinement and social prestige their position afforded them.[29]

A group of wealthy women of color established the *Société Cordon Bleu*, an organization whose goal was to use society balls known as *Bals de Cordon Bleu* as a means for securing their daughters' future with aristocratic white Creole males. These formal dances, sometimes called "quadroon balls," were similar to debutante balls in which Creole women of color presented their daughters to wealthy white Creole males. The admission fee for these dances was set high intentionally to discourage any but the wealthiest of men from attending. Chaperones in evening gowns lined the walls, fanning themselves with palmetto fans. Mothers or guardians kept a close eye on their elegantly attired daughters throughout the evening. After formal presentations had been made and compliments exchanged, a man would show his interest in a particular woman by asking her for a dance. If the girl did not like him for some reason, she would politely decline any additional invitations to dance with him. However, to indicate her reciprocation of his attention, she would send him to her mother for negotiation of their common-law arrangement. Once her mother and suitor reached an agreement, the girl was considered to be *placée*, a social condition comparable to a betrothal.[30]

Although *plaçage* arrangements undoubtedly occurred elsewhere in Louisiana, men who could afford such a luxury usually lived or conducted business in the bustling port city of New Orleans. Therefore, in order to prove his intentions honorable, the man normally purchased a small house on or near Rampart Street; but he was not permitted to see the girl without the presence of a chaperone until the home was finished. Once the couple began living together, he took on the full responsibility of providing for her and the children born to their union. Many of these mixed-race relationships were monogamous and lasted a lifetime. As a result, people began referring to these *plaçage* arrangements as *mariages de la main gauche*, or "left-handed marriages." Unlike "bastard" children whose fathers were unknown, the sons and daughters born into these left-handed marriages were considered to be "natural" offspring since their fathers legally recognized them. Many of these wealthy white Creole fathers not only acknowledged these children publicly, many also sent their natural children to France for higher education. They often left them sizable inheritances that enabled their mixed-race children to accumulate unprecedented wealth and social standing.[31]

Not knowing how to curtail the illegal liaisons that these popular quadroon balls spawned, Attorney General Gabriel Fonvergné tried to minimize white male patronage at black dances by asking the City Council to request that Governor Carondelet prohibit slaves from entering dance halls. The governor knew this would not be an acceptable solution since so many slave owners responded with numerous complaints and objections. Carondelet then decided to prohibit whites from attending these dances. The balls continued for several years, although Spanish authorities could boast little success in preventing white men from patronizing these establishments. Frustrated with their inability to regulate these social gatherings, the Spanish government finally decided to suspend the public dances altogether in the middle of the year 1800.[32]

Apparently white males were not the only men interested in keeping dance venues open in New Orleans. Louisiana militiamen of the Battalion of Octoroons and the Battalion of Quadroons requested permission to reestablish the weekly dances in a formal petition they sent to the Cabildo, or Spanish seat of government, on October 24, 1800. These soldiers had just returned from an expedition to Fort San Marcos de Apalache in Florida where, according to the statement they issued, "the men experienced bad times such as irregularity of weather and nourishment, blistering heat due to the harsh season in which the expedition was undertaken, mosquitoes, night air, humidity, and other nuisances harmful to human nature," as well as "shelling from the cannons which they expected to receive at any moment. . . ." They asked to reinstate the Saturday evening dances in order "to recompense them [militiamen] in some manner, [and] to cheer up their spirit, so that

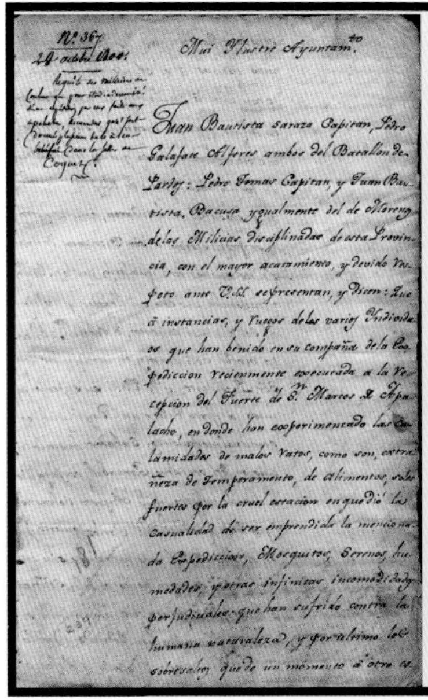
Nº 367

Mui Ylustre Ayuntamto.

Juan Bautista Saraza Capitan, Pedro
Galafate Alferes ambos del Batallon de
Pardos: Pedro Tomas Capitan, y Juan Bautista Bacusa ygualmente del de Morenos
delas Milicias disciplinadas de esta Provin-
cia, con el mayor acatamiento, y devido res-
peto ante V.S.S. se presentan, y dicen: Que
á instancias, y ruegos delas varios Individu-
os que han venido en su compañia dela Expedicion recienmente executada a la Re-
cepcion del Fuerte de Sn. Marcos de Apalache, en donde han esperimentado las Ca-
lamidades de malos ratos, como son, extra-
ñeza de temperamento, de alimentos, ...
fuertes por la cruel estacion en que dió la
casualidad de ser emprendida la menciona-
da Expedicion, Mosquitos, Serenos, hu-
medades, y otras infinitas incomodidades
perjudiciales que han sufrido contra la
humana naturaleza, y por ultimo los
sobresaltos que de un momento á otro es-

Public Dances

Louisiana's Spanish colonial government initially banned masquerade balls held by free people of color and slaves due to fear that these masked individuals would be able to slip into whites-only dances undetected or commit crimes anonymously. The Spanish government later prohibited masking at any ball as a result of their distress over the possibility of French revolutionaries or proponents of slave uprisings camouflaging themselves at these dances and infiltrating the local population.

Letter to the Cabildo requesting permission to reestablish weekly dances for the Battalion of Quadroons and the Battalion of Octoroons.

they can forget the hardships of the expedition which they undertook." They went on to explain, "The dance will not interfere with the one the white people regularly have, for they have their dance on Sundays." It is noteworthy that these men were successful in their attempts to reinstate the social event and that public dances for blacks continued well into the American period which began with the Louisiana Purchase in 1803.[33]

Although dancing never lost its popularity among both white Creoles and Creoles of Color, the influx of American settlers following the Louisiana Purchase brought about a clash of cultures, not between blacks and whites, slaves or free people of color, but between French-speaking Creoles and English-speaking Americans. Pierre Clément de Laussat, the French prefect who oversaw the transfer of Louisiana to the United States, recorded one such incident in his memoirs: "An unfortunate potential for trouble broke out between the French and Anglo-Americans at the regular public ball. Two quadrilles, one French, the other English, formed at the same time. An American, taking offense at something, raised his walking stick at one of the fiddlers. Bedlam ensued. . . ." Laussat went on to explain that William Charles Cole Claiborne, Louisiana's territorial governor and the American who later became the state's first governor in 1812, "resorted to persuasion rather than to rigorous measures in order to silence the American, who was a simple surgeon attached to the troops. The French quadrille resumed. The American interrupted it again with an English quadrille and took his place to dance. Someone cried, 'If the women have a drop of French blood in their veins, they will not dance.' Within minutes, the hall was completely deserted by the women."[34]

An 1866 engraving by Alfred Rudolph Waud depicts white Creoles at the French Opera House on a Sunday night in New Orleans.

According to historian R. Randall Crouch, many English and American travelers were shocked by the Creoles' fondness of dancing. Appalled at the idea of engaging in such frivolous activities on Sunday afternoons, a day normally reserved for sedate religious observances, Americans urged New Orleans's city council to shut down the dance halls and claimed that they were the cause of disorderly conduct and questionable morality. Much to the surprise of the Americans, however, Governor Claiborne did not eliminate these balls; he recognized that they were an integral part of local culture and attended them in order to exhibit his respect for longstanding Creole tradition. The city council, instead of banning public dances, passed a resolution in 1804 in an attempt to restrain the rowdiness that had come to be associated with some of these dance halls. For example, the resolution prohibited weapons in the ballrooms and required police presence to maintain order. Perhaps the most important factor in these peace-keeping efforts, however, was the council's decision to mandate the order in which the different dances took place—two French quadrilles were to be followed by an English quadrille, then a waltz.[35]

Regardless of where or how they gathered to dance, the musical instruments they played, or the language in which they sung the lyrics, South Louisiana's population has always enjoyed an extremely diverse musical heritage. As historian Thomas Fiehrer explains, "By the end of the colo-

Built in 1815, the Théâtre d'Orléans was located on Orleans Avenue between Royal and Bourbon streets in New Orleans's French Quarter.

nial regime the streets [of New Orleans] rang with operatic arias, African chants, West Indian ditties and popular French provincial refrains." Although white and black Creoles did move beyond the limits of New Orleans in order to settle the prairies of southwest Louisiana, only the Crescent City could boast such an impressive music scene at the turn of the nineteenth century. As early as 1808, two opera houses and hundreds of musicians worked to entertain a city whose population consisted of only fifteen thousand people.[36]

Fiehrer continues, "The most punctilious writers have assumed that French influence in Louisiana's culture abated with the end of migration in 1810. Actually, French and West Indian migration to Louisiana never stopped. The ingress of Frenchmen was very steady until the Civil War. Though reduced thereafter, it continued until after the First World War. Nor was French culture confined to the city: of the state's 17,462 free nonwhites in 1850, some 80 per cent [*sic*] were Creole, or mixed, distributed in sundry pockets throughout the state . . . coloured planters danced the quadrille, valse and fais-do-do, as did white counterparts."[37]

Although black and white Creole planters both inside and outside of New Orleans may have showcased their social standing by attending formal dances and hiring professionally trained musicians to provide entertainment, less affluent black Creoles of South Louisiana's prairie regions eventually developed their own style of music that has progressively been labeled Juré, La La, Creole, or Zydeco music.

Built in 1859, the French Opera House stood at the corner of Bourbon and Toulouse streets until it was destroyed by fire in 1919.

Field Hollers and House Dances: From Juré to La La

You see me there, well, I ain't no fool,
I'm one smart Frenchman—never been to school.
Want to go somewhere in a Creole town,
You stop and let me show you your way 'round
And let the bon ton roula . . .

At the church bazaar or the baseball game,
At the French la-la, it's all the same
You want to have fun now you got [to] go
Way out in the country to the Zydeco.

–Clarence Garlow[38]

Although no documentation indicates exactly when the style of music known as Juré emerged, it closely resembles the slave music being played in New Orleans's Congo Square during the antebellum period; it is possible these styles were contemporaries.[39] In fact, when Alan Lomax recorded a number of Juré songs in 1934, he called it "the most African sound I found in America."[40]

"*Juré*," a word derived from the French verb *jurer* meaning "sworn or testified," comes from the traditional expression "*Jurez* (testify), my Lord." As

Creole musicians from Frilot Cove pictured with their instruments—a guitar, twin fiddles, and a *'tit fer* or triangle, c. 1915.

Jeffery Broussard and his sisters performing a Juré song at Festivals Acadiens et Créoles.

folklorist Barry Ancelet explains, Juré is a "localized form of the African American 'ring shout,' consisting of a counterclockwise procession accompanied by antiphonal singing and the shuffling, stamping, and clapping of the dancers, occasionally supplemented by simple percussion such as the ubiquitous metal-on-jawbone scraper or its descendant, the washboard."[41] The blending of Afro-Caribbean, French-Acadian, and southern Protestant traditions of shouting and spirituals fused to form Louisiana's black Creole counterpart to French Acadian *danses rondes* (round dances) and Anglo-American play party songs.[42] When instrumental music was forbidden at certain times, such as during Lent or designated mourning periods, Juré singers were called upon to provide dance music. Since only improvised percussion such as clapping hands, stamping feet, and spoons rubbed on washboards accompanied the musicians' voices, this enabled musicians to comply with these compulsory periods of musical prohibition.[43]

Juré was originally spiritual music, but became progressively more secular as time passed. Although African in rhythm, and oftentimes religious in nature, Juré tunes also freely adapted popular Cajun songs. One example is the song "*Je fait tout le tour du pays*" ("I Went All Around the Land") whose title and theme emerged from an Acadian folk song, but whose melody reflects the Cajun tune "*J'étais au bal hier soir*" ("I Went to the Dance Last Night") which was based on an Anglo-American country song.[44]

The expression "*les haricots sont pas salés*" literally means "the green beans aren't salty." Figuratively, it implied that times were so tough, people could not afford to use salt meat to flavor their dishes. These green bean pickers in 1938 are waiting for trucks to pick them up along a highway near Gibson.

Touted as the origin for the term "Zydeco," the phrase "*les haricots sont pas salés*" first appeared in Lomax's collection of Juré songs. Canray Fontenot, a well-respected Creole fiddler, said, "They never had no such thing as Zydeco music. No such thing as Zydeco music. That's bullcorn . . . they had a thing they called Juré. The old people would sing for the young people, and clap their hands and make up a song." Clifton Chenier, known widely as the "King of Zydeco," told Canray, "No, I never went to one [a Juré dance], but my daddy used to go. My daddy played the [song] *'zaricots est [sic] pas salés'* on his accordion, but he didn't play it in the right speed, he played it like a Juré. I

Cedric Watson (front left) and members of Bijou Créole perform a Juré song a capella accompanied by a tambourine, hand clapping, and foot stomping.

thought it should go faster."[45] Despite the fact that Juré has virtually disappeared from the current Creole repertoire, some young artists like Cedric Watson have endeavored to reintroduce the genre. Using Lomax's collection as inspiration, Watson produced his own version of the Juré tune "*Je fait tout le tour du pays*" ("I Went All Around the Land") and released it on his self-titled record in 2008.[46]

In the decades before World War II, many Creoles worked hard all week as sharecroppers or day laborers and looked forward to a respite from their toil at weekend house dances, a social gathering that enabled them to catch up with family and friends. Creole accordionist Wilson "Boozoo" Chavis recalled, "In them days when we were small, Mama would carry us everywhere they would go. We had a wagon and horses. They'd go to those old house dances, and leave us sleeping in the wagon outside. We'd hear the music comin' through the windows."[47] Meanwhile, inside the house, furniture would be shoved aside to make room for the dancers while the musicians played from a makeshift "bandstand" consisting of chairs being placed on top of a homemade wooden table that had been nailed together.[48] These black Creole house dances, as well as the music played at these gatherings, were referred to as "French La Las" to distinguish them from the African American disco or soul parties that later gained popularity.[49]

Paydays were especially popular times for hosting house dances, although sharecroppers often found their pay from the landowner to be less than what they expected when the crops came in. Instead of verbalizing complaints outright,

A Louisiana sharecropper and his young child.

An accordion and washboard accompany these musicians in front of a store near New Iberia.

however, disappointed workers might tell their neighbors, "*Les haricots sont pas salés*," a French expression that literally means "the snap beans aren't salty." Since people often served snap beans with salted pork to guests at house dances, when times were lean and pay was short, it meant that the host could not afford to flavor the beans with salted meat. In other words, according to Jenelle Chargois, general manager for the Lafayette-based radio station KJCB, this was "their way of saying, 'I got shorted today' without actually saying it."[50]

Although the phrase "*les haricots sont pas salés*" had appeared in songs and conversations for many years before Lomax documented it in 1934, it was not until after World War II that the term "Zydeco" was applied to black Creole music.[51] Due to the frequent repetition of the phrase in many Juré and Creole songs, the expression gained popularity, and eventually "*les haricots*" (pronounced "layz-ah-dee-koh") evolved via numerous spelling variations into "Zydeco."[52]

Warren Caesar, a former member of Clifton Chenier's Red Hot Louisiana Band, grew up sharecropping and attending house dances like everyone else he knew. Although he was born into a family of musicians, it was not until later that he recognized the correlation between La La music and Zydeco. He recalled,

> I was seven years old when I went to the la-las, every Saturday night, with Bois-sec and Canray Fontenot, Canray is my uncle. I grew up in Basile. . . . I grew up there on a plantation, my daddy was a sharecropper. I was born in 1952.

> . . . Back in those days I was picking cotton for Bois-sec, too, man. Oh, yeah, I picked cotton, I dug sweet potatoes, I didn't cut no cane, but I did farm with my dad, he planted rice, soybeans. And my dad had a piece of land to plant his own corn and his beans, potatoes, okra.
>
> Bois-sec and my uncle Canray Fontenot, they always did have a band. . . . I was a little guy, I was seven years old, running around the clubs and stuff and I didn't know anything about no la-la. I was twenty-five or twenty-six years old, when I discovered that hey, this la-la, this is Zydeco music.[53]

The modern term "Zydeco" as applied to Creole music may have come into popular usage later, but the French La La music being played at these house dances was a simple style of music typically accompanied by just an accordion or an accordion and washboard combination. Sometimes a fiddle or harmonica chimed in. Other makeshift instruments like pots and pans, drums made from barrels, metal triangles, and spoons could be added to help the dancers keep rhythm.[54]

The time of the dance was often determined by how far people had to travel to get there. Born in 1900, accordionist Freeman Fontenot remembered, "I was young in those days. . . . There were no cars in those days, only horses. . . . The horses had to work in the fields, so we couldn't take them far at night and on weekends [to attend the house dances]."[55] Most dances occurred on Saturday night or Sunday afternoon, depending on whether or not people were riding in buggies or wagons or walking.[56]

Freeman's younger cousin Canray Fontenot, born in 1918, recalled, "Black dances almost always lasted all night long. The houses were so small that the people had to dance in shifts. One group would dance, then they had to leave to let another group come in. Then, the first group would come back. And that went on all night long."[57]

Without a doubt, the best-known Creole musician playing these house dances was Amédé Ardoin, an accomplished accordionist who was first recorded in 1929 along with Cajun fiddler Dennis McGee. After playing for a white dance one night, Amédé arrived late at a house dance where Canray Fontenot's father was playing. Canray's grandmother was selling bowls of gumbo for ten cents each, and Amédé promised to relieve Canray's father just as soon as he had finished off his bowl of gumbo. Canray remembered, "When Amédé came back, my father was playing a song. That's when I saw what those two men could do. My father stood up and let his bass side hand come out of the left strap [of his accordion]. Amédé put his hand in and the people never stopped dancing. Then, my father let the other hand out and Amédé took the accordion. They switched off on the accordion and the song never missed a beat."[58]

Amédé Ardoin, considered by many to be the "Father of Creole Music."

Although Cajun musicians have been recorded prolifically since the 1920s, unfortunately, there are relatively few Creole music recordings from those early years.[59] Ardoin is the notable exception, but even respected ethnomusicologists such as D. K. Wilgus mislabeled his music as "Negro-Cajun music" instead of crediting him as a Creole musician.[60] While Ardoin is considered to be the father of Creole music, and Canray Fontenot later became a legend in his own right, Canray's father refused to be recorded, despite the fact that blacks and whites routinely requested to document his musical talents. "No," the elder Fontenot would say, "when a person is dead, he is supposed to be gone. You're not supposed to hear him on the records. When I die, I want to be finished."[61]

With the introduction of new forms of entertainment such as radios and later television sets, the popularity of house dances began to wane. Urbanization and increased contact with African American music via the media also contributed to a shift from traditional to modern expressions.[62] For most elderly Creoles, these informal social gatherings persist only in their memories.

One of the last Creole musicians still playing French La La music is Goldman Thibodeaux. Born into a family of sharecroppers in 1932, Thibodeaux has witnessed the evolution of Creole music, but still stresses the importance of remembering and passing on the musical style of his youth. Along with his lifelong friend Joe Citizen, Goldman recalls attending house dances with his family. At one of these occasions, as a young boy of eight or nine years, Goldman met Amédé Ardoin. Recounting that experience, Goldman explained:

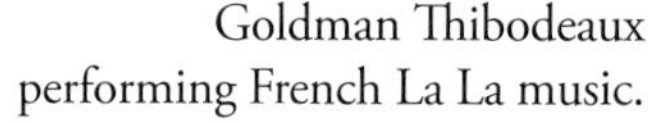

Goldman Thibodeaux performing French La La music.

Momma and Daddy would go to the house dances.
House dances was either Saturday night or mostly Sunday afternoon.
Why? [*rhetorically*]
Because we didn't have no transportation.
. . . People who had cars were people who had money.
We didn't have no car.
We had a wagon, buggy.
You'd always see people walking on the road headed to the Sunday afternoon dance.

Momma would work in the kitchen.
We had no electricity, just a big block of ice from the ice factory.
Break that ice.
Roll the lemons.
Make old-fashioned lemonade.
That's what they'd serve.
Momma was in the kitchen making popcorn, pies, and cook[ing].

That was the first time and the last time I saw Amédé Ardoin.
We were a bunch of little boys.
We was waitin.'
We didn't know [for] who.
We just heard the name.

He got down off his horse.
We opened the gate for him.
Had a lot of China ball trees there.
He went to the shade, tied his horse.
He got his accordion in a white goose sack.
He put it down.
He took the saddle off his horse,
put it on the fence,
took the blanket so it could dry off.
Boy, we were so happy!
He said, "Y'all can pack my accordion if y'all want."
Boy, we were so happy!
Brought it in the house.
[Amédé] met the people in the house,
the owner of the house,
and everything.
And he said, "When y'all want me to start playing?"
"Well," they said, "whenever you ready, you can start."

I remember they put him caddy corner—like in the corner right here—playing.
Just him.
But he was so short and tiny.
I guess soaking wet, he'd weigh about 95 pounds.
Small man.

He set up his accordion,
played for 3 hours,
just him.
No back up.
Sang and played.
This little, small man.

When he got to the payment, his pay—passed the hat.
A nickel.
A dime.
Prob'ly a quarter or two in the hat.
[Joe interjects]: That was a lot of money!—a quarter? Come on!
[Goldman continues]: Prob'ly *one*, Joe.
Maybe two.
A nickel.
A dime.
He didn't count it.
He said, "Thank you."
They said, "Don't leave. Stay here."
"No," he said, "I'd love to, but I got another dance."
He said, "[Got] to go play in Eunice."

I tell the musicians today,
I say, "Y'all got it made.
Y'all stand up there playing.
You got back-up.
You got a big towel on your shoulders to wipe your face."
I said, "How in the world they're gonna do that?"
He [Amédé] gotta keep going as long as they got people on the floor.
Once he quit, who they got?
Nothin.'"

He took off.
We brought the saddle back,
packed the accordion,
put his blanket on his horse.
"Ok, y'all, bye bye!"
Boy, he took off,
headed to Eunice for another dance.

. . . The next Sunday, they say, "Don't forget!
Next Sunday afternoon or Saturday night, it's gonna be at Jacque's!"

If it was over on Saturday night, momma had a lamp.
Remember that lantern?
A lantern—it was a good light at that time.

When the dance was over,
everybody [was] on the road,
maybe 50, 60, 70 people,
maybe more,
on the road walking back from the dance,
waitin' til the next weekend come for another [opportunity]
to go dance and waltz and two-step.
Go head, Joe.

[Joe]: There's one thing you forgot.
You say about the orange,
and the lemonade,
and the gumbo in the house.
You didn't say nothin' about what our daddy was doing outside.

My daddy, his brothers, and my uncles on my momma's side—
they out there with that corn whiskey . . .
those old men was drinking whiskey on the outside,
and the ladies was drinking lemonade on the inside,
and they had gumbo in the kitchen.
But they had corn whiskey that was against the law.
They couldn't sell that stuff in the store.
So they would make it at home.

[Goldman]: So what'd they call that?

[Joe]: White lightning.
It had no color to it.
It looked like there was nothing to it,
but you drank one or two of those things
and when it hit you,
it hit you so hard!

[Goldman]: Now listen.
They were sittin' down under the tree drinkin' that stuff.
Children of today—
they'd find out about it right now.
But I didn't know what it was.
You know what I thought it was?
"*My God*!" I'd say, "they keep sippin' on that water!"
It was white.
I thought it was water they were drinking![63]

Goldman Thibodeaux feeding his sheep at home in Lawtell.

When Thibodeaux relates his stories about attending French La La gatherings, he keeps the memory of this tradition alive for the current generation who did not grow up attending house dances. Although his other siblings eventually left the farm, Thibodeaux never did. He stayed around to help his aging parents and take care of his wife and two sons. Thibodeaux picked up the accordion at fifty years of age and subsequently released three CDs, but he does not consider his music to be an occupation.[64] Citizen explained, "Back in the '30s and '40s, you would go and play music for maybe two or three dollars a night. So quite naturally, you can't make a living off that. Everyone had families, and a lot of us country people were out there working in the fields. So, they'd play that just to have fun on the weekends and everybody would go back to work."[65]

Canray Fontenot began playing second fiddle with his father when he was about eleven years old and remembered that one night "when the [wedding] dance finished, I came out with four bits, fifty cents, and that was a lot of money in those days."[66] Playing music may not have helped to pay the bills, but it was a way of socializing with family and friends and helping others to dance their cares away.

There were drawbacks though. Being a musician meant you could not dance. Joe Citizen's father was a musician. He recalled, "I used to watch my daddy dance with my mother. When my daddy would get on the bandstand and start playing music, my mother had nobody to dance with. So, she'd make me get up at ten years old, and I had to dance in my daddy's place because he was busy beating his foot on the floor playing the accordion. And if I tried to do something that my daddy didn't do, my mother would slap [me] upside the head and say, 'Dance like your daddy, boy!' So, I stick with the old style, and that's the reason I can't dance like y'all [young people]."[67]

Thibodeaux and Citizen realize they are the last old-timers who still play French La La regularly, and they are working hard to make sure people understand what they play and why they play it. As Citizen commented, "We are the only band now in Southwest Louisiana that plays the old traditional music for hours. If we go to a dance, we're gonna play that music for four hours, talk French, sing French, and play French. We're not gonna mix it. If you ask us, we might want to help you out. But if you let us play our dance, we're gonna play the music from the '20s on up to the '50s and we're singing and playing in French."[68]

Canray Fontenot

Citizen observed, "We too old. The music is not interesting anymore. It's dying. We the last. After we leave, if Goldman die or if I die, you won't hear that kind of music anymore. That's it. You ain't gonna get nobody that plays it the way we play it 'cuz that's how our dad played it. The closest thing to what they were playing then is us. . . . If you don't go back to Amédé Ardoin . . . you ain't gonna find that music."[69]

French La La music may no longer be referred to as such, except by old-timers like Goldman Thibodeaux. However, elements of that old style of black Creole music are still being performed by younger musicians like Jeffery Broussard and Geno Delafose who play a variety of tunes ranging from traditional Cajun and Creole medleys to the more modernized rhythms of Zydeco.

As one of eleven musically gifted children, Jeffery was born in 1967. He began playing with his father Delton Broussard at the age of eight and has continued playing for the last thirty years. Although he fronted a band called Zydeco Force for nearly two decades, when Jeffery noticed that Zydeco music was shifting gears and incorporating more African American urban styles such as hip-hop, he realized that the new Zydeco, referred to as *nouveau Zydeco*, did not entice the older people to come out and dance like they did before. Recognizing this change, he decided to keep his father's legacy going and return to playing what he calls a more traditional Creole Zydeco. He stated, "I'm proud of keeping my daddy's legacy going. That's my main goal—to continue doing that, and pleasing the older people, you know, and giving them the type of music they are looking for."[70]

His band's name, Jeffery Broussard and the Creole Cowboys, reflects not only his interest in an older musical style, but also his rural upbringing. "Honestly speaking, as far as with Zydeco, I enjoyed the music back then more than the music that's being played now," he said. "I could relate more to that than what's going on right now. Because a lot of stuff that's being played with the younger bands, and I'm not knocking them—I love them all to death—[but] I just don't feel it. It's not me."[71]

Broussard commented that the younger Zydeco artists are great at what they do, but that he is from a different generation with different life experiences. As a father of five, he feels disconnected from the work of some of the younger musicians because of the generation gap that is reflected in their music. Broussard grew up speaking French and usually sings in his first language because the older people still prefer the old French songs. However, he recognizes that "with most of the young bands now, most—basically *everything*—they're singing now is in English." He added, "My advice to younger musicians is that they need to look back at what's going on and try to get back into the roots because if we don't do this, with the

Jeffery Broussard at Festivals Acadiens et Créoles in Lafayette.

style of music that's being played now, we're gonna lose this culture, this tradition. And I'm gonna fight it as long as I can."[72]

Like Jeffery Broussard, Geno Delafose also plays a traditional style of Creole music, speaks French, and grew up playing Creole music with his father. According to Delafose, if the music is not sung in French, then it is not Cajun or Zydeco music. Knowing that so many members of the younger generation do not speak French, he makes a conscious effort to sing in French so at least the young people can hear the language like he heard it growing up.[73]

Dancers at the Rhythm and Roots Festival in Charlestown, Rhode Island, enjoy music by Jeffery Broussard and the Creole Cowboys.

John Delafose and the Eunice Playboys

At the age of seven, Geno began playing the rubboard with his father John Delafose, "one of the hottest attractions on the Gulf Coast circuit."[74] By ten, he was playing the drums, and at thirteen years old, had already picked up the accordion. At his shows, Geno prefers to play a mixture of Cajun, Creole, and old Zydeco tunes. "I'm playing what I was brought up listening to," he said. "If everybody just goes with the times, the tradition gets lost."[75]

Living in his father's shadow presented some challenges for Geno as an upcoming artist because, despite the fact that he had played with his father in many different places for fifteen years before his father passed away, he still was not John Delafose. He had to prove himself. Although he really does not want to change the style of music that he plays, he understands that sometimes adjustments are necessary and that can be a good thing. "My goal is to please my fans, and we try our best," he explained.[76] As Joe Citizen observed, "You see, Geno found his own style, but Geno can play his daddy's music if you ask him. Sometimes, I get on him. 'Look! I want you to play that like your daddy used to play!' He look at me and laugh, and he gonna play, but he ain't gonna play it no more, 'cuz like I said, he want to be Geno. He don't want to be John Delafose."[77]

Delafose represents his Creole cowboy roots with Western attire like Wrangler jeans, boots, and a cowboy hat. Although he took a lot of grief over the style of music that he plays—from traditionalists for trying to be his own person instead of his father and from his own generation for liking country and Creole music when it wasn't "cool"—as well as criticism from outsiders be-

Geno Delafose performing at the Original Southwest Louisiana Zydeco Music Festival in Plaisance.

cause of the way he dresses, Delafose admits with a shrug, "I am what I am, and that's all I can be." He appreciates his rural upbringing and, despite the opportunities he has had to travel all over the world playing music, he says, "there's no feelin' like turnin' down that little gravel road and comin' to my house."[78]

In addition to playing music and taking care of his ranch, Delafose also drives a school bus and cuts grass. He knows what it means to work hard and says that life is already tough enough as it is. "I just want to make life pleasant for people," he explains. He understands that despite blistering heat during the summer or cold and rainy winter weather, at the end of a long week of work, people want to be able to let their hair down and go dancing, just like they looked forward to the house dances decades ago. "And God bless 'em for that!" he says with his characteristically wide smile.[79]

Unlike the house dances, which typically occurred in close-knit communities where mixed-race socialization rarely occurred, Delafose said, "I always wanted to bring blacks and whites together with my music."[80] As political scientist Mark Mattern explains in his article regarding South Louisiana race relations, despite the fact that Cajun and Creole musicians "draw from similar and sometimes identical individual musical sources," and that Creole musicians such as Amédé Ardoin (accordion), Freeman Fontenot (accordion), and Canray Fontenot (fiddle) are often cited as early influences on Cajun music, racial distinctions often kept Creole and Cajun dancers in separate dance halls.[81]

Delafose commented, "I would always tell myself, 'If they ever give me a chance, just *one* chance, to play in any of these Cajun clubs here in Louisiana, they're gonna see something.'" He was right. Geno made history when he and his band French Rockin' Boogie played for the first time at Whiskey River Landing, a popular Cajun dance hall on the Atchafalaya Basin levee in Henderson, Louisiana. Since most dances were held on Sunday afternoons, the club agreed to allow him to play on a Saturday night just to test the waters. His band drew over 350 people at that first show. About a month later, he was invited to play during the regular Sunday afternoon slot and drew a crowd of five hundred.[82]

Delafose made history again on August 29, 2009, when he and French Rockin' Boogie became the first all-Creole band to play at Breaux Bridge's La Poussière, the oldest Cajun dance hall still in existence.[83] Whether it is his country charm, wide smile, or combination of old-fashioned Creole, Cajun, and Zydeco tunes, Geno has found the key to successfully bring both young and old, Cajun and Creole together on the dance floor.[84]

Other Creole artists are continuing that trend. As Joe Citizen remarked approvingly, "Now there's another one that's starting out, and he wants to play John [Delafose]'s music. It's Cedric Watson. If you take Cedric off that violin and give him an accordion, he's going after John's music. He told me that he would like to play that music."[85]

Born in 1983, Cedric Watson grew up in East Texas where, unlike his urban neighbors, his family raised horses, cows, and hogs and were considered to be "cowboys." When he was just four years old, Watson's daddy put him on a horse and told him to ride. Growing up in a horse culture, he

Dancers move to the rhythms of a Zydeco band at Vermilionville's Performance Center.

Creole trail rides like Step-N-Strut draw thousands of participants who camp out for the weekend to enjoy good food and live Zydeco music. Young and old, representing their trail ride association, ride through the countryside on horseback.

oftentimes heard Zydeco music at trail rides, local events in which participants ride on horseback or on flatbed trailers throughout the countryside. He started dancing at the trail rides, then began thinking he could possibly play the music he liked. He got his first guitar at fourteen, his first fiddle at eighteen, and his first accordion shortly thereafter. He has been playing for the last fifteen years or so and has since made Lafayette, Louisiana, his home.[86]

Watson claims that his motivation for playing is being able to express himself, just like other musicians are able to do through their music. "I loved it so much what I heard, and felt it in my heart, you know, so whenever I started playing it, I figured since I learned it so much, I should just keep on going with it." As a young artist, Watson acknowledges that he looks up to people like Jeffery Broussard and John and Geno Delafose. When asked what kind of music he plays, Watson answers, "Creole French music or Creole Zydeco," but states that he can also play Cajun music.[87]

Through J.B. Adams, who has a Creole/Zydeco radio show in Houston, Watson met Goldman Thibodeaux, who was interested in mentoring a young musician in order to keep the Creole music tradition alive. Goldman offered

Cedric Watson performing at the Blue Moon Saloon in Lafayette.

Watson an opportunity to sit in with his band when Goldman Thibodeaux and the Lawtell Playboys performed at the Original Southwest Louisiana Zydeco Music Festival.[88] This formal introduction to the Louisiana Creole music scene helped Watson launch his successful career.[89]

Despite his youth, Watson and the bands he has performed with have already been nominated for four Grammy awards. He considers those nominations to be a gift from God, but is most proud of being able to work with different musicians and having the ability to write songs. "I'm proud of that—being able to create beautiful Creole music," he declared. In his shows, he plays a lot of his own music but also mixes in traditional songs. He admits, "Whatever I'm in the mood for is what I play."[90]

Like many members of the younger Creole generation, Watson did not learn how to speak French while growing up in East Texas. In order to play Creole music, however, Watson believes that he should sing the songs in French.

Therefore, at the age of twelve, he began learning the language by talking with older people and cousins. He also got a job working with a French woman at a store. Some six years later, he was speaking French well and attended a French immersion program in Canada. Now fluent in the language, Watson is able to sing all of his songs, including the ones he writes, in French.[91] Infusing traditional styles with his own innovations, Watson bridges the gap between old and new. As his website explains,

> Cedric has played with some of the great family names in Creole music, including . . . Jeffery Broussard and the Creole Cowboys.
>
> He plays old La-La French music (traditional Creole music) in a trio of accordion, fiddle and guitar with his two musical godfathers, Edward Poullard and James Adams, in Les Amis Créoles.
>
> With accordionist Corey "Lil' Pop" Ledet, Cedric turns to the more blues and R&B influenced songs of Clifton Chenier, John Delafose, Canray Fontenot, and Bébé Carrière.
>
> Now Cedric continues to explore the roots of Louisiana's Creole music with his own band, Bijou Créole. Playing a variety of old-school Zydeco styles, original material and Creole traditionals, the polyrhythmic and syncopated sounds of Africa and the Caribbean are unmistakable in this ensemble of talented musicians.[92]

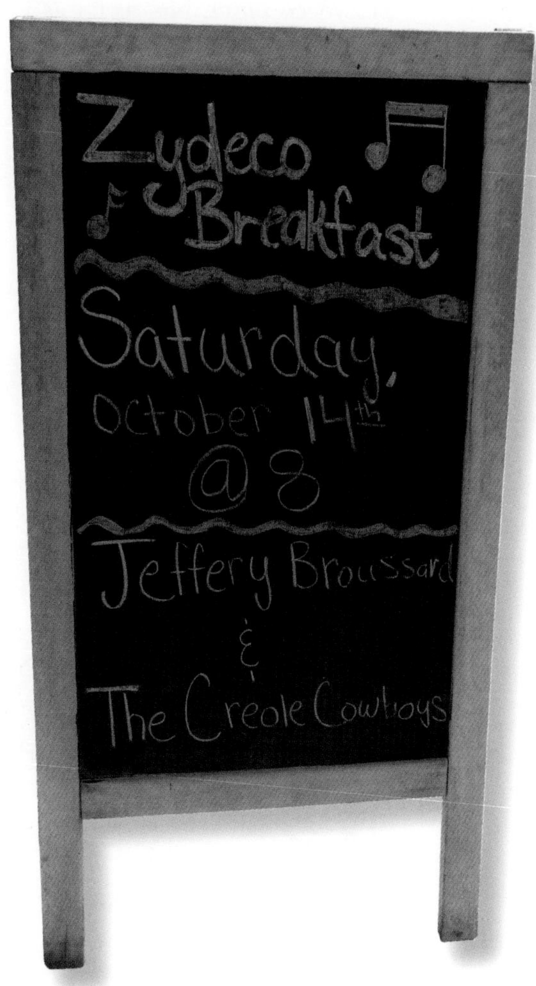

Through the conscious efforts of individuals like Goldman Thibodeaux, Joe Citizen, Jeffery Broussard, Geno Delafose, and Cedric Watson, the old sounds of Creole music can still be heard wherever they perform. Despite their efforts, however, most outsiders, and even many locals, associate Creoles with only what is currently known as "Zydeco" music.

Dance Halls and Festivals: From Creole to Zydeco

Following World War II, dance halls began replacing house dances. Musicians like Clifton Chenier took the old songs they were familiar with and added their own innovations. In the 1940s, Chenier was playing La La music.[93] What eventually set him apart from the other Creole musicians, however, was simply his ability to amp up that old style of music to fit the popular sound of his generation. As stated previously, Clifton knew the music his father played, but felt that it should be played faster.

Canray Fontenot remembered the story. "Clifton told me, 'I think I'm gonna make that *'zaricots est* [*sic*] *pas salés'* on a record, but I'm going to put some speed to it.' He went and made that record, and after people found out that our type of music was moving, everyone wanted to have an accordion, and everyone wanted to play Clifton's stuff." Fontenot continued on to explain that within the Creole communities, "Zydeco" initially referred to the dance itself and the dance halls where that style of music was played. "But they never had no such thing as Zydeco *music*. Not as far as I know. If you was black, you played Creole," he stated.[94] With the passage of time, however, the term "Zydeco" was applied to the revved-up style of Creole music that Clifton helped to popularize and market to the mass media.

The Chenier brothers—Cleveland on washboard and Clifton on accordion.

Clifton Chenier, "The King of Zydeco."

In addition to its Afro-Caribbean roots and rhythms, Zydeco music "also draws heavily on such mainstream African American styles as blues, soul, rhythm and blues, and, lately, rap [and hip-hop] music. Elements of rock, country, and reggae may also appear," notes folklorist and musician Ben Sandmel.[95] As with any musical form, Creole music has evolved over the years and undergone various name changes throughout those periods of transition. Musicians like Clifton Chenier may be credited with "inventing" Zydeco music, but what he really did was follow in the footsteps of other great Creole artists, adapt the old tunes and rhythms to fit his audiences' preferences, and change the name along the way.

Cars crowd the parking lot at Slim's Y-Ki-Ki in Opelousas.

Stanley "Buckwheat" Dural and his son Reginald performing on Festival International's main stage in Lafayette.

In an interview regarding his winning the Zydeco or Cajun Grammy Music Award in 2010, Stanley "Buckwheat Zydeco" Dural said that he came from a musical family in which all seven sisters and six brothers played something. Growing up, he refused to play the accordion because his dad played it all the time. "[Listening to] that was enough to give me the blues, man!" he exclaimed. However, when Clifton invited Buckwheat to play one night, a whole new world opened up to him. "In my daddy's generation, the music is what you played for family. It was only for home. . . ." Washboards were the kind you really washed clothes on and everyone in the family sang spirituals. Unlike most other Creole musicians of his day, Clifton performed in crowded dance halls with a full band consisting of horns, drums, piano note accordions, and washboards that wrapped around your shoulders.[96] "It blew me away. I had never seen that before. I had never been to a Zydeco concert before," Buckwheat remembered. The experience changed his life and affected his entire musical career. Before his passing in 2016, Buckwheat still traveled the road, bringing his Zydeco music to thousands, complete with a full band that featured rubboards, horns, and piano note accordions, just like Chenier did.[97]

When other Creole artists enter the music scene, it will be interesting to see where their musical journey will lead them since Louisiana boasts a long and proud tradition of musical preservation and innovation. As old-time musicians like Goldman Thibodeaux pass on their musical heritage, perhaps young musicians like Cedric Watson will continue the tradition by reintroducing old musical styles like Juré to younger generations. Maybe like Jeffery Broussard and Geno Delafose, these musicians will fuse the styles of their father's generation with their own innovations. Or, perhaps, like Clifton Chenier, their originality will change the face of traditional music and help to popularize an entirely new sound that infuses their own generation's styles and preferences.

Music, like heritage and culture, is not a static entity. In order to survive, it must preserve recognizable elements of the past while forging ahead into the future. From formal quadroon balls to pulsating Congo Square gatherings, from private house parties to public Zydeco dance halls, music and dancing has always played a significant role in the Creole cultural experience. Undoubtedly, South Louisiana's black Creole people will continue to carry on the tradition and contribute to the evolution of their music simply because, as Goldman Thibodeaux explained, "*c'est notre héritage*" [it's our heritage].[98]

Geno Delafose and French Rockin' Boogie
entertaining the crowd at the Boudin Festival in Scott.

Lil' Nathan Williams Jr.
Nathan Williams Sr.
Keith Frank

THE ACCORDION

THE WORD "AKKORDION" WAS FIRST USED WHEN A **VIENNESE** ORGAN BUILDER PATENTED HIS DESIGN ON **JUNE 6, 1829.**

IT'S LIKELY THAT DURING SLAVERY, BLACKS LEARNED TO PLAY THEIR MASTERS' ACCORDIONS. AN 1877 ILLUSTRATION DEPICTS A BLACK PRISONER PLAYING THE INSTRUMENT ALONG LOUISIANA'S CANE RIVER, IRREFUTABLE EVIDENCE THAT ACCORDIONS WERE ALREADY WIDELY AVAILABLE AND USED BY THIS TIME.

GERMAN-JEWISH IMMIGRANTS ARE CREDITED WITH INTRODUCING THE ACCORDION TO THE BAYOU STATE, BUT SOUTH LOUISIANA ACCORDIONISTS USED THE INSTRUMENT TO DEVELOP THEIR OWN STYLE OF FAST, SYNCOPATED RHYTHMS UNIQUE TO THE AREA. MANY EARLY CREOLE ACCORDIONISTS WERE PART OF A LARGE SETTLEMENT OF INDEPENDENT BLACK FARMERS IN THE PRAIRIES WEST OF OPELOUSAS. SINCE ACCOUNTS OF CAJUN DANCES DURING THIS PERIOD MENTIONED THE PREVALENT USE OF FIDDLES, BUT NEVER REFERENCED ACCORDIONS, **MANY BELIEVE BLACK CREOLES TAUGHT WHITE CAJUNS HOW TO PLAY THE INSTRUMENT.**

ACCORDIONS WERE CARRIED IN MAIL-ORDER CATALOGS AND LOCALLY-OWNED STORES AS EARLY AS THE 1870S. DURING WORLD WAR II, HOWEVER, IMPORTATION OF ACCORDIONS CEASED. THE DEVASTATION OF GERMAN FACTORIES PROMPTED MANY LOUISIANIANS TO BEGIN REPAIRING OR MAKING THEIR OWN ACCORDIONS, A TRADITION MANY CONTINUE TO THIS DAY. WHILE ZYDECO ARTISTS PLAY A VARIETY OF ACCORDIONS, INCLUDING LARGE PIANO ACCORDIONS AND TRIPLE-ROW BUTTON ACCORDIONS, THE SMALL **DIATONIC ACCORDION USED BY CAJUNS REMAINS THE POPULAR CHOICE OF MOST PRAIRIE CREOLES.**

Cedric Watson

Ed Poullard

D'Jalma Garnier III

FIDDLE

NEARLY EVERY TRAVEL WRITER WHO TRAVERSED LOUISIANA MENTIONED THE PREVALENCE OF FIDDLES AT DANCES THROUGHOUT THE REGION.

DESPITE THE POPULARITY OF FIDDLES, HOWEVER, THE ADVENT OF THE

ACCORDION NEARLY ECLIPSED THE STRINGED INSTRUMENT.

AT GATHERINGS SUCH AS *BALS DE MAISON* (HOUSE DANCES) THE ACCORDION COULD BE HEARD MORE EASILY ABOVE THE NOISE OF DANCING FEET, CLANGING DISHES, CRYING BABIES, AND VISITING FRIENDS AND FAMILY MEMBERS. ALTHOUGH FIDDLE MUSIC NEVER DISAPPEARED ENTIRELY, DANCE BANDS INCREASINGLY PREFERRED HIRING ACCORDIONISTS. AS A RESULT, FIDDLERS SOMETIMES FOUND THEMSELVES PLAYING AT HOME RATHER THAN FOR PAY.

WITH AMPLIFICATION AND THE ABILITY TO CONTROL VOLUME LEVELS IN THE

1930S CAME A RENEWED INTEREST

IN CREOLE FIDDLING. THOUGH NOT AS PREVALENT AMONG ZYDECO BANDS TODAY, CREOLE MUSICIANS STILL INCORPORATE THE FIDDLE INTO THEIR PERFORMANCES BOTH ON AND OFF THE STAGE. MANY PLAY RELATIVELY SIMPLE MELODIES USING BOW TECHNIQUES THAT EVEN CLASSICALLY TRAINED MUSICIANS FIND DIFFICULT TO DUPLICATE.

José Sanchez

Chubby Carrier

Oreun Joubert

PERCUSSION

PERCUSSIONISTS HAVE USED EVERYTHING FROM BARE HANDS AND FEET TO HIDES STRETCHED OVER WOODEN CHAIR FRAMES TO CREATE BEATS. UNLIKE OTHER SLAVE-HOLDING AREAS, **COLONIAL LOUISIANA DID NOT PROHIBIT ENSLAVED PEOPLE OF AFRICAN DESCENT FROM DRUMMING.** AS A RESULT, CERTAIN PLACES LIKE CONGO SQUARE IN NEW ORLEANS BECAME POPULAR LOCATIONS FOR MUSICIANS TO GATHER AND PERFORM MUSIC THAT EXHIBITED DIRECT AFRICAN ROOTS. THE SYNCOPATED, HARD-DRIVING RHYTHMS OF MODERN ZYDECO CAN BE TRACED TO THESE EARLY INFLUENCES.

HISTORICALLY, CREOLE AND CAJUN BANDS ALIKE USED THE TRIANGLE TO KEEP TIME. ALSO KNOWN AS THE **T'FER,** PRONOUNCED **"TEE-FARE"** AND MEANING "LITTLE IRON" IN FRENCH, THE TRIANGLE IS STILL USED IN SOME TRADITIONAL CAJUN AND CREOLE MUSIC. IT IS RARELY HEARD IN ZYDECO PERFORMANCES TODAY.

WITH FEW EXCEPTIONS, THE MODERN DRUM SET IS TYPICALLY THE ONLY PERCUSSIVE ACCOMPANIMENT FOUND ON ZYDECO STAGES. OCCASIONALLY, CONGAS, TAMBOURINES, AND OTHER INSTRUMENTS CAN BE HEARD, BUT THESE ARE EXCEPTIONS RATHER THAN THE RULE. ALONG WITH THE BASS, THE DRUMS KEEP THE BAND PLAYING AT THE SAME TEMPO AND HELP THE DANCERS AND THEIR PARTNERS KEEP TIME.

Paul "Lil' Buck" Sinegal

Kent Pierre-Auguste

Eric Singleton

GUITAR

ALTHOUGH LOUISIANA WAS ONCE A SPANISH COLONY, RELATIVELY FEW VISIBLE REMNANTS OF ITS SPANISH HERITAGE REMAIN.

ONE NOTABLE EXCEPTION IS THE GUITAR, AN INSTRUMENT STILL FOUND IN CREOLE AND ZYDECO BANDS TODAY. CAJUN BANDS AND SOME TRADITIONAL CREOLE BANDS IMPLEMENT ACOUSTIC GUITARS. MOST CONTEMPORARY ZYDECO MUSICIANS, HOWEVER, PLAY THE ELECTRIC GUITAR, A SIX-STRINGED INSTRUMENT INVENTED IN 1931 BY GEORGE BEAUCHAMP, THE NATIONAL GUITAR CORPORATION'S GENERAL MANAGER. MANY GUITARISTS TODAY PLAY BOTH RHYTHM, WHICH PLAYS THE CHORD SEQUENCE AND SETS THE BEAT, AS WELL AS LEAD GUITAR, WHICH PERFORMS SOLOS AND INSTRUMENTAL FILL PASSAGES.

& BASS

ALONG WITH THEIR PREFERENCE FOR ELECTRIC GUITARS COMES A STRONG DEPENDENCE ON THE FOUR-STRINGED BASS. THE STEADY RHYTHMS OF THE BASS NOT ONLY SUPPORT THE DRUMMER IN KEEPING THE BAND PLAYING ON TIME, BUT ALSO GIVE THE DANCERS CUES TO FOLLOW. THE BAND MAY PLAY WELL TOGETHER, BUT IF THE BASS PLAYER MISSES EVEN A SINGLE NOTE, EVERYONE ON THE DANCE FLOOR NOTICES THE DISCREPANCY AND USUALLY BLAMES A MISSTEP ON THE MISSED NOTE. THE BASS IS CRUCIAL TO ANY ZYDECO BAND'S OVERALL SOUND.

AS ONE ZYDECO ARTIST EXPLAINED, "THE DRUMS AND BASS GUITAR ARE THE RICE AND GRAVY OF THE GROOVE."

Brandon Delafosse

Kendrick Domingue

Joe Citizen

RUBBOARD

Also Known as a

FROTTOIR

IN SOUTH LOUISIANA, THE RUBBOARD IS CONSIDERED TO BE ONE OF THE FEW INSTRUMENTS INVENTED IN AMERICA. THE NAME FOR ZYDECO MUSIC'S MOST UNIQUE INSTRUMENT COMES FROM FROTTER, WHICH MEANS

"TO RUB" IN FRENCH.

INNOVATIVE MUSICIANS TOOK A COMMON HOUSEHOLD ITEM USED FOR WASHING CLOTHES AND TRANSFORMED IT INTO A SIGNATURE INSTRUMENT. THE SOUND PRODUCED EMULATES THE NOISE MADE BY SCRAPING SOMETHING LIKE A STICK ALONG AN ANIMAL JAWBONE. TODAY, EVERY ZYDECO BAND FEATURES A RUBBOARD PLAYER WHO MAY USE A VARIETY OF HAND-HELD DEVICES SUCH AS SPOONS, BOTTLE OPENERS, THIMBLES, WOODEN DRUM STICKS, AND EVEN WIRE WHISKS TO TAP, STROKE, OR BEAT OUT THEIR DISTINCTIVE RHYTHMS.

CLEVELAND CHENIER WAS THE FIRST TO TAKE THE TRADITIONALLY LAP-HELD WASHBOARD AND TIE IT AROUND HIS NECK, AN INNOVATION THAT SUCCEEDED IN GIVING HIM MORE MOBILITY ON STAGE, BUT WAS UNCOMFORTABLE TO WEAR.

IN 1946, CLEVELAND, ALONG WITH HIS BROTHER CLIFTON, THE "KING OF ZYDECO," CAME UP WITH A DESIGN AND ASKED WILLIE LANDRY, A CAJUN FRIEND AND METALWORKER, TO FABRICATE IT. LANDRY ELIMINATED THE WASHBOARD'S WOODEN FRAME AND CREATED A PIECE OF CORRUGATED SHEET METAL WITH SHOULDER STRAPS. THUS, THE ZYDECO RUBBOARD WAS BORN. TEE DON LANDRY, WILLIE'S SON, CONTINUES THE TRADITION OF MANUFACTURING RUBBOARDS BY HAND IN HIS

"KEY OF Z" SHOP IN SUNSET, LOCATED BETWEEN LAFAYETTE AND OPELOUSAS.

DANCERS

DANCERS ARE AS MUCH A PART OF CREOLE MUSIC AS THE INSTRUMENTS THEMSELVES. ZYDECO MUSICIANS WHO TRAVEL ABROAD HAVE COME TO EXPECT THAT SOME CROWDS OUTSIDE OF LOUISIANA MAY PREFER TO ENJOY THEIR MUSIC SITTING DOWN. WHILE AT HOME, HOWEVER, **IF THE DANCE FLOOR ISN'T CROWDED, THEY KNOW SOMETHING IS WRONG.**

FRENCH IMMIGRANT C.C. ROBIN'S OBSERVATIONS OF CAJUN CULTURE IN 1803, THE YEAR OF THE LOUISIANA PURCHASE, UNDOUBTEDLY COULD HAVE BEEN APPLIED TO CREOLES IN THE AREA AS WELL. HE NOTED,

"THEY LOVE TO DANCE MOST OF ALL, MORE THAN ANY OTHER PEOPLE IN THE COLONY. EVERYONE DANCES, EVEN GRANDMÈRE [GRANDMA] AND GRANDPÈRE [GRANDPA], NO MATTER WHAT THE DIFFICULTIES THEY MUST BEAR. THERE MAY BE ONLY A COUPLE OF FIDDLES TO PLAY FOR THE CROWD, THERE MAY BE ONLY FOUR CANDLES FOR LIGHT, PLACED ON WOODEN ARMS ATTACHED TO THE WALL; NOTHING BUT LONG WOODEN BENCHES TO SIT ON AND ONLY EXCEPTIONALLY A FEW BOTTLES OF TAFIA [CHEAP RUM] DILUTED WITH WATER FOR REFRESHMENT. NO MATTER, EVERYONE DANCES."

OVER TIME, **WALTZES, LINE DANCES,** AND **ZYDECO TWO-STEP** VARIATIONS DISPLACED OLD WORLD DANCES SUCH AS POLKAS, COTILLIONS, AND MAZURKAS; ELECTRIC LIGHTS REPLACED CANDLES; AND ACCORDIONS, RUBBOARDS, KEYBOARDS, HORN SECTIONS, AND DRUM SETS NOW ACCOMPANY THE UBIQUITOUS FIDDLE. HOUSE DANCES GAVE WAY TO **DANCE HALLS AND FESTIVALS** WHERE A VARIETY OF FOOD AND BEVERAGES TEMPT THE CROWDS. REGARDLESS OF THE TIME OR THE PLACE, HOWEVER, WHEN THE MUSIC STARTS IN SOUTH LOUISIANA, EVERYONE STILL DANCES.

Duke

L'Héritage Créole
Still Going Strong

Creoles in South Louisiana share an incredibly rich historical past. However, they are also very much a part of the present cultural landscape of South Louisiana, as evidenced by the various ways in which they have not only survived, but also continue to thrive in today's world. Through the food they eat, language they speak, and music they play, many Creoles are pushing their culture forward and doing all they can to preserve their heritage for future generations.

Although the quest for a specific identity still eludes some, many Creoles have discovered that it is not necessary to come up with a definition that creates lines of demarcation between people. Now, more than ever, people are beginning to understand that being Creole encompasses much more than family pedigree. It is about culture, how one views the world, and how one chooses to self-identify. Deborah J. Clifton, a Creole French language instructor and cultural activist, explained:

> I've heard anthropologists who'll give you ten or twenty definitions of what Creoles are. Maybe they're right, but for me and for the people I know who call themselves Creole, it's a nation, a national identity. It's total, it applies to language, to fashions, lifestyles, eating habits, houses, everything. Everything from Louisiana and native to Louisiana—that's part of us. Deep down, it's all part of being Creole. It's like no one ever thinks of asking what being an American is, but we're always asked what Creole is. It's like we were a *species* of rare animal or something. People want to come here and study our *blood lines* and everything, who slept with whom, or who married whom in the last two hundred years. But we're a nation, a people, we're not just a minority in the United States. There are people of every color who call themselves Creole, of every race and mixture of race who call themselves Creole. We're the people of Louisiana. The nation of Louisiana, our country.[1]

Creole People: From Invisible to Vocal

Just as other ethnic groups and nations around the world modernize to keep pace with those around them, Creoles throughout South Louisiana have also recognized that they must adapt in order to overcome new challenges and outside influences that impact their traditional way of life. For example, although *boucheries* (communal hog butcherings) are no longer necessary due to modern refrigeration, families still gather around the dinner table to enjoy smothered pork chops purchased at a local grocer's. Grandparents still tell children Bouki and Lapin stories, although most likely using English to communicate since so many youngsters do not learn Creole French growing up. House dances might exist only in the memories of a few elderly Creoles, but young people still fill up dance halls regularly and could not imagine missing their community's annual outdoor music festival. Creoles understand that change is inevitable; losing one's culture is not.

Yet despite their history and achievements, as well as their efforts to preserve their heritage, until fairly recently, black Creoles throughout South Louisiana's prairies have been an almost invisible culture overshadowed by the dominant Cajun communities with which they coexist. Largely due to the tourism industry that promotes the twenty-two parish Acadiana area in southwest Louisiana as "Cajun Country," Creoles have been overlooked or mislabeled. One Creole argued that it would be more accurate to call the area "Creole Country" since the region's ethnic blend is such a mixture of cultures. "It's really Cajun *and* Creole," he stated.[2]

Dancers enjoy a performance by Leroy Thomas and the Zydeco RoadRunners at Vermilionville.

C.R.E.O.L.E., Inc. members gathered to celebrate their twenty-fifth anniversary in 2013.

While Creoles still struggle to gain cultural recognition, there is no denying that Cajuns have overcome their humble beginnings as destitute exiles to become one of America's most widely celebrated ethnic groups. Following the bicentennial commemoration of their expulsion from Canada in 1955, Cajuns experienced a resurgence of cultural pride in the 1960s and 1970s that has continued to grow in the ensuing decades. Their distinctness as a French-speaking ethnic group within mainstream Anglophone American society has helped to propagate a sense of exoticism that fuels South Louisiana's vibrant cultural tourism industry today.[3] Cajun cuisine has become a global phenomenon with fast food chains around the United States and restaurants as far away as South Africa, Australia, Saudi Arabia, and Italy boasting menu items labeled "Cajun."[4]

Yet while "Cajun Craze" grips the nation, and even the world, black Creoles have remained caught between two worlds. Although culturally similar to Cajuns, they are not "Black Cajuns" as some have mistakenly labeled them. Outsiders may see their darker skin tones and consider them to be African Americans, but they are not that either. Although lagging behind the Cajun renaissance, within the last several decades, Creoles have attempted to establish their own *'tit monde* (little world) by becoming a more visible and vocal segment of the Bayou State.

At the head of much of this push for recognition has been C.R.E.O.L.E., Inc. One of its founding members, Herbert Wiltz, explained that a group of concerned Creoles got together in the 1980s and started the organization whose acronym stands for "Cultural Resource Education of Linguistic Enrichment." He said, "We knew basically that Cajuns could trace their heritage. And I wondered, 'Could we do the same thing?' And it is through those conversations that C.R.E.O.L.E., Inc. evolved as a way to get the community involved and thinking about that. And we found out that, yeah, we can, in a sense, for some of us. We're direct descendants from a cultural experience that started in Africa and diverted itself into many areas."[5] The organization's mission statement explains that their goal is "to develop the Creole language and culture in Louisiana" and to recognize that "this culture has been a major contributor to the foods, music, language, and spirit of south Louisiana" and, as a result, "merits acknowledgement and preservation."[6]

John Broussard, one of the cofounders of C.R.E.O.L.E., Inc., stated that Creoles do not want to take away anything from others, but simply wish to be recognized for who they are. He explained:

> We want to promote cultural exchange with groups of other black, French-speaking people. We want to connect with the other Creoles from Africa and the Caribbean. We host visiting journalists from those countries, and introduce them to our food and our Creole Zydeco music. We would like to assist in the development of tourism in Louisiana, bring in tourists from the Creole countries and from around the world.
>
> I want to emphasize that C.R.E.O.L.E., Inc., is not anti-Cajun. The Cajuns have plenty to be proud of, no question about it. If we were anti-Cajun, we would be denying some of our own identity, since we all speak French. We simply want to promote our culture along with that of the Cajuns. And the response to us from Cajuns is very positive, along the lines of "You should have done this long ago, to promote your particular corner of this bigger French culture." We also feel that the news media needs to recognize all segments of the community and realize that as black people we are not Cajuns, even though we do have a lot in common.[7]

John Broussard, host of KRVS radio program "Zydeco Est Pas Salé," welcomes audience members to the Creole Accordion Kings program at the Liberty theater in Eunice.

Although Creole musicians have always been a part of Lafayette's largest local event, as this poster illustrates, the name and programming of Festivals Acadiens emphasized Cajun culture for decades.

Although sometimes frustrated with the "Cajunification" of the area they also call home, many Creoles in Acadiana are beginning to see small changes that are long overdue in acknowledging their role in the region's heritage. For example, Lafayette's largest local cultural event Festivals Acadiens has featured Creole artists since its inception in the 1970s, but it just changed its name to Festivals Acadiens et Créoles in 2008.[8]

For over two decades, Vermilionville, one of Lafayette's primary tourist attractions, was branded as a "Cajun and Creole Heritage and Folklife Park." Although Vermilionville opened its doors to the public on April 1, 1990, and celebrated Acadian Culture Day annually, 2004 marked the first year that Vermilionville established a Creole Culture Day to recognize and celebrate the Creole contribution to the area.[9] Other places like the Jean Lafitte National Historical Park and Preserve unit in Lafayette[10] will undoubtedly take longer to change. Although exhibits inside the museum feature Creoles and park rangers often conduct programs that discuss elements of Creole culture, it would literally take an act of Congress to change the museum's name to something other than the "Acadian Cultural Center."[11]

As evidenced by the success of numerous attractions and venues that feature regional heritage, food, and music, cultural tourism plays a

This Creole Culture Day poster features Goldman Thibodeaux, the 2012 Richard J. Catalon Sr. Creole Heritage Award recipient.

The Lafayette Convention and Visitor Center markets the Hub City using the tagline "Genuine Cajun. Uniquely Creole."

major role in South Louisiana's economy. In order to help maintain that momentum, many individuals and organizations strive to promote the area. The primary catalyst for Lafayette's tourism industry is the Lafayette Convention and Visitors Commission (LCVC). The organization's first official logo promoted the city as "The Capital of French Louisiana," a label that included the region's entire French population, although the logo only featured the Acadian flag in the top left hand corner. Later on, LCVC labeled Lafayette "the Heart of Cajun Country," no doubt partly due to the parish's heart-like shape and partly due to its location in the center of Acadiana. It was not until sometime in the mid-1990s that LCVC's graphic artist Alicia Toups changed the tagline to "Genuine Cajun. Uniquely Creole" in a curvy font below the city's name.[12]

About that same time, LCVC cooperated with several surrounding parishes to develop a brochure known as the "Creole Country Guide" to serve as "A Guide to African-American and Creole Culture in South Louisiana."[13] The brochure's 2005 edition featured artwork by Dennis Paul Williams, a well-known Creole artist and musician from St. Martinville. The guide listed attractions and points of interest such as the Clifton Chenier Memorial Statue in Lafayette, the Creole Heritage and Folklife Center in Opelousas, and the African American Museum in St. Martinville. It also included churches and cemeteries like the Holy Ghost Catholic Church in Opelousas that boasts the largest Catholic congregation of blacks in the United States and St. Edward Catholic Church in New Iberia that was established in 1919 as the first black Catholic parish. The guide lists events that highlight the region's Creole heritage such as Creole Culture Day at Vermilionville, the Lebeau Zydeco Festival, Holy Ghost Creole Bazaar and Festival, Creole Zydeco Festival in St. Martinville, and Plaisance's Original Southwest Louisiana Zydeco Music Festival. Also included were dining options such as Vermilionville's La Cuisine de Maman, Josephine's Creole Restaurant, and the Creole Lunch House; Creole dance halls like El Sid O's Zydeco and Blues Club, the now-closed Slim's Y Ki-Ki, and Richard's Club (later known as Miller's Zydeco Hall of Fame before it burned down in 2017); and shopping venues such as record stores that sold Creole and Zydeco music.[14] Unfortunately, the guide is no longer available

As LCVC's Vice President of Media Relations and Special Projects Kelly Strenge explained, the guide was discontinued due to a number of reasons. One factor is simply that it is difficult to coordinate a project like that with so many other parishes. Businesses sometimes close while new ones open, making it a challenge to keep the information current. Additionally, most of the primary listings are already included in the regular tourism guide, so some consider printing a separate brochure an unnecessary expense.[15] Whether or not LCVC or other visitor centers are able or willing to create and distribute something comparable to the original "Creole Country Guide," it is significant to note that most of the major events and businesses listed in it are still actively promoting Creole culture.

Although no longer in print, this brochure once served as a reference material for those interested in exploring South Louisiana's Creole culture.

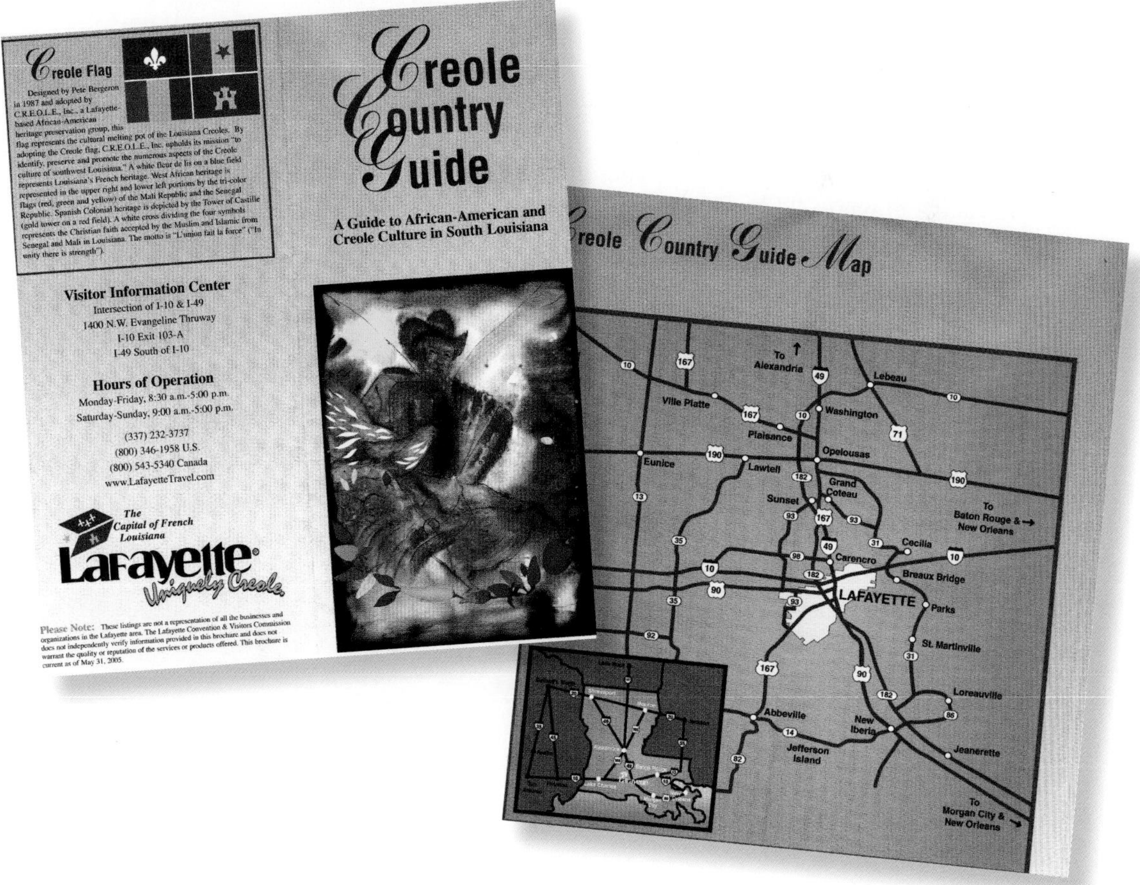

Creole Cuisine: Cookin' Up Something Good

Food is by far the most widely recognized cultural element of South Louisiana's Creole population, so it comes as no surprise that some of the area's main attractions are the numerous dining establishments that dot the prairie parishes. A testament to the popularity of Creole cuisine is the fact that a simple Google search for "Creole food" brings up nearly sixty million hits, which is more than a search for "Creole people" brings up and almost five times the number of hits resulting from a query for "Creole music."[16] Many people outside of Louisiana praise Creole cuisine, or at least what they have heard about it, but do not know much, if anything, about Creole people. Even fewer have heard of Creole music or danced to Zydeco. No doubt much of the outsider association with Creole food has to do with the city of New Orleans and its long history of serving visitors delectable delights. As we have seen in the chapter entitled "*Allons Manger!*: Cooking in Creole Country," however, good Creole food is not limited to New Orleans, and the prairies of South Louisiana boast a Creole cuisine distinctly different from its Crescent City counterpart. Regardless of where they live, however, Creoles throughout the Bayou State take food seriously, whether it be a steaming plate of crawfish étouffée served at a fine restaurant in town or a bowl of cornbread and milk at grandma's house.

Lafayette has garnered national attention through several culinary awards. For example, in 2012, Rand McNally Best of the Roads Rally selected the city to be home of the "Best Food in the USA." *Southern Living* named Lafayette "The Tastiest Town in the South" in its April 2012 issue.

Lafayette has received several accolades, including recognition for being the "Happiest City in America," as this banner welcoming travelers at the Lafayette Regional Airport indicates.

Magazine editors for *Southern Living* selected their tastiest towns based on the following criteria: food as a cultural identity, growth of a culinary-minded community, diverse cuisine at a variety of price points, local, sustainable food practices, hot chefs on the rise, and an abundance of buzz-worthy food events (i.e. festivals that celebrate food and drink).[17]

Despite its reputation as a great place to eat, Lafayette was not without its skeptics. One journalist from Texas did not believe that Lafayette could have possibly beaten larger cities around the country to earn such prestigious awards. As a result, she decided to travel to South Louisiana to make her own judgment. Although she visited several area restaurants, in an article she published about the experience, she wrote, "I was surprised to find some of the best food during my trip at La Cuisine de Maman, the unsuspecting café inside Lafayette's living history museum, Vermilionville. A plain old Sunday buffet was elevated by sweet cornbread, pork-fattened greens, livery spoonfuls of dirty rice, excellent fried chicken and a spicy cup of andouille sausage gumbo, the likes of which would be revered back home in Houston."[18]

La Cuisine de Maman serves up traditional fare to tourists and locals.

Vermilionville's menu is available in both English and French.

Vermilionville's La Cuisine de Maman ("Mama's Kitchen") caters to tourists, yet locals patronize it as well. Modeled after a Creole plantation overseer's house, La Cuisine de Maman offers daily plate lunches and weekend buffets that reproduce the same dishes typically eaten by Cajuns and Creoles at home. Linda Fontenot, the restaurant's former food and beverage coordinator, explained, "Tourists want to know 'What is an étouffée? What is a jambalaya?' Locals, on the other hand, come in and say, 'I remember my mom making this. Can you make this?'"[19] Veronica "Ronnie" Brown, a Lafayette native, has been responsible for making Vermilionville's gumbo for years. Although she left for a time, she said, "They called me back. I guess they like my gumbo." Mike Sam, also from Lafayette, said that he really enjoys being able to work "in a place that promotes our local culture."[20]

The front of La Cuisine de Maman's bilingual menu advertises it as a place "where taste meets tradition." The paragraph that follows that line illustrates the local emphasis on hospitality and authenticity:

> Be honest with me, honey. You're here because you're craving something authentic, right? And by the grace of good taste, you've found yourself at my kitchen. It may be small, but it's special. Because we put love into everything we make, and our cooking is an authentic experience in itself. Trust me, feeding loved ones is a family tradition for many of us here in Acadiana. So let us do what we do best. You just sit there and take it all in.[21]

For the convenience of tourists, part of the menu is dedicated to providing definitions for terms such as roux, *macque choux* (stewed corn), *boucherie,* and *lagniappe* (a little something extra); but locals enjoy the inviting atmosphere where they can gather with friends, family members, or co-workers for a home-style lunch in a glassed-in porch along the Vermilion River.

Since part of Vermilionville's mission statement is to "enlighten visitors and youth about the history and culture of Acadiana and to help ethnic groups of this area gain a better understanding and appreciation of their own cultures and those of others in this multi-ethnic region," it seems only natural that foodways would play a significant role in the site's interpretive programming. Although Vermilionville offered daily cooking demonstrations at scheduled times to visitors in the past, within the last few years, the museum has expanded to include a cooking school. For instance, one program, "From the Garden to the Table," teaches participants about life as it was when people relied more on their personal gardens.

Events like *boucheries* occur less frequently nowadays, so many people have lost that knowledge. Places like Vermilionville try to keep these traditions alive by hosting educational programs. For example, Vermilionville can not butcher a hog onsite; but, using meat purchased at a slaughterhouse, employees and volunteers can still demonstrate how to make sausage, boudin, and *gratons* (cracklins) the traditional way. Many elderly staff members grew up participating in *boucheries* with their families and neighbors and enjoy sharing their knowledge with visitors. [22]

Creoles in Lafayette and the surrounding areas certainly consider food to be a significant part of their cultural identity. Eric Cormier, a food columnist for the *American Press* newspaper in his hometown of Lake Charles, explained, "Well I'm legally, as the federal government says, I'm African American. In Louisiana culturally I fall under the umbrella of—of what they call Creole with a mix of French, Cajun, some Native American, African American, and Spanish. . . . Our family—kind of like all of Louisiana—especially South Louisiana, especially the area south of Interstate 10—is definitely a gumbo. We have a little bit of everything in us." [*Laughs*]

Boucheries involve butchering and cooking the slaughtered hog outdoors.

Cormier went on to explain that having family members from various Creole communities has influenced his cooking. He stated,

Food columnist Eric Cormier

> So when it comes to food, that's where my heritage really comes out, because I—we truly identify with smothering food and making gravies, experimenting with smoked meats, boudin, wild game, which is if you have—it's something that historically both blacks and whites in Louisiana have always loved whether it be rabbit or venison, wild—wild duck for gumbos and . . . So culturally I feel connected, and it's something that I like to define in this section of the state, whereas in New Orleans you have Creoles whose heritages [*sic*] is a little different than on this side of the state because—it hasn't been written down, but there's some folks here in this area who like to call ourselves Prairie Creoles because we come from areas like Lawtell and St. Martinville where folks were farming.

Cormier also related that much of what he learned was passed down to him informally by the men, not the women, in his family. Although many Creole cooks are women, a relatively little known aspect of South Louisiana's cooking culture is the fact that men cook. Not only do men cook, but they also cook well and take pride in their ability to do so. Cormier said,

> There's one thing that I think that's amazing and pretty cool is that men—and that's on both sides of the color spectrum, black or white—in most communities when it comes to cooking, you won't find a man who's going to run from the kitchen. And the ones who did, then their mama really was a dog-gone good cook; they had no reason to learn. [*Laughs*]. But every guy I know personally cooks—even guys I went to high school with and their dads and their grandfathers, and really and truly those recipes are passed down. And the thing is, it's not like it's written down. You pick up the recipe watching as a little kid. And it's amazing how much kids pick up when you're five years old and you're outside with the guys and they're passing around the whiskey bottle and drinking beer, joking, you know and playing the dozens—hanging out outside and the

Representatives of G&J Creole Foods man their booth at the Original Southwest Louisiana Zydeco Music Festival in Plaisance.

women are inside and—you'd just be amazed at how much you pick up and watch what these old guys do. And to me that's what's pretty cool, especially as a food writer. When I get a chance to go around some of the old-timers who are still alive, and they're at a festival and they're cooking, and just to sit there and watch them, and you feel a kinship with them because they're doing the same thing that you did and have learned. And it just—you just feel at home. And that's what makes writing about food, what makes watching these people even when I'm not worried about writing about food—you just feel this connection and it's—it's basic, and it's not macho at all. It's just guys who want to have good times and love cooking. And that's—I love that.[23]

Men cooking *gratons* (cracklins) at the Plaisance festival.

Many Creole men do not take lightly the responsibility of passing on the skills and knowledge acquired through their own life experiences. Joann Delafose related a poignant story about her father who had taught all of his children how to butcher a hog—all of them except for the youngest son who had gone into the Army at an early age. When Joann's brother came home from the military, her father said he wanted to make sure he knew how to kill and cut up a hog. The old man was not feeling well, but the family did not realize how serious it was at the time. He slept in his bed on a Friday night, and the next morning his son came to the house. After Joann's brother butchered the hog, he went indoors where his father was resting on the couch and told his dad he had finished the job. Her father asked, "Son, you sure you're the one who butchered that hog and cut it up?" His son said, "Yeah, I did it. You can come and look at it."

Joann explained that in those days, they hung the pig from the fence where it could be drained and rinsed off. Then it was cut up with a saw or a knife, not at a slaughterhouse. After her father went outside to the fence and saw the hog hanging there, he came back inside the house and told his son, "Good job." Some friends stopped in for a brief visit and after they left, the old man said, "Well, I'm going back to bed." Shortly after lying down he suffered a massive heart attack. His family, the priest, everyone was trying to save him; but when the ambulance arrived, he was already gone. Joann explained that it

Regional dishes like crawfish etouffée typically accompany events such as the Creole Renaissance Festival in Opelousas.

Though not fancy, makeshift kitchens like this one at the Catfish Festival in Washington offer some of the best local food available.

was as if her father could not breathe his last until he had taught each one of his sons how to butcher a hog the traditional way.[24]

As Eric Cormier mentioned, festivals are one of the primary places where Creoles, and especially male Creoles, demonstrate their cooking prowess and celebrate their rich culinary heritage in a public setting today. South Louisiana's music festival calendar is full year-round; and while the bands might draw crowds initially, dancers work up healthy appetites and expect good food to sustain them for hours of virtually uninterrupted dancing. Therefore, food plays an integral role in the success of Louisiana's festival scene. In addition to food vendors, many of these music-driven events also feature cook-offs that relate to the festival's theme.

The Catfish Festival, for instance, takes place every March in Washington, a small town in St. Landry Parish. Similar to festivals in other rural communities throughout South Louisiana, local cooks and churches often set up makeshift outdoor kitchens for the weekend in order to feed festival-goers. On the last day of the festival, a catfish cook-off generates friendly competition among local contestants. Also in St. Landry Parish, the one-day Lebeau Zydeco Festival takes place on the grounds of the Immaculate Conception

Hungry festival attendees line up to enjoy tasty meals prepared by local restaurants during Festivals Acadiens et Créoles.

Catholic Church on the first Saturday of July each year. In addition to cracklins, boudin, and other local favorites, this festival is known for its pork backbone dinners.[25] Naturally, St. Martinville's Okra Festival features okra dishes in its annual cook-off.[26]

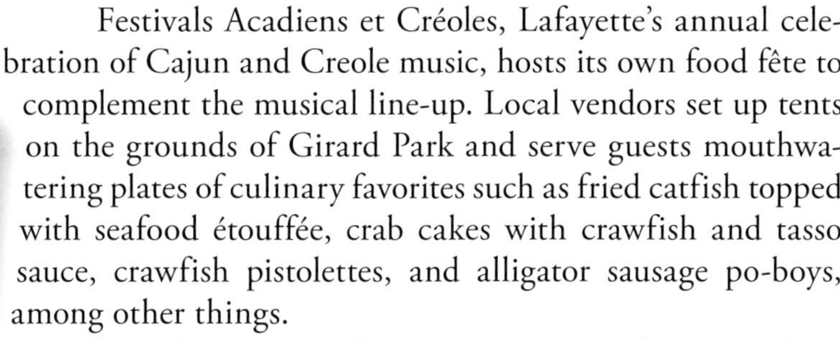

Festivals Acadiens et Créoles, Lafayette's annual celebration of Cajun and Creole music, hosts its own food fête to complement the musical line-up. Local vendors set up tents on the grounds of Girard Park and serve guests mouthwatering plates of culinary favorites such as fried catfish topped with seafood étouffée, crab cakes with crawfish and tasso sauce, crawfish pistolettes, and alligator sausage po-boys, among other things.

Festival organizers designate one particular tent to host forty-five minute cooking demonstrations in a program called *Culture sur la Table* ("Culture on the Table"). Chefs from area restaurants or representatives from local companies that sell products such as spice blends offer cooking classes or workshops to festival attendees. For example, in 2012, one of the cooking programs featured Tony Chachere's Original Creole Seasoning

Corporate chefs representing Tony Chachere's demonstrate how to make duck and andouille sausage gumbo under the "Culture Sur la Table" tent at Festivals Acadiens et Créoles.

blend, perhaps the most widely distributed food product in the world that carries a Creole label. The signature green containers can be found on most kitchen and restaurant tables throughout South Louisiana and the product line continues to expand as its consumer market grows.[27]

Whether someone learns to cook Creole food by observing his uncles outdoors, following instructions in a recipe book, or sitting in on workshops offered by cooks at festivals or heritage sites, judging by the popularity of South Louisiana's regional cuisine, traditional Creole dishes are far from being an endangered species. Although modern conveniences and urban lifestyles will no doubt continue to influence South Louisiana's culinary repertoire, Creoles know what good food is. The restaurant business continues to thrive as visitors flock to the area in order to get a taste for why locals wish to stay close to home. Nothing exhibits Southern hospitality better than a fine feast; and Creoles appreciate the art of dining, not just the necessity of it. Whether cooking up rice and gravy for dinner at home, hosting a crawfish boil for out-of-town guests, or competing in a festival cook-off, Creoles pride themselves on being able to produce and consume some of the best food in the world. As they like to say, "*Mais, ça c'est bon!*" ["Now that's good!"]

Creole French: Let's Talk About It

Creole food may be in no imminent danger of going extinct, but the Creole language has been slowly disappearing as fewer and fewer Creole French speakers are alive to continue the tradition. Although heard throughout South Louisiana for over three hundred years, Creole French is now only spoken in specific geographic locations by a relatively small number of individuals. In fact, many of the people who grew up speaking Creole face a challenge of finding others who are able to do the same. Even though immersion schools throughout Louisiana now offer local children the opportunity to become fluent in French, the type of International French these children are learning is not the Cajun and Creole French their grandparents speak but rather International French as spoken by their instructors who may be from Europe, Africa, Canada, or the Caribbean islands. South Louisiana may be known for its French heritage and culture, but the reality is that the struggle to maintain Creole French in spite of Anglo-American and even outside International French influences is far from over. Yet despite these challenges, several Creoles have clung tenaciously to their first language while simultaneously garnering

Children learn about their heritage by engaging in projects like recreating the Creole flag.

Street signs throughout South Louisiana bear French names like these found in downtown Lafayette, while interstate travelers crossing the state line are welcomed in French.

respect and attention from the academic world in literary and linguistic circles. By doing this, these individuals have made significant strides towards preserving the language of their ancestors for years to come.

For instance, Mary Alice Drake, a retired school teacher from Lafayette who taught French for thirty-three years, grew up speaking Creole French with her grandmother, aunts, and uncles. Raised primarily by her grandmother, Drake was an only child who rarely had the opportunity to play with other children. As a result, she often hid and listened in on her family's adult conversations. When she got older and began attending classes at the University of Louisiana at Lafayette (then known as the University of Southwestern Louisiana), the Creole French she spoke was subject to harsh criticism from her non-native instructors. One of her teachers, a Bostonian, told the white students, "If you speak Cajun French, forget that" and told the black students, "If you speak Creole French, forget that, too." Another instructor from Chicago told Drake and the other students in his class, "Blacks don't know

Educators Herbert Wiltz and Mary Alice Drake grew up speaking Creole French and promoted multilingualism in their classrooms for years.

how to speak French." Undeterred, Drake made good grades and eventually traveled to Angers, France; Quebec, Canada; and the island country of Guadeloupe to study French through various summer study abroad programs.

When Drake entered the workforce as an elementary teacher after completing her studies, she deliberately mixed Cajun and Creole French with Parisian French in order to enable her students to leave the classroom and be able to communicate with their grandparents at home. She did not want her students' grandparents thinking she did not know what she was doing in the classroom if what she taught the children was too different from the French they spoke at home.[28]

Like Mary Alice Drake, Herbert Wiltz is another retired French teacher who grew up speaking Creole French with his sharecropping grandparents. Wiltz was also an only child who spent much of his time listening to and talking with his grandparents and other family members in the Parks and Breaux Bridge areas of St. Martin Parish. After his graduation from Holy Rosary Institute, the nuns there helped Wiltz get a university scholarship in foreign languages. He completed his studies in French and Spanish, then returned to Holy Rosary where he taught for thirteen years. Although he initially taught

Spanish, he went back to teaching French and traveled with his students to Quebec every other year after that. He did not realize until later that language studies would take him to so many different places. "I guess language has become my life," he stated.[29]

Wiltz explained that many people over the years have looked down upon Creole speakers. He said, "We were considered ignorant. We were just slaves, you know, and those of us who went to school were just fortunate."[30] Drake agreed, explaining that early Creole speakers were far from ignorant. In fact, many of them were tri-lingual. She elaborated, "In those days, you had different types. The house woman [enslaved woman of African descent] spoke French with the white mistress and then she spoke another French with the slaves. . . . And the woman of the house [the white mistress] told everything to the slave woman so she learned perfect French. In other words . . . she spoke three languages: she had African, she had her [Creole] dialect from that area, and she had Parisian French."[31] Today, people like Drake and Wiltz not only speak Creole French, International French, Spanish, and English, but can teach in those languages as well. They are far from ignorant and strongly believe that Louisiana Creole should be recognized as a language in its own right.

Holy Rosary School

A rare exception to the *plaçage* system, Henriette DeLille was a free woman of color from New Orleans who was born in 1812 but refused to become a white man's concubine. She founded the Sisters of the Holy Family in 1842 to nurse the sick, care for the poor, and instruct the ignorant, whether they were slave or free, child or adult. On July 9, 1913, Father Keller purchased some land to establish the Holy Rosary Institute in Lafayette. In September 1913, the Institute opened as an industrial school for black females, but it became co-ed three decades later. Holy Rosary was staffed primarily by the Sisters of the Holy Family and the Priest and Brothers of the Divine Word. Serving commuter and boarding students from around the world, it was considered to be one of the best college preparatory schools in the country until it closed its doors in 1993.

As Wiltz pointed out, Louisiana Creole developed as a result of the need for Africans in the New World to be able to communicate with each other in spite of their various languages and dialects. He said, "Throughout studies and in conversations between members of C.R.E.O.L.E., Inc., we truly believe that a lot of the languages—if you want to, call them *patois*—but we call them languages because they are a way of communicating—came from Africa, mainly from Senegal and Mali and that area. The coastal areas of Africa. And that is the base of the [Louisiana Creole] language, with influences from French, Spanish, and of the Indians particular to that area. Because in Guadeloupe and Martinique, the Creole there is quite different. Haitian Creole and Louisiana Creole, and Creoles in other areas [speak different Creole]."

Wiltz expressed his concern that unless Louisiana Creoles use their language and speak it regularly, it will be lost forever. He hopes that does not happen and is trying to preserve it. In fact, he said, "I started something when I started working in the public school—to write what I heard and what I could remember from what people said in the Breaux Bridge area, what people said and what they did in conversations. So I have some lessons. I've never published them, but I have some lessons." He went on to state, "And a lot of expressions that we use, I try to put in conversation." He even tried to develop a system for people who study grammar to put the language into context since Creole verbs are not typically conjugated. When he acquired a Haitian Creole dictionary and realized that their vocabulary and pronunciation was similar to the Creole he grew up with in St. Martin Parish, he used that as a basis for writing his own lessons.[32]

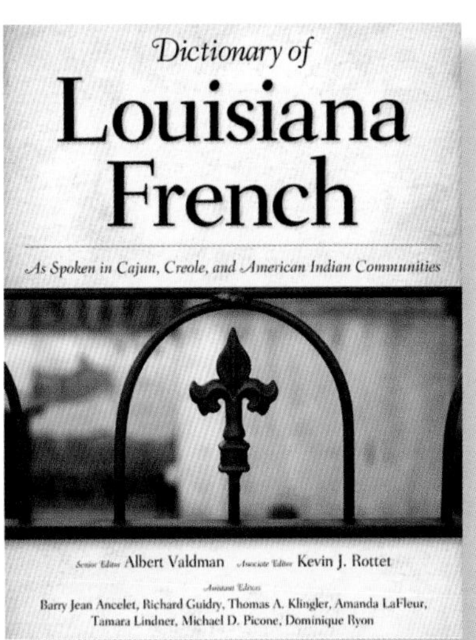

This dictionary consisting of over 900 pages is the most comprehensive collection of Louisiana French terms and expressions in existence.

Although Wiltz has not yet published his findings, several linguists and Louisiana scholars collaborated on a major project, the *Dictionary of Louisiana French: As Spoken in Cajun, Creole, and American Indian Communities* (2010). This dictionary not only provides words and definitions, but also includes illustrative examples of terms and phrases within context. Entries are labeled according to regions of usage as well. Overall, this volume is perhaps the most significant work documenting Louisiana French in existence.[33]

Unlike the days when Drake experienced negative attitudes from language instructors who belittled her Creole French and encouraged her to forget it, the Col-

La Maison Française welcomes students at the University of Louisiana at Lafayette.

lege of Liberal Arts at the University of Louisiana at Lafayette now offers an interdisciplinary minor in Cajun and Creole studies. Departments such as anthropology, architecture, geography, and history offer courses that feature Louisiana-specific topics. The English department offers Louisiana folklore and fieldwork classes. The music department has gotten on board with its Traditional Music major, which includes "Cajun and Zydeco Music" and "Creole and Black Music in Louisiana" classes. Even the Department of Modern Languages now offers courses such as "Cajun French" and "Louisiana Creole French" and hires native speakers to teach those classes.[34]

Although Creole French is now becoming more recognized and accepted as a legitimate language within the academic world, as Creole author Sybil Kein noted, "Thus far in the twentieth century, the Creole language has been with few exceptions a device to create and fortify negative stereotypes and racist thinking." As Kein states, it was not until Anne Rice published her novel *The Feast of All Saint's Day* in 1979[35] "that both the term and the people were restored to that degree of dignity demonstrated in [George Washington] Cable's nineteenth-century work [*The Grandissimes*]."[36]

Following closely on the heels of Rice's work, three Louisiana native Creole speakers published original literature that featured Creole French. In 1980,

Deborah Clifton, currently an adjunct faculty member at UL Lafayette who teaches the Louisiana Creole French course, published several poems in a collection entitled *Cris sur le bayou: naissance d'une poésie acadienne en Louisiane* (*Cries on the Bayou: Birth of Acadian Poetry in Louisiana*). In some poems, such as "Blackie Frugé," she blends Creole and English to give readers a sense of the bilingual culture of present-day Louisiana.[37] In her poem "Voyageur" she addresses the complexity of what it means to be Creole:

Mo connais premier fois-à yé pelé mo creole
Yé dit pas parler ça
C'est di villain moyèr
Yé rete tout quichoge, tout ça m'olé fait . . .
Yé ca massacre tout.

I remember the first time I was called Creole
They said, 'don't talk that.
It's an ugly way to speak.'
They blocked everything, all that I wanted to do . . .
Some people can destroy anything.[38]

As Dianne Guenin-Lelle, a French faculty member at Albion College, explains, "Until the publication of *Cris sur le bayou*, the literature of Cajuns and Creoles of Acadiana was primarily oral, consisting of songs, ballads, tales, stories, legends and jokes." Having a volume written and published in Louisiana French was an important means for demonstrating to the outside world that Louisiana Creole is indeed a language that merits literary attention. Folklorist Barry Ancelet contributed to the work and edited the volume. He stated,

> *Une littérature écrite semble tellement évidente pour une culture, mais il faut se rappeler que la grande majorité des franco-louisianais n'ont jamais eu l'occasion d'avoir une education en français. Leur langue maternelle orale, c'est bien le français, mais leur langue maternelle écrite, c'est l'anglais.*
>
> Written literature provides evidence for a culture, but it is important to remember that the large majority of French-speaking Louisianians never had the opportunity to receive an education in French. Their oral mother tongue is French, of course, but their written mother tongue is English.[39]

Herbert Wiltz lamented, "Creole was never a written language. It has always been a spoken language, and I think that's where we've lost a lot. Because there's no way of documenting all of it."[40] However, as more French Creole speakers find ways of expressing themselves on paper, more of the language will be documented and preserved for the future in written form. Children in French immersion programs who are completely literate and fluent in the language will undoubtedly be able to use these texts to help them reconstruct and relearn their grandparents' language even after the older generation has passed away.

Ulysses S. Ricard Jr., another Creole poet and educator, studied French in Paris and Spanish in Madrid. While a graduate student at Louisiana State University, he taught Spanish as well as the first course on Cajun French ever offered at the university level in the state. Having no prior publications to work with, he wrote the course textbook himself and included a chapter on Louisiana Creole. Before his death in 1993, he was compiling a dictionary of the Creole language. He served in several capacities to promote Creole culture, whether it was through presenting papers on Creole French, publishing *Souvenirs* (1980), a Creole newsletter, or acting as a consultant and assistant archivist for the Amistad Research Center in New Orleans.[41]

In 1981, Ricard also edited and oversaw the publication of the first anthology of poetry written in Creole French by a Louisiana Creole, Sybil Kein's *Gombo People.* As Kein explained, she wrote and published *Gombo People* as "an attempt to reclaim the full dignity of the Creole language and people. The poems seek to show the humanity of the Creole and claim a place for his language use."[42] Fifteen years later, she published another collection of poems entitled *An American South.* She wrote some poems in English with Creole words and phrases sprinkled in, but other poems are entirely in Creole with English translations as in the following poem "La Lumière."

Quand la lune est au visage plein,
Mo va posé un poème
sur so sein
De sorte que
Quand la lune té parti
To sera capable souffler mes paroles
Et connais que mo té là.

When the moon is full
I will place a poem
On your bosom
So that
When the moon is gone
You will breathe my words
And know that I was there.[43]

As Kein so eloquently demonstrates, Creole French is not a corruption of "proper" French comprised of poor grammatical structure, misused verbs, and other linguistic atrocities, but rather a beautiful language capable of expressing emotion and worthy of attention in its own right.

In his 1997 article on Louisiana French, Michael D. Picone commented on the current state of French in the Bayou State. He predicted a grim future that "is not promising, even though the Francophone population there far exceeds the population of all the other enclave dialects combined [such as Isleño Spanish and several American Indian languages like Coushatta and Jena Choctaw]." He went on to say,

> In all but a small minority of cases, French is no longer being transmitted to offspring at home. Furthermore, French is getting only minimal use in churches. Nor is its use prevalent in the workplace or in institutions, except for those serving Francophone tourists and the elderly. In the realm of education, some students are getting exposure to Louisiana French in public schools and universities, but, by and large, French instruction in Louisiana, though widespread, does not deviate from the standardized book-version found elsewhere. This is also true of excellent immersion programs being run in some elementary schools. These are producing a new cadre of young French speakers, but they are not speaking a dialect that is authentic to the region . . . French is getting only minimal air play on television, though it is faring much better on the radio. Only a small percentage of Francophones in Louisiana are actively literate in French, and there exists no widely distributed form of journalism to serve even this small minority.[44]

Despite the steady decline of regional French usage throughout Louisiana, not all is doom and gloom. As Picone pointed out, there is still hope for the future as more interest in preserving the language is coupled with a less negative connotation associated with speaking it. He explained:

> Nevertheless, the fact that use of regional French is on the rise in the communicative arts is a significant development. It is reflective of a new sense of pride among Louisiana Francophones in general. . . . This destigmatization is important and has manifested itself in various ways, including, in a small percentage of cases, a renewed commitment to transmission of regional French to children. Even some young adults are motivated to learn French from fellow workers or spouses. For these reasons the contraction of French in South Louisiana will not be as rapid or as complete as the most pessimistic assessments indicate.[45]

While many may lament the loss of Creole French in Louisiana, Kein, like Picone, is also optimistic about the future. Previously, Creole was almost

French Immersion programs in schools throughout Louisiana stimulate young minds by hiring native French speakers from around the world to teach various courses in French.

exclusively a spoken language. Therefore, knowledge was passed down from generation to generation in what evolved into a rich oral tradition. Although most Creoles lacked opportunities to become literate in French in the school systems in the early twentieth century, some Creoles have overcome that barrier by learning international forms of French at the university level while not forgetting their Creole French roots. Educators and linguists such as Herbert Wiltz, Mary Alice Drake, Deborah J. Clifton, Ulysses S. Ricard Jr., and Sybil Kein all demonstrate that it is not only possible, but also intellectually stimulating to be able to take the language of their ancestors that so many have denigrated over the years and weave it into their everyday lives and careers in such a way as to garner attention and respect from the academic world.[46]

Perhaps Sybil Kein summarized it best when she stated,

> Until the 1980s, the use and portrayal of Creole in literature was chameleonic at best. Now, as we begin the next century, it seems that this language—the only "foreign" language to be developed in the United States—is, at last, in the hands of capable Creole writers. The tongue once used to degrade and dismiss a people now shows evidence of a rebirth. From almost two hundred years of abuse in literature and *malgré* [despite] the concerted efforts of those who would crush it and its people, Louisiana Creole appears to be on the threshold of acceptance as a unique contribution from the Louisiana Francophone culture and a creative tool worthy of serious literature and serious scholarship.[47]

Creole Music: Play Me Some Zydeco

While few would consider musicians to be linguists, they, perhaps more than any other entity, are keeping Creole French alive in the public eye. For many young English-speaking Creoles, the only way for them to hear regional French is through the music they dance to at local dance halls and festivals. Deborah Clifton commented, "If it weren't for the musicians and for Zarico [Zydeco], there'd be no Creole culture left. Maybe I'm exaggerating things, but I think musicians, the role that the traditional musician plays, is of preserving our identity and keeping people together. They express true cultural values and help preserve the language."[48]

Since musical performances are by nature public events, perhaps the most obvious transmission of Creole culture from one generation to the next takes place on stage. For example, festival attendees and dance hall patrons frequently witness the convergence of multiple generations on stage as children squeeze accordions and rub spoons against metal *frottoirs* alongside their older family members. Despite the fact that many younger Creole artists sing in English, there is still a French sensibility in their music when shouts of common phrases like "*Eh, toi*!" ("Hey, you!") punctuate their performances. Whether gathered together in family living rooms, in local dance halls, or on festival stages overseas, Creole musicians take pride in their heritage and the music that stems from these deep roots.

Several generations of Frank family members perform together at Festivals Acadiens et Créoles.

Goldman Thibodeaux shares a moment with Guyland Leday on stage.

Most Creole and Zydeco artists developed an interest in the music because they grew up with it. Many of them had family members who played regularly, either at home or on the road. One young artist, Guyland Leday, is particularly gifted. He began playing the accordion at the age of three. Explaining his musical start, Leday shared, "I saw a picture of my great-grandfather playing accordion, and then he came to me in a dream. He taught me how to play." Before he turned eleven, Guyland had already performed at Carnegie Hall, been featured on a national Oscar Mayer commercial, and made guest appearances on *Oprah* and *The Ellen Show*.[49]

Goldman Thibodeaux, one of the most ardent defenders of the old Creole style of music known as La La, joined Leday for an interview leading up to Plaisance's Zydeco Festival in 2009. When Leday told the reporter, "I want other people to learn about Zydeco music. I want to bring this music to the world," Goldman inserted and said, "It makes me so happy to hear you say these things, because you're our future. I love how you love your music."[50]

Unlike the days of house dances that Goldman recalls, Leday is growing up in a world where dance halls and music festivals provide a stage for his accordion-driven music. Still, the significance of music within the local culture cannot be underestimated. Members of the older generation like Goldman can rest assured that music will continue to play an important role in future efforts to preserve Creole culture. Styles might change as younger musicians reflect the influences from their generation, but the essential elements and instrumentation will likely remain the same. Friends may no longer gather at house dances, but they still meet up and crowd the hardwood dance floors that dot the prairies of Acadiana. Ben Sandmel describes the current music scene in his book *Zydeco!*:

> On Saturday nights in southwest Louisiana, a weekly ritual unfolds in the bars and clubs along the "crawfish circuit." Working men and women exchange their work clothes for plumed Stetsons and fancy dresses, and converge on rural roadhouses to dance to Zydeco. Like the rough-and-tumble juke joints of the Mississippi Delta, few of these clubs maintain a slick appearance. Driving by in the daytime, one could easily assume that they closed down years ago and have languished in ramshackle neglect, their rutted and unpaved parking lots giving way to cane fields and pastures.
>
> Come Saturday night those lots fill quickly, however, and many patrons must park a half-mile down the highway. It's well worth the walk for the rollicking scene that awaits inside. Against a backdrop of low ceilings, plain plank floors, and year-round Christmas lights, the mood rises to fever pitch as Zydeco bands play marathon four-hour sets. These groups are led by an accordionist, who is apt to incite the crowd by playing on his

Dancers crowd the wooden floor at the Feed & Seed dance hall in Lafayette.

Hamilton's Place in Lafayette used to host Zydeco legends, but remains a relic after closing its doors in 2005.

> knees, behind the back, or even on the floor, limbo-style—a move which inspires shouts of "*fais 'tention!*" ("watch out, now!") and "go ahead on!" Then the accordionist "breaks it down," playing a frenzied double-time solo accompanied only by the drums and a "rubboard." Tireless couples dance on to sweaty euphoria, because Zydeco rivals oil as Louisiana's most potent source of energy.[51]

Local dance halls serve as more than just a place for people to experience Zydeco music played by old masters or up-and-coming artists. Oftentimes, these unassuming buildings are places where communities come together and individuals forge friendships that last a lifetime. One of Lafayette's best known Creole clubs opened in the mid-1950s just on the outskirts of town. Established during the Jim Crow era, Hamilton's Place served as an important location for Creoles to gather. William Hamilton recalls that when his father opened the place, "a lot of people then didn't have no way to go to town, and they had no place to go to have fun, to drink a beer, or two. So Daddy said, 'Let me open a little place for age-able people to drink beer and for the teenagers.'"[52]

For forty years, William Hamilton ran the place where Zydeco greats like Clifton Chenier, Boozoo Chavis, John Delafose, and Geno Delafose mesmerized dancers who pounded the hardwood floors and two-stepped beneath low ceilings. In 1982, Hamilton integrated his club with a weekly Wednesday event that became known as "White Night." From that point forward, blacks and whites came together on the dance floor and continued to do so for over two decades. The year 2005 marked the end of an era, however, when Hamilton was forced to close the historic dance hall's doors after undergoing an open heart surgery.[53]

Low ceilings and naked light bulbs did not deter dancers from filling up Slim's Y-Ki-Ki in Opelousas for sixty-nine years before it shut down in 2015.

John Broussard, in addition to his involvement with C.R.E.O.L.E., Inc., co-hosts a Saturday morning radio program on the University of Louisiana at Lafayette's station KRVS 88.7 aptly called "*Zydeco Est Pas Salé*." In between a playlist that includes old and new Zydeco tunes, as well as community announcements regarding trail rides, dances, and other events, Broussard frequently refers to Hamilton's Place. He grew up close enough to hear the music emanating from the dance hall and explained that the club was not just a bar. "People used to sit outside of it around a tree and listen to music and cook in a black pot, maybe make a cowboy stew. It was a time when people could gather and find enjoyment in that gathering," he recalled. Commenting on the closure of Hamilton's Place, he added, "We're going to lose that. We're going to miss that place. I don't think you can ever replace it."[54]

Although there was some informal discussion regarding trying to preserve the dance hall by moving it to a place like Vermilionville, folklorist Barry Ancelet opposed the idea, saying "if they move it to Vermilionville, all they're going to be doing is moving the building. They're not going to be moving what happened there. There was so much more than cultural stuff that happened there. You met people. You reinforced community ties. You exchanged news. You kept up with who's who and who's where. That's what's lost, too. We live increasingly in this thing that we call cyberspace. We stay in touch on the telephone, e-mails, instant messaging, and all that stuff. Our social interaction just doesn't happen the same way anymore, and no amount of wishing it did would make it come back." He went on to add, "Don't get me wrong. We all lament the passing of what we feel like was an important tradition. But we have to be careful not to confuse a romantic desire to preserve what we had in the past."[55]

Like Hamilton's Place, the Offshore Lounge in Lawtell served as another popular place for locals to gather. Following the death of its owner Roy Carrier in 2010, however, it also shut down. Carrier was a Zydeco musician and offshore worker who purchased the building in 1980 and opened it up for jam sessions. Many artists, including Geno Delafose, launched their careers in the rickety building where once upon a time dancers and music lovers could pay as little as two dollars for six bands in a row. Although Roy is gone now, he passed on his love of Zydeco music to his children long before he went.[56] His son Chubby Carrier and the Bayou Swamp Band earned the Best Zydeco or Cajun Music Album Grammy Award in 2011.[57]

Chubby Carrier playing accordion in his father's club before the Offshore Lounge closed in 2010.

Another son, Troy, also travels nationally as Dikki Du and the Zydeco Krewe. He recalled that three weeks before Roy passed away, his father told him, "Hey boy. Y'all better not sell my club." Troy said, "I told him, 'Daddy, why you talking like that?' But that's what my dad loved and he worked so hard offshore for it. He would hate to see the place go. I've been keeping his dream alive and keeping the club there. The dream now is to have the grand (re-opening) on a Thursday night [in 2013]. That's how it should be." To that end, Troy organized a three-day music tribute to his father with proceeds from the twenty dollar admission fee going towards renovation efforts. More than ten bands, including the Creole Zydeco Farmers and Jeffery Broussard and the Creole Cowboys, filled out the lineup that started on a Friday afternoon and concluded Sunday night, January 1, 2013. Organizers sold gumbo, fried chicken, red beans and rice, as well as barbecue every day.[58]

Just like Geno Delafose and Jeffery Broussard, Troy Carrier feels that he needs to maintain the original sounds of Zydeco he grew up hearing. "I'm following my daddy's tradition," Troy explained. "Plus, I'm trying to stick with the old-school stuff. I don't need the hip-hop Zydeco. I've got nothing against them. But my dad never did and I totally believe in the traditional Zydeco music. That's where I'm from, and that's what I'm doing."[59]

Although dance halls like Hamilton's Place, Slim's Y-Ki-Ki, and the Offshore Lounge have closed their doors, a few venues are still hanging

Open since 1985, El Sid O's Zydeco and Blues Club in Lafayette remains one of the last Zydeco dance halls still standing.

Lil' Nate and the Zydeco Big Timers performing at Café des Amis in Breaux Bridge.

on. For example, El Sid O's Zydeco and Blues Club on the opposite side of Lafayette from Hamilton's Place still draws crowds for artists like Keith Frank, Nathan "Lil' Nate" Williams Jr., and Chris Ardoin who emerged from deep family musical traditions, but who have forged their own identities while reflecting the influences of their generation.[60]

In recent decades, rap and hip-hop have influenced young Zydeco musicians who grew up in urban environments where English was the dominant language. Often criticized by purists for their English lyrics and, in the words of Ben Sandmel, "typically low standards of musical craft," many young Zydeco artists are nonetheless extremely popular.[61] Just as musicians of their parents' and grandparents' generation saw no problem incorporating soul, blues, and R&B into their traditional music, these young artists feel that infusing hip-hop into their Zydeco is a way of keeping the tradition alive while connecting with younger audiences.

Regardless of the style of Zydeco they play or the primary language they sing in, the Creole music world is thriving both at home and abroad. Whereas dance halls serve primarily local communities and area visitors, festival stages provide artists with the opportunity to share their music with wider audiences. Lafayette's Festival International de Louisiane and Festivals Acadiens et Créoles are two major events that attract hundreds of thousands of visitors to the area from all over the world annually.

Over 300,000 festival-goers flood downtown Lafayette annually to enjoy Festival International de Louisiane, the largest international music festival in the nation.

Every April, enormous crowds descend upon downtown Lafayette for a five-day music event in which multiple stages feature a variety of artists from around the globe. Festival International de Louisiane is the largest free Francophone-centered music festival in North America, and in 2012, the About.com World Music Reader's Choice Awards selected this event as the "Best World Music Festival," outvoting other global festivals such as Festival au Desert in Mali and Washington, D.C.'s Smithsonian Folklife Festival.[62] Focusing on connections between French-speaking Louisiana and the rest of the francophone world, this festival boasts a lineup of international stars alongside local Creole favorites like Cedric Watson and Bijou Créole and Keith Frank and the Soileau Zydeco Band.

Vendors and craftsmen from around the world sell their wares to Festival International attendees.

Budding musicians are encouraged to continue family traditions at Festivals Acadiens et Créoles.

Festivals Acadiens et Créoles is the world's largest Cajun and Creole music festival.[63] Boasting a lineup of over fifty Cajun and Zydeco bands spread over multiple days, this annual October fête showcases the region's rich musical heritage on a scale unmatched by other festivals in the area. Several stages scattered throughout Lafayette's Girard Park feature local musicians who play Cajun and Creole tunes. Many artists speak and sing only in Louisiana French on stage, proud to be able to publicly celebrate their Cajun or Creole heritage for a home crowd and for the thousands of visitors who come in from out of state.

Festivals Acadiens et Créoles, the world's largest Cajun and Creole music festival, has brought thousands of people together in Lafayette for more than forty years. These dancers are enjoying the sounds of Lil' Wayne and Same Ol' Two-Step.

Josephine "Jo" Charles.

Zydeco dance instructor Josephine "Jo" Charles said that being able to celebrate Creole culture in public "helps to keep it alive." She explained, "Festivals are a new expression of the culture. Before the festivals, it was grandma's house, you know, and families and friends would get together in one place and do their own thing. But now [through festivals] you're exposed to many, many different cultures and it's a melting pot." She added that it is an important way of getting the next generation involved. "If we don't expose it [our culture] to the young kids, it's gonna die down and they're not gonna know, you know, how important family was back in the Creole beginning and how important it is to keep families together. And that was one of the main things about the Creole culture—the way they kept families together." When asked if she thought festivals are serving that same purpose today, she said, "Absolutely! It's a family endeavor when everybody comes out. It's a place where you can come and take your family and expose them to the food, to the music, and that type of thing."[64]

Smaller in scale than Festivals Acadiens et Créoles, but perhaps more important to the Creole community specifically, is the Original Southwest Louisiana Zydeco Festival held every fall. Three decades ago, the festival began with a flatbed truck that had been transformed into a stage and parked in the middle of a field in the community of Plaisance located just north of Opelousas. Lena Charles, the Zydeco Festival director, stated, "The original

A large sign on the highway promotes Plaisance's annual Zydeco festival.

mission of the Zydeco Festival was to revive the [Creole] culture through the music. It's a proud culture, and in the time the festival has been around, we think it's been successful in its original mission."[65] Festival organizers take their role as cultural preservationists seriously. As Charles explained, "We see our mission now as preserving the old culture as the new generation comes in. Being the keeper of the old stories, making sure the new generation knows and preserves the old." She added, "We want to embrace the new generation and remember the original music as well. That's what our festival is all about."[66]

In addition to celebrating the area's musical heritage, the festival also offers opportunities to enjoy local foodways as various businesses and non-profit organizations set up temporary kitchens and sell Creole dishes such as jambalaya, red beans and rice, boudin, hog cracklins, sweet potato pies, and pralines to festival attendees.[67] On the Heritage Stage, participants offer workshops on topics like old-fashioned Creole storytelling methods, the evolution of Zydeco music and various styles of dancing, French Creole Juré traditions, and other related subjects.[68]

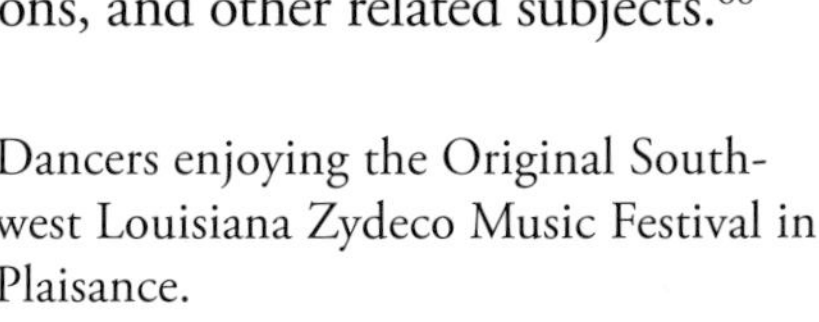

Dancers enjoying the Original Southwest Louisiana Zydeco Music Festival in Plaisance.

THE GRAMMY
Best Zydeco or Cajun Music Album

Efforts began in 2001 to recognize Cajun and Zydeco Music with its own Grammy category. Although the category was short-lived, those efforts paid off when the honor was awarded during the 50th, 51st, 52nd, and 53rd Annual Grammy Awards to "honor artistic achievement, technical proficiency, and overall excellence in the recording industry, without regard to album sales or chart position." In 2012 the Academy eliminated the award category but made Zydeco and Cajun recordings eligible for Best Regional Roots Music Album alongside other traditional American music styles such as Hawaiian, American Indian, and Polka.

Chubby Carrier

2008: *Live! Worldwide* by Terrence Simien and the Zydeco Experience
2009: *Live at the 2008 New Orleans Jazz and Heritage Festival* by Beausoleil avec Michael Doucet
2010: *Lay Your Burden Down* by Buckwheat Zydeco
2011: *Zydeco Junkie* by Chubby Carrier and the Bayou Swamp Band

To recognize how far Zydeco music has come within the last several decades, festival organizers decided to pick a theme that played on words in 2009: *"La Musique de Zydeco Était Salé"* (Zydeco music is salty). Although the music label originally came from the phrase "*les haricots sont pas salés*" (snap beans aren't salty), as Charles explained, "This music comes from a people that didn't have a lot. And look at us now. Zydeco music is mainstream. And the new artists are all so talented. Zydeco music is salty. We've gotten to this point and we're proud to be here."[69]

Indeed, Zydeco musicians do have much to be proud of. Several artists, including Chubby Carrier, Buckwheat Zydeco, Cedric Watson, Corey Ledet, Terrence Simien, and Geno Delafose, have all been nominated for a Grammy, and some of them have won the prestigious award, either in the short-lived Best Zydeco or Cajun Music Album category, or in the broader classification of Best Regional Roots Album.

Regardless of their success as musicians, many Creole artists still live in Louisiana, but spend much of their time traveling abroad exposing other people to their culture and style of music. For example, in 2011 Jeffery Broussard and the Creole Cowboys toured Europe and South America twice. In 2012, they went to Russia as part of a ten-day Library of Congress cultural exchange tour.

Jeffery Broussard draws a crowd on a Saturday morning at
Buck and Johnny's weekly Zydeco Breakfast in Breaux Bridge.

Recalling the experience, Broussard commented, "It was different, man. But once we started playing, the response was great, which surprised me because the music was so new to them." Ed Poullard, another well-respected Creole musician on tour with Jeffery, said, "They were kind of a conservative, somber-looking audience. But at the end of our set when Jeffery and I played, we had them dancing on the stage with us. It was really heartwarming to see that."[70]

The son of a sharecropper from Frilot Cove, a small community near Lawtell, Broussard often introduces children to Creole and Zydeco music through school assemblies in various classrooms throughout the country. "I get a kick out of the kids because there are so many interested in the culture." Like many other musicians, he decided to take his music on the road because of his father's example. "I decided to do what my daddy did and keep [the culture] going," he explained.[71]

Like Broussard, Terrence Simien and his band The Zydeco Experience, also tours abroad and conducts educational programs for children worldwide. His project "Creole

Military families at Fort Bliss in El Paso, Texas, enjoy a Mardi Gras-themed event featuring Disney's Creole princess Tiana.

for Kidz and the History of Zydeco" is, according to his website, a "multicultural arts-in-education 'informance' (informational performance) that has reached over 500,000 K-12 students, parents and educators at schools, art centers and festivals around the globe in places far away from Louisiana," such as Australia, Mali, Paraguay, and Canada.[72]

Terrence Simien and The Zydeco Experience are certainly enjoying a successful career as musicians and cultural ambassadors. In 2008, they won the first Grammy award in the Best Zydeco or Cajun Music Album category. The following December, Walt Disney included their music in the soundtrack for *The Princess and the Frog*, an animated film set in New Orleans that features Disney's first black princess. In 2012, Terrence and his band performed the song "Dance Everyday," which is their version of the classic Zydeco tune "Uncle Bud," for the Warner Brothers film *The Lucky One*, a movie based on a Nicholas Sparks novel. Terrence sees his music as a way to give South Louisiana's Creole culture the exposure it needs to continue to survive. He explained, "On screen images of a Zydeco band along with the word 'Zydeco' spoken in the script [of *The Princess and the Frog*] will allow us (with help from our friends at Disney!) to teach many generations about this indigenous American roots music genre known and loved worldwide."[73]

Whether they perform at home or abroad, in classrooms or on international stages, earn national honors or receive local praise, most artists believe that keeping the Creole tradition alive is critical not only to the musical heritage, but also to the culture as a whole. It is a way of respecting those who have gone before and giving the next generation something to be proud of. Through archived recordings, radio airwaves, dance hall gatherings, music festivals, and educational programs, Creole and Zydeco music is accessible to music lovers virtually anywhere in the world today and will continue to be for years to come.

Before his death in 2001, Wilson "Boozoo" Chavis, a legendary accordionist from Lake Charles, said that Zydeco music appeals to all ages and is more popular now than ever. He stated, "And they got youngsters at my dances and old people, too, all together, all dancing to my music—Friday, Saturday, Sunday—and they love it. It make me feel good. They want to follow that French music, that Zydeco. And they speaking that French language, that's coming back, too."[74]

Festivals Acadiens organizers may have added "et Créoles" to the festival's official name in 2008, but even five years later when Zydeco legend Boozoo Chavis was the festival honoree featured in the commemorative poster, the Acadian flag was incorporated into the background, not the Creole flag. Despite the ongoing struggle to be recognized as Creoles, some of Boozoo's relatives posed with his portrait backstage while the Dog Hill Stompers, comprised of other family members, performed on the festival's main stage.

Creole Culture: Preserving and Presenting Heritage

Although they may not have garnered the same level of recognition that Cajuns have experienced to date, it is clear that Creoles are in the midst of their own cultural renaissance. Perhaps some still struggle with the notion of a complex ancestry, but today, more and more Creoles are publicly celebrating their heritage and fighting to be seen and appreciated for who they are.

In addition to music festivals, Creoles have developed museums and special exhibits that highlight their culture. For example, the African American Museum in St. Martinville may have a name that appeals to a wider audience, but the site focuses on the rich history of the region's black Creole culture. At places like Vermilionville, a Cajun and Creole Heritage and Folklife Park in Lafayette, employees and volunteers wear historic costumes and share aspects of their Creole culture with locals and visitors from around the world on a daily basis.

Preserving Creole culture goes beyond showcasing a unique heritage to the outside world. For many Creoles, understanding their history creates a sense of self-worth and dignity as individuals and as a community. Before his death in 2001 at the age of seventy, Wilbert Guillory, founder of the Original Southwest Louisiana Zydeco Festival and advocate for the development of cultural tourism among Creoles spoke for many black Creoles from South Louisiana when he stated:

> What I want to spend the rest of my life doing is encourage people who still can speak Creole to continue to dig into our inheritance. We have a lot of culture out there that we need to know about as black Creoles, and a lot more to learn about our identity. Since I've learned more about myself I'm a much happier person. I'm proud of who I am.

Creole exhibit at the Lafayette Natural History Museum

Museum exhibit at the St. Martinville Cultural Heritage Center

> My role is to let people know very strongly that I'm not a Cajun, to let them know, no matter what anyone says, that Zydeco is not Cajun music. It is black Afro-American Creole music. Because I am a Creole. That's my best language, Creole French, which is different from Cajun French. So there's no way that I can accept myself as a Cajun, I'm not. I'm Creole and I was born in a small Creole community called Pointe Noire.[75]

Most folks in Louisiana can use almost any excuse to start a festival, so it comes as no surprise that the renaissance of Creole culture sparked a new event. September 1, 2012 marked the birth of the Creole Renaissance Festival, held at the Yambilee Building in Opelousas. The mission of this festival is "to celebrate all facets of our culture—the food, the music, the language, and most of all the fellowship." The homepage for the festival's website reflects much of what the current Creole community feels about their cultural identity:

> Throughout the world the word "Creole" can mean so many different things to so many people. But in Southwest Louisiana and East Texas, Creole is a way of life for French-speaking people of color who have dwelled throughout the region for over 300 years. While many believe Creole is a race identified by a particular skin tone, true Creoles throughout this area know firsthand that Creoles of color can be as pale as a crisp white sheet hanging from your *grand-mère*'s [grandmother's] clothesline, or as dark as a night on a Louisiana bayou; and yet both can be undeniably Creole. That's because being Creole is a lifestyle. From the French we speak, to the gumbo we eat, and the Zydeco we live and die by . . . Creoles are the heart and soul of Louisiana![76]

Under the shadow of the words "Arrête pas la musique" (don't stop the music), Rusty Metoyer and The Zydeco Krush continue the Creole tradition on the Heritage Stage.

The Creoles of South Louisiana boast a rich and complex history and culture reaching back across several centuries. Beginning with the first Europeans and Africans who set foot on Louisiana's soil and interacted with the American Indians they encountered, Creoles have been improvising, creating, and adapting ever since, embodying the hallmarks of a creolized culture. Far from homogenous, they celebrate their differences, understanding that the very definition of the term Creole is remarkably inclusive—ethnically, culturally, and linguistically. Every aspect of their culture reflects a long history of converging influences that create what we consider today to be the distinctive Creole culture of Louisiana's prairie regions.

Recipes include ingredients from European, African, Caribbean, and North American traditions. Cooking methods such as frying, boiling, and browning also reflect the cultural melting pot that defines creolized communities. Musical traditions incorporate African rhythms, Europeans instruments, and North American singing styles. Dancers express themselves passionately, whether crowded into a neighbor's home for a house dance, under shade trees at a festival, or below the bare light bulbs of a dance hall whose glory days have long since passed. Even the very language they speak exhibits the powerful influences of multiculturalism.

So what does the future hold for the next generation of Louisiana Creoles? How do we preserve and promote understanding and appreciation for our distinct past in today's modern world of globalization and homogenization?

While some may lament the loss of certain elements of Creole culture such as the widespread use of Creole French and the lack of *boucheries*, oth-

Musicians like Metoyer understand that mentoring the next generation is a critical means for keeping Creole culture alive.

ers recognize that despite the changing times, interest in preserving and promoting South Louisiana's Creole heritage is increasing, not decreasing. Although time changes things and outside influences cannot help but affect current trends, the centuries have proven that the Creole people of South Louisiana are resilient. Goldman Thibodeaux expressed his hope that young people of the future will "recognize the old-timers like me," and stated, "If you wait until I'm dead to send me flowers, what good does that do me?"[77] It seems that Goldman has no cause to worry. No one in the near future will need to send funeral arrangements to mark the end of Creole culture. Rather, as the next generation takes their place as cultural ambassadors, the seeds they are planting today will ensure that the flower of Creole culture continues to bloom for the enjoyment and appreciation of generations to come.

Artist Dennis Paul Williams created an exhibit for the St. Martinville Cultural Heritage Center to represent Creoles from all walks of life who have left their mark on Louisiana's rich past.

CREOLE *heritage*

Creole people have inhabited South Louisiana for over three hundred years. Today, many continue to honor their rich heritage by working or volunteering at various museums and historic sites throughout the region.

A Historic Creole Timeline

1560s: Earliest known use of the word "Creole"

1699: Louisiana founded as a French colony

1718: New Orleans founded and first slave ships arrived on the Gulf Coast

1722: First record of free blacks in New Orleans

1724: Louisiana adopted the *Code Noir*, establishing rights of enslaved and free blacks

1733: Earliest record of a slave freed in Louisiana

1751: Earliest published reference to Louisiana Creoles

1763: Spanish rule in Louisiana began

1765: Acadian refugees began arriving in Louisiana

1803: American period began with the Louisiana Purchase

1812: Louisiana attained statehood

1815: Free Men of Color helped Americans to victory at the Battle of New Orleans

January 1, 1863: Emancipation Proclamation celebrated in Congo Square

Sometimes wearing period clothing and using historic tools and methods, Creole people pass on their knowledge of certain traditional skills such as herbal remedies and quilting by hand. They address difficult topics like slavery to bring understanding of the past. By participating in commemorative events like the anniversary of the Battle of New Orleans in 1815, they remind people how Creoles played significant roles in some of the state's most defining moments.

CREOLE CUISINE

Creole cuisine enjoys international prestige as one of the world's most unique and flavorful ethnic foods. Restaurants at home and abroad offer everything from fine dining experiences to cozy kitchens that dish out plate lunches the way grandma made it.

MARKETING CREOLE

Food items ranging from pralines and seasoning blends to health bars and tortilla chips now bear the label "Creole," a phenomenon that prompted the Louisiana Department of Agriculture and Forestry to add a "Certified Creole" option alongside their "Certified Cajun" and "Certified Louisiana" labels. Companies meeting the criteria can now use the label to authenticate and distinguish local products from others.

A Los Angeles shopping mall food court includes a Creole restaurant that dishes up stick-to-your-rib plates of familiar menu items to hungry shoppers.

Creole food and flavors are a global phenomenon that can now be found around the world.

CREOLE

Chefs serve gourmet cuisine in an elegant atmosphere at the Creole Restaurant and Café established by a University of Louisiana at Lafayette graduate in his hometown of Al-Khobar, Saudi Arabia.

CREOLE French

Creole-speaking parishes

Creole French evolved as individuals from various continents blended African, European, and North American languages in the New World. Primarily an oral language, Creole French was widely spoken throughout Louisiana until legislation mandated that only English could be spoken on school grounds.

Louisiana French From A-Z

andouille (ahn-*doo*-ee) - a type of sausage

bébé (beh-*bay*)- baby

canaille (ka-*ny*)- mischievous

danser (don-*say*)- to dance

écrevisse (ay-cray-*vees*)- crawfish

faire le fou (fare luh foo)- to act the fool

gens de couleur (zhawn doo kuh-*lure*)- people of color

haricots (ah-dee-*koh*)- snap beans

ici (ee-see)- here

jolie blonde (zhoh-*lee* blawhn)- pretty blonde

kee-yaw- expression meaning "wow"

lagniappe (lohn-*yop*)- a little something extra

Mardi Gras (mar-*dee* grah)- "Fat Tuesday"

nonc (nonk)- uncle

ouaouaron (wa-wa-ron)- bullfrog

paillasse (*pie*-yahs)- clown

qui c'est ça (key say sah)- who is that?

riz (ree)- rice

sac-á-lait (sock-a-lay)- freshwater fish, perch

tracas (trah-*kah*)- trouble

uni (oo-*nee*)- united

veillée (vay-yay)- a visit

Who dat?- battle cry of New Orleans's NFL Saints

x- no "x"

yeux (zhuh)- eyes

Zydeco- a Creole style of music

Roundtable discussions keep Creole conversations going.

In recent years, French immersion programs have reintroduced French into the classroom, but instructors typically hail from Canada, Europe, Africa, and the Caribbean instead of Louisiana. Although Creole French is heard less frequently than before, there is a growing interest among young people to learn the language of their ancestors or at least sprinkle their songs and conversations with Creole phrases such as "*Eh, toi*!" (Hey, you!) and "*Ça fait chaud*!" (It's hot!). Once denigrated as a language of slaves, Creole French is now recognized as one of the few languages entirely developed in the New World.

CREOLE MUSIC

Creole music, like Creole French, is not written, so the passing down of tradition takes place on back porches, around kitchen tables, at jam sessions, and sometimes even on stages.

WHAT'S THE DIFFERENCE?

Rubboard vs. Washboard

Washboards were used for cleaning clothes, whereas rubboards are musical instruments created by eliminating the wooden frame and adding shoulder straps to the traditional washboard.

Fiddle vs. Violin

Despite popular belief, fiddles and violins are the same musical instrument. What distinguishes them from each other is typically the manner and context in which they are played. Violins are most often associated with classical music styles while fiddles are featured prominently in folk music around the world.

Fais-do-do vs. Zydeco

Both words are French derivatives containing three syllables and ending in an "o" sound, but their origins and meanings vary greatly. At pre-World War II house dances, Cajun mothers often rocked their babies in a back room saying "fais-do-do," a French expression meaning "go to sleep." These dances became known as fais-do-dos [fay-doh-doze]. The term "Zydeco" [pronounced "ZY-dee-koh"] came from the French expression *les haricots sont pas salés*, meaning that life is so tough, you cannot even afford the salt meat to flavor your snap beans. The phrase was incorporated into a popular song and has become a noun, verb, and adjective. Today, people go to the Zydeco (event) to dance the Zydeco (dance) to the sounds of Zydeco (music) played by Zydeco musicians.

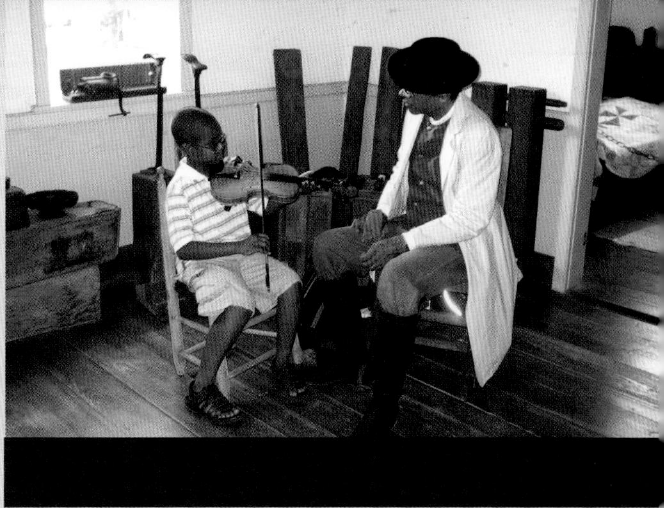

Understanding that living cultures must continue to evolve if they are to survive, young musicians use tradition as a platform to launch their own careers. They may perform songs they learned from older relatives, but contribute their own innovations, instrumentation, and inspiration to the repertoire. As people experience the syncopated rhythms and bluesy tunes of Zydeco music, the demand for artists continues to grow, assuring dancers and aficionados that Creole music will play on for generations to come.

CREOLE IDENTITY

Proud of their ancestry, culinary skill, linguistic abilities, and musical talent, Creoles and their descendants still call South Louisiana "home" after three centuries strong.

The Creole Flag

The Creole flag, adopted in 1987, celebrates the mixed lineage, culture, and religion of Creoles.

The white fleur-de-lis on the blue field symbolizes their colonial French past.

The gold Tower of Castille on the red field depicts their Spanish heritage.

The tri-color flags of Mali and Senegal on the upper right and lower left corners represent their African lineage.

A white cross unifies the four quadrants, representing the Christian faith adopted by most Creoles today.

Creole identity has always transcended traditional boundaries. In fact, the very term "creolization" indicates a process in which many elements that define a culture blend together to create a new one. Everything from colonial records to vehicle license plates bear the name "Creole," demonstrating that Creole people have not only played a role in Louisiana history from the beginning but also continue to preserve and present their distinct heritage wherever they go today.

NOTES

Introduction

1 This excerpt was taken from a poem entitled "*La Chaudrière Pèlè la Gregue*" or "The Pot Calls the Coffee Pot" by Louisiana Creole Sybil Kein in her collection of poems entitled *Gombo People* (New Orleans: Margaret Media, Inc., 1999), 30-31. In English, the word "gumbo" is usually spelled with a "u," but the French and African spellings incorporate an "o" in the middle of the word. Kein's decision to spell gumbo with an "o" in her poem reflects the Creole connection to both France and Africa.

2 Charles Gayarré, a native of New Orleans who served as president for the Louisiana Historical Society from 1860-1888, excluded Creoles of Color from his definition, as did Grace King, a genealogist Gayarré mentored. Novelist Edward Larocque Tinker introduced his major work *Toucoutou* in 1928 with a definition of Creole that asserted the term could only refer to pure whites born to European parents in Spanish or French colonies. See Shirley Thompson, "'*Ah Toucoutou, ye conin vous*': History and Memory in Creole New Orleans," *American Quarterly* 53, no. 2 (June 2001): 248-49. Other novels such as *The Creole Orphans; or, Lights and Shadows of Southern Life, A Tale of Louisiana*, published in 1856, also explained that "a Creole is a mere term taken from the Spanish, meaning a native descended from European ancestors." See James S. Peacocke, *The Creole Orphans; or, Lights and Shadows of Southern Life. A Tale of Louisiana* (New York: Derby and Jackson, 1856), 90-91. George Washington Cable provided a notable exception to the "whites-only" definition of Creole when he wrote in 1884 that "even in Louisiana the question [What is a Creole?] would be variously answered." He agreed that the term could "include any native, of French or Spanish descent by either parent," but went on to explain that "later, the term was adopted by—not conceded to—the natives of mixed blood. . . ." He added, "Besides French and Spanish, there are even, for convenience of speech, 'colored' Creoles; but there are no Italian, or Sicilian, not any English, Scotch, Irish, or 'Yankee' Creoles, unless of parentage married into, and themselves thoroughly proselyted in, Creole society." See George Washington Cable, *The Creoles of Louisiana* (1884; repr., Gretna, LA: Pelican Publishing, 2000), 41-42. Although a native of New Orleans like Gayarré, Cable's inclusive definition of Creole and his vocal opposition to the racial prejudice of his day drew sharp criticism from white Southerners. Cable eventually left Louisiana and made his home in the northeast to escape social persecution. For an excellent overview of Cable's life and career, see "Introduction: A Novelist Turns Historian," in Lawrence N. Powell, *The New Orleans of George Washington Cable: The 1887 Census Office Report* (Baton Rouge: Louisiana State University Press, 2008), 1-35.

3 *Creoles of Color in the Bayou Country* is an excellent examination of the origins and development of Louisiana's black Creole culture, especially in the prairie parishes located in the southwest region of the state. Although this work contributes significantly to better understanding the Creole world outside New Orleans, the final chapter concludes with the post-Civil War years; therefore, nearly a century and a half of subsequent Creole history is not addressed in this seminal work. See Carl A. Brasseaux, Keith P. Fontenot, and Claude F. Oubre, *Creoles of Color in the Bayou Country* (Jackson: University Press of Mississippi, 1994). Like its predecessor, James H. Dormon's collection of essays focuses on Creoles of

Color, but broadens its geographic sphere to include the city of New Orleans, other Gulf Coast ports like Mobile and Pensacola, as well as the rural prairie areas of South Louisiana. Experts in Louisiana's Creole culture such as Carl A. Brasseaux, Barry Jean Ancelet, and Nicholas R. Spitzer provide interesting discussions regarding topics such as the origins of New Orleans's free Creoles of Color, Creole Mardi Gras traditions, Zydeco music, and ethnic and identity issues among twentieth-century Creoles in South Louisiana. Much more than a strict historical overview, this book offers readers an excellent survey of specific historical and contemporary black Creole cultural elements. See James H. Dormon, ed., *Creoles of Color of the Gulf South* (Knoxville: University of Tennessee Press, 1996). Sybil Kein's *Creole: The History and Legacy of Louisiana's Free People of Color* also addresses a variety of topics related to the black Creole experience in South Louisiana. Some of the most interesting chapters in the first half of the book deal with nineteenth-century Creole composers, how the system of *plaçage* impacted the lifestyles of free women of color, and the use of Louisiana's Creole language in southern literature. The second half of the work focuses on their legacy and discusses topics such as their businesses, trades, and professions, racial passing, and the African origins of certain Creole foods. Kein's book complements Dormon's collection of essays in that it offers an examination of various hallmarks of black Creole culture. See Sybil Kein, ed., *Creole: The History and Legacy of Louisiana's Free People of Color* (Baton Rouge: Louisiana State University Press, 2000).

4 "Francophone" simply means "French-speaking," just as "Anglophone" refers to those who speak English.

5 See map, page 5.

6 The Cane River Creole community is located in Natchitoches, Louisiana. To protect and preserve the region's history and culture, the National Park Service oversees the Cane River National Heritage Area (see http://www.nps.gov/crha/index.htm) and the Cane River Creole National Historical Park (see http://www.nps.gov/cari/index.htm).

7 Acadiana, although perhaps more widely known for its distinctive swamp culture, is also home to vast prairies where ranching and farming provide livelihoods today as they have in the past. One noticeable difference between bayou and prairie culture is the way individuals prepare gumbo. Before refrigeration made virtually all ingredients transportable and therefore accessible, Cajuns and Creoles in the bayous used seafood as a staple ingredient, whereas those engaged in farming and ranching on the prairies used readily-available chickens and made their own sausage.

Chapter One

1 Unless noted otherwise, throughout this book, the word "Creole" will be spelled in English and written with an uppercase "c."

2 Charles R. Ewen, "From Colonist to Creole: Archaeological Patterns of Spanish Colonization in the New World," *Historical Archaeology* 34, no. 3 (2000): 36.

3 For a better understanding of Creole language studies worldwide, see "Egyptian Creole Origin Theory," *Oceanic Linguistics Special Publications* 14, *A Bibliography of Pidgin and Creole Languages* (1975): 53-55; Jonathan Owens, "Creole Arabic: The Orphan of All Orphans," *Anthropological Linguistics* 43, no. 3 (Fall 2001): 348-78; Suzanne Romaine, "Hawai'i Creole English as a Literary Language," *Language in Society* 23, no. 4 (December 1994): 527-54; Elizabeth Hume and Georgios Tserdanelis, "Labial Unmarkedness in Sri Lankan Portuguese Creole," *Phonology* 19, no. 3 (2002): 441-58; J.M. Carrière, "Creole Dialect of Missouri," *American Speech* 14, no. 2 (April 1939): 109-19; William F. S. Miles,

"The Creole Malaise in Mauritius," *African Affairs* 98, no. 391 (April 1999): 211-28; and Thomas L. Markey, "Afrikaans: Creole or Non-Creole?" *Zeitschrift für Dialektologie und Linguistik*, 49, no. 2 (1982): 169-207.

4 "Louisiana Folktales," *Journal of American Folklore* 7, no. 27 (October-December 1894): 317.

5 Robin Cohen and Paola Toninato, "The Creolization Debate: Analysing Mixed Identities and Cultures," in *The Creolization Reader: Studies in Mixed Identities and Cultures*, eds. Robin Cohen and Paola Toninato (New York: Routledge, 2010), 10.

6 For a more in-depth discussion regarding the disciplinary evolution of Creole studies, see the section "Beyond Discipline?" in Ibid., 9-14.

7 Ibid., 9.

8 Florence E. Borders, "Researching Creole and Cajun Musics in New Orleans," *Black Music Research Journal* 8, no. 1 (1988): 15. According to Edward K. Brathwaite, a scholar of Creole societies in the Anglophone Caribbean, "The word [creole] itself appears to have originated from a combination of two Spanish words *criar* (to create, to imagine, to establish, to found, to settle) and *colon* (a colonist, a founder, a settler) into *criollo*: a committed settler, one identified with the area of settlement, one native to the settlement though not ancestrally indigenous to it." Quoted in Cohen and Toninato, "The Creolization Debate," 3.

9 Carl A. Brasseaux, *French, Cajun, Creole, Houma: A Primer on Francophone Louisiana* (Baton Rouge: Louisiana State University Press, 2005), 90-91.

10 For a more detailed discussion regarding the creolization process in Cape Verde, see Tobias Green, "The Evolution of Creole Identity in Cape Verde," in Cohen and Toninato, *The Creolization Reader*, 157-66.

11 Ibid., 157.

12 Cohen and Toninato, "The Creolization Debate," 3.

13 The use of the Creole label in Mauritius refers to a wide variety of sub-ethnicities as exemplified by the terms "Creole Madras" (those with Tamil heritage), "Creole Sinwa" (Chinese ancestry), "Creole l'Ascar" (Arab descent), and "Creole Morisyen" (of African-Malagasy origin). See Cohen and Toninato, "The Creolization Debate," 8-9. For an additional source on Mauritius's Creole culture, see William F.S. Miles, "The Creole Malaise in Mauritius," *African Affairs* 98, no. 391 (April 1999): 211-28.

14 Cohen and Toninato, "The Creolization Debate," 8-9.

15 "Haiti,"https://www.cia.gov/library/publications/the-world-factbook/geos/ha.html, accessed April 17, 2012.

16 Ira Berlin first introduced the term "Atlantic Creole" in his article "From Creole to African: Atlantic Creoles and the Origins of African-American Society in Mainland North America," *The William and Mary Quarterly*, 3rd ser., 53, no. 2 (April 1996): 251-88.

17 For a discussion of Linda M. Heywood and John K. Thornton's emphasis on the West Central African contributions to the Atlantic Creole world, see their work *Central Africans, Atlantic Creoles, and the Foundation of the Americas, 1585-1660* (Cambridge: Cambridge University Press, 2007).

18 Berlin, "From Creole to African," 257.

19 Ibid., 251 and 265-66.

20 For an excellent explanation of why English-speaking colonists in North America chose to reject the term Creole, see Joyce E. Chaplin, "Creoles in British America: From Denial to Acceptance," in *Creolization: History, Ethnography, Theory*, ed. Charles Stewart (Walnut Creek, CA: Left Coast Press, 2007), 46-65.

21 Daniel Mouer, "Chesapeake Creoles: The Creation of Folk Culture in Colonial

Virginia," in *The Archaeology of 17th-Century Virginia*, eds. Theodore R. Reinhart and Dennis J. Pogue (Petersburg, VA: Dietz Press, 1993).

22 Trevor Burnard, *Creole Gentlemen: The Maryland Elite, 1691-1776* (New York: Routledge, 2002).

23 John Smolenski, *Friends and Strangers: The Making of a Creole Culture in Colonial Pennsylvania* (Philadelphia: University of Pennsylvania Press, 2010).

24 Although the Cane River Creoles form a significant segment of Louisiana's population, in the interest of time and space, this book will focus on the Creole communities of South Louisiana, particularly in the Acadiana and New Orleans areas. Those interested in learning more about Natchitoches's Creole people can consult Gary B. Mills's work entitled *The Forgotten People: Cane River's Creoles of Color* (Baton Rouge: Louisiana State University Press, 1977), Philip Gould's collection of captioned photographs entitled *Natchitoches and Louisiana's Timeless Cane River* (Baton Rouge: Louisiana State University Press, 2002), or Bill Rodman's documentary film *Reconstructing Creole: Cane River Creoles* (Louisiana Public Broadcasting, 2005).

25 Gwendolyn Midlo Hall, *Africans in Colonial Louisiana: The Development of Afro-Creole Culture in the Eighteenth Century* (Baton Rouge: Louisiana State University Press, 1992).

26 James H. Dormon, ed. *Creoles of Color of the Gulf South* (Knoxville: University of Tennessee Press, 1996).

27 Carl A. Brasseaux, Keith P. Fontenot, and Claude F. Oubre, *Creoles of Color in the Bayou Country* (Jackson: University Press of Mississippi, 1994).

28 Sybil Kein, ed., *Creole: The History and Legacy of Louisiana's Free People of Color* (Baton Rouge: Louisiana State University Press, 2000).

29 Joseph G. Tregle, Jr., "Creoles and Americans," in *Creole New Orleans: Race and Americanization*, ed. Arnold R. Hirsch and Joseph Logsdon (Baton Rouge: Louisiana State University Press, 1992), 137.

30 Cohen and Toninato, "The Creolization Debate," 4.

31 Tregle, "Creoles and Americans," 137.

32 Jean-Bernard Bossu, *Travels in the Interior of North America 1751-1762*, quoted in Virginia R. Domínguez, "Social Classification in Creole Louisiana," *American Ethnologist* 4, no. 4 (November 1977): 591.

33 Tregle, "Creoles and Americans," 137.

34 Brasseaux, "Creoles," http://ccet.louisiana.edu/tourism/cultural/The_People/creole.html, accessed April 22, 2010.

35 Jacques M. Henry and Carl L. Bankston, III, "Propositions for a Structuralist Analysis of Creolism," *Current Anthropology* 39, no. 4 (August-October 1998): 561.

36 Brasseaux, *French, Cajun, Creole, Houma*, 94-96.

37 Through the Treaty of Fontainebleau (November 3, 1762), France surrendered the Isle of Orleans and all of Louisiana west of the Mississippi River to Spain while the Treaty of Paris (February 10, 1763) ceded Louisiana east of the river to England.

38 Brasseaux, *French, Cajun, Creole, Houma*, 97-99.

39 Ibid., 92, 98-99.

40 Tregle, "Creoles and Americans," 136.

41 Following a series of late eighteenth century slave rebellions, Saint Domingue overthrew French rule and called itself Haiti in honor of its original Arawak name.

42 For a detailed study of Louisiana's Saint-Domingue immigrants, see Carl A. Brasseaux and Glenn R. Conrad, eds. *The Road to Louisiana: The Saint-Domingue Refugees, 1792-1809* (Lafayette: Center for Louisiana Studies, 1992).

43 Brasseaux, *French, Cajun, Creole, Houma*, 99-102.

44 Lyle Saxon, New Orleans *Times-Picayune*, February 11, 1926, quoted in William A. Read, "Creole and 'Cajan,'" *American Speech* 1, no. 9 (June 1926): 483.

45 Berquin-Duvallon, *Travels in Louisiana and the Floridas, in the year, 1802*, trans. by John Davis (New York: 1806) in "An Anti-Creole Observation," *Louisiana History: The Journal of the Louisiana Historical Association* 9, no. 2 (Spring 1968): 138.

46 Sarah Russell, "Intermarriage and Intermingling: Constructing the Planter Class in Louisiana's Sugar Parishes, 1803-1850," *Louisiana History: The Journal of the Louisiana Historical Association* 46, no. 4 (Autumn 2005): 407-434.

47 Beginning with French colonization of Louisiana in 1699 and continuing up to the brink of the Civil War in 1860, Louisiana was a three-tiered society with whites on top, enslaved blacks on the bottom, and a sizeable free people of color population in the middle.

48 It is safe to assume that these blacks were slaves since the first mention of a free man of color does not appear in Louisiana records until 1722. See Gwendolyn Midlo Hall, *Africans in Colonial Louisiana: The Development of Afro-Creole Culture in the Eighteenth Century* (Baton Rouge: Louisiana State University Press, 1992), 129.

49 Ibid., 57; and Daniel H. Usner, Jr., "From African Captivity to American Slavery: The Introduction of Black Laborers to Colonial Louisiana," *Louisiana History: The Journal of the Louisiana Historical Association* 20, no. 1 (Winter 1979): 25.

50 Thomas N. Ingersoll, "The Slave Trade and the Ethnic Diversity of Louisiana's Slave Community," *Louisiana History: The Journal of the Louisiana Historical Association* 37, no. 2 (Spring 1996): 137-38.

51 Brasseaux, *French, Cajun, Creole, Houma*, 90.

52 Ingersoll, "Louisiana's Slave Community," 151.

53 The *Code Noir* of 1724 was a compilation of "black codes" that regulated the treatment of slaves in Louisiana.

54 "Louisiana's Code Noir (1724)," http://www.blackpast.org/?q=primary/louisianas-code-noir-1724, accessed October 31, 2009; and Alice Moore Dunbar-Nelson, "People of Color in Louisiana," in Kein, *Creole*, 7.

55 Jerah Johnson, "New Orleans' Congo Square: An Urban Setting for Early Afro-American Culture Formation," *Louisiana History: The Journal of the Louisiana Historical Association* 32, no. 2 (Spring 1991): 122, 124.

56 Carl A. Brasseaux, "The Administration of Slave Regulations in French Louisiana, 1724-1766," *Louisiana History: The Journal of the Louisiana Historical Association* 21, no. 2 (Spring 1980): 143.

57 Gwendolyn Midlo Hall, "The Formation of Afro-Creole Culture," in *Creole New Orleans: Race and Americanization*, ed. Arnold R. Hirsch and Joseph Logsdon (Baton Rouge: Louisiana State University Press, 1992), 78-83.

58 Hall, *Africans in Colonial Louisiana*, 143-44.

59 Brasseaux, "Slave Regulations in French Louisiana," 142.

60 Hall, *Africans in Colonial Louisiana*, 143.

61 Jean-Pierre Leglaunec, "Slave Migrations in Spanish and Early American Louisiana: New Sources and New Estimates," *Louisiana History: The Journal of the Louisiana Historical Association* 46, no. 2 (Spring 2005): 185-209.

62 Berlin, "From Creole to African," 284-86.

63 Cabinda is a thumb-shaped province separated from the rest of Angola by a narrow strip of the Democratic Republic of the Congo (DRC). Jean-Marc Masseaut, editor of the scholarly journal *Cahiers des Anneaux de la Mémoire* [Shackles of Memory], provided statistics regarding the importation of slaves from Cabinda in an e-mail to the author on

September 15, 2017. Daniel Quinho, a Cabinda native and Luanda resident, sent the author a museum guidebook and shared his impressions of the *Museu Nacional da Escravatura* (National Slave Museum) during a phone interview conducted on June 19, 2016. For more information about Louisiana's Angola State Penitentiary, see www.angolamuseum.org, accessed November 15, 2017.

64 Although French policy typically honored Indian ownership of tribal land, the commandant at the Natchez settlement angered the Natchez when he broke with this tradition by ordering them to surrender their cultivated crop land and town to the French in 1729. When a group of Natchez Indians volunteered to provide wild game to the fort in exchange for goods later that year, the commandant agreed and furnished weapons for them to hunt with, as had been done in the past on numerous occasions. The Natchez shocked the French by attacking without warning, killing several soldiers and kidnapping their wives and children. To punish the Natchez, French governor Périer detached seven hundred men, laid siege, defeated the Indians, and "embarked upon a systematic, ruthless extermination of the entire Natchez tribe." By 1731, the Natchez hardly existed as an organized tribe. Most of the Indian prisoners, including their chief, were shipped to Saint-Domingue as slaves. Other survivors joined neighboring tribes. See "The Natchez War," *Louisiana: A History*, ed. Bennet H. Wall (Wheeling, IL: Harlan Davidson, 1997), 41-43.

65 Brasseaux, et. al, *Creoles of Color in the Bayou Country*, 3.

66 Dunbar-Nelson, "People of Color in Louisiana," 7.

67 Donald E. Everett, "Free Persons of Color in Colonial Louisiana," *Louisiana History: The Journal of the Louisiana Historical Association* 7, no. 1 (Winter 1966): 22.

68 Confidential correspondent, e-mail to author, November 7, 2012; and Brasseaux, et. al, *Creoles of Color in the Bayou Country*, 79-80.

69 Brasseaux, et. al, *Creoles of Color in the Bayou Country*, 4.

70 Everett, "Free Persons of Color in Colonial Louisiana," 35. The *plaçage* system will be discussed in greater detail in later chapters. For an excellent examination of Louisiana's *plaçage* system, see Joan M. Martin, "*Plaçage* and the Louisiana *Gens de Couleur Libre:* How Race and Sex Defined the Lifestyles of Free Women of Color," in Kein, *Creole*, 57-70. For a better understanding of how these relationships played out on the dance floor, see Ronald R. Morazan, "'Quadroon' Balls in the Spanish Period," *Louisiana History: The Journal of the Louisiana Historical Association* 14, no. 3 (Summer 1973): 310-15. Emily Clark's work *The Strange History of the American Quadroon: Free Women of Color in the Revolutionary Atlantic World* (Chapel Hill: University of North Carolina Press, 2013) serves to expose and examine some of the romanticized notions of the *plaçage* system and quadroon experience.

71 Mulatto children were half-black. Quadroons were one-fourth black. Octoroons were one-eighth black.

72 "The Journal of Dr. John Sibley, July-October, 1802," *Louisiana Historical Quarterly* 10 (October 1927): 478-79 in Everett, "Free Persons of Color in Colonial Louisiana," 37.

73 "Observations of Berquin Duvallon on the Free People of Colour in Louisiana in 1802," *Journal of Negro History* 2 (April 1917): 167.

74 Laura Foner, "The Free People of Color in Louisiana and St. Domingue: A Comparative Portrait of Two Three-Caste Slave Societies," *The Journal of Social History* 3, no. 4 (Summer 1970): 408, 411.

75 Everett, "Free Persons of Color in Colonial Louisiana," 29.

76 Ibid., 32-33.

77 Ibid., 23-25.

78 Foner, "Free People of Color," 407.

79 Ibid., 407, 424-26.

80 The chart shown was slightly modified from the one found in Juliet E. K. Walker, "Racism, Slavery, and Free Enterprise: Black Entrepreneurship in the United States before the Civil War," *The Business History Review* 60, no. 3 (Autumn 1986): 350, 354.

81 Loren Schweninger, "Socioeconomic Dynamics among the Gulf Creole Populations: The Antebellum and Civil War Years," in Dormon, *Creoles of Color of the Gulf South*, 54-55.

82 Foner, "Free People of Color," 417.

83 Mary Niall Mitchell, "'A Good and Delicious Country': Free Children of Color and How They Learned to Imagine the Atlantic World in Nineteenth-Century Louisiana," *History of Education Quarterly* 40, no. 2 (Summer 2000): 126-27.

84 Ibid., 135.

85 New Orleans *Daily Picayune*, November 11, 1860, in Ibid., 141.

86 Schweninger, "Socioeconomic Dynamics among the Gulf Creoles," 60-61.

87 Ibid., 62.

88 Ibid., 63.

89 Anthony G. Barthelemy, "Light, Bright, Damn *Near* White: Race, the Politics of Genealogy, and the Strange Case of Susie Guillory," in Kein, *Creole*, 262.

90 Henry and Bankston, "Propositions for a Structuralist Analysis of Creolism," 562.

91 Charles Gayarré, "Mr. Cable's Freedmen's Case in Equity," *New Orleans Times Democrat,* January-February 1885, quoted in Shirley Thompson, "'*Ah Toucoutou, ye conin vous*': History and Memory in Creole New Orleans," *American Quarterly* 53, no. 2 (June 2001): 248-49. For a full-text online version of Gayarré's four volumes entitled *History of Louisiana* (New York: William J. Widdleton, 1867), see http://penelope.uchicago.edu/Thayer/E/Gazetteer/Places/America/United_States/Louisiana/_Texts/GAYHLA/home.html, accessed November 5, 2012.

92 Ibid. Also see Grace King, *Creole Families of New Orleans* (New York: Macmillan, 1921) and *New Orleans: The Place and the People* (New York: Macmillan, 1895).

93 Edward Larocque Tinker, *Toucoutou* (New York: Dodd, Mead, and Co., 1928), 8, quoted in Thompson, "History and Memory in Creole New Orleans," 248.

94 Ibid., 256. For an interesting foray into the world of "passing," see Bliss Broyard, *One Drop: My Father's Hidden Life—A Story of Race and Family Secrets* (New York: Little Brown and Company, 2007).

95 August Fuselier, interview by Nick Spitzer in "'Zydeco': Creole Music and Culture in South Louisiana," *Flower Films*, 1986.

96 Thompson, "History and Memory in Creole New Orleans," 258.

97 Sara Le Menestrel, "The Color of Music: Social Boundaries and Stereotypes in Southwest Louisiana French Music," *Southern Cultures* (Fall 2007): 88.

98 Cajuns are the French-speaking descendants of Acadian settlers who were forced out of their homeland in Nova Scotia, sent into exile by the British in 1755, and eventually settled in the prairie and swamp regions of Louisiana. Until the introduction of the oil industry in the beginning of the twentieth century, most Cajuns lived off the land as hunters, trappers, fishermen, or farmers.

99 See "Creole Families in Black and White" pages 30-37 for a more in-depth explanation of this phenomenon.

100 James H. Dormon, "Ethnicity and Identity: Creoles of Color in Twentieth-Century South Louisiana," in *Creoles of Color of the Gulf South*, ed. James H. Dormon, 171.

101 Nicholas Spitzer, "'Zydeco': Creole Music and Culture in South Louisiana," *Flower Films*, 1986.

102 Known today as "Pine Prairie" in English, this small community in Evangeline Parish is comprised of less than 1.5 square miles.

103 Barry Jean Ancelet, *Cajun and Creole Music Makers* (Jackson: University Press of Mississippi, 1999), 83-85.

104 Ben Sandmel, *Zydeco!* (Jackson: University Press of Mississippi, 1999), 75.

105 Ibid., 121-22.

106 Michael Peter Smith, "Postmodernism, Urban Ethnography, and the New Social Space of Ethnic Identity," *Theory and Society* 21, no. 4 (August 1992): 512.

107 Cohen and Toninato, "The Creolization Debate," 9.

108 An anonymous black woman was quoted in Velesta Jenkins's work "River Road" as having said, "Honey, we's all Creoles." This quote can be found in the opening pages of Adam Fairclough's *Race and Democracy: The Civil Rights Struggle in Louisiana, 1915-1972* (Athens: University of Georgia Press, 2008), ix.

109 Phone interview with Theresa and Goldman Thibodeaux, October 12, 2017; Phone interview with Darrell Bourque, October 12, 2017.

110 Darrell Bourque was appointed poet laureate from November 2007-June 2008 and again from May 2009-May 2011. https://www.loc.gov/rr/main/poets/louisiana.html, accessed October 22, 2017.

Chapter Two

1 Louisiana historian Charles Gayerré, quoted in John D. Folse, *The Encyclopedia of Cajun and Creole Cuisine* (Gonzales, LA: Chef John Folse and Co. Publishing, 2010), 118.

2 John Egerton, *Southern Food: At Home, on the Road, in History* (New York: Alfred A. Knopf, Inc., 1987), 110.

3 Katrina Brown Hunt, "America's Best Cities for Foodies," http://travel.yahoo.com/p-interests-40686622, accessed September 23, 2011.

4 Patricia B. Mitchell, *French Cooking in Early America* (Chatham, VA: Mitchells Publications, 1991), 17.

5 James C. McCann, *Stirring the Pot: A History of African Cuisine* (Athens: Ohio University Press, 2009), 7.

6 Ibid., 26; Egerton, *Southern Food*, 13; and Reay Tannahill, *Food in History* (New York: Crown Publishers, Inc., 1988), 220.

7 Folse, *Encyclopedia of Cajun and Creole Cuisine*, 54. "The 'Columbian Exchange' is the phrase that describes the migration of foods and agricultural technology and know-how from Africa into the New World, the Americas, and from the Americas into Africa and the African Diaspora. It took place mostly during the fifteenth through nineteenth centuries, beginning when the Portuguese arrived on the west coast of Africa, landing first at the Cape Verde islands off the coast of Senegal and moving to Senegal and south along the Guinea coast. Eventually, the ships' captains discovered that the Africans being transported across the ocean in what is known a[s] the Middle Passage coped better when they were fed familiar foods. They thus gave them things such as yams, palm oil, and rice, along with peanuts, corn, plantains, and *melegueta* pepper." Fran Osseo-Asare, *Food Culture in Sub-Saharan Africa* (Westport, CT: Greenwood Press, 2005), 22.

8 Egerton, *Southern Food*, 129.

9 Folse, *The Encyclopedia of Cajun and Creole Cuisine*, 43.

10 Peter S. Feibleman, *American Cooking: Creole and Acadian* (New York: Time-Life Books, 1971), 18.

11 Breaux Bridge, located in St. Martin Parish, is the self-proclaimed "Crawfish Capital of the World."

12 C. Paige Gutierrez, *Cajun Foodways* (Jackson: University Press of Mississippi, 1992), 36.

13 John Laudun, "Gumbo This: The State of a Dish," in Ursula Mathis-Moser and Günter Bischof, eds., *Acadians and Cajuns: The Politics of Culture of French Minorities in North America* (Innsbruck [Austria]: Innsbruck University Press, 2009), 159.

14 Thomas "Big Hat" Fields, interview by author, Lafayette, LA, June 28, 2011. The author incorporated ethnopoetics for some of the lengthier interviews she conducted in order to more closely represent the contributors' way of speaking.

15 Folse, *The Encyclopedia of Cajun and Creole Cuisine*, 69.

16 Carolyn Shelton, *Zydeco, Blues 'n' Gumbo Cookbook* (n.p.: Chanel Zeno Publishing, 2009), 3.

17 French Chef Urbain Dubois (1818-1901), quoted in John-Bryan Hopkins, "Foodimentary: Celebrate Food Every Day," http://foodimentary.com/best-food-quotes-list/culture-quotes-food/, accessed September 4, 2012.

18 Folse, *The Encyclopedia of Cajun and Creole Cuisine,* 5.

19 Ibid., 6-7.

20 Feibleman, *American Cooking*, 39.

21 Folse, *The Encyclopedia of Cajun and Creole Cuisine*, 22-24.

22 Mitchell, *French Cooking in Early America*, 24.

23 Ibid., 2-3.

24 Gwendolyn Midlo Hall, *Africans in Colonial Louisiana: The Development of Afro-Creole Culture in the Eighteenth Century* (Baton Rouge: Louisiana State University Press, 1992), 57.

25 Ibid., 34-37.

26 McCann, *Stirring the Pot*, 37-40.

27 First known as the Mississippi Company (1684) then the Company of the West (1717), this corporation later became the Company of the Indies (1719). Holding a business monopoly in the French colonies of North America and the islands of the West Indies, this corporation became one of the earliest examples of an economic bubble. The Company of the Indies finally collapsed in 1731. For a more detailed discussion of the company's influence on the development of Louisiana, see Mathé Allain, *"Not Worth a Straw": French Colonial Policy and the Early Years of Louisiana* (Lafayette: Center for Louisiana Studies, University of Southwestern Louisiana, 1988).

28 Henry P. Dart, "The First Cargo of African Slaves for Louisiana, 1718," *The Louisiana Historical Quarterly* 14, no. 2 (April 1931): 173-76.

29 Thomas N. Ingersoll, "The Slave Trade and the Ethnic Diversity of Louisiana's Slave Community," *Louisiana History: The Journal of the Louisiana Historical Association* 37, no. 2 (Spring 1996): 135, 121-23.

30 Gutierrez, *Cajun Foodways*, 42.

31 The Superior Council was Louisiana's judicial and military oligarchy. See Daniel H. Usner, Jr., "From African Captivity to American Slavery: The Introduction of Black Laborers to Colonial Louisiana," *Louisiana History: The Journal of the Louisiana Historical Association* 20, no. 1 (Winter 1979): 32.

32 Hall, *Africans in Colonial Louisiana*, 127-28.

33 John Davis, "Observations on the Negroes of Louisiana," *Journal of Negro History* 2, no. 2 (April 1917): 170-71.

34 For an excellent discussion of the Saint-Domingue revolution, see *The Road to*

Louisiana: The Saint-Domingue Refugees, 1792-1809, edited an annotated by Carl A. Brasseaux and Glenn R. Conrad and translated by David Cheramie (Lafayette: Center for Louisiana Studies, 1992).

35 Davis, "Observations on the Negroes of Louisiana," 171-72.

36 Joe Gray Taylor, *Eating, Drinking and Visiting in the South: An Informal History* (Baton Rouge: Louisiana State University Press, 1982), 11, 20-21.

37 Gutierrez, *Cajun Foodways*, 43-44.

38 Davis, "Observations on the Negroes of Louisiana," 167, 173.

39 Carl A. Brasseaux, "The Administration of Slave Regulations in French Louisiana, 1724-1766," *Louisiana History* 21, no. 2 (Spring 1980): 154.

40 Usner, "From African Captivity to American Slavery," 28-29.

41 Ibid., 48.

42 McCann, *Stirring the Pot*, 154.

43 David Hunter Strother, a mid-nineteenth-century traveler, addressing a female tour group he was leading. In Patricia B. Mitchell, "The African Influence on Southern Cuisine," http://www.foodhistory.com/foodnotes/leftovers/african/infl/01/, accessed September 4, 2012.

44 R[obert]. Q. Mallard, *Plantation Life Before Emancipation* (Richmond, VA: Whittet and Shepperson, 1892), 18, http://docsouth.unc.edu/fpn/mallard/mallard.html, accessed August 22, 2012.

45 Patricia B. Mitchell, *Plantation Row Slave Cabin Cooking: The Roots of Soul Food* (Chatham, VA: Mitchells Publications, 1998), 14.

46 Mitchell, *Soul on Rice: African Influences on American Cooking* (Chatham, VA: Mitchells Publications, 1993), 18.

47 Ibid.

48 *The Magnolia Mound Plantation Kitchen Book, Being a Compendium of Foodways and Customs of Early Louisiana, 1795-1841, Interspersed with Anecdotes, Incidents and Observations* (1986; 3rd printing, Baton Rouge: Friends of Magnolia Mound Plantation, Inc., 2008), 10.

49 Lyle Saxon, *Old Louisiana* (New York: The Century Co., 1929), 279.

50 Ibid.

51 *Magnolia Mound Plantation Kitchen Book*, 9-10.

52 Taylor, *Eating, Drinking and Visiting in the South*, 54-55.

53 Egerton, *Southern Food*, 28.

54 Taylor, *Eating, Drinking and Visiting in the South*, 83.

55 Mitchell, *Soul on Rice*, 9-10

56 *Magnolia Mound Plantation Kitchen Book*, 11.

57 See http://memory.loc.gov/mss/mesn/163/113108.gif, accessed December 14, 2012.

58 Taylor, *Eating, Drinking and Visiting in the South*, 90-91.

59 Elliot Ashkenazi, ed., *The Civil War Diary of Clara Solomon: Growing Up in New Orleans, 1861-1862* (Baton Rouge: Louisiana State University Press, 1995), 110, 120, 211.

60 Egerton, *Southern Food*, 22-23.

61 Ibid., 23.

62 Taylor, *Eating, Drinking and Visiting in the South*, 96.

63 Egerton, *Southern Food*, 24.

64 Ibid., 113.

65 Christian Woman's Exchange, ed. *Creole Cookery* (1885; repr., Gretna, LA: Pelican Publishing Co., 2005), preface. The Christian Woman's Exchange was an organization founded in New Orleans in 1881 in order to provide a place for needy women to sell homemade products or family heirlooms anonymously since working outside the home was

still frowned upon. The title page explained that their purpose for publishing the cookbook was "to provide funds for the purchase or erection of a building to meet the demands of their constantly increasing business."

66 Lafcadio Hearn, *La Cuisine Creole: A Collection of Culinary Recipes from Leading Chefs and Noted Creole Housewives, Who Have Made New Orleans Famous for Its Cuisine* (New Orleans: F.F. Hansell and Bro., Ltd, 1885), http://archive.org/details/lacuisinereole00hearrich, accessed August 28, 2012.

67 Egerton, *Southern Food*, 114.

68 Thomas Fields, interview.

69 Laudun, "Gumbo This," 164. Laudun explained that the term "*ur*" was popularized by folklorists in the late nineteenth century and early twentieth century to refer to a speculative, idealized, or fictional origin of a term. In this case, Laudun used the word "*ur*-dish" to argue that the most significant dish of the region is not gumbo as many believe, but rather rice and gravy and other foods he lists. Many food writers like to begin a recipe with the phrase "first you make a roux," but Laudun argues that not all regional dishes begin with a roux; therefore, it would be more accurate to state, "first you brown something." John Laudun, phone interview by author, September 26, 2012.

70 Taylor, *Eating, Drinking and Visiting in the South*, 104, 139-40.

71 Ibid., 144-45; and "The Rockefeller Sanitary Commission for the Eradication of Hookworm Disease," http://www.rockarch.org/collections/rockorgs/hookwormadd.php, accessed September 24, 2012.

72 Taylor, *Eating, Drinking and Visiting in the South*, 139-40.

73 Ibid., 149.

74 Ibid., 11, 20-21, 104.

75 Eunice, located in St. Landry Parish, is "Louisiana's Prairie Cajun Capital."

76 Joann Delafose interview by author, Eunice, LA, June 15, 2010.

77 Nicknamed the "Frog Capital of the World," Rayne is a city in Acadia Parish.

78 Fields, interview.

79 Parks is a small community in St. Martin Parish.

80 New Iberia is the parish seat of Iberia Parish.

81 Brenda Placide, interview by Sara Roahen, New Iberia, LA, February 9, 2011, Southern Foodways Alliance, www.southernfoodways.org, accessed September 3, 2012.

82 Lesley "Les" Comeaux, interview by author, Lafayette, LA, August 8, 2010; and Fields, interview.

83 See page 92 for an explanation of couche-couche.

84 Opelousas, touted as the "Zydeco Capital of the World," is located in St. Landry Parish.

85 Comeaux, interview.

86 Fields, interview.

87 Delafose interview, 2010.

88 Fields, interview.

89 Comeaux, interview. The term "sweet bread" refers to potato bread as Comeaux's son Marvin explained in a phone conversation, September 26, 2012.

90 Merline Herbert, interview by Rien T. Fertel, Lafayette, LA, March 17, 2011, Southern Foodways Alliance, www.southernfoodways.org, accessed September 3, 2012.

91 Ibid.

92 Comeaux, interview.

93 Delafose, interview, 2010.

94 Fields, interview.

95 Delafose interview, 2010. "The good bread" referred to white bread, a modern luxury few could afford.

96 Comeaux, interview.

97 Ibid.

98 St. Martinville is the parish seat of St. Martin Parish.

99 Josephine Phillips Cormier, interview by Sara Roahen, St. Martinville, LA, August 20, 2008, Southern Foodways Alliance, www.southernfoodways.org, accessed September 3, 2012. The restaurant has since passed hands to Cormier's son who renamed it Jeaux's.

100 Comeaux, interview.

101 Placide, interview.

102 Madonna Broussard, interview by Rien T. Fertel, Lafayette, LA, March 14, 2011, Southern Foodways Alliance, www.southernfoodways.org, accessed September 3, 2012.

103 Herbert, interview.

104 See page 91 for an explanation of red and white boudin.

105 Placide, interview

106 Joann Delafose, interview by author, Eunice, LA, June 29, 2011.

107 Comeaux, interview.

108 Cormier, interview.

109 Placide, interview.

110 Broussard, interview.

111 For a brief explanation of cowboy stew, see fricassée on page 94.

112 Broussard, interview.

113 Most likely her mother came from either the Ibo tribe or the Ibo-speaking people of southern Nigeria.

114 Cormier, interview.

115 Ibid.

116 Herbert, interview.

117 Jessica Harris, *Iron Pots and Wooden Spoons: Africa's Gifts to New World Cooking* (New York: Macmillan Publishing Co., 1989), 151.

118 McCann, *Stirring the Pot*, 169.

119 Fields, interview.

120 For an excellent discussion of Cajun cuisine, consult Marcelle Bienvenu, Carl A. Brasseaux and Ryan A. Brasseaux, *Stir the Pot: The History of Cajun Cuisine* (New York: Hippocrene Books, Inc., 2005).

121 Mitchell, *Soul on Rice*, 29.

122 Ibid., 26.

123 Folse, "Foods of Africa," *A Taste of Louisiana*, DVD.

124 Soniat, *La Bouche Creole*, 198.

125 Gutierrez, *Cajun Foodways*, 60-61.

126 Belinda Hulin, *Roux Memories: A Cajun-Creole Love Story with Recipes* (Guilford, CT: Lyons Press, 2010), 201.

127 John Laudun, "Gumbo This: The State of a Dish," in Ursula Mathis-Moser and Günter Bischof, eds. *Acadians and Cajuns: The Politics and Culture of French Minorities in North America* (Innsbruck: Innsbruck University Press, 2009), 162.

128 C. Paige Gutierrez, *Cajun Foodways* (Jackson: University Press of Mississippi, 1992), 64. When recommending couche-couche for children, one suggested, "[It should be] good on de tongue en' easy on de stummick, da's how to cook fo' chilluns." Betty Fussell, *I Hear America Cooking* (New York: Elisabeth Sifton Books, Viking, 1986), 149.

129 See https://cracklinfest.com, accessed February 15, 2018.

130 Bienvenu, Brasseaux, and Brasseaux. *Stir the Pot*, 141.

131 Eric Cormier, interview, http://www.southerngumbotrail.com/cormier.shtml, accessed February 24, 2010. Cormier is described as a "Creole by ancestry, a Cajun by culture, an African American by complexion, and a Lake Charles native with a newspaper column devoted to the foodways of his peoples—all of them."

132 Gutierrez, *Cajun Foodways*, 57-58.

133 Eugene Walter, interview, http://www.southerngumbotrail.com/introduction.shtml, accessed February 24, 2010.

134 "Louisiana State Cuisine," http://www.statesymbolsusa.org/Louisiana/Gumbo LouisianaCuisine.html, accessed September 1, 2012.

135 Nicholas Spitzer, "*Monde Créole*: The Cultural World of French Louisiana Creoles and the Creolization of World Cultures," *Journal of American Folklore* 116, no. 459 (Winter 2003): 70.

136 John D. Folse, *Encyclopedia of Cajun and Creole Cuisine*, 38.

137 Frank Brigtsen, interview by Sara Roahen, New Orleans, LA, July 26, 2007, http://www.southerngumbotrail.com/images/oh/Frank%20Brigtsen.pdf, accessed February 24, 2010.

138 Armand Oliver III, interview by Amy Evans, New Orleans, LA, August 4, 2006, http://www.southerngumbotrail.com/olivier.shtml, accessed February 24, 2010.

139 Folse, "Foods of Africa," *A Taste of Louisiana with Chef John Folse and Co.: Our Food Heritage*, DVD, Louisiana Public Broadcasting, 2006.

140 Pierre Clément de Laussat, *Memoires of My Life to My Son during the Year 1803 and After, Which I Spent in Public Service in Louisiana as Commissioner of the French Government for the Retrocession to France of That Colony and for Its Transfer to the United States* (Baton Rouge: Louisiana State University Press, 1978), 86, quoted in Laudun, 156.

141 *The Magnolia Mound Plantation Kitchen Book, Being a Compendium of Foodways and Customs of Early Louisiana, 1795-1841, Interspersed with Anecdotes, Incidents and Observations* (1986; 3rd printing, Baton Rouge: Friends of Magnolia Mound Plantation, Inc., 2008), 13.

142 Marie Kimball, *Thomas Jefferson's Cookbook* (Charlottesville: University Press of Virginia, 1976), 44-45.

143 Ibid., 50.

144 Hulin, *Roux Memories*, 11.

145 Carolyn Shelton, *Zydeco, Blues 'n' Gumbo Cookbook* (n.p.: Chanel Zeno Publishing, 2009), no page.

146 Joann Delafose interview, 2010; and Shelton, *Zydeco, Blues 'n' Gumbo Cookbook.*

147 Fran Osseo-Asare, *Food Culture in Sub-Saharan Africa* (Westport, CT: Greenwood Press, 2005), 13.

148 Folse, "Famous African-Americans," *A Taste of Louisiana*, DVD.

149 Folse, "Foods of Africa," *A Taste of Louisiana*, DVD; and *Encyclopedia of Cajun and Creole Cuisine*, 86.

150 Folse, "Spanish Rule," *A Taste of Louisiana*, DVD.

151 Christian Woman's Exchange, *Creole Cookery*, 67.

152 Gutierrez, *Cajun Foodways*, 59-60.

153 Jessica Harris, *Iron Pots and Wooden Spoons: Africa's Gifts to New World Cooking* (New York: Macmillan Publishing Co., 1989), 74.

154 Patricia B. Mitchell, *Soul on Rice: African Influences on American Cooking* (Chatham, VA: Mitchells Publications, 1993), 26.

155 Mitchell, *Plantation Row Slave Cabin Cooking: The Roots of Soul Food* (Chatham, VA: Mitchells Publications, 1998), 23.

156 Christian Woman's Exchange, ed. *Creole Cookery* (1885; repr., Gretna, LA: Pelican Publishing Co., 2005), 10, 75, 76.

157 Lafcadio Hearn, *La Cuisine Creole: A Collection of Culinary Recipes from Leading Chefs and Noted Creole Housewives, Who Have Made New Orleans Famous for Its Cuisine* (New Orleans: F.F. Hansell and Bro., Ltd, 1885), 18, 85-86, http://archive.org/details/lacuisinereole00hearrich, accessed August 28, 2012.

158 Patricia B. Mitchell, *French Cooking in Early America* (Chatham, VA: Mitchells Publications, 1991), 9.

159 Veronica Wiese, "Cracking the Cooking Code: Deciphering Period Recipes, Tracking down Elusive Ingredients, and Locking in Great Flavor" (presentation, Arkansas Living History Association Annual Conference, Little Rock, AR, February 27, 2011).

160 Mitchell, *French Cooking in Early America*, 19.

161 Laudun, "Gumbo This," 163.

162 Leon E. Soniat, Jr., *La Bouche Creole* (Gretna, LA: Pelican Publishing Co., 1984), 18.

163 "Louisiana State Vegetable Plant," http://www.statesymbolsusa.org/Louisiana/VegetablePlant_LA.html, accessed September 1, 2012.

164 Osseo-Asare, *Food Culture in Sub-Saharan Africa*, 19-20.

165 Vicente Liumba, e-mail message to author, August 14, 2012.

166 Osseo-Asare, *Food Culture in Sub-Saharan Africa*, 20.

167 *Magnolia Mound Plantation Kitchen*, 21.

168 Bienvenu, Brasseaux, and Brasseaux, *Stir the Pot*, 39.

169 "History of the Louisiana Yambilee," http://www.yambilee.com/, accessed September 1, 2012.

170 "Louisiana State Vegetable," http://www.statesymbolsusa.org/Louisiana/Vegetable Louisiana.html, accessed September 1, 2012.

171 Sybil Kein, "Louisiana Creole Food Culture," in Sybil Kein, ed. *Creole: The History and Legacy of Louisiana's Free People of Color* (Baton Rouge: Louisiana State University Press, 2000), 250.

172 Folse "African Slavery in Louisiana," *A Taste of Louisiana*, DVD.

173 Kein, *Creole*, 250.

174 "Louisiana State Doughnut," http://www.statesymbolsusa.org/Louisiana/donut_beignet.html, accessed September 1, 2012.

175 Hulin, *Roux Memories*, 166.

176 Kein, *Creole*, 250.

177 Kein, *Creole*, 250.

178 Mitchell, *French Cooking in Early America*, 9.

179 Hulin, *Roux Memories*, 237.

180 Stacy Gibbons Moore, "'Established and Well Cultivated': Afro-American Foodways in Early Virginia," *Virginia Cavalcade* 39 (Autumn 1989): 74-75, in Mitchell, *Plantation Row*, 30.

181 "What is Pie?", http://www.foodtimeline.org/foodpies.html, accessed June 12, 2016.

182 "Sweet Dough Pie Festival." http://sweetdoughgc.com (accessed June 12, 2016).

Chapter Three

1 This African proverb was quoted by French immersion instructor Issiaka Diakité in André Gladu, *Marron: La Piste Créole en Amérique* ("Marroon: On the Trail of Creoles in North America"), DVD, National Film Board of Canada Production, 2005.

2 Unless otherwise noted, all stories and jokes are transcribed exactly how they appear

in the reference listed. This joke is found in Barry Jean Ancelet, *Cajun and Creole Folktales: The French Oral Tradition of South Louisiana* (Jackson: University Press of Mississippi, 1994), 100-101.

3 Michael D. Picone, "Enclave Dialect Contraction: An External Overview of Louisiana French," *American Speech* 72, no. 2 (Summer 1997): 117.

4 Quote from Maida Owens found in Carl Lindahl, Maida Owens, and C. Renée Harvison, eds., *Swapping Stories: Folktales from Louisiana* (Jackson: University Press of Mississippi, 1997), xix.

5 Richard Bauman, "The Migration of Folktales: Four Channels to the Americas [and Comments and Reply]," *Current Anthropology* 15, no. 1 (March 1974): 13.

6 Carl A. Brasseaux, *French, Cajun, Creole, Houma: A Primer on Francophone Louisiana* (Baton Rouge: Louisiana State University Press, 2005), 1-2.

7 Picone, "Enclave Dialect Contraction," 122.

8 Ira Berlin, "From Creole to African: Atlantic Creoles and the Origins of African-American Society in Mainland North America," *The William and Mary Quarterly*, 3rd ser., 53, no. 2 (April 1996): 257. Elmina is located in present-day Ghana.

9 Gwendolyn Midlo Hall, *Africans in Colonial Louisiana: The Development of Afro-Creole Culture in the Eighteenth Century* (Baton Rouge: Louisiana State University Press, 1992), 34.

10 Berlin, "From Creole to African," 272.

11 Hall, *Africans in Colonial Louisiana*, 26-27.

12 Ibid., 7-8.

13 Brasseaux, *French, Cajun, Creole, Houma*," 11.

14 Hall, *Africans in Colonial Louisiana*, 57.

15 Ibid., 27.

16 Daniel H. Usner, Jr., "From African Captivity to American Slavery: The Introduction of Black Laborers to Colonial Louisiana," *Louisiana History: The Journal of the Louisiana Historical Association* 20, no. 1 (Winter 1979): 26; and Henry P. Dart, "The First Cargo of African Slaves for Louisiana," *The Louisiana Historical Quarterly* 14, no. 2 (April 1931): 170.

17 Hall, *Africans in Colonial Louisiana*, 57.

18 Dart, "The First Cargo of African Slaves for Louisiana," 163.

19 Usner, "From African Captivity to American Slavery," 48.

20 Hall, *Africans in Colonial Louisiana*, 31-32.

21 Dart, "The First Cargo of African Slaves for Louisiana," 175-76.

22 Thomas N. Ingersoll, "The Slave Trade and the Ethnic Diversity of Louisiana's Slave Community," *Louisiana History: Journal of the Louisiana Historical Association* 37, no. 2 (Spring 1996): 140.

23 Ibid., 161.

24 Lyle Saxon, Edward Dryer, and Robert Tallant, eds., *Gumbo Ya-Ya: A Collection of Louisiana Folk Tales* (1945; Gretna, LA: Pelican Publishing Company, 1988), 224-26.

25 John A. Burrison, ed. *Storytellers: Folktales and Legends from the South* (London: University of Georgia Press, 1991), 2.

26 Linda Langley, Susan LeJeune, and Claude Oubre, *Les Raconteurs: Treasure Lore and More* (Eunice: Louisiana State University at Eunice, 1995), 18.

27 According to the 1989 edition of *The World Book Dictionary*, miscegenation is "intermarriage or interbreeding between different races, especially in the United States, between whites and blacks."

28 "Louisiana's Code Noir," http://www.blackpast.org/?q=primary/louisianas-code-noir-1724, accessed October 31, 2009.

29 Linda Langley, Susan LeJeune, and Claude Oubre, *Les Artistes: Crafters Tell Their Tales,* (Eunice: Louisiana State University at Eunice, 1995), 19-20.

30 According to folklorist Maida Owens, Louisiana boasts the largest Native American population within the eastern United States. However, due to extremely good relations with French and African immigrants to the area, they quickly adopted many of their cultural traits. As a result, many Louisiana Indians have lost distinctive cultural elements such as their language (many speak French as their mother tongue), a fact that makes it challenging for some to claim federal tribal status. For a brief overview of Louisiana's various native cultures, see Maida Owens, "Louisiana's Traditional Cultures: An Overview" in Lindahl, Owens, and Harvison, eds. *Swapping Stories: Folktales from Louisiana*, xliv-xlv.

31 Alcée Fortier, *Louisiana Folk-Tales in French Dialect and English Translation, Memoirs of The American Folk-Lore Society*, Vol. 2 (Boston: Houghton, Mifflin, and Company, 1895), v.

32 For a more in-depth discussion of various scholarly opinions regarding Louisiana's Creole French origins, see Fehintola Mosadomi, "The Origin of Louisiana Creole," in Sybil Kein, ed., *Creole: The History and Legacy of Louisiana's Free People of Color* (Baton Rouge: Louisiana State University Press, 2000), 223-43. Jean Raspail, a native of France born in 1925, has authored several award-winning books and novels in French. William Read chaired the English department at Louisiana State University from 1902-1940 and published *Louisiana French* in 1931 as an attempt to document and preserve some of the unusual French terms and phrases heard in Louisiana. Margaret Marshall served as one of the contributing editors in *The Dictionary of Louisiana Creole*, a work published in 1996.

33 Mosadomi, "The Origin of Louisiana Creole," in Kein, *Creole*, 242.

34 For a discussion of the French in Senegal, see John D. Hargreaves, "Assimilation in Eighteenth-Century Senegal," *The Journal of African History* 6, no. 2 (1965): 177-84.

35 Ibid., 226-30.

36 Usner, "From African Captivity to American Slavery," 36.

37 Berlin, "From Creole to African," 272-74.

38 Sybil Kein, "The Use of Louisiana Creole in Southern Literature," in Kein, *Creole*, 119.

39 Hall, *Africans in Colonial Louisiana*, 40. Père Jean Baptiste Labat, an eighteenth-century French missionary, scientist, soldier and slaveholder who spent many years in the West Indies, offered this description of the Fulbe women in a six-volume work of history he published in 1722.

40 Gwendolyn Midlo Hall, "African Women in French and Spanish Louisiana: Origins, Roles, Family, Work, Treatment," in Catherine Clinton and Michele Gillespie, eds., *The Devil's Lane: Sex and Race in the Early South* (New York: Oxford University Press, 1997), 247-48.

41 Mosadomi, "The Origin of Louisiana Creole," in Kein, *Creole*, 241.

42 Ibid., 237.

43 Example provided in Ibid., 233. English translation by author.

44 George Washington Cable, *Creoles and Cajuns: Stories of Old Louisiana*, ed. Arlin Turner (Gloucester, MA: Peter Smith, 1965), 396.

45 Fortier, "Memoirs of the American Folk-Lore Society," Vol. 2, 1895, Louisiana Folk-Tales, *The Journal of American Folklore* 8, no. 28 (January-March 1895): 72.

46 Note that the original Creole French transcription comes directly from the "Memoirs of the American Folk-Lore Society" cited in the previous note. The International French transcription and subsequent English translation are that of the author's.

47 Kein, "Use of Louisiana Creole in Southern Literature," 120. Much less formal than *Le Marseillaise* is the infinitely more humorous song that Cable documented in his work *Cajuns and Creoles*, 420-21.

48 Picone, "Enclave Dialect Contraction," 122.

49 For excellent discussions regarding this topic, see Mary Gehman, "Visible Means of Support: Businesses, Professions, and Trades of Free People of Color," in Kein, *Creole*, 208-22; and Kimberly S. Hangar, "Landlords, Shopkeepers, Farmers and Slave-Owners: Free Black Female Property-Holders in Colonial New Orleans," in David Barry Gaspar and Darlene Clark Hines, eds., *Beyond Bondage: Free Women of Color in the Americas* (Chicago: University of Illinois Press, 2004), 219-36.

50 Kein, "Use of Louisiana Creole in Southern Literature," 131.

51 Ibid., 127.

52 Picone, "Enclave Dialect Contraction," 122.

53 For a discussion of the history of education for blacks, see Ernest J. Middleton, "The Louisiana Education Association, 1901-1970," *The Journal of Negro Education* 47, no. 4 (Autumn 1978): 363-78.

54 Picone, "Enclave Dialect Contraction," 122.

55 Kein, "Use of Louisiana Creole in Southern Literature," 127.

56 See "CODOFIL," http://www.codofil.org/english/index.html, accessed November 1, 2012.

57 David Cheramie, e-mail to author, November 1, 2012.

58 James J. Natsis, "Legislation and Language: The Politics of Speaking French in Louisiana," *The French Review* 73, no. 2 (December 1999): 326; and 1921 Louisiana State Constitution, art. 12, sec. 12, http://archive.org/stream/cu31924030492163#page/n119/mode/2up/search/english, accessed November 1, 2012.

59 Picone, "Enclave Dialect Contraction," 123.

60 Elmo Authement, quoted in Natsis, 326.

61 Gladu, *Marron: La Piste Créole en Amérique*, 2005.

62 Ibid.

63 Ibid.

64 Gerald Istre, interview by author, Lafayette, LA, April 3, 2008.

65 This comment was posted by an individual identified as "CoCo" on October 24, 2010, in response to a website created to teach basic Louisiana Creole phrases. See http://learnlouisianacreole.wordpress.com/, accessed October 31, 2012.

66 Comment posted by an individual identified as "Lisa" on October 23, 2009. See http://learnlouisianacreole.wordpress.com/, accessed October 31, 2012.

67 As a child, the author remembers visiting a great-aunt who could speak no English. What communication occurred between the great-aunt and the younger children was primarily through body language and hand gestures. Verbal communication was cumbersome at best; storytelling, therefore, was impossible.

68 Ancelet, *Cajun and Creole Folktales*, xxv.

69 The word "folklore" was originally written in hyphenated form as seen here. The author has retained this spelling when appropriate to the historical frame of reference.

70 Rosan Augusta Jordan and Frank de Caro, "'In This Folk-lore Land': Race, Class, Identity, and Folklore Studies in Louisiana," *Journal of American Folklore* 109, no. 431 (1996): 46.

71 Ibid., 35-39.

72 Ancelet, *Cajun and Creole Folktales*, xxv.

73 Alcée Fortier, "Louisiana Folk-Tales," *Journal of American Folklore* 7, no. 27 (October-December 1894): 317.

74 Ancelet, *Cajun and Creole Folktales*, xxv.

75 Jordan and de Caro, "'In This Folk-lore Land,'" 52.

76 Ibid., 55.

77 Lindahl, Owens, and Harvison, eds. *Swapping Stories: Folktales from Louisiana*, 3-4.

78 Ancelet, *Cajun and Creole Folktales*, xxv.

79 Ibid., xxvii.

80 Ibid., xxv.

81 Bauman, "The Migration of Folktales," 14.

82 Philip M. Peek, "The Migration of Folktales: Four Channels to the Americas [and Comments and Reply]," *Current Anthropology* 15, no. 1 (March 1974): 19.

83 Alan Dundes, "African and Afro-American Tales," *Research in African Literatures* 7, no. 2 (Autumn 1976): 186-87.

84 See Introduction to Lindahl, Owens, and Harvison, eds. *Swapping Stories: Folktales from Louisiana.*

85 Mosadomi, "The Origin of Louisiana Creole," 230.

86 To date, no work currently exists that separates Creole folktales regionally. Barry Ancelet, the primary authority on South Louisiana's Creole repertoire, focuses on the Acadiana region.

87 Ancelet, *Cajun and Creole Folktales*, xlviii.

88 Ibid., xxviii

89 Quoted on the dedication page from Ancelet, *Cajun and Creole Folktales*, vi.

90 John David Smith, "The Unveiling of Slave Folk Culture, 1865-1920," *Journal of Folklore Research* 21, no. 1 (April 1984): 50.

91 For a more in-depth discussion of the African origins of Bouki, see Marcia Gaudet, "Bouki, the Hyena, in Louisiana and African Tales," *The Journal of American Folklore* 105, no. 415 (Winter 1992): 66-72.

92 Sand Warren Marmillion, ed. *Compare Lapin and Piti Bonhomme Godron (The Tar Baby) as Written by Alcée Fortier 1894* (n.p.: The Zoe Company, 1996).

93 Gaudet, "Bouki, the Hyena," 66-68.

94 Fortier, *Louisiana Folk-Tales in French Dialect and English Translation*, 110.

95 Ibid., 25-27.

96 Ibid., 112.

97 John W. Roberts, *From Trickster to Badman: The Black Folk Hero in Slavery and Freedom* (Philadelphia: University of Pennsylvania Press, 1989), 38.

98 Ancelet, "Louisiana French Oral Literature: An Overview," in Vaughan B. Baker and Jean T. Kramer, *Louisiana Tapestry: The Ethnic Weave of St. Landry Parish* (Lafayette: Center for Louisiana Studies, 1983), 51.

99 The original transcript can be found in Alcée Fortier, "Four Louisiana Folk-Tales," *The Journal of American Folklore* 19, no. 73 (April-June 1906): 125-26.

100 The author found this story included in the footnotes of Ronald M. Rassner, "The Transmission of the Oral Narrative from Africa to Brazil," in special issue on Lusophone African Writing, *Research in African Literatures* 13, no. 3 (Autumn 1982): 353. Rassner credits Alcée Fortier's article "Louisiana Nursery Tales" found in the *Journal of American Folklore* 2, no. 4 (1889): 37 as the source for this story. It appears here in a slightly abbreviated form.

101 Ancelet, *Cajun and Creole Folktales*, xxxii.

102 Ancelet, Jay Edwards, and Glen Pitre, *Cajun Country* (Jackson: University Press of Mississippi, 1991), 201-202.

103 Hall quoted this proverb to introduce her chapter entitled "The Bambara in Louisiana: From the Natchez Uprising to the Samba Bambara Conspiracy," in *Africans in Colonial Louisiana*, 96.

104 Saxon, *Old Louisiana* (New York: The Century Co., 1929), 354.

105 Cable, *Creoles and Cajuns*, 399. For other examples from Cable's collection see "Creole Slave Songs," in Ibid., 394-432.

106 Ibid., 403.

107 Ancelet, *Cajun and Creole Folktales*, 94-95.

108 Lindahl, Owens, and Harvison, eds. *Swapping Stories: Folktales from Louisiana*, 74-75.

109 Ibid., 75-76.

110 The exact transcript of this tale can be found in Ancelet, *Cajun and Creole Folktales*, 115.

111 Ibid., 127.

112 Ibid., 156-57.

113 Ibid., 175-78

Chapter Four

1 William Shakespeare, "Twelfth Night," http://shakespeare.mit.edu/twelfth_night/full.html, accessed September 29, 2012.

2 Clifton Chenier, the "King of Zydeco," quoted in Ben Sandmel, *Zydeco!* (Jackson: University Press of Mississippi, 1999), 14.

3 George Washington Cable, *Cajuns and Creoles: Stories of Old Louisiana*, ed. Arlin Turner (Gloucester, MA: Peter Smith, 1965), 390.

4 John Koegel, "Spanish and French Mission Music in Colonial North America," *Journal of the Royal Musical Association* 126, no. 1 (2001): 1-2.

5 For a brief history of St. Louis Cathedral, see http://stlouiscathedral.org/early_history.html, accessed September 29, 2012.

6 Koegel, "Spanish and French Mission Music," 45.

7 Ibid., 46.

8 Ibid., 45-46.

9 Gwendolyn Midlo Hall, *Africans in Colonial Louisiana: The Development of Afro-Creole Culture in the Eighteenth Century* (Baton Rouge: Louisiana State University Press, 1992), 57.

10 Daniel H. Usner, Jr., "From African Captivity to American Slavery: The Introduction of Black Laborers to Colonial Louisian," *Louisiana History: The Journal of the Louisiana Historical Association* 20, no. 1 (Winter 1979): 26; and Henry P. Dart, "The First Cargo of African Slaves for Louisiana," *The Louisiana Historical Quarterly* 14, no. 2 (April 1931): 170.

11 Mathé Allain, *"Not Worth a Straw": French Colonial Policy and the Early Years of Louisiana* (Lafayette: Center for Louisiana Studies, University of Southwestern Louisiana, 1988), 38; and Hall, *Africans in Colonial Louisiana*, 57.

12 Jerah Johnson, *Congo Square in New Orleans* (New Orleans: University of New Orleans, 1995), 6.

13 John Minton, "Creole Community and 'Mass' Communication: Houston Zydeco as a Mediated Tradition," *The Journal of Folklore Research* 32, no. 1 (January-April 1995): 15.

14 Florence E. Borders, "Researching Creole and Cajun Musics in New Orleans," *Black Music Research Journal* 8, no. 1 (1998): 18.

15 Minton, "Houston Creoles and Zydeco: The Emergence of an African Urban Popular Style," *American Music* 14, no. 4, New Perspectives on the Blues (Winter 1996): 490.

16 Borders, "Researching Creole and Cajun Musics in New Orleans," 18.

17 Louisiana was alternately under French and Spanish rule throughout the colonial period. French control began in 1699 and lasted until Spain acquired Louisiana in 1763. President Thomas Jefferson incorporated the territory into the United States of America via the Louisiana Purchase in 1803.

18 Gary A. Donaldson, "A Window on Slave Culture: Dances at Congo Square in New Orleans, 1800-1862," *The Journal of Negro History* 69, no. 2 (Spring 1984): 64-65.

19 Ibid., 63.

20 Ibid., 67.

21 Ibid., 65. For historian and writer George Washington Cable's memories of Congo Square, see "The Dance in Place Congo," in Cable, 366-93. In this selection, Cable gives excellent descriptions not only of the musical instruments being played and the songs sung, but also of the various ethnicities that participated and the different kinds of dances they performed.

22 Donaldson, "A Window on Slave Culture," 66. See Cable, *Cajuns and Creoles*, 383.

23 *Daily Picayune* (December 11, 1864), quoted in Donaldson, "A Window on Slave Culture," 68.

24 See Cable, *Cajuns and Creoles*, 372.

25 Borders, "Researching Creole and Cajun Musics in New Orleans," 18. Spanish governor Alejandro O'Reilly established new laws governing slavery in Louisiana known as *las Partidas Siete* or O'Reilly's Code. According to these laws, slaves who became priests or served the Spanish military were manumitted. The code also liberated slaves who had married free blacks and even granted freedom to enslaved females who had been hired out as prostitutes by their masters. Following the transfer of power from French to Spanish rule, some French families returned to France or relocated to the Caribbean without freeing their slaves. Under O'Reilly's Code, slaves who had been living independently from their masters for ten years could petition for their freedom. See Mary Gehman, *The Free People of Color of New Orleans: An Introduction* (Donaldsonville, LA: Margaret Media, Inc., 2009), 30-34. For a discussion of the Caribbean refugees who flooded Louisiana following the islands' slave uprisings, see Carl A. Brasseaux and Glenn R. Conrad, eds., *The Road to Louisiana: The Saint-Domingue Refugees, 1792-1809* (Lafayette: Center for Louisiana Studies, 1992).

26 Ronald R. Morazan, "'Quadroon' Balls in the Spanish Period," *Louisiana History: The Journal of the Louisiana Historical Association* 14, no. 3 (Summer 1973): 310.

27 New Orleans's quadroon balls may have originated in the French colony of Saint Domingue, where similar *redoutes des filles de couleur* took place.

28 Gehman, *The Free People of Color of New Orleans*, 59.

29 For an interesting discussion of this phenomenon, see Kimberly S. Hanger, "Landlords, Shopkeepers, Farmers, and Slave-Owners: Free Black Female Property-Holders in Colonial New Orleans," in David Barry Gaspar and Darlene Clark Hines, eds. *Beyond Bondage: Free Women of Color in the Americas* (Chicago: University of Illinois Press, 2004), 219-36; and Mary Gehman, "Visible Means of Support: Businesses, Professions, and Trades of Free People of Color," in Kein, *Creole*, 208-22.

30 Martin, "*Plaçage* and the Louisiana *Gens de Couleur Libre:* How Race and Sex Defined the Lifestyles of Free Women of Color," in Kein, *Creole*, 67. For a remarkable exception to the *plaçage* custom, see Virginia Meacham Gould, "Henriette Delille, Free Women of Color, and Catholicism in Antebellum New Orleans, 1727-1852," in Gaspar and Hine, eds., *Beyond Bondage*, 271-85. All of the women in Henriette Delille's family had cohabitated with white men for generations, but Delille refused to live in concubinage and never married. Instead, she founded the Catholic order of the Sisters of the Holy Family in New Orleans where she and other free women of color established schools, built orphanages and asylums for elderly, sick, and abandoned women, as well as provided food and clothing for the poor. Through their charitable work, Delille and the Sisters of the Holy Family made a difference in the lives of many enslaved and free women and children of African descent. See also page 227.

31 Ibid., 67-68.

32 Morazan, "'Quadroon' Balls in the Spanish Period," 310-11.

33 Ibid., 311-13. For a more thorough examination of this topic, see R. Randall Couch, "The Public Masked Balls of Antebellum New Orleans: A Custom of Masque outside the Mardi Gras Tradition," *Louisiana History: The Journal of the Louisiana Historical Association* 35, no. 4 (Autumn 1994): 403-31.

34 Pierre Clement de Laussat, *Memoires of my Life to my Son During the Years 1803 and After,* trans. Sister Agnes-Josephine Pastwa, ed. Robert D. Bush (Baton Rouge: Louisiana State University Press, 1978), 92-3.

35 Couch, "The Public Masked Balls of Antebellum New Orleans," 408-409.

36 Thomas Fiehrer, "From Quadrille to Stomp: The Creole Origins of Jazz," in "The 1890s," eds. David Horn and Dave Laing, special issue, *Popular Music* 10, no. 1 (January 1991): 25.

37 Ibid., 29.

38 Louisiana Creole Clarence Garlow recorded this song entitled "Bon Ton Roula" in 1949 and it became a hit in 1950, reaching #7 on the US *Billboard* R&B chart. The song's title is a phonetical spelling of the Louisiana phrase *laissez les bon temps rouler* ("let the good times roll"). Lyrics for the song are printed in Sandmel, *Zydeco!*, 42.

39 Ibid., 33.

40 Barry Jean Ancelet, "Zydeco/Zarico: Blues, Beans, and Beyond," *Black Music Research Journal* 8, no. 1 (1998): 45; and Sandmel, *Zydeco!*, 34.

41 Ancelet, "Zydeco/Zarico," 43; and Minton, "Houston Creoles and Zydeco," 490.

42 Ancelet, "Zydeco/Zarico," 43.

43 Ibid., 45.

44 Sandmel, *Zydeco!*, 34-35.

45 Ibid., 33-34 (first quote), 38-40 (second quote).

46 Cedric Watson, *Cedric Watson*, Track 4 "*J'ai été tout autour du Pays*" (Valcour Records), 2008. Although Cedric modified the title slightly, the musical arrangement remained essentially the same.

47 Sandmel, *Zydeco!*, 71

48 Ibid., 38.

49 Ancelet, "Zydeco/Zarico: Blues, Beans, and Beyond," 39.

50 Linda Langley, Susan G. Lejeune, and Claude Oubre, eds. "Just Exactly What Is Zydeco?" in *Le Reveil des Fetes: Revitalized Celebrations and Performance Traditions, Folklife Series*, Vol. 3 (Eunice: Louisiana State University at Eunice, 1995), 73.

51 This information appears in a footnote in Minton's article, "Creole Community and 'Mass' Communication," 13; and in Sara Le Menestrel, "The Color of Music; Social Boundaries and Stereotypes in Southwest Louisiana French Music," *Southern Cultures* (Fall 2007): 90.

52 Norm Cohen, "French-American Music," *The Journal of American Folklore* 102, no. 405 (July-September 1998): 336.

53 Sandmel, *Zydeco!*, 134.

54 Ibid., 38; and Langley, "Just Exactly What Is Zydeco," 73.

55 Barry Jean Ancelet, *Cajun and Creole Music Makers: Musiciens cadiens et creoles* (Jackson: University of Mississippi Press, 1999), 73-74.

56 Goldman Thibodeaux, interview by author, Lawtell, LA, February 7, 2009.

57 Ancelet, *Cajun and Creole Music Makers*, 78.

58 Ibid.

59 Sandmel, *Zydeco!*, 38.

60 D.K. Wilgus, "Cajun and Zydeco Music," *The Journal of American Folklore* 81, no. 321 (July-September 1968): 275.

61 Ancelet, *Cajun and Creole Music Makers,* 79.

62 Borders, "Researching Creole and Cajun Musics in New Orleans," 21.

63 Goldman Thibodeaux and Joe Citizen, interview by author, Lafayette, LA, Spring 2008.

64 Thibodeaux interview, February 7, 2009.

65 Thibodeaux and Citizen, interview.

66 Ancelet, *Cajun and Creole Music Makers*, 78.

67 Thibodeaux and Citizen, interview.

68 Ibid.

69 Ibid.

70 Jeffery Broussard, interview by author, Henderson, LA, February 22, 2009.

71 Ibid.

72 Ibid.

73 Geno Delafose, interview by author, Eunice, LA, January 31, 2009.

74 John Delafose Biography by Jason Ankeny, http://www.allmusic.com/artist/john-delafose-mn0000221165/biography, accessed 11 June, 2016.

75 Delafose, interview.

76 Ibid.

77 Thibodeaux and Citizen, interview.

78 Delafose, interview.

79 Ibid.

80 Ibid.

81 Mark Mattern, "Let the Good Times Unroll: Music and Race Relations in Southwest Louisiana," *Black Music Research Journal* 17, no. 2 (Autumn 1997): 161.

82 Delafose, interview.

83 "Dancing in the Dust," http://www.theind.com/lead-news/4902, accessed April 18, 2010.

84 The popularity of Creole and Zydeco music has steadily increased among white Cajuns and black Creoles alike, and it is fairly common to find a sea of shades on the dance floor nowadays. Perhaps this is due to the dancers' enjoyment of the rhythmic music's improvisational nature, or perhaps it is simply a reflection of changing attitudes towards race relations in more recent years.

85 Thibodeaux and Citizen, interview.

86 Cedric Watson, interview by author, Lafayette, LA, March 7, 2009.

87 Ibid.

88 The Original Southwest Louisiana Zydeco Music Festival is held annually in Plaisance, Louisiana, just outside of Opelousas. When it was established in 1982, four hundred people gathered in the middle of a farmer's field to celebrate the area's musical heritage.

89 Watson, interview.

90 Ibid.

91 Ibid.

92 "Cedric Watson Biography," http://www.cedricwatson.com/bio.html, accessed April 18, 2009.

93 Sandmel, *Zydeco!*, 40-41.

94 Ibid.

95 Ibid., 24.

96 Clifton Chenier highly valued his band's performance ability, in addition to their musicianship, and realized that having someone sitting on stage playing a washboard would detract from an otherwise electrifying show. Therefore, he and his brother invented the modern *frottoir*, and commissioned the corrugated metal instrument with extensions that rested on the player's shoulders to be built in a Lafayette metal shop. From Sandmel, *Zydeco!*, 24. See also pg. 203.

97 Stanley "Buckwheat Zydeco" Dural, interview by WMSE Radio host, http://www.wmseradio.wordpress.com/2010/02/15/interview-buckwheat-zydeco, accessed February 25, 2010.

98 Thibodeaux, interview.

Chapter Five

1 Deborah J. Clifton, interview by André Gladu in "*Zarico*," National Film Board of Canada Production, 1985.

2 Herbert Wiltz, interview by author, Lafayette, LA, June 28, 2011.

3 For a more in-depth discussion of this topic, see Elista Istre, "*'Laissez les Bon Temps Rouler!'*: Cajun Stereotypes and the Development of Cultural Tourism in South Louisiana," (master's thesis, University of Louisiana at Lafayette, 2002).

4 The author has traveled to over thirty countries and has seen so-called "Cajun" dishes on menus around the world.

5 Wiltz, interview.

6 Ben Sandmel, *Zydeco!*, (Jackson: University Press of Mississippi, 1999), 127.

7 Ibid., 129.

8 Moriah Istre, a stage manager and announcer who has worked *Festivals Acadiens et Créoles* for years, noted that many people, including the general public, festival organizers, and volunteers still consider the event to be primarily a Cajun festival. Following the name change, she noticed that festival t-shirts buried the "*et Créoles*" part of the name in the graphic art and used a much smaller font than the "*Festivals Acadiens*" part. She said that although the name change does reflect a more inclusive and representative title, many Creoles have trouble overlooking more than three decades of neglect. Moriah Istre, interview by author, Jonesboro, AR, February 7, 2013.

9 The author served as Vermilionville's Historic Programs Manager when the first Creole Culture Day took place. Since then, she has returned frequently as a visitor to enjoy the cooking demonstrations, craft lessons, and musical performances that occur each Creole Culture Day in June.

10 For more information on the Jean Lafitte units in Louisiana, see http://www.nps.gov/jela/index.htm.

11 The author worked as a seasonal interpretive park ranger at Jean Lafitte's Acadian Cultural Center in Lafayette, although she also helped at the Eunice location from time to time. Her primary task was to coordinate and execute summer camps for children that highlighted various aspects of South Louisiana's various cultures. Nearly all of the camp's participants were Cajun children; she can only recall one child in attendance who was black. She remembers that when the child's father came to pick him up one day, he wandered through the exhibit while his son finished a project. The man was shocked to see so many Creole faces included in the exhibit. Like most Creoles, he thought the site was only for Cajuns, a misconception that has persisted largely due to the unit's name.

12 Kelly Strenge, phone interview by author, February 7, 2013. Strenge has worked for LCVC since 1989.

13 Ibid.

14 "Creole Country Guide: A Guide to African-American and Creole Culture in South Louisiana," brochure published by the Lafayette Convention and Visitors Commission, 2005. Author's collection.

15 Strenge, interview.

16 The author conducted this internet search on January 25, 2013.

17 "Tastiest Town," http://www.lafayettetravel.com/eat/tastiest-town, accessed January 28, 2013.

18 Katharine Shilcutt, "Jambalaya, Crawfish Pie and File' Gumbo: The Bounty of Lafayette," http://blogs.houstonpress.com/eating/2012/01/lafayette_dining_scene.php, accessed January 29, 2013.

19 Linda Fontenot, interview by author, Lafayette, LA, July 10, 2012.

20 "About *La Cuisine de Maman* at Vermilionville of Lafayette, LA," http://www.lacuisinedemamanlafayette.com/about-la-cuisine-de-maman-at-vermilionville-lafayette-la.htm, accessed January 29, 2013.

21 Menu from *La Cuisine de Maman*, e-mail to author by Jesse Guidry, Vermilionville's Public Relations and Marketing Coordinator, February 1, 2013.

22 Fontenot, interview. While the author worked as Vermilionville's historic programs manager, cooking demonstrations were regular occurrences.

23 Eric Cormier, interview by Sara Roahen, Lake Charles, LA, September 11, 2007, Southern Foodways Alliance, http://www.southerngumbotrail.com/cormier.shtml, accessed February 24, 2010.

24 Joann Delafose, interview by author, Eunice, LA, June 29, 2011.

25 "22nd Annual Lebeau Zydeco Festival," http://louisiana.kitchenandculture.com/event/22nd-annual-lebeau-zydeco-festival, accessed January 31, 2013.

26 St. Martinville Cultural Heritage Center's African-American Museum sponsors the annual Okra Festival. Since Africans introduced the vegetable to the New World and since "gumbo" is the African word for okra, the vegetable's role in the region's cultural heritage is significant.

27 Tony Chachere [pronounced "sash-er-ee"], the creator of this well-known product, was born in Opelousas in 1905. After a second retirement at the age of sixty-seven, he started his company and began selling the first Creole seasoning blend on the market. He later became the first chef inducted into the Louisiana Chef's Hall of Fame in 1995, one week before his death. Referred to as simply "Tony's" by locals, the green containers that prominently display the label "Original Creole Seasoning" are perhaps the most widely-recognized Creole product on the market. Tony's is so popular, national chains like Subway promote the product line. Although the company is still owned and operated by Mr. Chachere's descendants and is still located in Opelousas, the product line has expanded beyond the seasoning blend to include injectable marinades, fish fry mixes, roux and gravy mixes, and most recently sandwich sauces. For more information about Tony Chachere and the company he founded, see http://www.tonychachere.com/, accessed January 28, 2013.

28 Mary Alice Drake, interview by author, Lafayette, LA, June 28, 2011.

29 Wiltz, interview.

30 Ibid.

31 Drake, interview.

32 Wiltz, interview.

33 Albert Valdman et al., eds., *Dictionary of Louisiana French: As Spoken in Cajun, Creole, and American Indian Communities* (Jackson: University Press of Mississippi, 2010).

34 "Francophone Studies: Minor in Cajun and Creole Studies," http://languages.louisiana.edu/French/minorcajun.html, accessed February 4, 2013.

35 Sybil Kein, "Use of Louisiana Creole in Southern Literature," in Kein, *Creole: The History and Legacy of Louisiana's Free People of Color* (Baton Rouge: Louisiana State University Press, 2000), 147. Although Rice is primarily known for her vampire novels, *The Feast of All Saint's Day* is a historical novel that focuses on the complexity and beauty of New Orleans's free people of color population. A made-for-television film adaptation of Rice's novel bearing the same name was released in 2001.

36 Kein, *Creole*, 148. Cable's *The Grandissimes: A Creole Life* chronicles the race and class struggles among New Orleans Creoles in the years following the Louisiana Purchase in 1803. One of the main characters is Honoré Grandissime, a white French Creole who is head of his prominent family, while his half-brother, also named Honoré Grandissime, is a quadroon who tries to help an enslaved African prince named Bras-Coupé.

37 Kein, *Creole*, 149.

38 Dianne Geunin-Lelle, "The Birth of Cajun Poetry: An Analysis of *Cris sur le bayou: naissance d'une poésie acadienne en Louisiane*," in *The French Review* 70, no. 3 (February 1997): 448. English translation provided by Deborah J. Clifton, e-mail to author, March 14, 2013.

39 Ibid., 440-41. English translation by author.

40 Wiltz, interview.

41 Kein, *Creole*, 150.

42 Ibid., 151.

43 Sybil Kein, *An American South* (East Lansing: Michigan State University Press, 1996), 63.

44 Michael D. Picone, "Enclave Dialect Contraction: An External Overview of Louisiana French," *American Speech* 72, no. 2 (Summer 1997): 143.

45 Ibid., 144.

46 Although some linguists are able to distinguish between different regional influences on Louisiana Creole, due to the limited number of fluent speakers, most Creoles emphasize differences between International French and Louisiana Creole as opposed to variations within Creole French. The works of various Creole scholars and poets such as New Orleans-born Sybil Kein (who now resides in Natchitoches) and Deborah J. Clifton from the prairie parishes, illustrates this united effort to preserve Louisiana Creole French.

47 Kein, "Use of Louisiana Creole in Southern Literature," 153-54. See Catharine Savage Brosman's work entitled *Louisiana Creole Literature: A Historical Study* (University Press of Mississippi, 2013) for not only an important historical overview of the state's diverse Creole population, but also, and perhaps more significantly, an excellent survey and analysis of their literary contributions. Brosman cited a variety of authors, including those who were famous and obscure, dark-skinned and light-skinned, native and non-native, male and female. Whether these writers expressed themselves in French or English, venerated or vilified Creole culture, published volumes of historical significance or wrote just a handful of poems, Brosman effectively demonstrated how they all contributed to Louisiana's Creole literary repertoire.

48 Clifton, interview in "*Zarico*."

49 Cody Daigle, "Sounding Through Generations," *The Times of Acadiana*, September 3, 2009.

50 Ibid.

51 Sandmel, *Zydeco!*, 12.

52 The club initially had two entrances. The adults drank and danced on one side of the building while teenagers danced to a jukebox on the other side.

53 R. Reese Fuller, "A Sense of Place," http://www.theind.com/cover-story/183, accessed February 7, 2013.

54 Ibid.

55 Ibid.

56 Herman Fuselier, "Tribute Remembers Carrier and His Legendary Lounge," *The Times of Acadiana*, December 27, 2012.

57 For a video clip of Chubby Carrier's Grammy speech, see http://www.chubbycarrier.com/grammyaward/, accessed February 8, 2013.

58 Fuselier, "Tribute Remembers Carrier and His Legendary Lounge."

59 Ibid.

60 Herman Fuselier, "El Sid O's Marks Thirty Years of Making 'em Dance," Lafayette *Daily Advertiser*, May 8, 2015. http://www.theadvertiser.com/story/entertainment/2015/05/08/el-sidos-marks-years-making-em-dance/27008359/, accessed 14 June 2016.

61 Sandmel, *Zydeco!*, 151.

62 "Best World Music Festival?", http://www.theind.com/a-a-e/arts-a-entertainment-stories/10118-best-world-music-festival, accessed February 11, 2013; and "2012 World Music at About.com Readers' Choice Awards Winners," http://worldmusic.about.com/od/newsarticles/ss/2012-World-Music-At-About-Com-Readers-Choice-Awards-Winners_5.htm, accessed February 11, 2013.

63 For an excellent discussion of this festival, see Moriah Istre, "*Festivals Acadiens*: Reflections of Cultural Identity through Print Media in Southwest Louisiana" (master's thesis, University of Louisiana at Lafayette, 2008).

64 Josephine "Jo" Charles, interview by author, Lafayette, LA, October 13, 2012.

65 Daigle, "Sounding Through Generations."

66 Ibid.

67 "The Original Southwest Louisiana Zydeco Music Festival," http://www.zydeco.org/, accessed February 12, 2013.

68 Ibid.

69 Daigle, "Sounding Through Generations."

70 "Jeffery Broussard: Taking Creole to the People," http://www.offbeat.com/2012/05/01/jeffery-broussard-taking-creole-to-the-people/, accessed February 12, 2013.

71 Ibid.

72 "Creole for Kidz," http://www.terrancesimien.com/creoleforkidz.html, accessed February 12, 2013.

73 "Terrance Simien and the Zydeco Experience," http://www.terrancesimien.com/news.html, accessed February 12, 2013.

74 Sandmel, *Zydeco!*, 90.

75 Ibid., 124.

76 "Creole Renaissance Festival," http://www.creolerenaissance.com/, accessed February 13, 2013.

77 Daigle, "Sounding Through Generations."

Bibliography

Books

Allain, Mathé.*"Not Worth a Straw": French Colonial Policy and the Early Years of Louisiana*. Lafayette: Center for Louisiana Studies, University of Southwestern Louisiana 1988.

Ancelet, Barry Jean. *Cajun and Creole Folktales: The French Oral Tradition of South Louisiana*. Jackson: University Press of Mississippi, 1994.

_____. *Cajun and Creole Music Makers: Musiciens cadiens et creoles*. Jackson: University of Mississippi Press, 1999.

_____. *One Generation at a Time: Biography of a Cajun and Creole Music Festival.* Lafayette: Center for Louisiana Studies, University of Louisiana at Lafayette, 2007.

Ancelet, Barry Jean, Jay Edwards, and Glen Pitre. *Cajun Country*. Jackson: University Press of Mississippi, 1991.

Ashkenazi, Elliot, ed. *The Civil War Diary of Clara Solomon: Growing Up in New Orleans, 1861-1862*. Baton Rouge: Louisiana State University Press, 1995.

Bienvenu, Marcelle, Carl A. Brasseaux, and Ryan A. Brasseaux. *Stir the Pot: The History of Cajun Cuisine*. New York: Hippocrene Books, 2005.

Brasseaux, Carl A. *French, Cajun, Creole, Houma: A Primer on Francophone Louisiana*. Baton Rouge: Louisiana State University Press, 2005.

Brasseaux, Carl A., and Glenn R. Conrad, eds. *The Road to Louisiana: The Saint-Domingue Refugees, 1792-1809*. Translated by David Cheramie. Lafayette: Center for Louisiana Studies, 1992.

Brasseaux, Carl A, Keith P. Fontenot, and Claude F. Oubre. *Creoles of Color in the Bayou Country*. Jackson: University Press of Mississippi, 1994.

Brasseaux, Ryan A. and Kevin S. Fontenot, eds. *Accordions, Fiddles, Two Step, & Swing: A Cajun Music Reader*. Lafayette: Center for Louisiana Studies, 2006.

Brosman, Catharine Savage. *Louisiana Creole Literature: A Historical Study*. Jackson: University Press of Mississippi, 2013.

Broyard, Bliss. *One Drop: My Father's Hidden Life—A Story of Race and Family Secrets*. New York: Little Brown and Company, 2007.

Burnard, Trevor. *Creole Gentlemen: The Maryland Elite, 1691-1776*. New York: Routledge, 2002.

Burrison, John A., ed. *Storytellers: Folktales and Legends from the South*. London: University of Georgia Press, 1991.

Cable, George Washington. *Creoles and Cajuns: Stories of Old Louisiana.* Edited by Arlin Turner. Gloucester, MA: Peter Smith, 1965.

_____. *The Creoles of Louisiana.* 1884. Reprint, Gretna, LA: Pelican Publishing, 2000.

Christian Woman's Exchange. *Creole Cookery.* 1885. Reprint, Gretna, LA: Pelican Publishing Co., 2005.

Clark, Emily. *The Strange History of the American Quadroon: Free Women of Color in the Revolutionary Atlantic World.* Chapel Hill: University of North Carolina Press, 2013.

Cohen, Robin, and Paola Toninato, eds. *The Creolization Reader: Studies in Mixed Identities and Cultures.* New York: Routledge, 2010.

de Laussat, Pierre Clement. *Memoires of my Life to my Son During the Years 1803 and After.* Translated by Sister Agnes-Josephine Pastwa. Edited by Robert D. Bush. Baton Rouge: Louisiana State University Press, 1978.

Din, Gilbert C. *The Canary Islanders of Louisiana.* Baton Rouge: Louisiana State University Press, 1999.

Dormon, James H., ed. *Creoles of Color of the Gulf South.* Knoxville: University of Tennessee Press, 1996.

Egerton, John. *Southern Food: At Home, on the Road, in History.* New York: Alfred A. Knopf, Inc., 1987.

Evans, Freddi Williams. *Congo Square: African Roots in New Orleans.* Lafayette: University of Louisiana at Lafayette Press, 2011.

Fairclough, Adam. *Race and Democracy: The Civil Rights Struggle in Louisiana, 1915-1972.* Athens: University of Georgia Press, 2008.

Feibleman, Peter S. *American Cooking: Creole and Acadian.* New York: Time-Life Books, 1971.

Folse, John D. *The Encyclopedia of Cajun and Creole Cuisine.* Gonzales, LA: Chef John Folse and Company Publishing, 2010.

Fortier, Alcée, ed. *Louisiana Folktales: In French Dialect and English Translation.* 1895. Reprint, Boston: Houghton, Mifflin, and Co., 1976.

_____. *Louisiana Folk-Tales in French Dialect and English Translation, Memoirs of The American Folk-Lore Society,* Vol. 2. Boston: Houghton, Mifflin, and Company, 1895.

_____. *Louisiana Folktales: Lapin, Bouki, and Other Creole Stories in French Dialect and English Translation.* Edited by Russell Desmond. Lafayette: University of Louisiana at Lafayette Press, 2011.

Fussell, Betty. *I Hear America Cooking.* New York: Elisabeth Sifton Books, Viking, 1986.

Gaspar, David Barry, and Darlene Clark Hine, eds. *Beyond Bondage: Free Women of Color in the Americas.* Chicago: University of Illinois Press, 2004.

Gehman, Mary. *The Free People of Color of New Orleans: An Introduction.* Donaldsonville, LA: Margaret Media, Inc., 2009.

Glassie, Henry. *All Silver and No Brass: An Irish Christmas Mumming.* Philadelphia: University of Pennsylvania Press, 1975.

Gould, Philip. *Cajun Music and Zydeco.* Baton Rouge: Louisiana State University Press, 1992.

____. *Natchitoches and Louisiana's Timeless Cane River.* Baton Rouge: Louisiana State University Press, 2002.

Gutierrez, C. Paige. *Cajun Foodways.* Jackson: University Press of Mississippi, 1992.

Hall, Gwendolyn Midlo. *Africans in Colonial Louisiana: The Development of Afro-Creole Culture in the Eighteenth Century.* Baton Rouge: Louisiana State University Press, 1992.

Harris, Jessica. *Iron Pots and Wooden Spoons: Africa's Gifts to New World Cooking.* New York: Macmillan Publishing Co., 1989.

Heywood, Linda M., and John K. Thornton. *Central Africans, Atlantic Creoles, and the Foundation of the Americas, 1585-1660.* Cambridge: Cambridge University Press, 2007.

Hirsch, Arnold R., and Joseph Logsdon, eds. *Creole New Orleans: Race and Americanization.* Baton Rouge: Louisiana State University Press, 1992.

Hulin, Belinda. *Roux Memories: A Cajun-Creole Love Story with Recipes.* Guilford, CT: Lyons Press, 2010.

Kein, Sybil, ed. *Creole: The History and Legacy of Louisiana's Free People of Color.* Baton Rouge: Louisiana State University Press, 2000.

_____. *An American South.* East Lansing: Michigan State University Press, 1996.

_____. *Gumbo People.* New Orleans: Margaret Media, Inc., 1999.

Kimball, Marie. *Thomas Jefferson's Cookbook.* Charlottesville: University Press of Virginia, 1976.

King, Grace. *Creole Families of New Orleans.* New York: Macmillan, 1921.

_____. *New Orleans: The Place and the People.* New York: Macmillan, 1895.

Kniffen, Fred B., Hiram F. Gregory, and George A. Stokes. *The Historic Indian Tribes of Louisiana: From 1542 to the Present.* Baton Rouge: Louisiana State University Press, 1987.

Langley, Linda, Susan LeJeune, and Claude Oubre. *Les Artistes: Crafters Tell Their Tales.* Eunice: Louisiana State University at Eunice, 1995.

_____. *Les Raconteurs: Treasure Lore and More.* Eunice: Louisiana State University at Eunice, 1995.

Lindahl, Carl, Maida Owens, and C. Renée Harvison, eds. *Swapping Stories: Folktales from Louisiana*. Jackson: University Press of Mississippi, 1997.

Marmillion, Sand Warren, ed. *Compare Lapin and Piti Bonhomme Godron (The Tar Baby) as Written by Alcée Fortier 1894*. N.p.: The Zoe Company, 1996.

McCann, James C. *Stirring the Pot: A History of African Cuisine*. Athens: Ohio University Press, 2009.

Mills, Gary B. *The Forgotten People: Cane River's Creoles of Color*. Baton Rouge: Louisiana State University Press, 1977.

Mitchell, Patricia B. *French Cooking in Early America*. Chatham, VA: Mitchells Publications, 1991.

_____. *Plantation Row Slave Cabin Cooking: The Roots of Soul Food*. Chatham, VA: Mitchells Publications, 1998.

_____. *Soul on Rice: African Influences on American Cooking*. Chatham, VA: Mitchells Publications, 1993.

Osseo-Asare, Fran. *Food Culture in Sub-Saharan Africa*. Westport, CT: Greenwood Press, 2005.

Peacocke, James S. *The Creole Orphans; or, Lights and Shadows of Southern Life: A Tale of Louisiana*. New York: Derby and Jackson, 1856.

Powell, Lawrence N. *The New Orleans of George Washington Cable: The 1887 Census Office Report*. Baton Rouge: Louisiana State University Press, 2008.

Roberts, John W. *From Trickster to Badman: The Black Folk Hero in Slavery and Freedom*. Philadelphia: University of Pennsylvania Press, 1989.

Sandmel, Ben. *Zydeco!* Jackson: University Press of Mississippi, 1999.

Saucier, Corinne L., ed. *Folk Tales from French Louisiana*. 1962. Reprint, Baton Rouge: Claitor's Publishing Division, 1972.

Saxon, Lyle, Edward Dryer, and Robert Tallant, eds. *Gumbo Ya-Ya: A Collection of Louisiana Folk Tales*. 1945. Reprint, Gretna, LA: Pelican Publishing Company, 1988.

Saxon, Lyle. *Old Louisiana*. New York: The Century Co., 1929.

Shelton, Carolyn. *Zydeco, Blues 'n' Gumbo Cookbook*. N.p.: Chanel Zeno Publishing, 2009.

Smolenski, John. *Friends and Strangers: The Making of a Creole Culture in Colonial Pennsylvania*. Philadelphia: University of Pennsylvania Press, 2010.

Soniat, Leon E., Jr. *La Bouche Creole*. Gretna, LA: Pelican Publishing Co., 1984.

Tannahill, Reay. *Food in History*. New York: Crown Publishers, Inc., 1988.

Taylor, Joe Gray. *Eating, Drinking, and Visiting in the South: An Informal History*. Updated ed., Baton Rouge: Louisiana State University Press, 2008.

The Magnolia Mound Plantation Kitchen Book, Being a Compendium of Foodways and Customs of Early Louisiana, 1795-1841, Interspersed with Anecdotes, Incidents and Observations. 1986. 3rd printing, Baton Rouge: Friends of Magnolia Mound Plantation, Inc., 2008.

Valdman, Albert, Kevin J. Rottet, Barry Jean Ancelet, Richard Guidry, Thomas A. Klinger, Amanda LaFleur, Tamara Lindner, Michael D. Picone, and Dominique Ryon, eds. *Dictionary of Louisiana French: As Spoken in Cajun, Creole, and American Indian Communities.* Jackson: University Press of Mississippi, 2010.

Wall, Bennet H., ed. *Louisiana: A History.* Wheeling, IL: Harlan Davidson, 1997.

Journal Articles and Chapters in Books

Ancelet, Barry Jean. "Louisiana French Oral Literature: An Overview." In *Louisiana Tapestry: The Ethnic Weave of St. Landry Parish*, edited by Vaughan B. Baker and Jean T. Kramer, 49-69. Lafayette: Center for Louisiana Studies, 1983.

____. "Zydeco/Zarico: Beans, Blues, and Beyond." *Black Music Research Journal* 8, no. 1 (1988): 33-49.

Bauman, Richard. "The Migration of Folktales: Four Channels to the Americas [and Comments and Reply]." *Current Anthropology* 15, no. 1 (March 1974): 13-14.

Berlin, Ira. "From Creole to African: Atlantic Creoles and the Origins of African-American Society in Mainland North America." *The William and Mary Quarterly,* 3rd ser., 53, no. 2 (April 1996): 251-88.

Bernard, Shane, and Julia Girouard. "'Colinda': Mysterious Origins of a Cajun Folksong." *Journal of Folklore Research* 29, no. 1 (January-April 1992): 37-52.

Berquin-Duvallon. "An Anti-Creole Observation." *Louisiana History: The Journal of the Louisiana Historical Association* 9, no. 2 (Spring 1968): 138.

Borders, Florence E. "Researching Creole and Cajun Musics in New Orleans." *Black Music Research Journal* 8, no. 1 (1988): 15-31.

Brasseaux, Carl A. "The Administration of Slave Regulations in French Louisiana, 1724-1766." *Louisiana History: The Journal of the Louisiana Historical Association* 21, no. 2 (Spring 1980): 139-58.

Carrière, J.M. "Creole Dialect of Missouri." *American Speech* 14, no. 2 (April 1939): 109-19.

Chaplin, Joyce E. "Creoles in British America: From Denial to Acceptance." In *Creolization: History, Ethnography, Theory,* edited by Charles Stewart, 46-65. Walnut Creek, CA: Left Coast Press, 2007.

Cohen, Norm. "French-American Music." *The Journal of American Folklore* 102, no. 405 (July-September 1998): 336-37.

Couch, R. Randall. "The Public Masked Balls of Antebellum New Orleans: A Custom of Masque outside the Mardi Gras Tradition." *Louisiana History: The Journal of the Louisiana Historical Association* 35, no. 4 (Autumn 1994): 403-31.

Dart, Henry P. "The First Cargo of African Slaves for Louisiana, 1718." *The Louisiana Historical Quarterly* 14, no. 2 (April 1931): 163-77.

Davis, John. "Observations on the Negroes of Louisiana." *Journal of Negro History* 2, no. 2 (April 1917): 164-85.

Domínguez, Virginia R. "Social Classification in Creole Louisiana." *American Ethnologist* 4, no. 4 (November 1977): 589-602.

Donaldson, Gary A. "A Window on Slave Culture: Dances at Congo Square in New Orleans, 1800-1862." *The Journal of Negro History* 69, no. 2 (Spring 1984): 63-72.

Dundes, Alan. "African and Afro-American Tales." *Research in African Literatures* 7, no. 2 (Autumn 1976): 181-99.

"Egyptian Creole Origin Theory." *Oceanic Linguistics Special Publications* 14, *A Bibliography of Pidgin and Creole Languages* (1975): 53-55.

Everett, Donald E. "Free Persons of Color in Colonial Louisiana." *Louisiana History: The Journal of the Louisiana Historical Association* 7, no. 1 (Winter 1966): 21-50.

Ewen, Charles R. "From Colonist to Creole: Archaeological Patterns of Spanish Colonization in the New World." *Historical Archaeology* 34, no. 3 (2000): 36-45.

Fiehrer, Thomas. "From Quadrille to Stomp: The Creole Origins of Jazz." In "The 1890s," edited by David Horn and Dave Laing. Special issue, *Popular Music* 10, no. 1 (January 1991): 21-38.

Foner, Laura. "The Free People of Color in Louisiana and St. Domingue: A Comparative Portrait of Two Three-Caste Slave Societies." *The Journal of Social History* 3, no. 4 (Summer 1970): 406-30.

Fortier, Alcée. "Four Louisiana Folk-Tales." *The Journal of American Folklore* 19, no. 73 (April-June 1906): 123-26.

_____. "Louisiana Folk-Tales." *Journal of American Folklore* 7, no. 27 (October-December 1894): 317.

_____. "Memoirs of the American Folk-Lore Society," Vol. 2, 1895, Louisiana Folk-Tales. *The Journal of American Folklore* 8, no. 28 (January-March 1895): 72.

Gaudet, Marcia. "Bouki, the Hyena, in Louisiana and African Tales." *The Journal of American Folklore* 105, no. 415 (Winter 1992): 66-72.

Geunin-Lelle, Dianne. "The Birth of Cajun Poetry: An Analysis of *Cris sur le bayou: naissance d'une poésie acadienne en Louisiane.*" *The French Review* 70, no. 3 (February 1997): 439-51.

Gould, Virginia Meacham. "Henriette Delille, Free Women of Color, and Catholicism in Antebellum New Orleans, 1727-1852." In *Beyond Bondage: Free Women of Color in the Americas*, edited by David Barry Gaspar and Darlene Clark Hines, 271-85. Chicago: University of Illinois Press, 2004.

Hall, Gwendolyn Midlo. "African Women in French and Spanish Louisiana: Origins, Roles, Family, Work, Treatment." In *The Devil's Lane: Sex and Race in the Early South*, edited by Catherine Clinton and Michele Gillespie, 247-62. New York: Oxford University Press, 1997.

Hangar, Kimberly S. "Landlords, Shopkeepers, Farmers and Slave-Owners: Free Black Female Property-Holders in Colonial New Orleans." In *Beyond Bondage: Free Women of Color in the Americas*, edited by David Barry Gaspar and Darlene Clark Hines, 219-36. Chicago: University of Illinois Press, 2004.

Hardy, James D., Jr. "The Transportation of Convicts to Colonial Louisiana." *Louisiana History: The Journal of the Louisiana Historical Association* 7, no. 3 (Summer 1966): 207-20.

Hargreaves, John D. "Assimilation in Eighteenth-Century Senegal." *The Journal of African History* 6, no. 2 (1965): 177-84.

Henry, Jacques M., and Carl L. Bankston, III. "Propositions for a Structuralist Analysis of Creolism." *Current Anthropology* 39, no. 4 (August-October 1998): 558-66.

Hume, Elizabeth, and Georgios Tserdanelis. "Labial Unmarkedness in Sri Lankan Portuguese Creole." *Phonology* 19, no. 3 (2002): 441-58.

Ingersoll, Thomas N. "The Slave Trade and the Ethnic Diversity of Louisiana's Slave Community." *Louisiana History: The Journal of the Louisiana Historical Association* 37, no. 2 (Spring 1996): 133-61.

Istre, Elista. "De l'Angola à l'Acadiana: Les Traditions Orales en Afrique Centrale Atlantique et dans le Sud de la Louisiane." *Cahiers des Anneaux de la Mémoire: L'Afrique Centrale Atlantique*, no. 14 (2011): 276-96.

_____. Les Créoles du Sud de la Louisiane: Origines et Évolution d'une Identité Culturelle Moderne." *Cahiers des Anneaux de la Mémoire: Créolités aux Amériques Françaises/Creolization in the French Americas*, no. 15 (2014): 147-91.

Johnson, Jerah. "New Orleans's Congo Square: An Urban Setting for Early Afro-American Culture Formation." *Louisiana History: The Journal of the Louisiana Historical Association* 32, no. 2 (Spring 1991): 117-57.

Jordan, Rosan Augusta, and Frank de Caro. "'In This Folk-lore Land': Race, Class, Identity, and Folklore Studies in Louisiana." *Journal of American Folklore* 109, no. 431 (1996): 31-59.

Koegel, John. "Spanish and French Mission Music in Colonial North America." *Journal of the Royal Musical Association* 126, no. 1 (2001): 1-53.

Langley, Linda, Susan G. Lejeune, and Claude Oubre, eds. "Just Exactly What *Is* Zydeco?" In *Le Reveil des Fetes: Revitalized Celebrations and Performance Traditions, Folklife Series*, vol. 3., 73-74. Eunice: Louisiana State University at Eunice, 1995.

Laudun, John. "Gumbo This: The State of a Dish." In *Acadians and Cajuns: The Politics and Culture of French Minorities in North America*, edited by Ursula Mathis-Moser and Günter Bischof, 155-66. Innsbruck (Austria): Innsbruck University Press, 2009.

Le Menestrel, Sara. "The Color of Music: Social Boundaries and Stereotypes in Southwest Louisiana French Music." *Southern Cultures* (Fall 2007): 87-105.

Leglaunec, Jean-Pierre. "Slave Migrations in Spanish and Early American Louisiana: New Sources and New Estimates." *Louisiana History: The Journal of the Louisiana Historical Association* 46, no. 2 (Spring 2005): 185-209.

Markey, Thomas L. "Afrikaans: Creole or Non-Creole?" *Zeitschrift für Dialektologie und Linguistik* 49, no. 2 (1982): 169-207.

Mattern, Mark. "Let the Good Times Unroll: Music and Race Relations in Southwest Louisiana." *Black Music Research Journal* 17, no. 2 (Autumn 1997): 159-68.

Middleton, Ernest J. "The Louisiana Education Association, 1901-1970." *The Journal of Negro Education* 47, no. 4 (Autumn 1978): 363-78.

Miles, William F.S. "The Creole Malaise in Mauritius." *African Affairs* 98, no. 391 (April 1999): 211-28.

Minton, John. "Creole Community and 'Mass' Communication: Houston Zydeco as a Mediated Tradition." *The Journal of Folklore Research* 32, no. 1 (January-April 1995): 1-19.

____. "Houston Creoles and Zydeco: The Emergence of an African Urban Popular Style." *American Music* 14, no. 4, *New Perspectives on the Blues* (Winter 1996): 480-526.

Mitchell, Mary Naill. "'A Good and Delicious Country': Free Children of Color and How They Learned to Imagine the Atlantic World in Nineteenth-Century Louisiana." *History of Education Quarterly* 40, no. 2 (Summer 2000): 123-44.

Morazan, Ronald R. "'Quadroon' Balls in the Spanish Period." *Louisiana History: The Journal of the Louisiana Historical Association* 14, no. 3 (Summer 1973): 310-15.

Mouer, Daniel. "Chesapeake Creoles: The Creation of Folk Culture in Colonial Virginia." In *The Archaeology of 17th-Century Virginia*, edited by Theodore R. Reinhart and Dennis J. Pogue. Petersburg, VA: Dietz Press, 1993.

Natsis, James J. "Legislation and Language: The Politics of Speaking French in Louisiana." *The French Review* 73, no. 2 (December 1999): 325-31.

"Observations of Berquin Duvallon on the Free People of Colour in Louisiana in 1802." *Journal of Negro History* 2 (April 1917): 167-74.

Owens, Jonathan. "Creole Arabic: The Orphan of All Orphans." *Anthropological Linguistics* 43, no. 3 (Fall 2001): 348-78.

Peek, Philip M. "The Migration of Folktales: Four Channels to the Americas [and Comments and Reply]." *Current Anthropology* 15, no. 1 (March 1974): 19.

Picone, Michael D. "Enclave Dialect Contraction: An External Overview of Louisiana French." *American Speech* 72, no. 2 (Summer 1997): 117-53.

Rassner, Ronald M. "The Transmission of the Oral Narrative from Africa to Brazil." In special issue on Lusophone African Writing. *Research in African Literatures* 13, no. 3 (Autumn 1982): 327-58.

Read, William A. "Creole and 'Cajan.'" *American Speech* 1, no. 9 (June 1926): 483.

Romaine, Suzanne. "Hawai'i Creole English as a Literary Language." *Language in Society* 23, no. 4 (December 1994): 527-54.

Russell, Sarah. "Intermarriage and Intermingling: Constructing the Planter Class in Louisiana's Sugar Parishes, 1803-1850." *Louisiana History: The Journal of the Louisiana Historical Association* 46, no. 4 (Autumn 2005): 407-34.

Smith, John David. "The Unveiling of Slave Folk Culture, 1865-1920." *Journal of Folklore Research* 21, no. 1 (April 1984): 47-62.

Smith, Michael Peter. "Postmodernism, Urban Ethnography, and the New Social Space of Ethnic Identity." *Theory and Society* 21, no. 4 (August 1992): 493-531.

Spitzer, Nicholas. "*Monde Créole*: The Cultural World of French Louisiana Creoles and the Creolization of World Cultures." *Journal of American Folklore* 116, no. 459 (Winter 2003): 57-72.

Thompson, Shirley. "'*Ah Toucoutou, ye conin vous*': History and Memory in Creole New Orleans." *American Quarterly* 53, no. 2 (June 2001): 232-66.

Tregle, Joseph G., Jr., "Creoles and Americans." In *Creole New Orleans: Race and Americanization*, edited by Arnold R. Hirsch and Joseph Logsdon, 131-88. Baton Rouge: Louisiana State University Press, 1992.

Usner, Daniel H., Jr. "From African Captivity to American Slavery: The Introduction of Black Laborers to Colonial Louisiana." *Louisiana History: The Journal of the Louisiana Historical Association* 20, no. 1 (Winter 1979): 25-48.

Walker, Juliet E. K. "Racism, Slavery, and Free Enterprise: Black Entrepreneurship in the United States before the Civil War." *The Business History Review* 60, no. 3 (Autumn 1986): 343-82.

Wilgus, D.K. "Cajun and Zydeco Music." *The Journal of American Folklore* 81, no. 321 (July-September 1968): 274-76.

Unpublished Works

Istre, Elista. "'*Laissez les Bon Temps Rouler!*': Cajun Stereotypes and the Development of Cultural Tourism in South Louisiana." Master's thesis, University of Louisiana at Lafayette, 2002.

Istre, Moriah. "*Festivals Acadiens*: Reflections of Cultural Identity through Print Media in Southwest Louisiana." Master's thesis, University of Louisiana at Lafayette, 2008.

Online Sources

"1921 Louisiana State Constitution, art. 12, sec. 12." http://archive.org/stream/cu31924030492163#page/n119/mode/2up/search/english (accessed November 1, 2012).

"2012 World Music at About.com Readers' Choice Awards Winners." http://worldmusic.about.com/od/newsarticles/ss/2012-World-Music-At-About-Com-Readers-Choice-Awards-Winners_5.htm (accessed February 11, 2013).

"22nd Annual Lebeau Zydeco Festival." http://louisiana.kitchenandculture.com/event/22nd-annual-lebeau-zydeco-festival (accessed January 31, 2013).

"About *La Cuisine de Maman* at Vermilionville of Lafayette, LA." http://www.lacuisinedemamanlafayette.com/about-la-cuisine-de-maman-at-vermilionville-lafayette-la.htm (accessed January 29, 2013).

"Best World Music Festival?" http://www.theind.com/a-a-e/arts-a-entertainment-stories/10118-best-world-music-festival (accessed February 11, 2013).

Brasseaux, Carl A. "Creoles." http://ccet.louisiana.edu/tourism/cultural/The_People/creole.html (accessed April 22, 2010).

"Cedric Watson Biography." http://www.cedricwatson.com/bio.html (accessed April 18, 2009).

Council for Development of French in Louisiana (CODOFIL). "CODOFIL." http://www.codofil.org/english/index.html (accessed November 1, 2012).

"Creole for Kidz." http://www.terrancesimien.com/creoleforkidz.html (accessed February 12, 2013).

"Creole Renaissance Festival." http://www.creolerenaissance.com/ (accessed February 13, 2013).

"Dancing in the Dust." http://www.theind.com/lead-news/4902 (accessed April 18, 2010).

"Francophone Studies: Minor in Cajun and Creole Studies." http://languages.louisiana.edu/French/minorcajun.html (accessed February 4, 2013).

Fuller, R. Reese. "A Sense of Place." http://www.theind.com/cover-story/183 (accessed February 7, 2013).

"Haiti." https://www.cia.gov/library/publications/the-world-factbook/geos/ha.html (accessed April 17, 2012).

Hearn, Lafcadio. *La Cuisine Creole: A Collection of Culinary Recipes from Leading Chefs and Noted Creole Housewives, Who Have Made New Orleans Famous for Its Cuisine.* New Orleans: F.F. Hansell and Bro., Ltd, 1885, http://archive.org/details/lacuisinereole00hearrich (accessed August 28, 2012).

"History of the Louisiana Yambilee." http://www.yambilee.com/ (accessed September 1, 2012).

Hopkins, John-Bryan. "Foodimentary: Celebrate Food Every Day." http://foodimentary.com/best-food-quotes-list/culture-quotes-food/ (accessed September 4, 2012).

Hunt, Katrina Brown. "America's Best Cities for Foodies." http://travel.yahoo.com/p-interests-40686622 (accessed September 23, 2011).

"Jeffery Broussard: Taking Creole to the People." http://www.offbeat.com/2012/05/01/jeffery-broussard-taking-creole-to-the-people/ (accessed February 12, 2013).

"Louisiana State Cuisine." http://www.statesymbolsusa.org/Louisiana/GumboLouisianaCuisine.html (accessed September 1, 2012).

"Louisiana State Doughnut." http://www.statesymbolsusa.org/Louisiana/donut_beignet.html (accessed September 1, 2012).

"Louisiana State Vegetable." http://www.statesymbolsusa.org/Louisiana/VegetableLouisiana.html (accessed September 1, 2012).

"Louisiana State Vegetable Plant." http://www.statesymbolsusa.org/Louisiana/VegetablePlant_LA.html (accessed September 1, 2012).

"Louisiana's Code Noir (1724)." http://www.blackpast.org/?q=primary/louisianas-code-noir-1724 (accessed October 31, 2009).

Mallard, R[obert]. Q. *Plantation Life Before Emancipation.* Richmond, VA: Whittet and Shepperson, 1892. http://docsouth.unc.edu/fpn/mallard/mallard.html (accessed August 22, 2012).

Mitchell, Patricia B. "The African Influence on Southern Cuisine." http://www.foodhistory.com/foodnotes/leftovers/african/infl/01/ (accessed September 4, 2012).

"The Original Southwest Louisiana Zydeco Music Festival." http://www.zydeco.org/ (accessed February 12, 2013).

"Port Barre Cracklin Festival." https://cracklinfest.com (accessed February 15, 2018).

"The Rockefeller Sanitary Commission for the Eradication of Hookworm Disease." http://www.rockarch.org/collections/rockorgs/hookwormadd.php (accessed September 24, 2012).

"St. Louis Cathedral." http://stlouiscathedral.org/early_history.html (accessed September 29, 2012).

Shakespeare, William. "Twelfth Night." http://shakespeare.mit.edu/twelfth_night/full.html (accessed September 29, 2012).

Shilcutt, Katharine. "Jambalaya, Crawfish Pie and File' Gumbo: The Bounty of Lafayette." http://blogs.houstonpress.com/eating/2012/01/lafayette_dining_scene.php (accessed January 29, 2013).

"Sweet Dough Pie Festival." http://sweetdoughgc.com (accessed June 12, 2016).

"Tastiest Town." http://www.lafayettetravel.com/eat/tastiest-town (accessed January 28, 2013).

"Terrance Simien and the Zydeco Experience." http://www.terrancesimien.com/news.html (accessed February 12, 2013).

"Tony Chachere." http://www.tonychachere.com/ (accessed January 28, 2013).

"What is Pie?" http://www.foodtimeline.org/foodpies.html (accessed June 12, 2016).

Interviews

Bourque, Darrell. Interview by author. Lafayette, LA. October 12, 2017.

Brigtsen, Frank. Interview by Sara Roahen. New Orleans, LA. July 26, 2007. http://www.southerngumbotrail.com/images/oh/Frank%20Brigtsen.pdf (accessed February 24, 2010).

Broussard, Jeffery. Interview by author. Henderson, LA. February 22, 2009.

Broussard, Madonna. Interview by Rien T. Fertel. Lafayette, LA. March 14, 2011. Southern Foodways Alliance. www.southernfoodways.org (accessed September 3, 2012).

Charles, Josephine "Jo." Interview by author. Lafayette, LA. October 13, 2012.

Comeaux, Lesley "Les." Interview by author. Lafayette, LA. August 8, 2010.

Cormier, Eric. Interview by Sara Roahen. Lake Charles, LA. September 11, 2007. Southern Foodways Alliance. http://www.southerngumbotrail.com/cormier.shtml (accessed February 24, 2010).

Cormier, Josephine Phillips. Interview by Sara Roahen. St. Martinville, LA. August 20, 2008. Southern Foodways Alliance. www.southernfoodways.org (accessed September 3, 2012).

Delafose, Geno. Interview by author. Eunice, LA. January 31, 2009.

Delafose, Joann. Interview by author. Eunice, LA. June 15, 2010.

____. Interview by author. Eunice, LA. June 29, 2011.

Drake, Mary Alice. Interview by author. Lafayette, LA. June 28, 2011.

Dural, Stanley "Buckwheat Zydeco." Interview by WMSE Radio host. http://www.wmseradio.wordpress.com/2010/02/15/interview-buckwheat-zydeco (accessed February 25, 2010).

Fields, Thomas "Big Hat." Interview by author. Lafayette, LA. June 28, 2011.

Fontenot, Linda. Interview by author. Lafayette, LA. July 10, 2012.

Herbert, Merline. Interview by Rien T. Fertel. Lafayette, LA. March 17, 2011. Southern Foodways Alliance. www.southernfoodways.org (accessed September 3, 2012).

Istre, Gerald. Interview by author. Lafayette, LA. April 3, 2008.

Istre, Moriah. Interview by author. Jonesboro, AR. February 7, 2013.

Oliver, Armand, III. Interview by Amy Evans. New Orleans, LA. August 4, 2006. http://www.southerngumbotrail.com/olivier.shtml (accessed February 24, 2010).

Placide, Brenda. Interview by Sara Roahen. New Iberia, LA. February 9, 2011. Southern Foodways Alliance. www.southernfoodways.org (accessed September 3, 2012).

Quinho, Daniel. Phone interview by author. June 19, 2016.

Strenge, Kelly. Phone interview by author. February 7, 2013.

Thibodeaux, Goldman and Joe Citizen. Interview by author. Lafayette, LA. Spring 2008.

Thibodeaux, Goldman. Interview by author. Lawtell, LA. February 7, 2009.

Thibodeaux, Theresa. Interview by author. Lafayette, LA. October 12, 2017.

Watson, Cedric. Interview by author. Lafayette, LA. March 7, 2009.

Wiltz, Herbert. Interview by author. Lafayette, LA. June 28, 2011.

Audio and Video Recordings

Folse, John D. "A Taste of Louisiana with Chef John Folse and Company: Our Food Heritage," DVD. Louisiana Public Broadcasting, 2006.

Gladu, André. *Marron: La Piste Créole en Amérique* ("Marroon: On the Trail of Creoles in North America"), DVD. National Film Board of Canada Production, 2005.

Istre, Moriah. *First Cousins: Cajun and Creole Music in South Louisiana*, DVD. Fleurish Films, 2016.

Rodman, Bill. *Reconstructing Creole: Cane River Creoles*, DVD. Louisiana Public Broadcasting, 2005.

Spitzer, Nicholas. "'Zydeco': Creole Music and Culture in South Louisiana," DVD. *Flower Films*, 1986.

Watson, Cedric. *Cedric Watson*, Track 4 "*J'ai été tout autour de Pays.*" Valcour Records, 2008.

Additional Sources

Cheramie, David. E-mail to author. November 1, 2012.

Clifton, Deborah J. E-mail to author. March 14, 2013.

"Creole Country Guide: A Guide to African-American and Creole Culture in South Louisiana." Brochure. Lafayette Convention and Visitors Commission, 2005.

Daigle, Cody. "Sounding Through Generations." *The Times of Acadiana*. September 3, 2009.

Fuselier, Herman. "Tribute Remembers Carrier and His Legendary Lounge." *The Times of Acadiana*. December 27, 2012.

____. "El Sid O's Marks Thirty Years of Making 'em Dance." Lafayette *Daily Advertiser*. May 8, 2015.

Guidry, Jesse. E-mail to author. February 1, 2013.

Liumba, Vicente. E-mail to author. August 14, 2012.

Masseaut, Jean-Marc. E-mail to author. September 15, 2017.

Wiese, Veronica. "Cracking the Cooking Code: Deciphering Period Recipes, Tracking down Elusive Ingredients, and Locking in Great Flavor." Presentation, Arkansas Living History Association Annual Conference. Little Rock, AR. February 27, 2011.

Image Credits

All photos are © Elista Istre except for the following:

Chapter 1

xvi, Thibodeaux wedding photo, courtesy of Goldman and Theresa Thibodeaux; 4, *Portrait of an African Slave Woman,* attributed to Annibale Carracci, c. 1580, from Wikimedia Commons; 5, Map of Creole parishes in Louisiana, courtesy of Center for Louisiana Studies; 6, *Linen Day, Roseau, Dominica—A Market Scene* by Agostino Brunias, c. 1780, from Wikimedia Commons; 7, *The seat of Mr. Duplantier, near New Orleans & lately occupied as Head quarters by Genl. J. Wilkinson*, courtesy of New York Public Library Digital Collections; 8, Frontspiece from the book *Saint-Domingue, ou Histoire de Ses Révolutions*, published c. 1815, entitled *Burning of Cape Français. General revolt of the Blacks. Massacre of the Whites*, courtesy of Center for Louisiana Studies; 9, Laura Plantation, photo by Elisa Rolle, from Wikimedia Commons; 10, Advertisement for a New Orleans slave auction in the *Orleans Gazette* on November 11, 1810, courtesy of America's Historical Newspapers database; 11 top, *Sale of Estates, Pictures and Slaves in the Rotunda, New Orleans* by William Henry Brooke, engraving with watercolor from *The Slave States of America*, vol. 1, 1842, public domain; 11 bottom, Ad from the *Orleans Gazette* on May 17, 1820, courtesy of America's Historical Newspapers database; 12, The *Code Noir*, from Wikimedia Commons; 13 top, *Negroes Hiding in the Swamps of Louisiana*, in *Harper's Weekly*, May 10, 1873, courtesy of the Library of Congress Digital Collections; 13 bottom, Runaway slave illustration recreated in pen and watercolor by Bernarda Bryson, c. 1935, courtesy of the Library of Congress Digital Collections; 14, Enslaved female field hand, sketch by E.W. Kemble, from *Century Magazine*, courtesy of Center for Louisiana Studies; 15 top and center, *Museu Nacional da Escravatura* (National Slave Museum) in Luanda, Angola, all images courtesy of Daniel Quinho; 15 bottom, Angola Penitentiary, 1934, courtesy of the Library of Congress Digital Collections; 16, Marie Philomene Donato Olivier, c. 1865, from private collection; 17 top, Painting *Creole in a Red Turban*, c. 1840, by Jacques Amans, from Wikimedia Commons, permanently held at the Historic New Orleans Collection; 17 bottom, *Colored Lady of New Orleans*, courtesy of New York Public Library Digital Collections; 18, Detail from *Free Women of Color with their Children and Servants in a Landscape*, (c. 1764–96) by Agostino Brunias, from Wikimedia Commons; 21, Melrose Plantation, courtesy of the Library of Congress Digital Collections; 22, Louisiana Creole of Color family with their darker-skinned servant, from private collection; 24, Unidentified Creole girl with her doll in Frilot Cove, Louisiana, from private collection; 29, Metoyer family crawfish boil, courtesy of the Metoyer family; 35, Telesmar Fontenot, Alicia Matte Leday, and John Leday, all courtesy of Goldman and Theresa Thibodeaux; 36, Théodule Thibodeaux, courtesy of Darrell Bourque; 36, Anatole Thibodeaux and Josephine Carriere, courtesy of Goldman and Theresa Thibodeaux; 37, Philomene Latiolais Thibodeaux, courtesy of Darrell Bourque.

Chapter 2

45 top, Paul Prudhomme, photo by Marvin Joseph, from the *Washington Post*; 45 middle, Leah Chase, photo by Matthew Hinton, from the *New Orleans Advocate*; 45 bottom, John Folse, photo by Kerry Maloney, from the *New Orleans Advocate*; 47, Thomas "Big Hat" Fields,

photo by Ezra Istre; 49, *Communal Venison Hunt*, by Antoine Simon Le Page du Pratz, 1758; 50 top, *Louisiana Indians Walking Along a Bayou* by Alfred Boisseau, 1847, from Wikimedia Commons, permanently held at the New Orleans Museum of Art; 51 bottom, botanical drawing of sassafras plant, 1890, from Wikimedia Commons; 53, *African women pounding rice* and *Negre du Senegal*, both by Jacques Grasset de Saint-Sauveur, c. 1797, from Wikimedia Commons; 54, Illustration of rice cultivation in South, courtesy of the Library of Congress Digital Collection; 55, *Carrying a Bushel of Corn*, by Mary Hallock Foote, courtesy of the New York Public Library Digital Collection; 58, *Southern Scenes—Cooking Shrimps*, in *Frank Leslie's Popular Monthly*, July 1877, vol. IV, no. 1: 100; 61, *Clear Starching in Louisiana* by Auguste Hervieu, 1837; 62, Kitchen scene at Destrehan Plantation, courtesy of Ian McKellar, from Wikimedia Commons; 63, *Courrier de la Louisiane*, May 21, 1821, courtesy of America's Historical Newspapers database; 64, La San Mire, courtesy of the Library of Congress Digital Collection; 65, Black army cook, courtesy of the Library of Congress Digital Collection; 66, *The starving people of New Orleans fed by the United States military authorities*, in *Harper's Weekly*, June 14, 1862, courtesy of the Library of Congress Digital Collection; 67, Antoine's Restaurant postcard, from Wikimedia Commons; 68, Lepine family, c. 1922, courtesy of the Library of Congress Digital Collection; 70, Detail of black workers pitching bundles of rice into a wagon in Crowley, Louisiana, by Lee Russell, 1938, Farm Security Administration, courtesy of the Library of Congress Digital Collection; 71, "Negro laborers employed by Joseph La Blanc [*sic*], wealthy Cajun farmer, Crowley, Louisiana, with possum and birds they shot," by Lee Russell, 1938, Farm Security Administration, courtesy of the Library of Congress Digital Collection; 73, Unidentified young men working on their farm in Frilot Cove, from private collection; 74 top, "Negro sugarcane worker drinking water in the field near New Iberia, Louisiana," by Lee Russell, 1938, Farm Security Administration, courtesy of the Library of Congress Digital Collection; 74 bottom, Sharecropper tenant preparing a meal in the kitchen, courtesy of the Library of Congress Digital Collection, by Lee Russell, 1938, Farm Security Administration, courtesy of the Library of Congress Digital Collection; 76, Merline Herbert, courtesy of Denny Culbert for the Southern Foodways Alliance; 77, Children heading off to school in Mix, Louisiana, by Lee Russell, 1938, Farm Security Administration, courtesy of the Library of Congress Digital Collection; 78, Children fishing in the ditch in Thomastown, Louisiana, 1940, by Marion Post Wolcott, courtesy of the Library of Congress Digital Collection; 79, Family going to town in wagon near Opelousas, Louisiana, by Lee Russell, 1938, Farm Security Administration, courtesy of the Library of Congress Digital Collection; 81, Smothered sausage and rice with corn, greens, and cornbread, courtesy of Denny Culbert for the Southern Foodways Alliance; 82, Brenda Placide with grandson Typann, courtesy of Sara Roahen for the Southern Foodways Alliance; 83, Madonna Broussard, courtesy of Denny Culbert for the Southern Foodways Alliance; 84, Josephine Phillips Cormier, courtesy of Sara Roahen for the Southern Foodways Alliance; 85, Cormier's shrimp and okra gumbo, courtesy of Sara Roahen for the Southern Foodways Alliance; 91 top, Red beans and rice and po-boy, photo by Gary J. Wood, from Wikimedia Commons; 94, Chicken fricassee, courtesy of Denny Culburt for the Southern Foodways Alliance; 96, Chicken and sausage gumbo, from Wikimedia Commons; 98 bottom, Bowl of gumbo at the Creole Restaurant and Café in Saudi Arabia, courtesy of Ahmed Al-Omair; 102, Cooking a roux, courtesy of Mary Duhé; 104, "A Marchande des Calas," sketch by E.W. Kemble from *Century Magazine*, courtesy of the Center for Louisiana Studies; 105, Beignets at Café du Monde, from Wikimedia Commons; 105 bottom, Calas cakes at Elizabeth's Restaurant in New Orleans, from Wikimedia Commons.

Chapter 3

110, "Negroes talking on porch of small store near Jeanerette, Louisiana," by Lee Russell, 1938, Farm Security Administration, courtesy of the Library of Congress Digital Collection; 111, *The Acadians driven into exile*, by Darley, Felix Octavius Car, 1877, courtesy of the New York Public Library Digital Collection; 112 top, *Marchand d'Esclaves de Gorée*, by Jacques Grasset de Saint-Sauveur, c. 1797, from Wikimedia Commons; 112 bottom, Illustration of the stowage of the British slave ship *Brookes*, courtesy of the Library of Congress Digital Collection; 113, Map of Africa with noted slave ports, courtesy of the center for Louisiana Studies; 114, *A Slave-Pen at New Orleans—Before the Auction*, in *Harper's Weekly*, January 24, 1863; 115, *Hoisting of American Colors over Louisiana*, by Thure de Thulstrup, 1904, permanently held in the Louisiana State Museum collection; 117, Slaves emancipated from New Orleans, 1863, courtesy of the Library of Congress Digital Collection; 120 top, Notices for runaway slaves in the New Orleans *Daily Picayune*, courtesy of America's Historical Newspapers database; 120 bottom, *Bambara Man* and *Bambara Woman*, by Abbé David Boilat, 1853, from Wikimedia Commons; 121, *Wolof Woman carrying her baby*, by Abbé David Boilat, 1853, from Wikimedia Commons; 123, *Negro cabins on a rice plantation*, by Edward King, c. 1874, courtesy of the New York Public Library Digital Collections; 124, *The American Soldier, 1814—Free Men of Colour and Choctaw Indian Volunteers at New Orleans, Louisiana*, courtesy of the U.S. Army Center of Military History; 125 bottom, "Three generations of Louisiana negroes," 1910, courtesy of the New York Public Library Digital Collections; 126, "Negro School, Destrehan, Louisiana," by Lee Russell, 1938, Farm Security Administration, courtesy of the Library of Congress Digital Collection; 127 top, "Negro mother teaching children numbers and alphabet in home of sharecropper. Transylvania, Louisiana," by Lee Russell, 1939, Farm Security Administration, courtesy of the Library of Congress Digital Collection; 127 bottom, "A French-speaking Louisiana Negro and his grandchild," 1910, courtesy of the New York Public Library Digital Collections; 128, "A French-speaking negress seamstress in Louisiana," 1910, courtesy of the New York Public Library Digital Collections; 131, Alcée Fortier, *Popular Science Monthly Volume* 43, 1893, from Wikimedia Commons; 132, Alcée Fortier teaching French at Tulane University, c. 1905, courtesy of Tulane University Archives; 133, Lyle Saxon, courtesy of Tulane University Archives; 134, "Negroes in front of post office, Lafayette, Louisiana," by Lee Russell, 1938, Farm Security Administration, courtesy of the Library of Congress Digital Collection; 135, Wilson "Ben Guiné" Mitchell and Barry Jean Ancelet, photo by Caroline Ancelet; 140, Brer Rabbit in *Uncle Remus, His Songs and His Sayings: The Folk-Lore of the Old Plantation*, by Joel Chandler Harris, 1881, illustrations by Frederick S. Church and James H. Moser, from Wikimedia Commons; 141, Hyena, from Wikimedia Commons; 142, Rabbit, courtesy of the Center for Louisiana Studies; 144, Fish, from Wikimedia Commons; 145, Hoe, from Wikimedia Commons; 146, Two men and passing lady, *Family Friend*, Vol. IX, 1854, from Wikimedia Commons; 147, *Attakapas herdsman*, by Allen C. Redwood, in *Scribner's Monthly* 19 (1879-1880), courtesy of Center for Louisiana Studies; 148, *Black courier*, by Allen C. Redwood, in *Scribner's Monthly*, 18 (May 1879-October 1879), courtesy of Center for Louisiana Studies; 149, *Negro fisherman*, by Edward King, in "The Great South," *Scribner's Monthly*, 8 (May, 1874-October, 1874), courtesy of the Center for Louisiana Studies; 150, Cathedral Woods, Intervale, White Mountains, c. 1900, courtesy of the Library of Congress Digital Collections; 153, Wagon and cabin, from Wikimedia Commons.

Chapter 4

156, St. Louis Church architectural drawing, 1794, from Wikimedia Commons; 157 top, Sheet music cover from "The Tri-Colored Quadrilles," c. 1830, from Wikimedia Commons; 157 bottom left, *The Fiddler*, sketch by E.W. Kemble from George W. Cable, "Creole Slave Songs," *Century Magazine*, 31 (April 1886), courtesy of the Center for Louisiana Studies; 157 bottom right, ad from the *Orleans Gazette*, November 23, 1807, courtesy of America's Historical Newspapers database; 158, *Calinda, dance of the Negroes in America*, by François Aimé Louis Dumoulin, 1783, from Wikimedia Commons; 159, *Sunday in New Orleans—The French Market*, Alfred R. Waud, *Harper's Weekly*, August 18, 1866; 160 top, *Bamboula*, sketch by E.W. Kemble from George W. Cable, "Creole Slave Songs," *Century Magazine*, 31 (April 1886), courtesy of the Center for Louisiana Studies; 162, Illustration of drum played at Congo Square by Benjamin Henry Latrobe, 1819, from Wikimedia Commons; 160 bottom, Jawbone, from Wikimedia Commons; 163 top, *The Love Song*, sketch by E.W. Kemble from George W. Cable, "Creole Slave Songs," *Century Magazine*, 31 (April 1886), courtesy of the Center for Louisiana Studies, University of Louisiana at Lafayette; 163 bottom, Robinson Atlas of New Orleans, Faubourg Tremé, 1883, courtesy of the Clerk of Civil District Court for the Parish of Orleans; 164, Quadroon ball newspaper ad, December 18, 1884, courtesy of America's Historical Newspapers database; 165, Free woman of color with daughter painting, from Wikimedia Commons; 166, Mask, from Wikimedia Commons; 167, Letter to the Cabildo, from www.neworleanspast.com/;168, *Sunday Amusements in New Orleans—A Creole Night at the French Opera House*, Schomburg Center for Research in Black Culture, Photographs and Prints Division, New York Public Library Digital Collections; 169 top, Théâtre d'Orléans from plan of the city and suburbs of New Orleans, 1815, by Wlliam Rollinson, courtesy of New York Public Digital Library; 169 bottom, French Opera House, c. 1890s, by William Henry Jackson, from Wikimedia Commons; 170, Family of Creole musicians, from private collection; 172 top, "String bean pickers waiting along highway for trucks to pick them up, near Gibson, Louisiana," by Lee Russell, 1938, Farm Security Administration, courtesy of the Library of Congress Digital Collection; 173, "Negro sharecropper and child who will be resettled, Transylvania Project, Louisiana,"by Lee Russell, 1938, Farm Security Administration, courtesy of the Library of Congress Digital Collection; 174, "Negro musicians playing accordion and washboard in front of store, near New Iberia, Louisiana," by Lee Russell, 1938, Farm Security Administration, courtesy of the Library of Congress Digital Collection; 176 top, Amédé Ardoin, public domain; 177, "Belmont Plantation ruins and cabin, Maringouin, Iberville Parish, Louisiana,"by Frances Benjamin Johnston, 1938, courtesy of the Library of Congress Digital Collection; 178-79, "Columbia Plantation cabins, Louisiana," by Frances Benjamin Johnston, 1938, courtesy of the Library of Congress Digital Collection; 181, Canray Fontenot, photo by Philip Gould; 184, John Delafose and the Eunice Playboys, courtesy of the Center for Louisiana Studies; 188, Cedric Watson and Bijou Creole performing at the Blue Moon Saloon in Lafayette, photo by Ezra Istre; 190, The Chenier brothers, courtesy of the Center for Louisiana Studies; 191 top, Clifton Chenier, courtesy of Arhoolie Records.

Chapter 5

210, John Broussard in Eunice, 2017, courtesy of David Simpson; 211 top, Festivals Acadiens poster, courtesy of the Center for Louisiana Studies; 216, Vermilionville's La Cuisine de Maman menu, courtesy of Vermilionville; 218, Eric Cormier, courtesy of Sara Roahen for the Southern Foodways Alliance; 225 top, Downtown Lafayette street signs in French, photo by Daniel Schwen, from Wikimedia Commons; 225 bottom, State welcome sign in French, from Wikimedia Commons;

227, Henriette DeLille, public domain, permanently held at the Historic New Orleans Collection; 231, *Die Sentimentale*, by Johann Peter Hasenclever, c.1846, from Wikimedia Commons; 235, Goldman Thibodeaux with Guyland Leday at a Zydeco Breakfast in Opelousas, 2009, courtesy of David Simpson; 239 top, Sign for Offshore Lounge in Lawtell, La., courtesy of Chubby Carrier; 239 bottom, Chubby Carrier performing at the Offshore Lounge in Lawtell, La., courtesy of David Simpson; 240, Lil' Nate and the Zydeco Big Timers performing at Café des Amis in Breaux Bridge, photo by Ezra Istre; 245 bottom, Dancers at the Original Southwest Louisiana Zydeco Music Festival in Plaisance, courtesy of David Simpson; 246, Chubby Carrier with Grammy award, photo by Kenny Champagne, courtesy of Chubby Carrier; 253 top, Metoyer and young musicians, courtesy of the Metoyer family; 257 right bottom, Creole coffee cup and Creole restaurant in Saudi Arabia, courtesy of Ahmed Al-Omair; 258, Map of Creole-speaking parishes, courtesy of the Center for Louisiana Studies; 261 bottom, Goldman and Brock Thibodeaux, courtesy of David Simpson; 263, "I am Creole" t-shirt, courtesy of Tracey Colson; Creole license plate, courtesy of Louisiana Department of Public Safety, Office of Motor Vehicles.

Index

A

Acadiana, 5, 33, 44, 46, 70, 89, 103, 113, 137, 208, 211-12, 216-17, 230
Acadian refugees, 33, 155, 255. *See also* Cajun
accordions, 174-75, 192, 194-95
Adams, James (J.B.), 187, 189
African: enslaved, 10-11, 15, 28, 53-55, 112-15, 135, 155, 158; foodways, 44, 48, 54, 57, 59; languages, 110, 118-19, 121-22, 227; music, 159-64
African American Museum (St. Martinville, La.), 212, 250
Alciatore, Antoine, 67
American Indians, 135, 156, 252; Choctaw, 51; Coushatta, 232; enslaved, 7, 16, 114, 158; foodways, 48-50, 92, 102; languages, 110-11, 118-19, 228, 232; music, 156; oral tradition, 135-36, 147; population, 7, 67, 118; wars, 16, 55, 156
American Revolution, 3
Ancelet, Barry Jean, 131-32, 134-36, 138-39, 143, 145, 171, 230, 238
Angelle, Donna, 98
Anglo-Americans, 8-9, 12, 41, 67, 125, 167, 171, 224
Angola, 15, 54, 77, 89, 100, 103, 114, 118-19; State Penitentiary, 15
animal trickster tales, 134-35, 139-42. *See also* Bouki and Lapin stories
Antoine's Restaurant (New Orleans, La.), 67
Arceneaux, Jean, 140
Ardoin, Alphonse "Bois Sec," 27
Ardoin, Amédé, 36, 175-77, 182, 185
Ardoin, Chris, 241
Aurore (ship), 54
Auzenne, Norbert, 25

B

Bambara, 119-21
bamboula dance, 160
Barthé, Earl, 130
Battalion: of Octoroons, 166; of Quadroons, 166
Battle of New Orleans, 123-24, 255
Bauman, Richard, 111, 135
beignets, 105
Berlin, Ira, 4
Bernard, Raphael, 19
Berquin-Duvallon, Pierre Louis, 9, 56-57
Bienville, Sieur de, 52, 158. *Also* Moyne, Jean-Baptiste Le.
Black Code. *See* Code Noir
black-eyed peas, 44, 80-81, 90-91
Blue Moon Saloon (Lafayette, La.), 188
Borders, Florence E., 164
Bossu, Jean-Bernard, 6, 49, 102
boucherie (hog butchering), 25, 80, 92, 94, 208, 217, 220-21, 252
boudin, ix, 80, 90-91, 217-18, 222, 245
Boudin Festival (Scott, La.), 193
Bouki and Lapin stories, 132, 139-42, 145, 208
Bourque, Darrell, 36-37
Brandon, Elizabeth, 134
Brasseaux, Carl A., xiii, 41, 57, 104, 111
Breaux Bridge, La., 46, 73, 186, 226, 228, 241, 247
Brenda's Dine-In and Take-Out (New Iberia, La.), 81-82
Brigtsen's Restaurant (New Orleans, La.), 95

Broussard, Delton, 182
Broussard, Jeffery, 27, 171, 182-83, 187, 189, 193, 240, 246-47; and the Creole Cowboys, 182-83, 189, 240, 246
Broussard, John, 210, 238
Broussard, Laura Williams, 82-84
Broussard, Madonna, 79, 82-83
Broussard, Prosper, 64
Brown, Veronica "Ronnie," 216
Brüe, André, 53, 120
Burnside Plantation, 63
Burrison, John A., 115

C

Cabildo, 166-67
Cabinda, 15, 103. *See also* Angola
Cable, George Washington, 122, 146, 156, 162-63, 229
Caesar, Alfred, 129-30
Caesar, Warren, 174
Café des Amis (Breaux Bridge, La.), 241
Café du Monde (New Orleans, La.), 105
Café Pontalba (New Orleans, La.), 46
Cajun, 24-25, 27, 30-37, 209-10; dance halls, 185-86; foodways, 44, 46, 82, 84-85, 89-90, 209; language, 118, 123, 128, 226; music, 155, 158, 171, 176, 185, 195, 197, 205; oral tradition, 134-36, 147; origins, xiii, 5, 111; tourism, xii, 44, 46, 128, 208-12
calas cakes, 104-105
calinda dance, 158, 160
Cane River Creoles, xv, 5, 47. *See also* Natchitoches, La.
Cape Verde, 2, 3
Caro, Frank de, 131, 133
Carondelet, barón de, 55, 164, 166
Carrier, Chubby, 198, 246; and the Bayou Swamp Band, 239
Carrier, Roy, 239-40
Carrier, Troy "Dikki Du," 240
Carrière, Bébé, 189
Carriere, Josephine, 36
Catalon, Inez, 150
Catfish Festival (Washington, La.), 221
Catholicism, 12, 18, 78, 81, 93, 107, 109, 156-58, 212, 222
Chaplin, Joyce E., 4
Chargois, Jenelle, 174
Charles, Josephine "Jo," 244
Charles, Lena, 244-46
Chase, Leah, 45, 98
Chaudenson, Robert, 2
Chavis, Wilson "Boozoo," 173, 237, 249
Chenier, Cleveland, 190, 203
Chenier, Clifton, 155, 172, 174, 189-93, 203, 212, 237; and the Red Hot Louisiana Band, 174
Cheramie, David, 128
Citizen, Joe, 176-84, 186, 189, 202
Civil War, 15-16, 22, 61, 63, 65-67, 70, 91, 125, 132, 161, 169
Claiborne, William Charles Cole, 167-68
Claudel, Calvin, 133-34
Clifton, Deborah J., 207, 230, 233-34
Code Noir, 12-13, 16, 19, 116, 255
coffee, 44, 62-63, 66, 102
Cohen, Robin, 2
Comeaux, Lesley "Les," 74-79, 81
Coming, Fortescue, 96-97
Company of the Indies, 54-55, 121, 158
Company of the West. *See* Company of the Indies
Congo, 115, 118-19, 121
Congo Square, 159-64, 170, 193, 255
Cormier, Eric, 93, 217-19, 221
Cormier, Josephine Phillips, 78, 81, 84-85
corn, 44, 49, 53, 55-57, 65-66, 71-72, 75, 92, 100, 102, 129, 146, 175, 217
cornbread, 48, 55-56, 60, 63-64, 75-76, 80-81, 214-15
couche-couche, 64, 74, 76, 92
Council for the Development of French

in Louisiana (CODOFIL), 128
cowboy stew, 70, 83, 89, 94, 238
Cracklin Festival (Port Barre, La.), 92
cracklins, 80, 90, 92, 217, 219, 245. *See also* gratons
crawfish, xiii, 29, 50, 70, 81, 90, 93, 214, 222-23, 236
Creole: cooking, *See* chapter 2, 214-23; heritage, See chapter 5; identity, See chapter 1, 207-213; language, *See* chapter 3, 224-33, 258-59; music, *See* chapter 4, 234-49; plantations, 2, 6, 9, 15, 16, 21, 60-62, 116, 133, 216; race, 7-10, 22-25, 126, 185, 207, 251; slavery, 10-22, 64, 115-17, 119-21, 159-63; stories, 140-53; surnames, 38-41
C.R.E.O.L.E., Inc., 209-10, 228, 238
Creole Cookery, 68-69, 99-100
Creole French, 109-12, 118-23, 125-30, 224-33
Creole Heritage and Folklife Center (Opelousas, La.), 212
Creole Lunch House (Lafayette, La.), 81, 85-89, 212
Creole Renaissance Festival, 26, 220, 251
Creole Zydeco Festival, 212
Cris sur le bayou: naissance d'une poésie acadienne en Louisiane, 230
Crouch, R. Randall, 168

D

Dahomey (Republic of Benin), 119
dance halls, 27, 164, 166, 168, 185, 190, 192-93, 205, 208, 213, 234-35, 237-38, 240-41, 252
Deetz, James, 1
Delafose, Geno, 72, 98, 182-87, 189, 193, 237, 239-40, 246; and French Rockin' Boogie, 185-86
Delafose, Joann, 71-72, 75-77, 80, 98, 220
Delafose, John, 98, 184, 186, 189, 237; and the Eunice Playboys, 184
Delafosse, Brandon, 202
DeLille, Henriette, 227
Dennis, Westley "Kit," 151-53
De Soto, Hernando, 49
Dictionary of Louisiana French: As Spoken in Cajun, 228
Domingue family, 30-33, 37; Camille, 31; Ellis and Edma Meyers, 32; Elista Elizabeth, 32
Domingue, Kendrick, 202
Dominguez family, 31-32, 37
Donaldson, Gary A., 161
Donato, Martin, 16
Dormon, James H., xiii
Dorsin, Edmée, 143-44
Drake, Mary Alice, 225-28, 233
Duparc, Guillaume, 9
Du Pratz, Le Page, 49, 121
Dural, Reginald, 192
Dural, Stanley "Buckwheat Zydeco," 27, 192, 246
Duvallon, Berquin, 56-57

E

education, 36, 109, 125, 127, 151, 230
Egerton, John, 43, 65-66, 69
Elmina, 112
El Sid O's Zydeco and Blues Club (Lafayette, La.), 213, 241
enslaved. *See* slavery
étouffée, xiii, 81, 90, 93, 99, 214, 216, 222

F

Faine, Jules, 121
fairy tales. *See* magic tales
Feibleman, Peter, 44
Fernandes, Valentim, 54
Festival International de Louisiane, 192, 241-42
Festivals Acadiens et Créoles, 171, 183, 211, 222-23, 234, 241, 243-44, 249

feux follets, 150
Fiehrer, Thomas, 168-69
field hands, 7, 14, 59, 63-64
Fields, Thomas "Big Hat," 47, 70, 73-75, 77, 89
filé, xi-xii, 51, 94, 95-97
Fils family, 23
folklorists, 110, 131-32, 134-38, 140
Folse, John, 44-45, 48, 95
Fontenot, Canray, 172, 174-76, 180-81, 185, 189-90
Fontenot, Freeman, 175, 185
Fontenot, Keith P., xiii
Fontenot, Linda, 216
Fontenot, Telesmar, 34-36
Fonvergné, Gabriel, 166
Fortier, Alcée, 118, 122, 131-33, 140-41
Frank, Keith, 194, 234, 241; and the Soileau Zydeco Band, 242
free black population. See *gens de colour libre*
French: colonization, 11-14, 118, 120-21, 158-59, 169; foodways, 52-53, 55, 57-58; language, *See* International French and Creole French; music, 156-57, 167; slave trade, 10, 53, 113-16; transfer of Louisiana, 7, 115
French and Indian War, 34
French Opera House (New Orleans, La.), 169
fricassée, xiii, 52, 70, 86, 89, 94, 100
Frilot Cove, La., 24, 73, 170, 247
frottoir, 202-03, 234. *See also* washboard
Fulbe nation, 121

G

Galam trading post, 112
Gambia, 53, 118-19
Garlow, Clarence, 170
Garnier, D'Jalma, III, 196
gateau de sirop (syrup cake), 104
Gayerré, Charles, 23, 43
gens de colour libre (or "free people of color"), 16-22, 29, 116, 124, 164, 259
Ghana, 100, 119
G&J Creole Foods, 219
Gombo People, xi, 231
Gorée Island, 112, 114
Grammy awards (Best Zydeco or Cajun Music Album category), 188, 192, 239, 246, 248
gratons, 92, 217, 219. *See also* cracklins
green beans, 44, 80, 95, 172. *See also* snap beans and haricots
Guadeloupe, 10, 226, 228
Guenin-Lelle, Dianne, 230
Guillory, Wilbert, 250-51
gumbo, xi-xii, xv, 25, 47, 51, 61, 68, 70, 78, 80-81, 85, 89, 92-100, 102, 121, 145, 175, 179, 216-18, 223, 240, 251
Gumbo Ya-Ya: Folktales of Louisiana, 133
Gutierrez, C. Paige, 46, 92, 94

H

Haiti, 4, 21; Creole, 228; slave revolt, 8, 14. *See also* Saint-Domingue
Hall, Gwendolyn Midlo, 96, 113-14, 121
Hamilton's Place (Lafayette, La.), 237-41
Hamilton, William, 237
haricots (green beans), 95, 172, 174, 246, 259, 260. *See also* snap beans
Harris, Joel Chandler, 132
Harvison, C. Renée, 136
Hearn, Lafcadio, 68-69, 145
Héctor, Francisco Luis, 164
Herbert, Merline, 75, 76, 79, 85-88
Heywood, Linda M., 4
historical tales, 135, 151-153
Holy Ghost Catholic Church, (Opelousas, La.), 212
Holy Rosary Institute (Lafayette, La.),

226-27
house dances, 170, 173-180, 185, 190, 208, 235-36, 252, 261
Hulin, Belinda, 97

I

Iberville, Sieur d', 52. *Also* Moyne, Pierre Le
Immaculate Conception Catholic Church (Lebeau, La.), 221-22
immersion schools, French, 189, 224, 231-33, 259
Indians. *See* American Indians
Ingersoll, Thomas, 115
Inseparable Friends Benevolent Society, 25
International French, 118, 121-23, 125, 224, 227, 233, 258-59
Istre family, 32-34, 37; Fastin, 33; Denis, 34; Evelyn Amelia Trahan, 34

J

jambalaya, 25, 70, 81, 87, 99, 103, 216, 245
James, Samuel, 15
Jeanerette, La., 110
Jean Lafitte National Historical Park and Preserve, 211
Jeannot (slave), 18-19
Jefferson, Thomas, 97, 106, 115
Jim Crow era, 25, 33, 237
jokes, 109-10, 134-35, 138-40, 145, 147, 153, 230
Jordan, Rosan Augusta, 131
Josephine's Creole Restaurant (St. Martinville, La.), 81, 84, 212
Joubert, Oreun, 198
Juré music, 155, 169-74, 193, 245

K

Kein, Sybil, xiii, 104, 229, 231-33
King, Grace, 23
Koegel, John, 156

L

La Cuisine Creole, 68, 100
La Cuisine de Maman (Lafayette, La.), 212, 215-16
Lafayette, La., 28, 30, 75, 81-82, 85-86, 134, 174, 183, 187-88, 192, 211-17, 222, 225, 236-37, 240-43, 250
Lafayette Convention and Visitors Commission (LCVC), 111, 212-13
Lake Charles, La., 25, 30, 47, 217, 249
La La music, 155, 173-76, 180-82, 189-90, 235
la Nériède (ship), 15, 114
Lanusse, Armand, 125
La Poussière (Breaux Bridge, La.), 186
La Salle, Nicolas de la, 158
La Salle, René-Robert Cavelier de, 49
Latrobe, Benjamin 161-62
Laudun, John, 46, 70, 92, 102
Laura Plantation (Vacherie, La.), 9
Laura's II (Lafayette, La.), 81-84
Laussat, Pierre Clément de, 96, 167
Lebeau Zydeco Festival, 212, 221
Leday family, 35; Alicia Matte, 35; John, 35, Leroy, 35
Leday, Guyland, 235
Ledet, Corey "Lil' Pop," 189, 246
legends, 147-50; *See also* tall tales
Le Meschacébé, 125-26
Les Cenelles, 125
"les haricots sont pas salés," 95, 172, 174, 246, 261
Liberia, 54, 119
Lindahl, Carl, 133, 135
Lil Wayne and Same Ol' Two-Step, 243
Lomax, Alan, 170-74
Louisiana: Americanization of, 8-9, 67, 125, 138, 209, 224; French colonization, 11-14, 52-53, 118, 120-21, 158-59, 169; Purchase, 7-8, 55, 115, 167, 255; slavery, 10-15, 53, 55, 58, 70, 112-15, 116-17,

120-21, 148, 156, 158-64, 255; societal hierarchy, 16, 18, 19, 117; Spanish administration, 1, 4, 11-14, 16-17, 19, 31, 55, 112, 115, 160-61, 164, 166-67, 255
Louisiana Association of the American Folk-lore Society, 131
Louisiana Constitution of 1921, 128
Louisiana Department of Culture, 135
Louisiana Folklife Program, 135
Louisiana Writers' Project, 64, 133
Luxembourg, Raphael de, 156

M

magic tales, 132-35, 139, 143-44, 145, 153
Mali, 54, 92, 228, 242, 248, 263
Mallard, R.A., 58
Mandatory Attendance Act of 1916, 128
Mandingo language, 119, 121
maroons, 12-14
Marshall, Margaret, 118, 120
Martinique, 10, 228
Mattern, Mark, 185
McCann, James C., 44
McGee, Dennis, 175
Metoyer family, 20-21, 29
Metoyer, Rusty, 136, 253; and the Zydeco Krush, 252
Middle Passage, 103, 112-13
Mire, La San, 64
miscegenation, 22, 116-17. *See also* plaçage
Mississippi River, 28, 43, 49, 55, 57, 88, 121, 159, 236; Valley, 114, 158
Mitchell, Patricia B., 52
Mitchell, Wilson "Ben Guiné," 135, 148
Mosadomi, Fehintola 118-19, 121
Moyne, Jean-Baptiste Le (Bienville, Sieur de), 52, 158
Moyne, Pierre Le (Iberville, Sieur d'), 52
mulatto, 10, 17-18, 27, 122, 126, 146, 165

N

Natchez Wars, 16
Natchitoches, La., 5, 20-21, 52
Native American. *See* American Indian
New Orleans, La.: foodways, 3, 43-44, 46-47, 65-69, 88-89, 96-97, 99, 101, 103-105, 214; founding, 52, 255; music, 28, 156-58, 160-69; race, xiv, 6 -11, 17, 19, 20-21, 23-24; slavery, 10-11, 114-115, 117, 120-21
Nigeria, 119
Nova Scotia, 3, 27, 34-35, 111

O

octoroon, 165
Offshore Lounge, (Lawtell, La.), 239-40
okra, xi, xii, 44, 51, 59, 66, 73, 79, 81, 84-85, 94-95, 97, 100, 103, 121, 175, 222
Olivier, Armand, III, 95-96
Olivier, Marie Philomene Donato, 16
Olivier's Creole Restaurant (New Orleans, La.), 96
Opelousas, La., 26, 45, 74, 79, 104, 130, 191, 212, 220, 238, 244, 251
Original Southwest Louisiana Zydeco Music Festival (Plaisance, La.), 185, 188, 212, 219, 244-45, 250
Osseo-Asara, Fran, 103
Oubre, Claude F., xiii
Owens, Maida, 111, 135
Owens, William, 140

P

pain perdu, 101
Peek, Philip M., 135
Picayune Creole Cook Book, 69
Picone, Michael D., 110, 112, 125, 128, 232

Pierre-Auguste, Kent, 200
plaçage, 17-18, 22, 164-66, 227
Placide, Brenda, 73, 79-80, 82
Plaisance, La., 185, 212, 219, 235, 244-45
plantation system, 2, 7, 9, 16, 20, 57, 60-64, 84, 116, 131, 133
Port Barre, La., 92
Poullard, Edward, 189, 196, 247
pralines, 104, 106, 245, 257
proverbs, 110, 145-46, 153
Prudhomme, Paul, 44-45
public dances, 157, 164, 166-68

Q

quadroon, 17, 165
quadroon balls, 17, 164-66, 193. *See also* plaçage

R

Randolph, Anne Cary, 106
Randolph, Mary, 90, 100
Raspail, Jean, 118
Rayne, La., 47, 73
Read, William, 118
Reconstruction era, 16, 22, 69-70, 125
Reunion Island, 28
Rhythm and Roots Festival, 183
Ricard, Ulysses S., Jr., 231, 233
rice, 44, 52-55, 57, 59, 66, 70, 74, 76, 78-81, 83-84, 86-87, 90-92, 94, 99-100, 104-105, 175, 223, 245, 259
rice and gravy, 48, 70, 81, 86, 90, 99, 102, 223
Rice, Anne, 229
Richard's Club/Miller's Zydeco Hall of Fame (Lawtell, La.), 213
Roberts, John, 142
Robin, C.C., 55-56, 205
Roman Plantation, 62
roux, xi-xii, 47, 51, 83-84, 89, 94-95, 97, 102-103, 217
rubboard. *See* washboard
Russell, William Howard, 62-63

S

Saint-Domingue, 8-10; refugees, 8, 41, 56; slave revolts, 9; surnames, 41. *See also* Haiti
Sam, Mike, 216
Sanchez, José, 198
Sandmel, Ben, 191, 236-37, 241
sassafras, xi, 51, 95, 97
Saucier, Corinne, 133-34
Saxon, Lyle, 8, 133, 145
Senegal, 2, 19, 53-54, 89, 114, 118-20, 141, 228, 263
Senegambia, 15, 53, 113-14, 119
sharecropping, 70-71, 73-74, 84, 127, 173-74, 176, 226, 247
Sierra Leone, 3, 119
Simien, Terrence, 246-47; and the Zydeco Experience, 247-48
Sinegal, Frank, 73
Sinegal, Paul "Lil' Buck," 200
Singleton, Eric, 200
Singleton, Theresa, 139
Singleton, Wayne. *See* "Lil Wayne and Same Ol Two-Step"
Slaves: arrival in Louisiana, 14-16, 53-54, 114-115, 158, 255; Creole, 1, 6, 10-14, 20-21, 115, 117, 124; foodways, 55-57, 59-60, 63-64, 70, 103; language, 118-22, 227; marketplace tradition, 12, 16, 96, 104, 159; music, 160-64; population, 10-11, 14-15, 18, 115, 160; ports, 112-13; revolt in Haiti, 8-9, 14; runaways, 12-14; trade, 2-3, 10, 110, 112-15; treatment of, 9, 21, 55-56, 64, 116-17. *See also* Code Noir, Bambara, and Wolof
Slim's Y-Ki-Ki (Opelousas, La.), 191, 213, 238, 240
snap beans, 75, 95, 174, 246, 259-60. *See also* green beans and haricots

Société Cordon Bleu, 165
Solomon, Clara, 65
Soniat, Leon E., Jr., 91, 102
Southwest Louisiana Zydeco Music Festival. *See* Original Southwest Louisiana Zydeco Music Festival.
Spitzer, Nicholas, 95
St. Charles Catholic Church (Grand Coteau, La.), 107
St. Edward Catholic Church (New Iberia, La.), 212
St. Louis Cathedral (New Orleans, La.), 23, 104, 156
St. Louis Hotel (New Orleans, La.), 11
St. Louis, Military Order of, 7
St. Louis (ship), 54, 114
St. Louis trading post, 112
St. Martinville, La., 78, 84, 212, 218; African American Museum, 212, 250-51; Creole Zydeco Festival, 212; Cultural Heritage Center, 251, 253; Okra Festival, 222
Strenge, Kelly, 213
sugarcane, 8-10, 44, 64, 74
sweet dough pies, 107
sweet potatoes, 44, 59, 64, 66, 80, 103-104, 107, 175. *See also* yams

T

tall tales, 134-35, 139, 147, 149-51
Théâtre d'Orléans, 169
The Princess and the Frog, 45, 248
Thibodeaux, Anatole, 36
Thibodeaux, Goldman, 34-37, 137, 176-82, 187-89, 193, 211, 235, 253; and the Lawtell Playboys, 188
Thibodeaux, Philomène Latiolais, 36-37
Thibodeaux, Théodule, 36-37
Thomas, Leroy: and the Zydeco RoadRunners, 208
Thornton, John K., 4
Tinker, Edward Larocque, 23
Tiocou, François, 19
tobacco, 53
Togo, 119
tomato, 2-3, 44, 65, 70, 75, 97-100, 103
Toninato, Paola, 2
Tony Chachere's Original Creole Seasoning, 222-23
tourism, xii, 135, 208-13, 217, 250
trail rides, 25, 187, 238, 262
triangle (tit' fer) instrument, 170, 175, 198-99
Triangle Club (Frilot Cove, La.), 27

U

Uncle Remus stories, 132, 140
University of Louisiana at Lafayette, 36, 225, 229, 238, 257
Ursuline nuns, 156

V

Vacherie, La., 9, 140
Vega, Garcilaso de la, 5
Vermilionville, Lafayette, La., 129, 139, 186, 208, 211-12, 215-17, 238, 250; Creole Culture Day, 139, 211-12
Verret, Zoeanna, 51

W

Warden, D.B., 103
washboard, 171, 174-75, 190, 192, 202-03, 261
Watson, Cedric, 172-73, 186-89, 193, 196, 246; and Bijou Créole, 172, 242
Whiskey River Landing (Henderson, La., 185
Wilgus, D. K., 176
Williams, Dennis Paul, 212, 253
Williams, Lil' Nathan, Jr., 194; and the Zydeco Big Timers, 241
Williams, Nathan, Sr., 194
Wiltz, Herbert, 209, 226-28, 231, 233
Wolof, 54, 103, 119, 121, 141

Y

Yambilee Festival (Opelousas, La.), 104
yams, 44, 79, 103-104. *See also* sweet potato

Z

Zydeco music, 28, 155, 169, 234-249; artists, 27, 182-93, 235; Grammy award, 188, 192, 239, 246, 248; instruments, 194-206; origins, 95, 170-75, 190; at trail rides, 187